Real Estate Appraisal Terminology

SOCIETY OF
REAL ESTATE APPRAISERS

Real Estate
Appraisal
Terminology

REVISED EDITION

Compiled and Edited by
Byrl N. Boyce, Ph.D., SRPA
*Center for Real Estate and Urban
Economic Studies*
University of Connecticut

Ballinger Publishing Company • Cambridge, Massachusetts
A Subsidiary of Harper & Row, Publishers, Inc.

Published in the United States of America by Ballinger Publishing Company, Cambridge, Mass.

Library of Congress Catalog Card Number: 80-23713

International Standard Book Number: 0-88410-597-0

Printed in the United States of America

Library of Congress Cataloging in Publication Data

Boyce, Byrl N
  Real estate appraisal terminology

  1. Real property—Valuation—Terminology. I. American Institute of
Real Estate Appraisers. II. Society of Real Estate Appraisers. III. Title.
HD1387.B69 1980   333.33′2′0321   80-23713
ISBN 0-88410-597-0

Contents

Preface and Acknowledgments

Terms and definitions are subject to continuous modification. This fact is particularly true in the dynamic field of real estate appraisal, where changing client requirements have increased the need to interface with other disciplines. In the five-year interim since the publication of the first edition of *Real Estate Appraisal Terminology*, much change has occurred within the profession which has produced substantial constructive criticism of existing terms and definitions by users. It was in response to that constructive criticism that the current revision was undertaken. Therefore, much of this revision was directed toward refinement of existing terms; there was also a major effort to degenderize terms that was warranted, necessary, and long overdue. In addition, there was some modest broadening of terms in the areas of finance, statistics and energy.

The number of individual appraisers and appraisal or appraisal-related organizations responding to the review of existing materials and suggestions for changes and additions is too numerous to mention. Without their efforts, however, the task of revision would have been much more difficult. Those who can be identified and acknowledged for their advice and direction throughout the preparation of these materials are O. J. Clontz, Jr., MAI; John Doerr, MAI; and John G. Hoppe, MAI, SREA. Representing SREA were William E. Coyle, Jr., SREA, MAI; R. J. Frank, Jr., SREA; and H. Grady Stebbins, SREA, MAI. To these gentlemen, I would like to express my sincere appreciation.

There were a number of colleagues at the Center for Real Estate and Urban Economic Studies at the University of Connecticut who aided me in this project and for which special recognition is appropriate. Stephanie C. Coleman assisted by noting changes suggested by members of appraisal organizations. Judy Paesani provided general direction of Stephanie's activities as well as some of my own and updated the Sources of Information that appear in the Appendix. Nancy J. Easton and Sandra J. Mazzola provided their normal top quality assistance in the areas of typing and production. Last but not least, a special thank you to my colleague, Dr. William N. Kinnard, Jr., Director, Center for Real Estate and Urban Economic Studies, University of Connecticut, for his continued inspiration and direction in virtually all projects that I undertake.

As in the earlier edition, editorial comments have been reduced to a minimum. What appears here truly represents the culmination of advice and suggestions offered by individuals as well as appraisal and appraisal-related organizations. As editor, however, I accept the responsibility for the final product, including any shortcomings.

Storrs, Connecticut   **Byrl N. Boyce**
January 1980

Terminology

AAE – Accredited Assessment Evaluator. A professional designation conferred by the International Association of Assessing Officers upon real and personal property appraisers in the assessment field not employed by an assessment agency.

A HORIZON – Upper horizon, surface soil from which material is being removed by percolating water. See also B, C, and D Horizons.

ABC ROADS – Collective term for federal-aid primary roads, federal-aid secondary roads, and urban extensions of federal-aid systems.

ABC SOIL – A soil having well-developed A, B, and C horizons, is said to have complete soil profile.

ABANDONMENT – The relinquishment of all interests in real property and/or fixtures thereon with no intention to reclaim or use again. Sometimes called "vacation".

ABATEMENT
1. An official reduction or cessation of an assessed valuation for ad valorem taxation after the initial assessment has been completed.
2. Termination of a nuisance.
3. Correction of an unlawful building condition.

ABSCISSA – The distance along the horizontal axis of a curve, diagram, or chart. See also Ordinate.

ABSENTEE LANDLORD – An owner, lessor, or sublessor who owns real estate from which rental income is derived, but who does not reside in the place or area in which the real estate is located.

ABSTRACT OF TITLE – A summary of all conveyances, such as deeds or wills, and legal proceedings, giving the names of the parties, the description of the land, and the agreements, arranged to show the continuity of ownership. See also Title.

ABSTRACTION – The distribution of the appraised value of the property between land and building. This is accomplished by subtracting a figure representing building value from the appraised total value of the improved property. Although a distribution of a price or value between land and improvements can be useful at times, the procedure has limitations.

1

ABUT — To touch or border on, as a property abutting on a highway or sharing a common boundary with another property.

ABUTMENT — That part of a wall or pier on or against which an object abuts or presses; that part which receives the pressure of an arch or strut, as the supports at either end of a bridge.

ABUTTER'S RIGHTS — The right of visibility, that is, the right to see and be seen from the street; and the right to the flow of light and air from the street to the property. Synonymous with right to light, air, and view.

ACCELERATED DEPRECIATION

1. A method of cost write-off in accounting practice in which allowances for depreciation of a wasting asset are greater in early years and decline according to a formula. Note: Technically, the depreciation decelerates with respect to time, but the term "accelerated depreciation" has gained acceptance through popular usage and refers to "accelerated" or faster recovery of capital during the early years as compared to straight-line recovery.
2. Permission, granted by the federal government, allowing faster write-off of a wasting asset for purposes of tax shelter. It is also used to describe depreciation methods, e.g., double-declining balance and sum of the year's digits, among others. See illustration, page 338.

ACCELERATION CLAUSE — A condition in a loan contract or mortgage note which permits the lender to require immediate repayment of the entire balance if the contract is breached or conditions for repayment occur, such as sale or demolition.

ACCELERATION LANE — An additional traffic lane which permits entering traffic to merge with through traffic with minimum delay and risk. It is also referred to as "Access Connection."

ACCESS

1. The means or way by which a property is approached.
2. The means or method of entrance into or upon a property.

ACCESS RIGHTS

1. The right of ingress to and egress from a property which abuts upon an existing street or highway. It is an easement in the street which is appurtenant to abutting property and is a private right as distinguishable from rights of the public. The right of access cannot be denied or unreasonably restricted unless other reasonable access is available or provided or compensation is awarded. See Landlock.
2. The right of a riparian owner to pass to and from the waters upon which the premises border.

ACCESSIBILITY
1. The relative degree of effort (time and cost) by which a site can be reached. Indicates ease of entrance upon a property.
2. A location factor which will implement the most probable and profitable use of a site in terms of ease and convenience.

ACCESSION – Acquisition rights of a property owner through additions or improvements attaching to the property either naturally or by the labor or materials of another. See Accretion.

ACCESSORY BUILDINGS – Secondary buildings on the same property which are appurtenant to a main building; any out buildings used in connection with the main building, such as garage, pump, and well houses.

ACCRETION – The increase of dry land by the gradual deposit of solid material, water borne, over former riparian land, i.e., accretion by alluvion. The owner of the riparian land becomes the owner of the title to land formed by accretion. It is the opposite of erosion.

ACCRUALS FOR DEPRECIATION – Provisions for (usually credits to reserves on accounting statements) anticipated depreciation.

ACCRUED DEPRECIATION – The difference between reproduction cost new or replacement cost new of the improvements and the present worth of those improvements, both measured as of the date of appraisal. In measuring accrued depreciation, the appraiser is interested in identifying and measuring the loss in utility experienced by the subject structure in its present condition, as compared to the utility it would have as a new improvement representing the highest and best use of the site. Accrued depreciation is sometimes referred to as diminished utility.

ACID SOIL – See Types of Soil, page 351.

ACOUSTICAL MATERIAL – Materials having sound-absorbing qualities which are applied to walls and/or ceilings. They may be tile, fiber or mineral board, cork, special plaster, etc.

ACOUSTICAL TILE – Any tile having the inherent property to absorb sound; usually made of mineral fiber, or insulated metal materials.

ACQUISITION APPRAISAL – An appraisal for market value of a property to be acquired by negotiation or condemnation for some public use by a governmental body or other duly authorized condemning authority for the purpose of establishing the amount of compensation to be offered to the property owner.

ACRE – A land measure of 160 square rods or 43, 560 square feet.

ACREAGE – Acres collectively. For example, farm acreage, industrial acreage, or residential acreage.

ACREAGE CONTROLS – The limits set by the federal government on the acres which can be planted to price-supported crops.

ACRE–FOOT (FOOT–ACRE)

1. A volume of water equivalent to one acre in area with a depth of one foot. It is 43,560 cubic feet of water. See also Measures, page 274.
2. Used in estimating the amount of coal in place, that is, a horizontal bed of coal which is five feet thick over an area of one acre would comprise five acre-feet of coal.

ACRE–INCH – A volume of water equivalent to one acre in area with a depth of one inch. See also Measures, page 274.

ACRES–IN–CROPS – The area of land on which crops, exclusive of permanent pasture and woods, are either growing or harvested in a year.

ACRES–OF–CROPS – The total acreage of crops growing or harvested in a year, exclusive of annual crops planted for harvest during the following year. It may be larger than the number of acres actually in crops because of the production of more than one crop on a part or all of the cropland.

ACROSS THE FENCE VALUE (ATF) – Used in the valuation of corridor real estate. It refers to prices or values of land adjacent to or "across the fence" from railroad, pipeline, highway, or other corridor real estate.

ACTUAL AGE – The number of years elapsed since an original structure was built. Sometimes referred to as historical or chronological age.

ADDITION

1. Part of a building added to original structure; a wing or ell.
2. Synonymous with subdivision, particularly in legal descriptions.

ADJOINING – Touching or contiguous, as distinguished from lying near or adjacent. See Abut.

ADJUSTED BASIS – The original cost of a property plus allowable additions including capital improvements, certain carrying costs and assessments minus depreciation taken and partial sales. See also Book Value.

ADJUSTED INTERNAL RATE OF RETURN (AIRR) – An internal rate of return concept where the reinvestment rates for both positive and negative cash flows have been adjusted. The adjusted internal rate applies a safe rate to all negative cash flows, discounting them to time period zero and adding them to the initial investment. Further, the adjusted internal rate applies a market rate to all positive cash flows and carries them forward to the end of the investment holding period. The calculated adjusted internal rate of return is then a function of the original investment, the terminal value, and the time period separating those two amounts.

ADJUSTMENTS

1. Net—Those figures which are added to or subtracted from the time adjusted sales prices of comparable properties to obtain an adjusted sales price of each comparable property. The result is the appraiser's best estimate of what each comparable property would have sold for if it had possessed all of the salient characteristics of the subject property.

2. Dollar—The identification of individual differences between comparable sales and the subject property in terms of plus or minus dollar amounts. To obtain an adjusted sales price for the comparable property, additions are made to or deductions taken from the time adjusted sales prices of comparable properties (not the subject property) for the differences identified.

3. Percentage—The identification of individual differences between comparable sales and the subject property in terms of plus or minus percentage differentials. Individual percentage adjustments are then summed and converted to dollar amounts based upon the time adjusted sales price of the comparable in order to form the net adjustment.

4. Cumulative Percentage—The identification of individual differences between comparable sales and the subject property in terms of plus or minus percentage differentials, cumulating them by multiplication or division. The process assumes a causal relationship among the various factors for which adjustments are made; i.e., it carries the implication that there is intercorrelation among the factors. Cumulative percentage adjustments are not recommended.

ADMINISTRATIVE EXPENSES—The expenses incurred in directing or conducting a business as distinct from the expense of manufacturing, selling, etc. The items depend upon the nature of the business, but usually include salaries of officers, rent of offices, office and general expenses, etc. Also, the costs for personnel (not custodial in nature) and services used or needed in operating a real estate property.

ADMINISTRATOR—A person to whom letters of administration, i.e., authority to administer the estate of a deceased person, have been granted by the proper court. A representative of limited authority, whose duties are to collect assets of estate, pay its debts, and distribute residue to those entitled. An administrator resembles an executor, but, being appointed by the court, and not by the deceased, has to give security for the due administration of the estate, by entering into a bond with sureties, called the administration bond.

ADMINISTRATOR'S DEED – A deed by a person lawfully appointed to manage and settle the estate of a deceased person who has left no executor.

ADOBE – See Types of Soil, page 351.

ADOBE CONSTRUCTION – Exterior walls built of blocks made from adobe soil mixed with straw and hardened in the sun.

AD VALOREM – According to the value.

AD VALOREM TAX – A tax varying with the value of a good or commodity; a real estate tax based on the value of the property.

ADVERSE LAND USE – A land use that detrimentally affects and is incompatible with other properties in its vicinity; for example, an industrial land use in a residential neighborhood.

ADVERSE POSSESSION – The actual, exclusive, open, notorious, hostile, and continuous possession and occupation of real property under an evident claim of right or title. The time required legally to obtain title by adverse possession varies from state to state and does not apply to federal lands.

AEOLIAN SOIL – See Types of Soil, page 351.

AERATION ZONE – The upper ground water zone which retains water for use of plants, permitting excess water to seep into the saturation zone.

AERIAL PHOTO – Any photo of the earth's surface taken from the air. Airplane photography of entire U.S. land mass taken by Federal Government every few years. Available from County Agricultural Stabilization and Conservation Service Office.

AESTHETIC – Pertaining to a sense of the beautiful. In common usage, describes that which has a beautiful or pleasing appearance as distinguished from purely utilitarian considerations.

AESTHETIC VALUE – The intangible, psychic enhancement of the value of a property due to such factors as a site offering an unusually pleasing view; a property located in an area, the overall layout and design of which is exceptionally attractive and wherein all the properties are harmonious.

AFFORESTATION – The establishment of a forest on land or in areas, such as abandoned or submarginal farm land, where no forest existed before. Should not be confused with "Reforestation."

AFM – Accredited Farm Manager. A professional designation conferred by the American Society of Farm Managers and Rural Appraisers.

AFTER-TAX CASH FLOW (ATCF) – The residual obtained by deducting Income Tax Liability from Cash Throw-Off to Equity (Before-

Tax Cash Flow). In the case where Taxable Income is negative, After-Tax Cash Flow is equal to Cash Throw-Off to Equity plus Tax Savings (presumes that negative Taxable Income can be offset against other income).

AFTER-TAX EQUITY YIELD RATE — The annual rate of return on equity after payment of income taxes; the Internal Rate of Return (IRR) after taxes. See Internal Rate of Return.

AFTER-TAX INCOME (ATI) — The residual obtained by deducting Income Tax Liability from Taxable Income; an accounting term not to be confused with After-Tax Cash Flow, i.e., the terms are not synonymous.

AFTER-TAX NET CASH PROCEEDS OF RESALE (ATNCPR) — The after-tax reversion to equity; generally, the estimated resale price of the property less commissions, outstanding debt, and tax claims on the ownership interest. Also represents a cash flow and is incorporated into after-tax internal rate of return (IRR) calculations.

AGE (of structure) — See Actual Age, Effective Age.

AGE-LIFE METHOD — A method of estimating physical deterioration incurable as a percentage applied to current reproduction cost new of the improvements. The percentage reflects the ratio of estimated effective age to typically anticipated economic life (the sum of the effective age plus estimated remaining economic life). The Age-Life Method may also be applied to current replacement cost new of improvements, in which case the percentage calculated may differ from that percentage used for application to current reproduction cost new of improvements.

AGE-LIFE METHOD, MODIFIED — A method of estimating accrued depreciation which recognizes the possibility of curing certain items of accrued depreciation. The cost to cure all curable items, both physical and functional, is estimated, and this sum is deducted from reproduction cost new of the improvements. A percentage lump-sum deduction covering all incurable items is then derived by applying to the remaining reproduction cost new of the improvements a percentage computed by the Age-Life Method.

AGENT — A person who acts for another person by the latter's authority. The distinguishing characteristics of an agent are that the agent acts on behalf and subject to the control of the principal; that the agent does not have title to the property of the principal; and that the agent owes the duty of obedience to the principal's orders.

AGENTS IN PRODUCTION — See Factors in Production.

AGGREGATE

1. Materials used in the manufacture of concrete or plaster except water and the bonding agents (cement, lime, plaster). May include sand, gravel, cinders, rock, slag, etc.
2. It may refer to any summation process, such as aggregate income. See also Soil Aggregate.

AGREEMENT OF SALE — A written contract of sale between buyer and seller in which they reach a meeting of minds as to the conditions necessary for the transfer of ownership but before the actual transfer of title or assumption of ownership.

AGRICULTURAL ECONOMICS — That part of the study of economics which deals with the production and distribution of agricultural products together with the economic agencies serving agriculture, such as credit institutions, marketing associations, etc.

AGRICULTURAL EXTENSION AGENT — The representative of the Department of Agriculture stationed in a county to advise the farming community on new agricultural developments and methods to improve farming and rural living. Synonymous with County Extension Agent and County Farm Advisor.

AGRICULTURAL PROPERTY — Land improved or unimproved which is devoted to or available for the production of crops and other products of the soil, as fruits and timber, and for the raising of livestock.

AGRICULTURAL RESEARCH ADMINISTRATION — A major division of the United States Department of Agriculture, which is responsible for coordinating most of the department's bureaus and offices engaged in experimental, demonstration, or research activities. The administration has direct responsibility for the department's special research funds and for departmental research laboratories.

AGRICULTURAL RESEARCH SERVICE — A major division of the United States Department of Agriculture engaged in experimental, demonstration, and research activities relating to the production and utilization of farm products. It is also responsible for the control and regulatory programs involving the enforcement of plant and animal quarantines, the eradication of animal and plant diseases, meat inspection, and related work. Projects are carried on at the Agricultural Research Center, Beltsville, Md., as well as in other localities in the United States and in foreign countries. Much of the research is in cooperation with state agricultural experiment stations.

AGRICULTURAL USE VALUE — Value estimate premised on earnings/income approach based on agricultural productivity. Utilized by assessors for land devoted to farming, i.e., preferential assessment of farm land.

AGRICULTURE, DEPARTMENT OF – One of the more important administrative units of the federal government with a secretary of cabinet rank, created February 9, 1889. Traditionally, its prime objective has been the conduct of educational and research activities of immediate benefit to the farm community. In recent decades, however, the department has acquired additional responsibilities of a regulatory and enforcement nature. It now has direct or indirect responsibility for the administration of many federal agricultural-aid programs, among them programs for the stabilization and extension of agricultural markets; the extension of various forms of credit to the agricultural community; the administration of agricultural price-support policies; the promotion of land resource conservation; and other programs to assist farmer and rancher. Some of its principal subsidiary units are the Soil Conservation Service, the Forest Service, the Agricultural Marketing Service, the Farmers Home Administration, and the Commodity Credit Corporation.

AIR CONDITIONING – A system designed to control room temperature and humidity by means of ventilation, air circulation, and air cleaning; the process of treating air for simultaneous control of temperature, humidity, cleanliness, and distribution.

AIRPORT ZONING
1. A system of control of the height of structures and natural growth, and of land uses around an airport for the purposes of eliminating hazards to aircraft, such as smoke, electronic, and structural interference.
2. A right granted by the State, which empowers the regulatory agency to impose the restrictions.

AIR RIGHTS – The right to undisturbed use and control of a designated air space within the perimeter of a stated land area and within stated elevations. Such rights may be acquired for the construction of a building above the land or building of another, or for the protection of the light and air of an existing or proposed structure on an adjoining lot. Not synonymous with air space.

AIR SPACE – Suprasurface space owned by the property owner and to which the owner has all rights of possession, enjoyment, and disposition. The full use of suprasurface space, as with surface or subsurface space, may be subject to regulation or restriction (both public and private). Not synonymous with air rights.

ALCOVE – A recessed area connected with a room or hallway.

ALKALI – Applies to certain soluble salts which, when accumulated in soils in abnormal concentrations, are toxic to economic plant growth. Not acid. Black alkali is a term applied to alkali salts containing a preponderance of the toxic sodium carbonate and sodium chloride salts; white alkali refers to the neutral salts, sodium chloride, and sodium sulfate, as distinguished from sodium carbonate (black alkali) when occurring in concentrations sufficient to interfere with plant growth.

ALKALINE SOIL – See Types of Soil, page 351.

ALLEY – A relatively narrow way, publicly or privately owned, which serves as a secondary means of access and affords light and air to abutting properties. In the older, built-up cities alleys are often characterized by structures built out to the edge of narrow sidewalks or to the curb line. In some areas where the grid pattern of development has been prevalent, it is located at the rear of rows of properties facing parallel, public streets and is used for deliveries and other service functions.

ALLEY INFLUENCE – The effect caused by a side or rear alley on the value of abutting property, especially with respect to commercial property.

ALLOCATION – The distribution of the appraised value of the property between land and building. This is accomplished on a ratio basis (utilizing percentage breakdowns from comparable locations) by subtracting a figure representing the percentage contribution of buildings to total value from total value of the improved property (100%). Although a distribution of a price or value between land and improvements by statistical ratio can be useful at times, the procedure has limitations.

ALLOTMENT
1. A tract of land which has been divided into smaller parts; a subdivision.
2. An allowance as set forth by the USDA designating the specific amount of crops which may be produced or the acreage which can be devoted to the production of a specific crop.
3. Funds allocated by an institutional investor for the purchase of mortgages for its portfolio within a designated period of time.

ALLOWANCE FOR VACANCY AND INCOME LOSS – That amount deducted from Potential Annual Gross Income to reflect the effect of probable vacancy, turnover, or non-payment of rent by tenants; commonly expressed as a percentage of Potential Annual Gross Income and then converted to a dollar figure; the percentage of vacancy and income loss is the complement of the occupancy ratio.

ALLUVIAL – Deposits made by flowing water.

ALLUVIAL FAN – The outspread sloping fan-shaped deposit of boulders, gravel, and sand left by a stream or river where it spreads out into a level plain or meets a slower stream or river. The delta at the mouth of a river.

ALLUVIAL SOIL – See Types of Soil, page 351.

ALLUVION – The addition made to land by the washing of the sea, a navigable river, or other streams, whenever the increase is so gradual that it cannot be perceived in any one moment of time. See also Accretion.

ALLUVIUM – A fine material, such as sand, mud, or other sediments, carried by water and deposited on land.

ALTERNATIVE MORTGAGE INSTRUMENTS (AMIs) – A generic term which relates to a whole range of new mortgage forms which differ from the standard fixed-rate, level-payment mortgage instrument widely used today. See, for example, Graduated Payment Mortgage (GPM); Flexible Loan Insurance Plan (FLIP); Reverse Annuity Mortgage (RAM); and Variable Rate Mortgage (VRM).

AMENITIES – The pleasant satisfactions that are received through using rights in real property but that are not necessarily received in the form of money. The tangible and intangible benefits generated by a property.

AMENITY VALUE – The increment in value above the utility or rental value alone.

AMERICAN BOND – A masonry process in which every 5th, 6th, or 7th course of bricks is laid with the length perpendicular to the wall as a header course.

AMORTIZATION – The process of retiring debt or recovering a capital investment through scheduled, systematic repayments of principal; a program of periodic contributions to a sinking fund or debt retirement fund; that portion of a fixed mortgage payment applied to reduction of the principal amount owed.

AMORTIZATION FACTOR – See Partial Payment.

AMORTIZATION RATE – The ratio of the periodic amortization payment to the total principal amount to be amortized; corresponds to a sinking fund factor or rate; the difference between the Mortgage (Annual) Constant and the nominal rate of interest.

AMORTIZED MORTGAGE – A mortgage requiring periodic payments which include both a partial repayment of the debt and interest on the outstanding balance.
 1. Fully Amortized Mortgage Loan – equal periodic payments, most often on a monthly basis, which provide for both a return on investment (interest) and full return of investment (recovery of principal) over the term of the loan. The proportion of the principal is reduced, and the proportion represented by principal repayment increases correspondingly.
 2. Partially Amortized Mortgage Loan – occurs when the loan is not fully amortized over its maturity and the portion of the loan principal outstanding at maturity must be repaid as one

lump sum. Partial Amortization is often achieved by writing a loan for one maturity but calculating debt service payments on the basis of a longer amortization period. See Balloon.

AMOUNT OF ONE (FUTURE WORTH OF ONE) – The basic compound interest factor from which all others are derived. Indicates the amount to which a single lump-sum investment made today (at time period zero) will grow at compound interest, given the rate of interest and the number of periods (of equal length) over which compounding is to occur. See Basic Formulas, page 333.

AMOUNT OF ONE PER PERIOD (FUTURE WORTH OF AN ANNUITY OF ONE, ACCUMULATION OF ONE PER PERIOD) – The factor applied to an ordinary level annuity to derive the total sum to which all the payments will accumulate if they are left on deposit to earn compound interest, at a specified rate over a specified number of time periods. See Basic Formulas, page 333. See also Annuity.

ANALYST – See Real Estate Analyst.

ANCHOR BOLT – A bolt used to secure a structural member to a masonry support. A common form is the anchor bolt set into a concrete foundation and extending up through the sill, secured with a nut at the top. It is designed to prevent upward and lateral movements by the superstructure.

ANCHOR TENANT – The major store or stores within a shopping center considered to be the magnet or traffic generator for the shopping center. The type of anchor or anchors depends upon the size of the shopping center and ranges from the supermarket in a neighborhood center to a major chain or department store(s) in the larger (regional) shopping centers.

ANIMAL UNIT – Generally, a mature beef or dairy animal. An animal weighing 1,000 pounds is the standard of measure; thus, a 500-pound weaner calf represents one-half animal unit, or 4 to 6 sheep or goats equal one animal unit. Generally, cows with nursing calves, or bulls, are counted as one animal unit regardless of weight in ranching operations. Horses are generally considered to equal 1.2 to 1.25 animal units each. The term is subject to some local variation. See also Animal Units Per Month Table, page 293.

ANIMAL UNIT MONTH (AUM)
1. The number of animal units which can be grazed for one month on tame pasture or native range without injurious effect to forage production.
2. The number of animal units held in a herd for one month.
3. Frequently the measure of hay, silage, and feed grain is converted from weight or other unit of measure to animal unit

months of feed as a unit of measure. See Animal Units Per Month Table, page 293.

ANNUAL PERCENTAGE RATE (APR) — A requirement of truth in lending legislation that loan instruments and loan advertising show the interest cost to the borrower in the form of an annual rate.

ANNUALS — See Types of Range Vegetation, page 349.

ANNUITY — An income in the form of a series of payments collectible at even intervals, the basic characteristic being equality of the time interval between collections. Otherwise defined as:

1. A periodic income.
2. The return from an investment of capital, in a series of periodic payments which comprise both return on and a partial return of capital.
3. The periodic return may be in equal annual amounts, called a level annuity, or in increasing or decreasing annual amounts, called an increasing or a decreasing annuity. See also Amount of One per Period, Declining Annuity, Declining Annuity Method, Deferred Annuity, Increasing Annuity, Inwood Factor, Variable Annuity.
4. An annuity in advance or annuity due, depending upon whether the income payments are prepaid or postpaid.
5. The phrase "characteristics of an annuity" implies a high degree of reliability to the quantity, quality, and durability of the income projection.

ANNUITY CERTAIN — An annuity assured for a specified period of time as distinguished from a life annuity which terminates with the death of an individual.

ANNUITY IN ADVANCE — An annuity with payments due at the beginning of each time interval as opposed to an annuity payable in arrears (at the end of each time interval).

ANNUITY METHOD

1. A procedure of capitalization or discounting which is based on common formulas or tables used for the valuation of annuities, e.g., leases. The method provides for both return on and return of investment.
2. A method in which one component of the value of an income-producing property is the present worth of the right to receive the net income over a stipulated period of time. The process involves the discounting of future annual Net Operating Income to a present value.
3. The application of the annuity principle to determine the amount, rate, or time necessary to liquidate an interest-bearing debt, or to determine the periodic amount, rate, or time required to accumulate a specified capital sum.

ANODIZED ALUMINUM – Aluminum which has had a hard, corrosion-resistant, oxide film applied to it by an electrochemical process. A color anodizing process may be used to produce a number of colored finishes.

ANTICIPATION, PRINCIPLE OF – Affirms that value is created by the anticipation of future benefits. (Value may be defined as the present worth of all rights to future benefits.)

ANTICIPATED USE METHOD – A method of estimating the value of vacant land. The usual application is to raw, unsubdivided land by deducting from the estimated gross selling price, the direct expense of development such as cost of streets, utilities, sales, advertising, and overhead (taxes, carrying charges, inspection). Profit and "time lag" (interest on the money invested for the time needed to complete the project) are also deducted, after which the land value is indicated. Also known as development method.

ANTILOGARITHM – The natural number corresponding to a logarithm.

APARTMENT – A dwelling unit comprised of one or more rooms designed to provide complete living facilities for a family or an individual(s).

APARTMENT HOTEL – A furnished apartment building, the tenancy of which is more or less permanent, but which offers such hotel facilities as reception desk, telephone switchboard, maid service, utilities, etc.

APARTMENT BUILDING – A building containing separate residential units, commonly not less than three, and providing such facilities as central heating, common main entrance, stairs or elevators, and janitor services. See also Flat, Cooperative Apartment, High-rise Apartment Building, Condominium, Tenement.

APPLIED ECONOMICS – The application of economic theory to the solution of economic problems.

APPORTIONMENT – An allocation of funds by one governmental unit to another based on a prescribed formula for the accomplishment of specific purposes.

APPRAISAL
1. An estimate or opinion of value.
2. "An evaluation of the nature, quality or utility of any parcel of real estate, or any interest in or aspect of real property." (Regulation No. 10, AIREA Code of Professional Ethics and Standards of Professional Conduct).
3. The solution or conclusion concerning any real estate problem.
4. The act or process of estimating value or conducting an evaluation study. The resulting opinion or conclusion derived from the appraisal may be informal, transmitted orally; or it may be formal, presented in written form. Usually it is a written statement

setting forth the opinions or conclusions of the appraiser concerning an adequately described property as of a specified date, supported by the presentation and analysis of relevant data.

APPRAISAL CERTIFICATE — See Certificate.

APPRAISAL DATE — The date as of which the conclusion or opinion rendered in an appraisal is applicable and valid. The date of appraisal identifies the market conditions that existed when the appraisal was made.

APPRAISAL METHODS — The investigative methods or valuation approaches used in the appraisal of real property.

APPRAISAL PROCESS — A systematic analysis of the factors that bear upon the value or utility of real estate. An orderly program by which the problem is defined, the work necessary to solve the problem is planned, and the data involved are acquired, classified, analyzed, and interpreted into a final opinion or conclusion.

APPRAISAL REPORT — Although abbreviated forms of appraisal reports (including verbal) may be acceptable depending upon the requirements of the client, the type of property, and the nature of the appraisal assignment, the narrative appraisal report is a formal written document which contains (a) the purpose of the appraisal, (b) the result of the appraisal (the opinion of value or other estimate or conclusion formed by the appraiser), (c) the effective date of the appraisal, (d) the certification and signature of the appraiser, (e) the qualifying conditions, (f) an adequate description of the neighborhood and identification of the property and its ownership, (g) the factual data, (h) an analysis and interpretation of the data, (i) the processing of the data, and (j) other descriptive supporting material (maps, plans, charts, photographs).

APPRAISAL SUMMARY — A recapitulation of significant facts and conclusions contained in an appraisal report.

APPRAISAL TECHNIQUE — Traditionally, in the context of capitalization in appraisal practice, one of the physical residual techniques (Land Residual, Building Residual, or Property Residual). Current practice would suggest, however, a much broader definition: Any technique or techniques by which data are processed into an opinion or conclusion concerning a real estate problem. See Ellwood Premise, Mortgage Equity, Residual Process.

APPRAISED VALUE — An opinion of an appraiser which is based upon an interpretation of facts and judgments and their processing into an estimate of value, as of a stated date. While the term "appraised value" is general in nature, it is precisely defined in the statement of purpose. The value most commonly sought is market value, although there are other types of value, depending on the use for which the client requires the appraisal.

APPRAISEMENT – Synonym: appraisal.

APPRAISER – One who conducts appraisals; specifically, one who possesses the necessary qualifications, ability, and experience to execute or direct the appraisal of real or personal property. See also Professional Appraiser.

APPRECIATION – Increase in value due to increase in cost to reproduce, value over the cost, or value at some specified earlier point in time, brought about by greater demand, improved economic conditions, increasing price levels, reversal of depreciating environmental trends, improved transportation facilities, direction of community or area growth, or other factors.

APPROACH NOSE – An area of land between highways which faces the approaching traffic that may pass to either or both sides of this land.

APPROACH ZONE – A path or corridor which represents the legal altitude through which aircraft descend to, or take off from an airport.

APPROACHES (to value) – The traditional basic methods or techniques by which market data may be processed into an indication of value:
1. Direct Sales Comparison Approach – variously referred to as Comparison Approach, Sales Approach, Comparative Sales Approach, Market Data Approach, and Market Approach.
2. Cost Approach – sometimes referred to as Summation Approach.
3. Income Approach – sometimes referred to as Capitalization Approach and Income Capitalization Approach. See also Appraisal Methods.

APPROPRIATION
1. The taking of a public thing for private use, particularly personal use.
2. The doctrine of appropriation affirms that the water of natural streams belongs to the public generally, but a person may appropriate if for a beneficial use. The first person making such use of the water thereby establishes a prior right to the continued use of the water for that particular use against all others.
3. Incorrectly used as a synonym for either condemnation or expropriation.

APPURTENANCE – That which has been added to another thing; that which has been added or appended to a property and which becomes an inherent part of the property, and usually passes with it when it is sold, leased, or devised.

A PRIORI – From the past; from what has previously transpired.

APRON
1. A hard-surfaced entrance to a loading dock or portion of a building.

2. The connecting portion of a private driveway or roadway with a public street or road.
3. That portion of a wharf or pier lying between the waterfront edge and the buildings thereon.
4. A wooden protection along a sea wall or face of a dam.
5. The inside wood finish piece of a window underneath the sill.

AQUEDUCT — An artificial channel for conveyance of water from place to place; a major conduit either open or covered. The similar structure by which a canal is carried over a river (aqueduct-bridge).

ARA — Accredited Rural Appraiser. A professional designation conferred by the American Society of Farm Managers and Rural Appraisers.

ARABLE — Land fit for the plow; suitable for purposes of cultivation. Tillable.

ARCADE — A series of arches on the same plane, either open or closed. A walkway or passageway with arched roof, frequently with shops along one or both sides. A passageway open on street side, usually colonnaded. A colonnaded sidewalk.

ARCH — A convexly curved vertical span of steel, concrete, stone, or wood. A structural section with end base supports, so constructed as to have supporting ability for itself, superstructure, and attached or suspended structure. See illustration, page 303.

ARCHITECTURAL CONCRETE CONSTRUCTION — Concrete with little or no reinforcement, poured against a form which bears a design producing a decorative treatment to simulate stone masonry.

ARCHITECTURE
1. Generally, the art or science of building design and construction.
2. Style, appearance, character of buildings, etc.

ARCHITRAVE — The molding above and on both sides of a door or other square opening.

AREA
1. The surface extent, measured in square units, of a building, a site, neighborhood, section of a city, a tract, or a region. See also Blighted Area, Gross Area; Standard Area Measurement, page 295.
2. In residential design this term is used to indicate function, as work area, recreation area, etc.

AREA CONTROLS — A zoning provision controlling use densities; the ratio of building area to site area.

AREA SAMPLE — A limited number of observations selected from an entire aggregate of phenomena on the basis of geographical subdivisions.

AREAWAY — An uncovered space next to a building, for entrance of light, air or access. See Light Well.

ARITHMETIC MEAN — The quotient of a sum of a series of values divided by the number of values in the group. It is the most commonly used average, being easily understood. Its disadvantage is that its value may be distorted by extreme figures. Synonym: arithmetic average. For illustration, see page 314.

ARM'S LENGTH — A transaction freely arrived at in the open market, unaffected by abnormal pressure or by the absence of normal competitive negotiation as might be true in the case of a transaction between related parties.

ARPENT — An old French land measure of area used in Canada and in some parts of southern United States; varying slightly but approximating 0.84625 acre. The side of a square arpent equals 2.909 chains or 191.994 feet.

ARRANGEMENT OF DATA — In a statistical table the items are most commonly arranged:
1. Alphabetically — according to the alphabetic order of the items.
2. Chronologically — according to the time of occurrence in comparing subjects over a period of time. Generally, the dates should move from the earliest at the top to the latest at the bottom of the column, or from left to right.
3. Geographically — according to location.
4. Magnitude — according to size. The largest or smallest number is placed at the top of the column and the others follow in order of size, or by largest or smallest number from left to right.
5. Sequence — according to the order of succession, continuity, connection, or possibly, uniformity.

ARRAY — The listing of a set of observations, usually in order of magnitude from "low" to "high" or "high" to "low."

ARROYO — A dry gully.

ARTERIAL HIGHWAY — A general term designating a major highway, usually on a continuous or through route. Descriptive of character of use and not of character of improvement.

ASBESTOS — A non-flammable natural mineral fiber.

ASHLAR — Squared stone carefully laid in a wall with uniform joint thickness. May be further defined according to the coursing as range, broken range, or random. When the stone exceeds 12 inches in thickness, it becomes rough ashlar.

ASPECT

1. Position facing, fronting, or regarding a particular direction; as a house with a southern aspect. Synonym: exposure.
2. The part so fronting.
3. In forestry, the direction toward which a slope faces according to the main points of the compass.

ASPHALT TILE — A resilient floor covering laid in mastic, available in several colors. Standard size is 9″ × 9″ (also comes in several other sizes). Asphalt is normally used only in darker colors, lighter colors having a resin base.

ASPHALTIC CONCRETE — Asphalt binder and stone or other aggregate, used as a hard surface for streets, airstrips, and other paved areas.

ASSEMBLAGE — The combining of two or more parcels (usually but not necessarily contiguous) into one ownership or use. See also Plottage.

ASSEMBLAGE COST — That excess cost of acquiring individual adjacent parcels of real estate into a single ownership beyond the estimated cost of similar sites not forming the specifically desired assemblage.

ASSESS

1. The official valuation of property as a basis for taxation.
2. To fix or determine, as by a court or commission, the compensation due a property owner (condemnee) in a condemnation of real property ownership.

ASSESSABLE IMPROVEMENT — An improvement that increases the value of a property and hence (in the absence of a contrary law) should also increase the assessment.

ASSESSED VALUATION

1. The figure at which the property is put on the assessment roll and, unless altered by a higher authority, the basis upon which the property tax levy is distributed among the property owners. Assessed values may differ from market values for these major reasons: fractional assessment laws, partial exemption, and problems in keeping assessed values current.
2. The assessor's estimate of market value before deductions for partial exemptions and before the application of any factor prescribed by law or tradition concerning the level of assessment.

ASSESSED VALUE — A dollar amount assigned to taxable property, both real and personal, by the assessor for the purpose of taxation. Assessed value is frequently a statutorily determined percentage of market value.

ASSESSMENT
1. The official valuation level of property for ad valorem tax purposes and, in this sense, synonymous with Assessed Value.
2. A single charge levied against a parcel of real estate to defray the cost of a public improvement which presumably benefits only the properties it serves, and in an amount at least equal to the property owner's share of the cost of the improvement: e.g., assessment for installation of sidewalks, curbs, sewer or water line. Also referred to as a Special Assessment.

   In this sense, the improvement for which the assessment is levied is usually immediately adjacent to or a part of the properties benefited and does not always invade or encroach upon them.
3. An official determination of the amount(s) to be paid by or to the owners of real estate to defray the cost of a public improvement which is presumed to benefit the properties it is declared to serve in an amount at least equal to the cost of the improvement; e.g., assessment of benefits and damages for trunk sewer or trunk water line.

   In this sense, the improvement, depending upon its layout or location, may or may not encroach upon or actually invade the properties benefited.
4. An official determination of the amount to be paid property owners for the taking of all or part of their property for an improvement which is presumed and, in fact, is designed to benefit the public generally; e.g., assessment of benefits and damages for highway or school construction.

   In this usage, jurisdictional rules will determine in cases of a partial taking whether (a) benefits may be employed to offset only severance damages to the remainder area, (b) only special, as opposed to general, benefits may be used as an offset against damages, or (c) both general and special benefits may represent an amount that offsets all damages. See also Special Assessment.

ASSESSMENT BASE—The assessed value of all property within a designated area, such as an assessment or tax district. Synonym: property tax base.

ASSESSMENT DISTRICT—A jurisdiction, such as a county or other political subdivision, under the authority of an assessor. It may be identical to a tax district or may encompass several tax districts.

ASSESSMENT PERIOD (ASSESSMENT CYCLE OR FREQUENCY)— The period during which all property in the assessment district must be reassessed.

ASSESSMENT PROCESS—The discovery, listing, and valuation (or appraisal) of property for taxation. See Cadastral Program.

ASSESSMENT RATIO—The relationship an assessed value bears to market value. See also Assessed Value.

ASSESSMENT ROLL—The basis upon which the property tax levy is allocated among the property owners in a jurisdiction with taxing powers. The assessment roll usually lists an identifier for each taxable parcel in the jurisdiction, the name of the owner of record, the address of the parcel or the owner, the assessed value of the land, the assessed value of the improvement(s), application exemption codes if any, and the total assessed value.

ASSESSMENT–SALES RATIO—The ratio derived by dividing the assessed value by the selling price; used as a measure of assessments to market value.

ASSESSOR—One whose duty it is to assess property for ad valorem taxes.

ASSESSOR'S MANUAL—A manual giving specific requirements for property assessment. Primarily structured to provide a base or guide for property assessment and thus a more uniform treatment of similar properties.

ASSET—Any property which is owned and has value. Assets are either financial, as cash or bonds; or physical, as real and personal. See also Capital Assets, Cash Assets, Current Assets, Deferred Assets, Diminishing Assets, Fixed Assets, Intangible Assets, Liquid Assets, Physical Assets, Working Assets.

ASSIGNEE—The person(s) or corporation to whom a contract is assigned.

ASSIGNMENT—The transfer of an interest in a bond, mortgage, lease, or other instrument, by writing.

ASSIGNOR—The person(s) or corporation from whom a contract is assigned.

ASSUMED MORTGAGE—An existing mortgage for which a new owner agrees to assume the liability when the property is purchased and transferred.

ASSUMPTION OF MORTGAGE—When buyers take ownership to real estate encumbered with a mortgage, they may assume the responsibility as the guarantor of the unpaid balance of the mortgage. Such buyers are liable for the mortgage repayment.

ATRIUM—Typically, a central area of a structure with a ceiling of a translucent material admitting nurturing sunlight to interior ornamental plants.

ATTIC—Accessible space between roof rafters and ceiling joists.

AUM—See Animal Unit Month.

AUSTRIAN SCHOOL—See Marginal Utility School.

AUTHORITY — An agency of government, usually independent, established for a specific purpose, such as constructing and/or operating housing projects, toll roads and turnpikes, ports, public transportation, etc.

AUTOMATION — A productive system wherein the various production processes are executed by self-acting and self-regulating machines, replacing the use of human labor to perform the same tasks.

AUXILIARY LANE — That portion of pavement which is adjacent to the travelway and designed for parking, speed acceleration or deceleration, or other use supplementing the through traffic flow.

AVERAGE — A value which is typically used to sum up or describe a mass of data. It is a measure of central tendency. See also Arithmetic Mean, Geometric Average, Median, Mode, Moving Average, Trend, Weighted Average. See illustration, page 314.

AVERAGE DAILY TRAFFIC (ADT) — The average one-day traffic volume measured at a selected highway location. It is the sum of all traffic recorded for a given period of time divided by the number of days in that period. It is usually reported as the ADT for a specific year.

AVERAGE (MEAN) DEVIATION — The value obtained by first subtracting the arithmetic mean of all items from each item, then adding up these differences without regard to sign (plus or minus), and finally dividing this sum by the number of items. See illustration, page 318.

AVIGATION EASEMENT — The right granted by the owner of land adjacent to an airport to the use of the air space above a specific height for the flight of aircraft. The easement may prohibit the owner from using the land for structures, trees, signs, stacks, etc., higher than the altitude specified. The degree of such restriction will vary in accordance with the glide angle necessary for the safe use of an airfield's runway.

AVULSION — The sudden removal of land from the property of one owner to that of another, as by inundation or a change in the course of a river; the land so removed continues in the original ownership.

AWNING — A roof-like shelter extending over a doorway, window, porch, etc., which provides protection from the sun or rain.

AWNING WINDOW — A type of window having sash with hinges at the top, permitting the window to open horizontally, forming an awning over the opening. See illustration, page 301.

AXIOM — A fundamental principle widely accepted on its intrinsic merit; a proposition regarded as a self-evident truth. Some basic rules of arithmetic and algebra are stated as axioms, e.g., equals will remain equal if equal amounts are added to, or subtracted from, or multiplied by, or divided into the equals.

AZIMUTH—The angle between true north or true south and an object. In surveying, it is measured clockwise from north.

AZONAL SOIL—See Types of Soil, page 351.

B HORIZON—The subsoil; a horizon of deposition to which materials are being added by percolating water. The horizon lying beneath the A horizon. See also A, C, and D Horizons.

BACK BAND CASING—A common or butt casing with a molded and/or mitered trim piece around its outer edge. See illustration, page 308.

BACKFILL—To replace earth material removed during excavation. The subsurface material placed against structures, foundations, or footings.

BACKUP—The lower-cost material in a masonry wall which is covered by more expensive and ornamental material facing such as face brick, stone, marble, metal panels, etc.

BACKWATER VALVE—An automatic valve set in the sewer lateral to prevent sewage from backing up into the cellar or plumbing fixtures during flood periods.

BALANCE, PRINCIPLE OF—Holds that value is created and maintained in proportion to the equilibrium attained in the amount and location of essential uses of real estate. The degree of value of a property is governed by the balance or apportionment of the four factors in production.

BALANCE SHEET—A statement of the financial position of an undertaking at a specified date, prepared from books kept by a double entry system of bookkeeping. A statement showing a reconciliation of the assets with the liabilities, capital, and surplus in a business as of a certain date.

BALANCED OPERATION

1. In ranching, a livestock enterprise which provides sufficient feed and forage resources at each season to sustain continuous satisfactory maintenance of its livestock and game throughout the year.
2. An enterprise in which the gross income either equals or exceeds, by a suitable margin for profit, the cost of production.

BALCONY

1. A balustrade or railed platform projecting from the face of a building above the ground level with an entrance from the building interior, usually cantilevered or supported by columns.
2. In a theater or auditorium, a partial upper floor with seats.

BALLOON
1. In finance, the unamortized principal amount of a mortgage or long term loan which is paid off in a lump sum at the end of the term – Balloon Payment.
2. In construction, a type of framing in which the studs extend from the sill to the roof; support for the second floor is provided by a horizontal ribbon or ledger board and joists which are nailed to the studs – Balloon Frame.
3. A parcel of land which does not have frontage on a public road.

BALUSTER – A short pillar or post, usually circular, slender above and bulging below, supporting a rail; the uprights supporting the handrail of a staircase.

BALUSTRADE – A row of balusters surmounted by a rail, coping, or cornice.

BAND OF INVESTMENT – A widely used and conceptually defensible approach to estimating a Discount (Risk) Rate. It is based on the premise that financing is typically involved in a real estate transaction, and that equity investors seek to obtain the best available financial package in order to maximize the potential benefits of leverage.

The Rate developed is a weighted average of the return on investment required to cover mortgage interest and the return on investment required to provide a competitive equity return.

In simple mortgage-equity analysis, the band of investment technique is used to derive the Overall Rate. In this instance, the Overall Rate is a weighted average of the mortgage constant and the equity rate (simple mortgage-equity analysis assumes no change in the value of the equity position over the holding period, i.e., equity dividend rate and equity yield rate are equal).

BAR CHART – A graphic method of presenting data in which bars of uniform width are used to indicate differences in the size of two or more variables by means of varying length or height.

BARN – A specially designed building for housing farm animals and for the storage of hay and grain. This original use is becoming obsolete in much current farm operation and the buildings are being converted to equipment storage and other uses.

BARREL – A unit of measure equal to 31½ gallons for liquids; 42 gallons for oil; or 376 pounds (4 sacks) of cement.

BARREN – See Types of Range Vegetation, page 349.

BASAL AREA – In forestry, the breast height cross section area of a single tree or all trees in a stand, expressed in square feet.

BASAL AREA FACTOR (BAF) – The basal or stem area per unit of stand area for a given angle for each tree intercepted from a sampling point. The factor gives basal area in square feet per acre if multiplied by the average number of trees counted per sample point.

BASE

1. In compound interest (discount) tables, one plus the periodic rate; denoted by the symbol S in mortgage-equity and Ellwood formulations.
2. In building construction, the lowest part of a wall, pier, pedestal, or column.

BASEBOARD — A finishing piece of material carried around the bottom of interior walls which conceals the base of the wall where it meets the floor.

BASEBOARD HEATING — A system of perimeter heating with radiators, convectors, or air outlets located in the wall, replacing the baseboard; also called base panel heating. May be hot water, forced air, or electric.

BASE LINE

1. A survey line running due east and west through the initial point of a principal meridian from which township lines are established by the government survey.
2. A topographic centerline of a survey as for the route of a highway.

BASE MAP — A map having sufficient points of reference, such as state, county, or township lines, and other selected physical features, to allow the plotting of other data.

BASEMENT — The lowest story of a building, partially or wholly below ground level; not a cellar. For measurement of, see Standard Area Measures, page 295.

BASE MOLD — An ornamental, decorative strip of molded material laid along the top of a baseboard; sometimes called a bed mold. See illustration, page 305.

BASE PERIODS — Time intervals or reference points used for business and economic data. In the formulation of index numbers the figures for a base period are usually averaged and the average is adopted as 100. The base period of an index number is sometimes erroneously regarded as a "normal" period.

BASE PLATE — The horizontal member at the bottom of a column or post which transmits the column loads to its foundation. See Anchor Bolt.

BASE PROPERTY — The private holdings of a stock raiser, either fee owned land, water sources, or private leased property which is used as the base required for the issuance of a grazing permit on public domain under the Taylor Grazing Act.

BASE RENT — The minimum rental stipulated under a percentage lease.

BASIC ACTIVITIES — In economic base analysis, those activities with outputs primarily intended for export to other areas.

BASIC CAPACITY — The maximum number of passenger cars that can pass a given point on a lane or roadway during one hour under the most nearly ideal roadway and traffic conditions obtainable. It is often reported as automobile units of capacity.

BASIC CROPS — Certain staple commodities, such as corn, wheat, cotton, tobacco, rice, and peanuts; often subject to price supports.

BASIC RATE — The portion of the overall (composite) rate which covers all of the income requirements except provision for depreciation or appreciation; in the Ellwood formula, designated by the symbol r.

BASIS — That portion of total property value likely to be affected by depreciation or capital improvement.

BASIS POINT — One one-hundredth of one percentage point.

BATCH PROCESSING — A computer operation which involves the processing of a number of programs utilizing the same data base in a single continuous run.

BATHROOM — A room containing, as a minimum, a toilet, lavatory, and a bathtub, with or without shower. FHA counts three plumbing fixtures equal to one bathroom; two plumbing fixtures equal to one-half bathroom. In some areas, real estate brokers count a toilet, lavatory, and shower as three-fourth bathroom.

BATTEN — A narrow strip of wood to cover a joint between boards, or to simulate a covered joint for architectural purposes.

BATTER — The slope of a wall, terrace, pier, or bank from the perpendicular, the vertical incline of which is generally expressed as so many inches horizontal to so many inches vertical.

BATTURE LAND — Land situated between the water's edge at low tide or at low water stage, and the river bank or the levee. Generally, the land is held in the same ownership as that of the abutting land; but it can be sold separately from the adjoining land.

BAY
1. An opening in a wall.
2. The space between columns or piers.
3. A division of a barn or other buildings, such as industrial, warehouse, service stations.

BAY WINDOW — A window forming a bay in a room and which projects outward from the wall and is supported by its own foundation, in contrast to an oriel or box bay window which is similar but lacks foundation support. See illustration, page 301.

BAYES' THEOREM — Used to incorporate information gathered (sample information) about a particular situation into the total amount at hand; the formula used in the revision of probabilities; central to the Bayesian Approach to statistical estimation.

BAYESIAN ANALYSIS (STATISTICS) — A statistical technique in which probabilities (referred to as "prior probabilities") are assigned to a set of mutually exclusive and exhaustive events on the basis of whatever evidence (information) is currently available. Then, if additional evidence is subsequently obtained, the initial (prior) probabilities are revised on the basis of this evidence by means of Bayes' Theorem. The probabilities resulting from the revision process are known as posterior probabilities.

BAYESIAN DECISION RULE — To choose that action which has the best expected payoff; to optimize the expected payoff — minimize the expected loss — where payoffs and losses are defined in terms of utility or dollars and cents.

BEAM
1. A principal load supporting member of a building; may be of wood, steel, or concrete.
2. Lumber of rectangular cross section, five or more inches thick and eight or more inches wide, graded with respect to its strength when loaded on the narrow face. See also Bond Beam, Cantilever Beam, Constrained Beam, Grade Beam.

BEAMED CEILING — A ceiling with beams exposed. A false beamed ceiling has ornamental boards or timbers which are not load-bearing.

BEARING
1. The situation or horizontal direction of one point or object with respect to another, or to the points of the compass.
2. That portion of any member of a building that rests upon its supports.

BEARING VALUE (OF SOIL) — The character and ability of the soil and other underlying material to support a load such as foundations and building.

BEARING WALL (BEARING PARTITION) — A wall which supports a part of a building, usually a floor or roof above it. See also Wall Bearing Construction.

BED-A-TREE — To prepare the path on which a tree is to fall so that it may not shatter.

BED MOLD — An ornamental strip laid horizontally at the juncture of the frieze and cornice soffit; also see Base Mold. For illustration, see page 305.

BEDROCK — The solid rock underlying soils and other surficial formations.

BEFORE-TAX CASH FLOW — The cash available to the owner-investor after necessary operating expenses and contractual debt service are covered, but before deducting income tax liability. It is the cash flow generated by the property under any ownership (assuming normal competent management) and available as a return on the owner's equity. Before-tax cash flow is frequently called cash throw-off.

BELT — A horizontal course of decorative stone or brick encircling a masonry building.

BELT COURSE — A continuous course of distinctive masonry usually, but not necessarily, of decorative natural or cast stone, around an exposed wall or walls of a masonry building, laid at one or more levels between the water table and the cornice.

BELT HIGHWAY — An arterial highway for carrying traffic partially or entirely around an urban area or portion thereof and connected by principal streets or highways with the city. Synonyms: bypass, circumferential highway.

BENCH MARK — Identification symbols on stone, metal, or other durable matter permanently fixed in the ground and from which differences of elevation are measured as in tidal observations or topographical surveys. A datum.

BENCHMARK — The standard or base from which specific estimates are made.

BENEFICIAL INTERESTS — Benefits, profits, or advantages resulting from a trust contract. The equitable title in a property as distinguished from the trustee who holds only legal title.

BENEFICIAL USE
1. The right to the enjoyment of property where legal title is in one person and the right to use the property is in another.
2. Regarding water rights, this doctrine holds that the water resources (of the state) must be put to the most beneficial use of which they are capable. In some states, it supersedes the doctrine of riparian rights.

BENEFITS — The beneficial factors which arise from a public improvement for which private property has been taken in condemnation. There are two classifications of benefits, General Benefits, Special Benefits. See also Set-off Rule.

BENT
1. A transverse frame designed to support either horizontal or vertical loads, e.g., elevated railroad trackage.
2. Sections of a tobacco shed.

BERM
1. A horizontal ledge or bench part way up a slope.
2. A mound of earth, sometimes paved, used to divert or control the flow course of surface drainage, mark property boundaries, or alter topography.
3. The earthen or paved extension of a roadway; the shoulder along a highway.

BETTERMENT — An improvement which adds to the capital cost of the structure. A capital expenditure which increases the utility or market desirability of the property. It is distinguished from repairs or replacements in that the original character is improved and the capital investment is increased. A physical change in an existing property or equipment which increases its value and usefulness, and is not a mere restoration. It is reflected in accounting by an equivalent increase in book value. It does not result from an acquisition of new property or enlargement of an old one; also may arise from a physical change external to the property as street improvements, improved drainage facilities, etc. Measure of value is not in actual cost, but in enhanced value imparted to the property.

BEVELED SIDING — Clapboard.

BIKEWAYS — A continuous way designated for use of bicycles and other vehicles propelled by human power.

BI-LEVEL — A house built on two levels; a split-level house.

BINOMIAL DISTRIBUTION — In statistics, a discrete distribution characterizing situations in which samples are taken from a population of attributes having only two values (yes or no, success or failure, etc.)

BIRTH RATE — The number of births per 1,000 persons per year.

BLACKTOP (BITUMINOUS CONCRETE) — Bituminous or asphalt material used in hard surface paving.

BLANKET MORTGAGE — A mortgage which covers several properties. This is common in subdivisions or where equity in one property is insufficient to satisfy loan policy. Usually individual properties are released from the blanket mortgage as they are sold.

BLIGHT
1. Decay; withering away, as of a neighborhood. Decay caused by failure to maintain the quality of real estate and that of public services.

2. Applied to plant diseases which cause withering and, generally, death of parts, as leaves, or of the entire plant.

BLIGHTED AREA – Area or district subject to detrimental influences (such as adverse land use mixture) sufficient in number and/or extent to affect desirability adversely; characterized by retrogression, decline of property values, and no recognizable prospect of a change for the better.

BLOCK

1. A segment of a city; usually (but not always) a square area formed by and lying between intersecting streets or other physical boundaries. Also, the length of one side of such a square.
2. Preformed structural component made of concrete and used in construction. See Concrete Block.

BLOCK BUSTING – A method of obtaining property at depressed prices in a changing neighborhood. It involves the introduction into the area of a family of another race or class and then, taking advantage of the fears and prejudices of the inhabitants, buying their property at low prices and then reselling such property to the newcomers at inflated prices.

BLOWDOWN – A tree blown down by the wind. Also, an area on which the trees have been so blown down. Synonyms: windfall, wind slash.

BLUEPRINT – A working plan used on a construction job by tradesmen; an architectural drafting or drawing which is transferred to chemically treated paper by exposure to strong light causing the paper to turn blue thus reproducing the drawing in white.

BLUE SKY LAWS – Laws which are intended to protect the inexperienced investor against fraud and misrepresentation in the purchase of securities or real estate.

BOARD AND BATTEN – A type of siding, typically vertical, composed of wide boards and narrow battens. The boards are nailed to the sheathing so that there is one-half space between them. The battens are nailed over the open spaces between the boards.

BOARDFOOT – A unit of lumber measurement, one foot long, one foot wide, and one inch thick, i.e., one square foot, one inch thick (144 cubic inches). A boardfoot differs from a square foot in that (1) thickness is added as a third dimension, (2) the dimensions are "nominal" rather than actual, i.e., board measurements are quoted as "full" before dressing or planing.

BOARD MEASURE

1. A system of measurement for lumber. Quantities of lumber are designated and prices determined in terms of board feet. See Boardfoot.

2. The volume of logs, trees, or stands in terms of the estimated amount of lumber which may be cut therefrom according to various log rules. Usually abbreviated B.M. Units of larger quantities stated in thousands are abbreviated M.B.M. or M. See also Log Rules.

BOARD OF APPEALS – See Board of Equalization.

BOARD OF EQUALIZATION – A nonjudicial board whose function is to review assessments to see that all districts are assessed at a uniform level of value; to raise or lower the assessments to achieve this purpose, so that a uniform basis of taxation is achieved. Also referred to as Board of Tax Review, Board of Appeals.

BOARDS – Yard lumber 8 or more inches wide, and less than 2 inches thick.

BOG SOIL – See Types of Soil, page 351.

BOLE – The trunk of a tree.

BOLSTER – A horizontal timber on a post for lessening the free span of a beam.

BOLT
1. Any of several types of strong fastening rods, pins, or screws, usually threaded to receive a nut.
2. A movable bar or rod which, when slid into a socket, fastens a door, gate, etc.

BOND
1. The arrangement of individual masonry units in certain overlapping patterns to give the finished structural unit additional strength and to allow the individual elements to act together as a cohesive, integrated unit. See also Brick Masonry.
2. In finance, an interest-bearing certificate of private or public indebtedness.

BOND BEAM – A continuous beam, usually of reinforced concrete, but sometimes of reinforced brick or concrete block, placed in masonry walls to tie them together and add lateral stability. It also distributes concentrated vertical loads along the wall.

BOND FOR DEED – An executory contract for the sale of property with the title remaining in the grantor until the purchase price is paid; ordinarily binding on both parties.

BOOK COST – The cost of acquisition shown in the general ledger of an individual, partnership, or corporation, which generally includes direct and indirect financing, and all development costs, except preliminary operating losses.

BOOK DEPRECIATION—In accounting, the amount reserved upon the books of an owner to provide for the retirement or replacement of an asset, as distinguished from accrued depreciation. See also Accrued Depreciation.

BOOK VALUE—The capital amount at which property is shown on the books of account. Usually, it is the original cost less reserves for depreciation plus additions to capital. See also Adjusted Basis.

BOOM
1. Rapid growth in market values and expansion of business facilities and activities. Antonym: Bust.
2. Heavy construction crane or lift arm.
3. Logboom; for water transportation of logs.

BOOT—Any asset or liability transferred as part of an exchange of realty. Most typical forms include cash and debt existing prior to the exchange, purchase money mortgages created within the exchange, and debt instruments transferred in lieu of cash.

BORING TEST—A study of load-bearing qualities of subterranean surface by analysis of bore or drilling residue (core samples).

BORROW—Suitable material (soil) used for regrading or backfilling that is introduced from outside of the construction project.

BORROW BANK—The source from which borrow material is obtained.

BORROW PIT—The depression resulting from the removal of borrow material.

BORROWED LIGHT—Usually glazing in an interior partition that will allow light to enter interior areas from exterior fenestration.

BOTEL—An adjunct to a marina which offers accommodations to guests traveling by boat and services comparable to those of a motel for automobile travelers.

BOTTOM RAIL—A horizontal member forming the bottom of a window or paneled door; sometimes referred to as "bottom stile." For illustration, see pages 304 and 310.

BOULEVARD—A broad street or promenade, planted with rows of trees either along its border or in a median strip.

BOWSTRING TRUSS—A truss whose top member is formed in such a manner as to look like a bow or an arch. It is made of either steel or wood.

BOX CONSTRUCTION—A construction system using horizontal framing members to which vertical siding is attached. Frequently used in the construction of farm buildings.

BOX GIRDER—A girder having a hollow cross section similar to that of a rectangular box.

BRACE—A structural member which reinforces a frame or truss.

BRACED FRAMING—A type of heavy timber framing in which the frame is reinforced by the use of posts, girts, and braces, thus forming a more rigid structure than in balloon framing.

BRACKET—A horizontally projecting support for an overhanging weight such as a cornice or eaves.

BRADLEY FOUNTAIN—A large circular basin with a center column containing faucets or spray heads to provide washing facilities for several persons at one time. Frequently found in industrial buildings.

BRANCH STORE—A secondary or outlying store owned, supplied, and operated by a main store which is generally larger and more centrally located. Common in shopping centers.

BREAK–EVEN POINT—In financial analysis, the intersection of the total cost line and the total revenue line represents the break-even point. In real estate, it is that point where effective gross income from a property just covers normal operating expenses and debt services.

BREAST–HEIGHT—A height of 4½ feet above the average ground surface, or above the root collar. The diameter of a standing tree ordinarily is measured at this height. The abbreviation d.b.h. means diameter at breast height. See also Diameter-Breast-High.

BREATHER ROOF—A roof on a storage tank which expands and contracts with the level of the stored material, usually liquid, and which prevents loss through rapid vaporization or the mingling of gases with the outside air.

BREEDING HERD—The livestock retained to provide for the perpetuation of the herd or band, not including animals being prepared for market.

BRICK CAVITY WALL—A wall in which a space is left between inner and outer tiers of brick. The space may be filled with insulation.

BRICK MASONRY (BOND)—The arrangement or overlapping of brick, blocks, or stones to tie a masonry wall together longitudinally (stretchers) and transversely (headers), and of great importance to the strength of the wall. For illustrations of the various forms of Brick Masonry Bonds, Joints, Courses and Patterns, see page 302.

BRICK VENEER—A non-loadbearing single tier of brick applied as the facing to a wall of other materials.

BRICK VENEER WALL—Usually used to describe a wall made up of brick veneer applied over wood framing or masonry block.

BRIDGING—Small wood or metal structural members inserted between horizontal (joists) or vertical (studs) framing to provide lateral rigidity to the members to which applied. See illustration, page 305.

BRITISH THERMAL UNIT (Btu) — A standard unit for measuring heat. One Btu is the amount of heat required to raise the temperature of 1 pound of water 1 degree Fahrenheit. In the United States the rated capacity of furnaces and boilers is expressed in terms of the number of Btus emitted per hour. Fuel oil, natural gas, electricity, and all other heat sources are also rated in Btus.

BROAD-LEAVED TREES — See Types of Range Vegetation, page 349.

BROODER HOUSE — A heated building for raising young fowl.

BROWSE-SHRUB — See Types of Range Vegetation, page 349.

BUCK

1. Wood framework in a door opening in masonry wall to which jambs and casings are attached.
2. Fabricated steel frame, prefitted for doors in a masonry wall; sometimes inclusive of the entire assembly, except the door. Commonly referred to as "door buck," meaning the entire assembly.

BUCKED — Cut into log lengths.

BUFFER STRIP — A parcel of land which separates lands of differing uses. It is frequently unimproved except for landscaping and screening. Its purpose is to prohibit immediate adjacency of incompatible or inharmonious uses, such as commercially or industrially zoned land which is adjacent to residentially zoned land.

BUILDING — A structure erected to stand more or less permanently and designed for human use and occupancy or as a shelter for animals or goods.

BUILDING CAPITALIZATION RATE — A rate which includes return on and return of capital invested in improvements, separate from capital invested in the underlying land; used in the residual techniques which separate property income into components attributable to land and to improvements.

BUILDING CODE — Locally or State adopted ordinance or regulation, enforceable by police powers under the concept of health, safety, and welfare, which control the design, construction, alteration, repair, quality of materials, use and occupancy, and related factors of any building or structure within its jurisdiction.

BUILDING ENERGY PERFORMANCE STANDARD (BEPS) — A standard requiring that a building be designed to meet a specified level of energy use per year. See also Energy Budget.

BUILDING LINE — Line established by ordinance or statute between which line and the street line no structure is permitted.

BUILDING RESIDUAL TECHNIQUE—The process of estimating the contribution of improvements to the present worth or value of the entire property, over and above the value of the site, in which
1. Return attributable to the land, valued independently of the building, is deducted from Net Operating Income;
2. The residual income, representing return to the building (including recapture) is capitalized to indicate building value.

BUILDING SERVICE SYSTEMS—Those systems and their components which provide plumbing, sewerage, heating, ventilating, air conditioning, lighting, power, vertical transport, fire protection, and special services such as public address or oxygen to a building.

BUILT-INS—Items such as cabinets, counters, desks, benches, shelving, equipment, which are permanently attached to the building structure and could not be removed without leaving evidence of removal. Not considered personal property.

BUILT-UP METHOD—A method of identifying the basic elements of compensation contribution in the development of a Discount Rate. There are considered to be four basic components of the Discount Rate: the pure or riskless rate, management, non-liquidity, and risk. This method is utilized for demonstration purposes. Often referred to as the Summation Method of rate selection.

BUILT-UP ROOFING—Roofing that is built up by laying felt paper with overlapping seams, sealed by mopping with hot asphalt or roofing compound. The final coat may be asphalt or asphalt covered with small gravel.

BULB TEE—A rolled steel shape with a cross section resembling a bulbous T, often used as a purlin.

BULKHEAD
1. A retaining wall erected along the water behind which solid fill is usually placed, thus extending the upland out to the bulkhead line. It also serves as a protection against tidal or water course erosion of the land.
2. The wall beneath a store display window.

BULKHEAD LINE—A line established by an authoritative body (federal government through the Army Corps of Engineers) in navigable waters beyond which no solid filling is permitted. It is always inshore from the pierhead line except where they are coincident.

BUMPER STRIPS—Timbers placed along the outer edge of a loading dock to protect it from damage caused by the "bumping" of loading and unloading trucks.

BUNDLE OF RIGHTS THEORY—Ownership of a parcel of real estate may embrace a great many rights, such as the right to its occupancy and use; the right to sell it in whole or in part; the right to bequeath;

the right to transfer, by contract, for specified periods of time, the benefits to be derived by occupancy and use of the real estate. These rights of occupancy and use are called beneficial interests.

BUSINESS CYCLE — A recurring sequence of changes in economic activity. Beginning with a period of prosperity, business activity declines until a low point is reached. A period of recovery then follows when economic conditions become more and more active until prosperity is again restored and a cycle is thus completed.

BUTT — Door hinges.

BUTT CASING — A very plain casing formed by installing a piece across the top of an opening, and bringing up two side pieces to butt against it from beneath. See illustration, page 307.

BUTTERFLY ROOF — An inverted gable roof with two sides sloping downward and inward, forming a reversed ridge in the center. The two gables resemble the wingspread of a butterfly. See illustration, page 300.

BUTT JOINT — The joint formed when two timbers or members are joined by butting (meeting) end to end.

BUTT LOG — That log in a tree which is first above the stump.

BUTTRESS — An external structure, usually brick, stone or concrete, which supports a wall or building by receiving lateral pressures acting at a particular point and in a single direction.

BUYER'S MARKET — The condition which exists when, under competitive conditions, the schedules of supply and demand are such that market prices are at a relatively low level, giving the buyers an advantage. An oversupply causing prices to decline.

BX — Electrical cable consisting of a flexible metal covering enclosing two or more wires.

BYPASS — See Belt Highway.

CAE — Certified Assessment Evaluator. A professional designation conferred by the International Association of Assessing Officers upon real property appraisers employed by a government assessment agency.

C HORIZON — Horizon of relatively unweathered material underlying the B Horizon; parent material; the substratum. See also A, B, and D Horizons.

CABINET WORK — Any interior finish usually in hardwoods, and which involves the skills of cabinetmakers rather than carpenters. Built-in fixtures, such as kitchen cupboards, counters, etc.

CADASTRAL PROGRAM – A complete inventory of land in an area by ownership, descriptions or maps, and values. See also Assessment Process.

CAISSON – A large strong water-tight box or casing in which work is conducted below water level, usually under artificial air pressure. It it also used as a retaining structure in an open excavation to prevent cave-in; or when sunk to a high bearing stratum and filled with concrete, as a supporting member of a structure.

CAISSON FOUNDATION – A foundation system in which holes are drilled in the earth to bearing strata and then filled with concrete.

CALCAREOUS SOIL – See Types of Soil, page 351.

CALF-CROP – The number of calves produced by a given number of cows, usually expressed in percent of calves weaned of cows bred.

CALIFORNIA RANCH ARCHITECTURE – A modern residential style which originated in California, involving a spread-out one story design easily adapted to extensive floor plan variations.

CAMBER
1. A slight convex arching given to a load-bearing beam, girder, or timber, to compensate for, and thus tend to eliminate, sagging or concavity due to superimposed weight.
2. The slight arching of a structure, such as a road or deck of a ship.

CAMPANILE – A bell tower; usually a tall tower built separate from a church.

CANAL
1. An artificial, open water course uniting rivers, lakes, or seas for inland navigation.
2. A channel used in irrigation.

CANDLE – A measure of light intensity. A standard candle is approximately equal to the intensity of light from a 78-inch sperm candle burning at the rate of 120 grains per hour.

CANDLE POWER – The luminous intensity of a light expressed in candles.

CANTILEVER
1. That part of a structural member which extends beyond its support, and by virtue of its rigidity is capable of supporting loads and resisting lateral pressure.
2. Either of the two structural members, projecting from piers toward each other, which, when joined directly or by a suspended span, form the span of a cantilever bridge.

CANTILEVER BEAM—A beam with one end projecting beyond the point of support, free to move vertically under the influence of vertical loads placed between the support and the free end.

CANTILEVER CONSTRUCTION—A building technique in which a portion of the structure is supported by a cantilever beam or cantilever beams.

CAP

1. The top part of a structural member, such as columns, doors, moldings; a cornice, a lintel.
2. A threaded plumber's fitting used to close a pipe end.
3. Short for capitalization as in Cap Rate.

CAPACITY

1. In land utilization, the input of labor and capital in terms of the number of dollar units that can profitably be expended on any given area.
2. The ability of land, through its vegetative cover, to continuously support livestock, ordinarily expressed as number of acres required to furnish feed for an animal unit for one month (AUM), or for a year (CYL), or number of head a specific ranch will carry on a year-long basis.
3. The ability of a roadway to carry traffic. See also Basic Capacity, Possible Capacity, Practical Capacity, Range Capacity Formula.

CAPE COD HOUSE—A type of architectural style which is a development of the one-story cottage. Generally, the main cornice line is at the second-story level; the roof is sloping and there may be rooms on the second floor, served by dormer windows. A detailed entrance features pilasters and cornices. These houses are most authentic when built of frame with clapboard or shingle walls, and painted white. In some sections, however, stone or brick is used for the first story.

CAPITAL

1. Accumulated wealth. The entire stock of goods from which income is derived. The accumulated wealth employed to produce other goods or additional wealth. Land, tools, machines, stocks, bonds, and any materials used to create, alter, extract, or transport goods can be termed capital.
2. In building construction, the uppermost part of a column; usually ornamented.

CAPITAL ASSETS—An accounting term signifying the moving and/or readily convertible assets of a corporation as of a certain date; cash, accounts receivable, and merchandise inventories. See also Current Assets.

CAPITAL EXPENDITURES—Investments of cash or the creation of liability incurred for additions or betterments; usually land, buildings, machinery, and equipment.

CAPITAL EXPENSE—The annual amount required to pay return on and provide for the ultimate return of (depreciation or amortization) the investment. See also Capital Expenditures, Operating Expenses.

CAPITAL GAIN—The amount by which the net proceeds from resale of a capital item exceed the adjusted cost (or "book value") of the item; used primarily in income tax computations. It may be short or long term depending upon whether resale occurs more or less than one year after the acquisition of the asset.

CAPITAL GOOD—A material economic good created by man which is used in the production of wealth; that is, raw material, machinery, factories.

CAPITAL GRANT—The cash contribution, usually by government, to the cost of a project undertaken in a locality.

CAPITAL RECOVERY (RECAPTURE)—The return to investors of that portion of their property investment expected to be lost over the Income Projection Period. Capital Recovery may be viewed in either a physical sense as reflected in the traditional physical residual techniques of capitalization or in a financial sense as reflected in mortgage-equity analysis. It is not interchangeable with the term depreciation.

CAPITAL RECOVERY (RECAPTURE) METHOD—Alternative methods of providing for recovery of capital; each method can be expressed in the form of a sinking fund. See Straight Line, Safe Rate and Level Annuity Capital Recovery.

CAPITAL RECOVERY (RECAPTURE) PAYMENTS—Annual amounts to cover the forecast decline from initial investment to reversion.

CAPITAL RECOVERY (RECAPTURE) PERIOD—A definite time period over which income is forecast to be produced and based upon either (1) physical life of improvements; (2) useful life of improvements; (3) remaining economic life of improvements; (4) lease term; (5) mortgage amortization period; or (6) investment holding or turnover period.

CAPITAL RECOVERY (RECAPTURE) RATE—The return of invested capital, expressed as an annual rate. It is often applied in a physical sense to wasting assets having a finite economic life. Synonymous with "amortization rate" to express investors' desire to recover their equity investment over some specified time period.

CAPITAL REQUIREMENTS — The total monetary investment essential to the establishment and operation of an enterprise; usually the appraised investment in plant facilities and normal working capital. May or may not (for certain purposes) include appraised cost of business rights, such as patents, contracts.

CAPITAL STOCK — The permanently invested capital of a corporation contributed by the owners either at or subsequent to the time the corporation is organized. Capital stock is divided into shares, each share representing a proportionate ownership in the corporation. Shares are issued in the form of a stock certificate which is usually transferable only by endorsement.

CAPITALIZATION

1. The process of converting into present value (or obtaining the present worth of) a series of anticipated future periodic installments of net income. In real estate appraising, it usually takes the form of discounting.

2. The accountant sometimes uses the word "capitalization" to mean, in effect, what appraisers call an addition to capital. "In the broadest sense, the capital of a business is measured by the total of the resources available to carry on its operations. Capital so defined comprehends a creditor interest as well as the entire proprietary equity. Excluding the liabilities, corporate capital consists of the amount of funds specifically contributed by the stockholders plus the undistributed profits." (From Accountants Handbook, third edition.)

   Acquisitions of assets are capitalized when their value extends beyond the current accounting period which is usually twelve months either on the calendar basis or on the fiscal year basis. Assets are classified as current, fixed, and often, intangible assets. Current assets are valued at cost or market, whichever is lower. Fixed assets are valued at cost less depreciation. The accepted theory by the accounting profession is that the cost of these assets should be distributed over their useful life.

   Intangible assets are usually valued by capitalizing earning power. In business this value is called goodwill, and, while it is not considered good practice to carry the value on the books unless purchased directly as such, it is necessary in determining the real value of a going business and is necessary in the sale or purchase of a business. After the profits have been normalized, there is deducted from the average net profit a fair rate of return on the tangible assets. The balance is then capitalized at an agreed upon percentage. See also Income Approach.

CAPITALIZATION APPROACH — See Income Approach.

CAPITALIZATION IN PERPETUITY — Capitalization of income which is expected to endure indefinitely with no change; capitalization of income generated by a property which can be sold in the future for a price equal to the original investment; capitalization at a rate which provides a return on the investment but no return of the investment.

CAPITALIZATION RATE — The sum of a Discount Rate and a Capital Recapture Rate. It is applied to any income stream with a finite term over which the invested principal is to be returned to the investor or lender.

A rate which represents the relationship between future income and value. Except for Capitalization in Perpetuity (where capital value remains intact), the capitalization rate contains, either implicitly or explicitly, provision for return on and full recovery of capital invested.

The term "Capitalization Rate" (Cap Rate) has been traditionally used colloquially in reference to overall rate. Proper terminology would distinguish between these two terms and avoid the colloquial usage of the term "Cap Rate."

CAPITALIZE — To convert future incomes into current value. It involves discounting future incomes into present value.

CAPITALIZED VALUE — A value indication resulting from a capitalization process. The present worth of anticipated future benefits usually in the form of income.

CAPRICIOUS VALUE — The value indicated when the price paid is a consequence of a whim or fanciful idea. Not a market value.

CAR FLOAT BRIDGE — A landing place (or movable section of a lighterage pier to accommodate itself to the change in water elevation) where railroad cars are transferred from shore tracks to tracks on floats or vice versa.

CARPORT — An opensided, roofed auto shelter.

CARRYING CAPACITY — The maximum number of animals that can be grazed without inducing a downward trend of forage production, quality and soil of the range. See Capacity.

CARRYING CHARGES — Expenses necessary for holding idle property or property under construction, such as taxes, insurance premiums, standby water and sewer rents, and, on occasion, security or other protective service.

CASE — The framework of the structure; the external facings of a building when made of material superior to the backing.

CASEMENT WINDOW — A type of window having sash with hinges on the side. See illustration, page 301.

CASH — Money, especially ready money; money on deposit or due on demand.

CASH ASSETS — Cash on hand and in working funds immediately available for the current needs of a business.

CASH CROP — Farm crops grown for direct sale as opposed to those which are fed to livestock on the farm.

CASH EQUIVALENT — A price expressed in terms of cash as distinguished from a price which is expressed all or partly in terms of the face amount of notes or other securities which cannot be sold at their face amount.

The cash equivalent price of a sale property may differ from its contract price and should represent the present worth at time of sale of all cash and other considerations paid for the real property as opposed to other portions of stated consideration which may be paid for services, fees and/or other non-realty items.

CASH FLOW — Any flow of cash, in or out, of an investment. In any investment a variety of "cash flows" can be identified on both a before- and after-tax basis. For real estate investments in particular, See Net Operating Income, Cash Throw-off (Before-Tax Cash Flow), After-Tax Cash Flow, Operating Expenses, Debt Service.

CASH FLOW DIVIDEND — Same as Equity Dividend.

CASH ON CASH — The ratio of cash throw-off to the original down payment (dollar investment in equity); equity dividend rate. See Before-Tax Cash Flow.

CASH RENT
1. The amount of rent paid in money; not inclusive of services rendered in lieu of cash.
2. A fixed and agreed upon money rent for a farm, usually in dollars per acre per year.

CASH THROW-OFF — Net Operating Income less annual debt service; also known as Before-Tax Cash Flow. See also Equity Dividend.

CASING — A piece of trim material around the sides and top of doors, windows, and other openings in a wall. For illustrations of Clam Shell, Colonial, Corner Block, and Mitered Casings, see page 307. See also Back Band Casing and Butt Casing.

CATENA — See Types of Soil, page 351.

CATTLE GUARD — An opening in a fence which is not closed by a gate but has a ground grill that cattle will not cross.

CATTLE SQUEEZE — A mechanism installed in a corral chute which closes on an animal and immobilizes it so various treatments, such as branding or dehorning, can be accomplished.

CATWALK — A narrow footing on a bridge or along a girder of a large building. It may also be a walkway strung from one girder to another or placed over uncovered attic joists.

CAULKING — A flexible material used to fill gaps at fixed joints on a building in order to reduce the passage of air and moisture. Also includes materials known as "sealants," "putty," and "glazing compounds."

CAUSEWAY — A raised roadway on fill or a bridge-like structure over a low area, such as a swamp, lake or bay.

CAVEAT — Notice not to do an act, given by an interested party, until that party is heard in the matter.

CAVITY WALL — See Hollow Wall.

CEILING JOISTS — The horizontal structural members to which the ceiling is fastened. Some members may support a floor above.

CEILING LOAN — That part of a total loan that will be disbursed when special requirements are met, such as rent roll achievement. See Floor Loan.

CELLAR
1. A storage space, usually, but not always, below ground.
2. An underground chamber.

CELLULAR CONCRETE — A lightweight insulating concrete.

CELLULAR STEEL DECK — A structural floor system, consisting of two layers of sheet metal shaped to form cells and welded together. Cells serve as electrical raceways.

CEMENT BLOCKS — Blocks of which the principal component materials are cement and gravel formed into shape under pressure. Used principally for walls.

CENTER TO CENTER — The measurement between centers of two adjoining parallel structural members. Also referred to as "on center."

CENTRAL ASSESSMENT — An assessment of property, such as railroads, public utilities, commercial and industrial property located in more than one assessment district and held under a single ownership.

CENTRAL BUSINESS DISTRICT (CBD) — The core area in the center of a city in which is concentrated the major retail, financial, governmental, professional, recreational, and service activities of the community. Downtown and core area of the city center.

CENTRAL CITY — The primary city in a standard metropolitan area, and from which the name of the metropolitan area is usually taken.

CENTRAL LIMIT THEOREM — In statistics, a principle which identifies the tendency of the arithmetic mean to be normally distributed as n increases in size, almost regardless of the shape of the distribution of the original population.

CERTIFICATE

1. An instrument giving formal assurance of the existence of some fact or set of facts. Such an instrument is used as evidence of some right or obligation.
2. That part of an appraisal report containing the limiting conditions, the conclusions, and the appraiser's signed certification that to the best of his or her knowledge and belief these conclusions are correct.

CERTIFICATE OF BENEFICIAL INTEREST—A document which identifies an owner's interest in the assets and earnings of a business enterprise. Such certificates may be issued to stockholders when the stock of a corporation is surrendered to a trustee or trustees.

CERTIFICATE OF TITLE—A document usually given to a homebuyer with the deed, stating that the title to the property is clear. It is usually prepared by an attorney or qualified person who has examined the abstract of title for the property. It is only an opinion that title is good; not to be confused with title insurance.

CERTIFICATION OF VALUE—A statement that appraisers, in their professional capacity, personally conducted the appraisal in an objective manner. Such a statement permits appraisers to state their precise position, thus protecting their integrity and the validity of their appraisals.

CERTIORARI—A writ from a superior to an inferior court officer, board, or tribunal directing a certified record of its proceedings in a designated case to be sent up for review. A remedy for judicial review. In New York State, an owner's remedy for judicial review of an alleged illegal or erroneous assessment of real estate for the purpose of taxation.

CESSPOOL—An underground catch basin for household sewage or other liquid waste.

CHAIN—A chainlike measuring instrument consisting of wire links. A surveyor's chain is 66 feet long, each link being 7.92 inches long. A mile is 80 chains; one acre 10 square chains. An engineer's chain consists of 100 wire links, each a foot long. A mile is 52.8 chains. See Measures, page 271.

CHAIN OF TITLE—See Abstract of Title.

CHAIN STORE—One of a number of retail stores or shops under the same ownership, under central management, selling uniform merchandise, and following a uniform policy.

CHAMFER—To bevel or round off a right angle corner.

CHANGE, PRINCIPLE OF—Holds that economic, physical, governmental, and social forces are constantly at work and because changes brought about by these forces affect real property, the appraiser views real property and its environment as in transition, observing evidence of trends which may affect the property in the future.

CHANNEL
1. The bed of a stream of water. The deeper part of a river, harbor, strait, or bay where the main current flows; a ship's channel or passageway.
2. A long gutter, groove, or furrow.
3. A closed course or conduit through which anything flows or passes, as a duct.

CHANNELIZATION — The direction of traffic flow into definite paths, by means of traffic markings, islands, or other means.

CHARACTERISTIC — In decimal arithmetic, the characteristic specifies the location of the decimal point. See also Mantissa.

CHATTEL — In law, any property other than a freehold or fee estate in land. Chattels are treated as personal property, although they are divisible into chattels real and chattels personal.

CHATTEL INTEREST — A non-ownership right in real estate, such as leaseholds; easements, and liens.

CHATTEL MORTGAGE — A mortgage on chattels.

CHATTELS PERSONAL — Movable things.

CHATTELS REAL — All interests in real estate which do not constitute a freehold or fee estate in land; such chattels include leasehold estates and other interests issuing out of or annexed to real estate.

CHECK RAIL — The horizontal members which form the top of the lower sash and the bottom of the upper sash in a double hung window; also termed "meeting rail."
    While this member in each sash is referred to as a rail, the two in combination, when a window is assembled, are designated the check rail. See illustration, page 309.

CHECK ROW — A type of planting in which the plants are grown at the intersections of lines, as on a checkerboard. A method frequently used for corn, melons, tomatoes.

CHECK VALVE — A plumbing valve which closes automatically preventing the backflow of water or other liquids.

CHERNOZEM — See Types of Soil, page 351.

CHIMNEY BACK — The rear lining or wall of a furnace or fireplace.

CINDER BLOCK — A concrete block using cinders as coarse aggregate to achieve lighter weight. Sometimes used as a generic term for all lightweight block.

CIRCLEHEAD WINDOW – A small half-oval window used for decorative purposes, usually over a door. It is shaped like an open fan, the ribs of which are simulated by the sash bars. See illustration, page 301.

CIRCUIT BREAKER – In property taxation, a method of effecting property tax relief for the elderly and/or poor by rebating to qualifying taxpayers, by income tax credits or cash payments, that portion of the taxpayers' property tax payments which exceeds a certain percentage of the taxpayers' incomes. Usually limited to tax relief for residential property taxes, and may apply to both homeowners and renters.

CIRCULATING CAPITAL – See Current Assets.

CIRCULATION PATTERN – The traffic pattern, either pedestrian or automotive, established in moving from one place to another, as from home to business or to or past a specific location.

CIRCUMFERENTIAL HIGHWAY – See Belt Highway.

CISTERN – An artificial reservoir or tank, often underground, for storing rain water.

CITY – In the United States, a municipal corporation occupying a definite area and subject to the state from which it derives its power. In Canada, a municipality of the highest class.

CIVIL LAW – The legal system prevailing in the European, Asiatic, Central American, and South American countries which inherited their legal systems from Rome; that is, in practically all except the English-speaking countries of the United States and the British Commonwealth. See also Common Law.

CLAPBOARD – An exterior wood siding having one edge thicker than the other and laid so that the thick butt overlaps the thin edge of the board below.

CLASSICAL SCHOOL – A school of economic thought that originated in England with Adam Smith's *Wealth of Nations* (1776) and which included the writings of such English economists as David Ricardo, Thomas R. Malthus, and John Stuart Mill, as well as the French economist Jean Baptiste Say. In the writings of the Classical economists, one's self-interest is assumed, and a person's economic behavior is generalized in the form of principles or laws which are believed to be universally applicable.

CLASSICAL STATISTICS – In the "classical" theory of statistical inference, the decision to accept or reject an hypothesis is based on the evidence of sample information alone as opposed to the "Bayesian" approach where the analysis is extended to include the judgment of the decisionmaker and the economic payoffs involved.

CLASSIFIED BASAL AREA—In forestry, the grouping of total land area tallied per sample point into diameter classes to record and better describe forest growing stock.

CLASSIFIED PROPERTY TAX—An ad valorem tax under which the effective tax rate varies with the classification of property, that is, with the character and/or use of the property (residential commercial, agricultural). The different classes may be assessed at different percentages of market value and taxed at uniform rates, or they may be assessed uniformly and taxed at different rates.

CLASS OF CONSTRUCTION—The classification of buildings according to the fire resistant materials of which they are constructed; for example, structural steel, reinforced concrete, masonry, frame.

CLAY—See Types of Soil, page 351.

CLAY LOAM—See Types of Soil, page 351.

CLAYPAN—See Types of Soil, page 351.

CLEARANCE—A type of urban renewal project undertaking in which land acquisition; demolition and removal of structures; relocation of families, individuals, and businesses; and preparation of the land for redevelopment are the predominant activities.

CLEAR HEADWAY—The vertical measurement of the area from the floor to the lowest overhead framing member.

CLEAR LUMBER—Lumber practically devoid of defects, such as knots.

CLEAR-SPAN—The term is used to describe portions of a structure built without internal supporting columns.

CLERESTORY WINDOW—A window or series of windows placed in a building above the roof of other parts of the structure, providing additional light and ventilation for the interior. A style of architecture usually found in churches and similar structures but also used in modern residential design.

CLIMATIC ZONE—An area across the country which reflects similar climatic conditions as established by the number of heating and cooling degree days.

CLOCK THERMOSTAT—A device which is designed to reduce energy consumption by regulating the demand on the heating or cooling system of a building. See Thermostat.

CLOUD ON TITLE—An encumbrance which may affect the fee holder's ownership and marketability of the title.

CLOVERLEAF—A grade-separated intersection designed to eliminate all left turn and cross traffic conflicts and to accommodate turning movements from four directions achieved by use of loops for left turns and outer connections for right turns, or two-way ramps for these turns. A full cloverleaf has ramps for two turning movements in each quadrant.

CLUSTER SAMPLING—In statistics, a two-stage sampling procedure by which a population is divided into several groups or clusters, a number of which are then drawn into the sample and then a sub-sample of elements is selected from each of the specified clusters.

COARSE TEXTURED SOIL—See Types of Soil, page 351.

COAT—A single layer of paint, plaster, or other material.

COEFFICIENT
1. A dimensionless statistic, useful as a measure of change or rela-tionship, as the coefficient of multiple regression, coefficient of determination, etc.
2. A number, a letter, a group of letters, or a combination of num-bers and letters which precedes another and by which that letter is to be multiplied, as 2 is the coefficient of X in the expression, $2X$.

COEFFICIENT OF CORRELATION (r)—In statistics, the measure of degree of relationship between variables and the way in which they change together. The correlation coefficient can range in value from -1 (perfect negative correlation) through 0 (independence) to $+1$ (perfect positive correlation).

COEFFICIENT OF DETERMINATION (r^2)—In statistics, the propor-tion of the total variance in the dependent variable which is ex-plained by the independent variable; the proportion of total vari-ance explained by the regression. The coefficient of determination is preferred to the coefficient of correlation for most applications in business and economics because it is a more clear-cut way of stating the proportion of the variance in the dependent variable which is associated with the independent variable. The coefficient of corre-lation may suggest a higher degree of correlation than really exists.

COEFFICIENT OF DISPERSION—In statistics, the ratio of a measure of absolute dispersion to an appropriate average usually expressed as a percent. It may be computed from either the quartile or mean deviation but is usually expressed as a ratio of the standard devia-tion to the mean. A measure of relative dispersion.

In assessment administration, the median is frequently the "aver-age" for which a coefficient of dispersion is calculated. Sometimes referred to as an "index of assessment inequality" or the "Russell Index." See also Coefficient of Variation.

COEFFICIENT OF MULTIPLE CORRELATION (R)—In statistics, the square root of the coefficient of Multiple Determination.

COEFFICIENT OF MULTIPLE DETERMINATION (R^2) – In statistics, indicates the proportion of total variance in the dependent variable explained by all independent variables in the regression equation; the ratio of explained variance to total variance.

COEFFICIENT OF PARTIAL DETERMINATION – In statistics, indicates the increase in explained variance, relative to prior unexplained variance, caused by adding a given variable to the regression equation.

COEFFICIENT OF PERFORMANCE (COP) – A measure of operating efficiency, expressed as a ratio of useful output energy to input energy. In percentage terms, the COP indicates what portion of the fuel input is converted to useful heating or cooling.

COEFFICIENT OF SKEWNESS – In statistics, a measure in standard deviation units that is used for comparison purposes between distributions that differ in unit of measurement or in average size; of limited practical use. Skewness is ordinarily treated in descriptive terms rather than being summarized by a single measure.

COEFFICIENT OF VARIATION – In statistics, the standard error of the estimate divided by the mean value of the dependent variable; a measure of the relative chance for error in a forecast or estimate of the dependent variable. See also Coefficient of Dispersion.

COFFERDAM – A temporary watertight enclosure from which water is pumped to expose the bottom of a river, etc., and to permit work to be done there; a caisson. A watertight structure on the side of a ship used in making repairs below waterline.

COIGNES – In architecture, stone or contrasting material used at a corner in a masonry wall, normally of alternating size and comprising larger units than the remainder of the wall.

COINSURANCE – The coinsurance or average clause in a fire insurance policy is a device to penalize the underinsured. The most common clauses provide for insurance in the amount of 80%, or 90%, or 100% of the value of the building. The New York Standard Average Clause reads: "This Company shall not be liable for a greater proportion of any loss or damage to the property described herein than the sum hereby insured bears to eighty percentum (80%) of the actual cash value of said property at the time such loss shall happen, nor for more than the proportion which this policy bears to the total insurance thereon."

The "value of the building" means the cost to rebuild or reproduce the destructible portion of a building just as it was at the time of the fire, with the same kind and quality of materials, as of the date of the fire, less depreciation.

The cost, as here used, ordinarily includes architects' fees, superintendence during construction, and builders' profit. It does not include interest or taxes during the construction, legal expenses, or the cost of or interest on the mortgage. Those parts of the building foundations which are below the lowest floor usually are excluded.

The depreciation includes loss from wear and tear, exhaustion and deterioration, but, as a rule, does not include depreciation from economic causes, or actual or potential obsolescence.

COLD STORAGE — Refrigerated storage of perishable commodities.

COLINEARITY — In statistics, the relationship between independent variables in a multiple regression. When highly correlated, they may affect the reliability of the net regression coefficients. While colinearity affects the reliability of individual variables in a regression, it may not alter the predictive power of the total regression equation.

COLLAR TIE — See Tie Beam.

COLLUVIAL SOIL — See Types of Soil, page 351.

COLONIAL ARCHITECTURE — Traditional design, most commonly following the characteristics of New England colonial homes; usually two-story houses with balanced openings along the main facade, windows subdivided into small panes, shutters and dormer windows. There is an effect of painstaking attention to detail, kept small in scale.

COLONNADE — A range of columns at regular intervals, usually supporting an architrave.

COLUMN — A vertical structural member supporting horizontal members (beams, girders, etc.). Designed to transmit load to bearing material at base of column.

COLUMN FOOTINGS — Reinforced concrete footings which support loadbearing columns.

COLUMN LOTS — Small sections of land acquired with air rights for the placement of columns, piers, and/or caissons which are needed in the construction of the foundation of the air rights structure.

COLUMN STEEL — The vertical bars of reinforcing steel in concrete columns. Also the H-shaped structural steel member used as a column.

COMBINATION DOOR — An outer door frame having an inside removable section for year-round utility. A screen panel is inserted in warm weather and a glass panel in winter.

COMBINATION SEWER — A sewer that carries both sewage and surface water (rainwater).

COMBINATION WINDOWS — An outer window frame having an inside removable section for year-round utility. In warm weather a screen may be inserted and in winter a glass storm panel is used. This same feature is available in doors as well as windows.

COMMENSURATE PROPERTY – The measure of a rancher's ability to take care of livestock while not on public land. It is referred to as the rancher's commensurability and the property so used is commensurate property. See also Base Property.

COMMERCIAL CONDOMINIUM – The application of the condominium concept to commercial, industrial, or office space.

COMMERCIAL PROPERTY – Real property acquired for investment except apartment houses, housing projects, and other dwelling units, including stores, shops, and recreational facilities connected with them.

COMMITTEE DEED – A deed by a committee or commission appointed by a court of competent jurisdiction to sell a property.

COMMON BASE – A single-member base, usually from four to six inches high. See illustration, page 307.

COMMON LAW
1. The body of customs, usages, and practices developed and administered by the Anglo-Saxons. The body of English Law as distinguished from Roman Law, canon law, and other systems.
2. The ancient unwritten law founded on immemorial customs and precedents as distinguished from statute law.
3. A system of elementary rules and general judicial declarations of principles, which are continually expanding with the progress of society, adapting themselves to the gradual changes of trade, commerce, arts, inventions, and the exigencies and usages of the country.

COMMON PROPERTY – Land generally, or a tract of land, considered as the property of the public in which all persons enjoy equal rights. A legal term signifying an incorporeal hereditament consisting of a right of one person in the land of another, as common of estovers, of pasture, or of piscary; property not owned by individuals or government, but by groups, tribes, or in formal villages.

COMMON STOCK – A share of ownership in a corporation which usually but not always possesses voting power.

COMMON WALL – A single wall used jointly by two buildings or sections of a single building. See Party Wall.

COMMUNITY DEVELOPMENT BLOCK GRANT (PROGRAM) – A federal funding program created by Title I of the Housing and Community Development Act of 1974. A flexible grant which can be used for a wide variety of community development activities as opposed to designated uses for specific funds in categorical funding programs which block grants replace.

COMMUNITY DEVELOPMENT CORPORATION — A corporation set up within the Department of Housing and Urban Development in 1970 to administer the new communities program. The corporation establishes policy for new communities on a wide range of subjects including loan guarantees, project selection, and work-out problems.

COMMUNITY FACILITY LOAN — Loans made available by the Farmers Home Administration to communities with less than 10,000 population and which can show that commercial credit is not available at reasonable terms. Long-term low interest loans are available for such projects as water and waste disposal systems, relocation of roads, and acquisition of land and rights of way for development of community facilities, as well as for the purchase and construction of a wide range of equipment and buildings.

COMMUNITY PROPERTY — Property acquired by either husband or wife during their marriage, excepting gifts for inheritances, and which then belongs to them as a unit and not individually. The death of either one results in a full ownership to the other.

COMMUNITY REINVESTMENT ACT — A provision of the Housing Act of 1977 requiring the Federal Home Loan Bank Board, the Federal Reserve Board, and the Federal Deposit Insurance Corporation to assess and periodically report to Congress progress of their constituent lending institutions to meet the credit needs of their communities, especially low income neighborhoods.

COMMUNITY RENEWAL PROGRAM — An urban planning program under which governmental grants may be made for preparing community wide blueprints for urban renewal. The law specifically contemplates such broad activities as:
1. Identification of blighted or deteriorating areas in the community.
2. Measurement of the nature and degree of blight and blighting factors in the areas.
3. Determination of the financial, relocation, and other resources needed to renew the areas.
4. Identification of potential project areas and types of urban renewal action contemplated.
5. Scheduling of urban renewal activities.

COMMUNITY SHOPPING CENTER — A tract of land improved with a coordinated group of retail buildings having a variety of types of stores. The Community Center provides, in addition to "convenience goods," a wide range of facilities for the sale of "shopping goods," such as apparel and furniture, and may include banking, professional services, and recreational facilities. A junior department store or variety store is the principal tenant in this type of center.

COMPARABLES — An abbreviation for comparable property sales, rentals, incomes, etc., used for purposes of comparison in the appraisal process.

COMPARATIVE UNIT METHOD — A method of estimating construction costs which involves lumping together all components of the structure on a unit basis (cost per square foot of building area, cost per square foot of foundation area, cost per cubic foot of building volume, etc.). The costs estimated are completed construction costs including all installation expense and builder's overhead and profit, but do not include architect fees and financing during construction. See Cubic Foot Method, Square Foot Method.

COMPARISON METHOD — See Direct Sales Comparison Approach, Market Data Approach.

COMPENSABLE DAMAGES — Those damages for which a condemnor is required by law to compensate the owner and/or tenant of a property which has been or will be wholly or partially condemned. In most jurisdictions, a physical invasion of a property by a condemning authority or a taking of some of the property rights must occur before damages arising therefrom become compensable. See Consequential Damages, Inverse Condemnation.

COMPENSABLE INTEREST — A property right which if acquired for public purposes would entitle the owner to receive just compensation.

COMPENSATION — See Just Compensation.

COMPETITION, PRINCIPLE OF — Holds that profit tends to breed competition and excess profit tends to breed ruinous competition.

COMPILE — To prepare a machine language program from a computer program written in another programming language.

COMPLEMENT — The difference between a fraction (less than 1) or a proportion and the whole number 1; e.g., if a mortgage loan is amortized by 35%, the complement of the 35% principal paid off equals the unamortized balance (65%).

COMPONENT — Construction elements such as the complete exterior walls, framing, floor and roof construction, interior finish, building service systems, considered individually.

COMPONENT CONSTRUCTION — See Prefabrication.

COMPONENT DEPRECIATION — See Depreciation Methods, page 341.

COMPONENT (SPLIT) FINANCING — In recognition of the fact that rights in real estate are both separable and divisible, this concept splits the property between its fee and leasehold interests, financing each component in order to obtain optimum benefits from the financial package. Component financing involves such financial packages as sale leaseback and fee subordination combined with a leasehold mortgage.

COMPONENT PANEL—A wall unit ready for installation. It comprises a panel which is a complete wall unit with finished inner and outer surfaces (skins), framing, insulation, etc., either of solid construction or with door and/or window framing.

COMPOSITE RATE—An overall rate; a blend or weighted average of multiple rates of return applicable to a single investment, R in the Ellwood formulation.

COMPOSITION SIDING—A manufactured exterior wall covering often finished in an imitation brick pattern.

COMPOUND AMOUNT OF ONE—See Amount of One.

COMPOUND AMOUNT OF ONE PER PERIOD—See Amount of One Per Period.

COMPOUND DISCOUNT—Successive deductions from a future sum or sums receivable at specified future dates to the present. Mathematically it is the obverse of compound interest. See also Discounting.

COMPOUND INTEREST—The continuous and systematic additions to a principal sum over a series of successive time periods. The rate is constant, time periods are of equal length, and the number of periods is specified (finite).

COMPOUND SLOPE—One which is made up of two or more slopes with different gradients.

COMPUTER—An electronic machine for automatically performing simple or complex calculations according to a program of instructions.
1. Analog computer—Numbers are represented by measurable physical quantities such as voltages, resistances, rotations or pressures.
2. Digital computer—Numbers are expressed directly as digits in the decimal, binary, or other number system.

COMPUTER ASSISTED MASS APPRAISAL PROGRAM—The application of computer technology and statistical techniques to the solution of appraisal problems; in assessment administration computer assisted mass appraisal programs are used to produce cost and market approach estimates of value, as well as to perform other functions such as assessment ratio analysis.

COMPUTER PROGRAM—A set of instructions which automatically controls the operation of the computer in the solution of a problem.
1. ALGOL (ALGORITHMIC LANGUAGE)—An international computer programing language for problem solutions which can be expressed algebraically.

2. COBOL (COMMON BUSINESS ORIENTED LANGUAGE)—A computer programing language designed primarily for processing data involved in business.
3. FORTRAN (FORMULA TRANSLATOR)—A computer programing language for problem solutions which can be expressed algebraically.

COMPUTER SYSTEM—The collection of mechanical and electrical equipment that performs the actual data manipulations of an electronic data processing system.

CONCEALED HEATING—See Radiant Heating.

CONCENTRATES—In agriculture, milled and blended high protein feed used to supplement farm grown forage.

CONCESSION
1. A franchise for the right to conduct a business granted by a governmental body or other authority.
2. Floor space or the right to conduct a business within a premise controlled by another. The latter condition usually is controlled by a lease.

CONCLUSION OF VALUE—See Certificate.

CONCRETE—A hard stonelike material made by mixing sand, an aggregate such as crushed stone or gravel, and cement with water and allowing mixture to harden. See also Poststressed Concrete, Prestressed Concrete.

CONCRETE BLOCK—Concrete compressed into the shape of a block and allowed to set until it hardens. Used as a masonry unit.

CONCRETE CONSTRUCTION—See Architectural Concrete Construction, Reinforced Concrete Construction.

CONCRETION—Local concentrations of certain chemical compounds, such as calcium carbonate or compounds of iron, which form hard grains or nodules of mixed composition and of various sizes, shapes, and coloring.

CONDEMNATION—The act of government (federal, state, county, municipal), and of duly authorized units of government and public utility companies invested with right of eminent domain, to take private property for public use and benefit, upon the payment of just compensation. It is the act of the sovereign in substituting itself in place of the owner and/or the act of taking all or a part of the rights of an owner.

CONDEMNATION VALUE—A misconception. Value sought under the laws applicable in condemnation is market value.

CONDEMNEE—Owner of property taken in eminent domain proceedings.

CONDEMNOR – Taking agency or body (federal, state, county or municipal government) or some other public authority or utility corporation vested with right of eminent domain.

CONDITIONAL PROBABILITY – The probability of the occurrence of one event, given that some other event has occurred.

CONDITIONAL SALE – See Contract Sale.

CONDOMINIUM – A form of fee ownership of whole units or separate portions of multi-unit buildings by statute which provides the mechanics and facilities for formal filing and recording of a divided interest in real property, where the division is vertical as well as horizontal. Fee ownership of units in a multi-unit property and joint ownership of the common areas. Not to be confused with "Cooperative."

CONDOMINIUM CONVERSION – Conversion of rental projects (residential, commercial, office, or industrial) to the condominium form of ownership.

CONDUCTION – Transmission through or by means of a conductor; in heating, by the transfer of heat from one object to another as distinguished from convection or radiation.

CONDUCTION, THERMAL – The transmission of heat through or within a solid object.

CONDUCTOR
1. A substance or body capable of transmitting heat, electricity, etc.
2. A wire or cable through which electricity flows.
3. A rod used to carry lightning to the ground, a lightning rod.
4. A pipe to convey rain water from the roof gutter to the drain pipe; a down spout.

CONDUIT
1. An artificial or natural channel for conveyance of water or other fluid, as a pipe, canal, aqueduct, flume. A pipe or tube used to convey and protect electric wires or cables.
2. The conveyance of income from one entity to another so that the final recipient incurs tax liability.

CONDUIT SYSTEM – An electrical wiring system having conductors encased in metal tubing.

CONFIDENCE INTERVAL – In statistics, the specification of a zone based upon a sample mean and its standard error within which one may be confident that the true population mean does lie.

CONFORMITY, PRINCIPLE OF – Holds that the maximum of value is realized when a reasonable degree of homogeneity is present. Thus conformity in use is usually a highly desirable adjunct of real property, since it creates and/or maintains value.

CONGRUOUS — That which, by comparison, corresponds, conforms, or agrees. Antonym: incongruous.

CONIFER — See Types of Range Vegetation, page 349.

CONNECTION — A part which fastens, joins, links or unites such as plate and angle riveted or bolted connections which unite structural steel columns, girders, and trusses in a building.

CONSEQUENTIAL DAMAGES — A damage to property arising as a consequence of a taking and/or construction on other lands. In many states owners may be compensated for damage as a consequence of a change in grade of a street which adversely affects ingress to and egress from the affected property. In some states property owners are not legally entitled to consequential damages which occur to their real estate. Owners may not be compensated for damage to business, frustration, and loss of goodwill which result as a consequence of a taking or construction by the government. See also Inverse Condemnation.

CONSERVATION

1. As applied to real estate, the protection of good neighborhoods and structures from blight or other influences which may adversely affect desirability or value.
2. As applied to natural resources, the care and preservation in such a way as to prolong their use or make for their more effective use.

CONSIDERATION — The price or subject matter which induces a contract; may be in money, commodity exchange, or a transfer of personal effort. In appraising, usually the actual price at which property is transferred.

CONSISTENT USE THEORY — Affirms that a property in transition to another use cannot be valued on the basis of one use for the land and another for improvements (i.e., improvements must contribute to the value of the land in order to have value attributed to them). For example, a building that has several years of physical life remaining may not enhance the value of land that has a higher use (except as an interim-use taxpayer while the land itself is in transition). Where the transition to highest and best use is deferred, the element of interim use should be considered. See Interim Use.

CONSOLIDATION — The combining of two or more corporations into one; implying the dissolution of one or more of the individual corporations. See also Merger.

CONSTANT — A number, characteristic, or item that does not vary in value or amount. See Mortgage Constant.

CONSTRAINED BEAM–A beam rigidly fixed at one or both points of support.

CONSTRUCTION COST–The cost to build, particularly an improvement, usually including direct costs of labor and material plus contractors overhead and profits, or may include all direct and indirect costs incidental to the development.

CONSTRUCTION LOAN–A short term loan to finance construction of real estate improvements with or without a takeout commitment for permanent financing.

CONSTRUCTIVE NOTICE–Notice given by the public records. (The law presumes that everyone has the same knowledge of all instruments properly recorded as if that person were actually acquainted with them.)

CONSULTING–See Counseling.

CONSUMER GOOD–An economic good used directly to satisfy human want. Consumer goods may be either durable or nondurable.

CONTEMPORARY–A type of modern architecture which takes many forms. It is designed to promote close relationship to the outdoors, to incorporate new construction methods and materials, and to create new uses of old materials. Large windows, open planning, horizontal lines, and simple details characterize this style. In residential architecture, contemporary houses may be one or two stories or split-levels to harmonize with the site conditions. Roofs may be flat, shed, gabled, or various combinations thereof.

CONTIGUOUS–Adjacent; in actual contact; touching.

CONTINGENT FEES–Remuneration based or conditioned upon future occurrences or conclusions, or results of services to be performed.

CONTINUOUS DISTRIBUTION–In statistics, a distribution where the random variable can take on any value within an interval rather than only a restricted set of values (e.g., only integers).

CONTINUOUS GROWTH–Growth as it occurs in nature as distinguished from periodic growth as it occurs in finance when interest is compounded at regular intervals; growth at compound interest with instantaneous compounding or compounding at infinitely small intervals of time.

CONTINUOUS WINDOWS–Windows designed for sawtooth roofs or roof monitors of industrial buildings; generally top hinged and opened by mechanical operators.

CONTOUR FURROWS–Furrows plowed at right angles to the direction of slope, at approximately the same level throughout and ordinarily at comparatively close intervals. Together with the ridges produced by making the furrow, they intercept and retain run-off water and thereby facilitate erosion control, moisture distribution, penetration, and retention.

CONTOUR LEVELING – Land leveling within a limited change in elevation resulting in a terraced land form.

CONTOUR LINE – Outline of a figure, body, mass; lines representing such an outline as the edge of the water of a lake. A line as on a topographic map or chart connecting the points on a land surface which have the same elevation.

CONTOUR MAP – A map showing the configuration of a surface by means of contour lines representing regular intervals of elevation.

CONTRACT – An agreement of two or more persons upon a sufficient consideration to do or not to do a particular thing. When real property is involved, a dated, written, signed agreement between two or more competent parties to do or not to do a legal act, for a legal consideration, within a specified time.

CONTRACTOR'S OVERHEAD – The general burden of costs assumed by a contractor on any construction work other than the direct costs of material and labor; consisting of such costs as are represented in the use of and return upon the investment in the construction equipment and normal office and executive expense. See also Contractor's Profit.

CONTRACTOR'S PROFIT – The margin or the amount by which the price received by a contractor for work performed exceeds the total direct cost of materials and labor, plus overhead. See also Contractor's Overhead.

CONTRACT RENT – Payment for the use of property as designated in a lease. Used to establish the fact that the actual rent designated, or contract rent, may differ from market rent.

CONTRACT SALE – A sale in which the title to property or goods remains with the seller until the purchaser has fulfilled the terms of the contract, usually payment in full. Synonym: conditional sale. See also Land Contract.

CONTRIBUTION, PRINCIPLE OF – A valuation principle which states that the value of an agent of production or of a component part of a property depends upon how much it contributes to the value of the whole; or how much its absence detracts from the value of the whole. The Principle of Contribution is sometimes known as the Principle of Marginal Productivity. See also Increasing and Decreasing Returns.

CONTRIBUTORY VALUE OF IMPROVEMENTS – The dollar amount that a building adds to the market value of a given property as based on the building reproduction cost less accrued depreciation.

CONTROL DATA — A method of using transactions of real properties to adjust the market data utilized in the comparative approach to valuation. Such control data are necessary in order to segregate certain influences which have caused changes in real estate values, either generally or specifically. An example would be two or more sales of each of several properties, the first sales of which were made during a certain period, and the subsequent sales having taken place after a lapse of some time. Any trend shown by an increase or decrease in the prices of such properties between the two periods would indicate a change because of the time element, assuming no other specific causes. Such changes in value could be utilized in adjustment for time, where only older sales of properties comparable to the subject property in the immediate area are available. Control data are also useful where it is necessary to identify and segregate causes affecting values in specific areas due to a public improvement, such as a freeway.

CONTROLLED ACCESS HIGHWAY — A highway especially designed for through traffic, and over, from, or to which owners or occupants of abutting land or other persons have no easement rights or only controlled easement rights of access, light, air, or view. Synonym: limited access highway.

CONTROLS — The conditions in an urban renewal plan, usually of a limiting nature, concerned with land use, density, height, parking requirements, etc.

CONVECTOR — A radiator designed to furnish a maximum amount of heat by convection; has many fins or plates closely fitted on pipes carrying hot water or steam, the fins heating the circulating air.

CONVECTION — Motion within a fluid or gas resulting in a difference in density and the action of gravity. In heat transmission, this meaning has been extended to include both natural motion and that due to forced circulation.

CONVENIENCE GOODS — Those commodities purchased frequently and automatically, without extensive comparison of style, price, and quality.

CONVENTIONAL LOAN — A permanent loan which is neither insured nor guaranteed by an agency of the federal government (e.g., FHA or VA), although it may carry private mortgage insurance.

CONVERSION FACTOR — In forestry, a factor that is multiplied by tree count or volume for a given size class to give number of trees or volume per acre for that size class.

CONVERSION PERIOD — The interval of time used in the computation of compound interest.

CONVEYANCE — A written instrument which passes an interest in real property from one person to another; may be a deed, mortgage, lease, but not a will.

CONVEYOR BELT — A belt used in manufacturing processes which continually moves items in production. It may also be used, as in mining, to convey mined materials from their source to a place of transport or usage.

COOLING TOWER — A water tower designed to cool water by evaporation.

COOP — Usually associated with housing for chickens or other fowl.

COOPERATIVE — A form of ownership whereby the owner of stock in a cooperative apartment or housing corporation pays a proportionate share of the interest and real estate taxes paid by the corporation. This proportionate share is based on the proportion of the total stock owned, and the interest that is deductible can relate to any debt incurred by the corporation to acquire, construct, alter, rehabilitate or maintain the building or land. The cooperative must be bona fide, i.e., stock ownership must give the stockholder the right to live in an apartment or house on the property owned or leased by the corporation though the stockholder need not actually be required to live there. See Cooperative Apartment.

COOPERATIVE APARTMENT — An apartment owned by a corporation, either for or not for profit, or by a trust, in which each owner purchases stock to the extent of the value of the apartment, title being evidenced by a proprietary lease.

COOPERATIVE HOUSING (FHA Section 213) — A section of Title II of the National Housing Act under which FHA insures mortgages, including construction advances, on sales-type and management-type cooperative housing projects of eight or more units.

COORDINATES — Any of a number of magnitudes which determine position as of points, planes, lines, etc.

COPING — Covering course of a wall or roof, usually sloping on its upper surface to permit run-off of water.

CORBEL — A beam or bracket projecting from a wall to support some other object or structural part of the building; also may be an embellishment rather than structural.

CORD — A cubic measure, especially of wood; the quantity of wood in such a measure. A pile of cut wood 8 feet long, 4 feet high, and 4 feet wide (128 cubic feet) is the recognized measure in the United States.

CORDAGE — In forestry, a forest product measured in cords.

CORN CRIB — A farm building designed to store harvested unshelled and undried corn.

CORNER — The point or place where two converging lines, sides, etc., meet, as where two streets intersect. In surveying, a point marked by a monument.

CORNER INFLUENCE — The value effect of location at or in proximity to the intersection of two streets. The increment of value resulting from such location or proximity.

CORNER INFLUENCE TABLE — A table purporting to reflect the increment in value accruing to a parcel of land (usually commercial) by reason of its location on a corner, used primarily in mass appraising such as in assessment work.

Most corner influence tables are based on some percentage combination of the front foot land values on the main street and secondary street, in relation to the proximity to the corner of the frontage on the high value street.

These tables are hazardous to use unless related directly to the property under appraisement through comparison with market rents and/or sales.

CORNER LOT — A lot abutting upon two intersecting streets.

CORNICE
1. A molded projection at the top of a wall, either exterior or interior.
2. A horizontal projection, usually molded, which finishes or crowns an exterior wall.
3. Commonly used to designate the enclosure at the roof eaves or at the rake of a roof, and includes a crown mold, fascia, soffit, bed mold and frieze. See illustration, page 305.

CORPORATION — In law, a form of organization enjoying legal personality for the purpose of carrying on certain activities, usually business for profit; but also, charitable, educational, and religious corporations. In the United States, all governmental units smaller than a state.

CORPOREAL — Pertaining to a right or group of rights of a visible and tangible nature.

CORPOREAL PROPERTY — Tangible property.

CORRAL — A small enclosure for handling livestock at close quarters.

CORRECTION LINES — See Standard Parallels.

CORRELATION
1. In statistics, an estimation of the degree (closeness) with which two or more variables are associated.
2. In appraising, see Reconciliation.

CORRELATION ANALYSIS — A statistical technique which relates a dependent variable to one (simple correlation) or more (multiple correlation) independent variables in order to determine the extent to which, and the direction in which, change in the dependent variable is associated with change in the independent variable(s).

CORRELATION COEFFICIENT (r) — A statistic that measures the degree of relationship between two or more sets of numbers.

CORRELATION MATRIX — A table of numbers used to display the correlation coefficients for each pair of variables when three or more variables are thought to be correlated.

CORRIDOR
1. A passageway or hall connecting parts of a building.
2. A strip of land between two termini within which traffic, topography, environment, land uses, and other characteristics are evaluated for transportation purposes.

CORRUGATED SIDING — Siding made of sheet metal or asbestos cement composition board; used for siding on some industrial facilities and other inexpensive buildings. Corrugation increases the structural strength of the material.

CORRUGATED WALL TIE — A piece of thin sheet metal about six inches long and one inch wide that has been crinkled. It is laid in the mortar courses between brick to tie a wall together where a brick bond cannot be used.

COST — The price paid or obligated for anything. The amount of money or its equivalent worth which is exchanged for use of ownership of property. See also, Cubic Foot Cost, Replacement Cost, Reproduction Cost, Square Foot Cost.

COST APPROACH — That approach in appraisal analysis which is based on the proposition that the informed purchaser would pay no more than the cost of producing a substitute property with the same utility as the subject property. It is particularly applicable when the property being appraised involves relatively new improvements which represent the highest and best use of the land or when relatively unique or specialized improvements are located on the site and for which there exist no comparable properties on the market.

COST-BENEFIT RATIO — The relationship (ratio) of benefits generated by an improvement related to the cost of that improvement: the calculation (ratio) must exceed 1:00 for the improvement to be considered "desirable." The alternative term, benefit-cost ratio, is actually more descriptive.

COST-BENEFIT STUDY — The calculation of all benefits which a proposed investment will create (often nonpecuniary benefits) weighted against the cost of creating the improvement. Generally used by public agencies to aid them in decisions about the construction of capital improvements.

COST EFFECTIVENESS – The comparison of alternative courses of action in terms of their dollar costs and their relative effectiveness in achieving a specific goal.

COST ESTIMATING – In construction, the cost to build based on a quantity survey of the cost of all materials and labor to be employed and other essential costs incurred in the process. In appraising, estimating the reproduction or replacement cost of an improvement by one of several methods. See also Quantity-survey Method, Unit Cost-in-place Method, Cubic Foot Method, Square Foot Method.

COST OF ADMINISTRATION – That portion of indirect cost represented in management and related expenses. All expense involved in handling the business affairs of an estate, a minor, or a similarly delegated obligation.

COST OF BETTERMENTS – The expenditures made or required for improvement in a property which are considered to add to the investment or capital cost, as distinguished from the cost of repairs and replacements.

COST OF DEVELOPMENT METHOD – A method of valuing undeveloped acreage. Derivation of an estimate of the maximum amount an investor-developer would be warranted in paying for land, given the cost of developing it, the probable proceeds from the sale of the developed sites and appropriate discounting techniques. Also called Subdivision Method or Subdivision Analysis Method.

COST OF OCCUPANCY – The periodic expenditure of money necessary to occupy a property, exclusive of the expenses directly attributable to the conduct of a business.

COST OF REMODELING – Expenditures made or required on alterations for the purpose of changing the plan, form, or style of a structure or its use potential.

COST OF REPAIRS – Expenditures made or required to mend or restore deterioration brought about by decay, wear and tear, or partial destruction. An expenditure to recapture depreciation due to deterioration or damage. A repair is to be distinguished from a betterment (capital improvement) inasmuch as a repair is intended merely to maintain the utility of the property repaired.

COST OF REPLACEMENT – See Replacement Cost.

COST OF REPLACEMENT LESS DEPRECIATION – See Replacement Cost Less Depreciation.

COST OF REPRODUCTION – See Reproduction Cost.

COST-PLUS CONTRACT – A contract in which the contractor's profit is fixed at a stated percentage of the actual direct costs of labor and materials or at a flat sum above such costs.

CO-TENANT – A tenancy in common; a joint ownership or common unity of possession.

COTERMINOUS – The quality of having the same boundaries.

COUNSELING (CONSULTING) – Providing competent, disinterested and unbiased advice, professional guidance and sound judgment on diversified problems in the broad field of real estate involving any and all segments of the business. Counseling/consulting may involve any or all of the following services: merchandising, leasing, management, planning, financing, renovation, appraising, court testimony, market and feasibility analysis, etc. In counseling/consulting, the appraiser simulates the decision-making framework and criteria of the client to provide the client with direction in choosing from among alternative courses of action. The American Society of Real Estate Counselors confers upon those who qualify the professional designation CRE (Counselor, Real Estate). See also SREA, Real Estate Analyst.

COUNT PLOTS – In forestry, sampling points at which tallied trees are counted by species to determine average basal or stem area per unit of area.

COUNTY – The largest division for local government in all states except Louisiana and Alaska where the comparable units are the parish and borough respectively.

COUNTY EXTENSION AGENT – See Agricultural Extension Agent.

COUNTY FARM ADVISER – See Agricultural Extension Agent.

COUNTY HIGHWAY – A road under the jurisdiction of a county. In many states the term includes all rural public roads outside the state highway system; other states have township roads in addition.

COURSE
1. A continuous horizontal layer of brick or masonry; one of a series of layers of materials in construction.
2. The natural course of a stream; a natural channel for water.

COURT
1. An uncovered area partly or wholly bounded by buildings or walls.
2. An open space such as a short street.
3. In law, the place where justice is administered; the persons duly assembled under the authority of law to administer justice; a tribunal established for administration of justice; the session of a judicial assembly.

COURT AWARD – Any decision following a contested trial or hearing before a jury, commission, judge, or other legal entity having the authority to establish the amount of compensation for a taking under the laws of eminent domain.

COVE – A concave molding; the edge of a ceiling which is curved or arched at its junction with the side walls.

COVENANT – A promise, between two or more parties, incorporated in a trust indenture or other formal instrument, to perform certain acts or to refrain from the performance of certain acts. See also Restrictive Covenant.

COVER CROP – A crop planted principally for the purpose of controlling wind or water erosion during the dormant season. It is normally plowed under and not harvested.

COW UNIT – See Animal Unit.

COW-YEAR-LONG (CYL) – The total number of head of stock which can be nourished properly for a full year on a given piece of land without harming the natural adult vegetative cover on the land divided by the number of cows that are available in that total to produce calves. See also Animal Unit Month (AUM's) Animal Units per Month Table, page 293.

CPE – Certified Personality Evaluator, a professional designation conferred by the International Association of Assessing Officers upon personal property appraisers in the assessment field. See also CAE.

CRADLE – A bed into which large trees are felled to prevent breakage. It is made by preparing the ground surface either by excavating or filling, or both.

CRANE – A device for lifting and moving heavy weights. Three types of traveling cranes are: overhead crane, a bridgelike structure which moves on parallel tracks above inside work areas; gantry cranes supporting the bridge on its own legs which move on fixed track, usually outdoors at ground level; and a one-leg gantry which combines features of each. Jib crane has arm guyed at a fixed angle to the head of a rotating mast; the boom of a derrick.

CRANEWAY – The steel or concrete column and girder supports and rails on which a crane travels.

CRAWL SPACE – An unfinished, accessible space below the first floor, generally less than full story height.

CREATIVE SELLING – The creation of a market for a property. Creating a property from bare land or underimproved land which will suit the particular needs of prospects, and selling it to them.

CREDITOR'S POSITION – That portion of the market price of a property which is represented by or can be obtained through debt financing.

CREOSOTE BUSH – See Types of Range Vegetation, page 349.

CRITICAL ASSUMPTION – A statement in the appraisal, of expectations and beliefs in applying factual data (and judgments) believed appropriate and plausible which cannot be expected to be accomplished (or changed) before the effective date of the appraisal (or completion of transaction). No invalidation occurs if the assumptions turn out to be incorrect.

CROP – The harvest or yield of a single field or single variety which is gathered in a single season or partial season.

CROP ACRES – See Cropland.

CROP ALLOTMENT – The acreage alloted to farms under the Crop Production Program of the federal government. See also Acreage Controls.

CROP ROTATION – The practice of alternating, usually on an annual basis, field crops, such as corn or wheat, with legumes in order to maintain or improve the structure and productivity of the soil.

CROP SHARE RENT – A rent which is an agreed percentage of the crops grown by the tenant. The share may vary depending upon local custom and the landowner's contribution of seeds, fertilizer, harvesting costs, irrigation, water supply, etc.

CROPLAND – That part of the farm acreage normally used for the production of annual crops or for summer fallow or rotation pasture, as distinguished from wood lots, marshes, etc.

CROSS-BRIDGING – Cross-bracing between floor joists to provide rigidity and permit the transfer of isolated heavy bearing weight to a broader supporting area. Also to prevent warping.

CROSS CONNECTING ROAD – A connecting roadway between two nearby and generally parallel roads.

CROSS FENCE – An interior fence on a farm or ranch which divides the property into fields or pastures. See also Division Fence.

CROSS SECTION – A transverse section viewed at right angles to the longitudinal axis of a piece of wood, drawing, or other work.

CROSS TIE – A lightweight structural member attached to and used to brace rafters on opposite roof slopes. See illustration, page 306.

CRUISE – A survey of land to locate standing timber and estimate its quantity for species, products, size, quality, or other characteristics. The estimate obtained in such a survey.

CUBIC CONTENT – The cubic volume of a building, usually measured from the outer surfaces of the exterior walls and roof and a level related to that of the lowest floor; common practice accepts six inches below finished surface of lowest floor for measuring standard cubic content. See illustration, pages 296–297.

CUBIC FOOT COST – The quotient of the cost of a building divided by the cubic content.

CUBIC FOOT METHOD – One of the methods of estimating reproduction or replacement cost of a building by multiplying the cubic foot units of building content by an appropriate unit construction cost figure. For illustration, see page 296.

CUBIC FOOT PER SECOND – A flow of water equivalent to a stream having a width and depth of one foot each (one square foot) and flowing at the rate of one foot per second. See Measures, page 274.

CUBIC YARD – A measure of volume that is three feet wide, three feet high and three feet deep. There are 27 cubic feet in a cubic yard.

CUERDA – A Spanish unit of land measurement. See Measures, page 273.

CUL DE SAC – A street open at one end only; having an enlarged turn-around area at the closed end.

CULTURAL FEATURES – Those additions and changes to the face of the land created by man, as distinguished from natural attributes; for example, structures, highways, fences, etc.

CULVERT – Any structure, generally small, which provides drainage under a travelway, parking lot or other area requiring it.

CUPOLA – A small building-like structure on a roof.

CURABLE DEPRECIATION – Those items of physical deterioration and functional obsolescence which are economically feasible to cure and hence are customarily repaired or replaced by a prudent property owner. The estimate of this depreciation is usually computed as a dollar amount of the cost-to-cure.

CURB – The stone or concrete edging of a sidewalk or paved street; the raised edge of a floor or well opening.

CURB LINE – The dividing line between the roadway and that portion reserved on each side of the roadway for the use of pedestrians.

CURRENT ASSETS – Moving and/or readily convertible assets. Quick or liquid assets, such as cash, accounts receivable, and merchandise inventory.

CURRENT LIABILITIES – A liability which will be paid in the normal operation of a business; a short-term debt.

CURTAIN WALL—An exterior wall which encloses but does not support the structural frame of a building. Synonym: panel wall.

CURTESY—The estate to which, by common law, the husband is entitled in the lands of his deceased wife. The extent varies with statutory provision.

CURTILAGE—The fenced-in ground surrounding a building.

CURVILINEAR—Consisting of, or bounded by, curved lines, as curvilinear streets.

CUT—The output of a sawmill for a given period of time. A season's output of logs.

CUT-OVER LAND—An area from which there has been removed by logging all or most of the original virgin forest.

CUTS—In highway construction, excavations through lands of higher elevation to establish the grade of the right of way.

CYCLICAL MOVEMENT—The moving from prosperity through recession, depression, recovery, and back again to prosperity. This movement varies in time, length, and intensity. See Business Cycle.

D HORIZON—Calcareous material showing some oxidation, underlying the C horizon. See also A, B, and C Horizons.

DAM—A barrier across a water course to restrict the flow of water or confine it. It may be a simple earthen bank or masonry wall across a minor stream, or a large engineering structure across a river as for a hydro-electric plant.

DAMAGES—In condemnation, the loss in value to the remainder in a partial taking of a property. Generally, the difference between the value of the whole property before the taking and the value of the remainder after the taking is the measure of the value of the part taken and the damages to the remainder. Two types of damages are recognized; consequential and severance.

DAMPER—A hinged plate in the flue of a furnace or fireplace which, acting as an air valve, is used to regulate the draft. Also, a device to deaden vibrations.

DAMPPROOFING—The coating of a surface to prevent the passage of moisture.

DARK STORE CLAUSE—Clause in a lease which provides that the tenant must continue to do business at that site or location during the full term of the lease. This is vital in a straight percentage lease involving a major tenant. It also prevents the tenant from opening a competitive store 6 months prior to the expiration of the lease which may place the subject property in a very poor releasing position.

DATA—In appraising, it is the information pertinent to a specific assignment. Such data may be divided into two classes, general (relating to the economic and demographic background, the region, the city and the neighborhood) and specific (relating to the subject property and comparable properties in the market).

In statistics, information or facts, most generally in numerical form, which can be classified by qualitative characteristics (ratios), by size (frequency distributions) or by time (time series or regression analysis).

DATA PROCESSING—Any operation or combination of operations performed on data.

DATE OF APPRAISAL
1. The date on which, or as of which, the value estimate applies.
2. Most frequently, the date of inspection for purposes of appraisal, though often fixed at some prior time, or, in the case of proposed construction or development, at some future time when the construction is presumed to be complete.

DATUM—The horizontal base line from which heights and depths are measured. The datum level which has been adopted as a base or starting point for the grades or levels of the municipality as recorded in the building codes which control the building standards.

DBH—See Diameter Breast High.

DEAD-END STREET—A street which is open at one end, closed at the other, and not having special enlarged turning provisions at the closed end as a cul de sac.

DEAD LOAD—The permanent inert weight of a structure itself and such fixed loads as boilers, heavy machinery, and equipment; does not include variable live loads such as furniture, merchandise, or people.

DEAD RENT—A fixed, annual sum paid for a mine or quarry, in addition to payment of royalties, which vary in amount according to the yield.

DEAD STORAGE—Used by garage owners to designate the storage of automobiles which are not in use, as those which are stored for a period of time or a season, as distinguished from "live" storage, of automobiles which are in active or daily use.

DEATH LOSS—The reduction of animals through loss of life from such causes as plant poisoning, accident, or disease as differentiated from reduction by causes such as straying, theft, or sales.

DEATH RATE—The number of deaths per 1,000 persons during the period of a year. This is called the crude death rate. The refined death rate makes corrections for the number of people in each age group.

DEBENTURE — An obligation that is not secured by specific lien on property, as an unsecured note of a corporation.

DEBT — Borrowed money; money which has been borrowed usually for a specified period of time. May be either secured or unsecured.

DEBT COVERAGE — The ability of a property to meet its debt service out of operating income (NOI).

DEBT COVERAGE RATIO — The ratio of net operating income (NOI) from an income-producing property to the annual debt service (ADS). An underwriting tool utilized by mortgage lenders which varies depending upon the type of property offered as security for the debt and that property's cash flows.

DEBT FINANCING — The payment (either partial or full) for a capital investment with borrowed funds. In real estate, the property itself usually serves as security for the debt.

DEBT SERVICE — The periodic payment for interest on and retirement of the mortgage loan (principal).

DEBTOR'S POSITION — That portion of the market price or value of property which is in excess of a prime first mortgage or mortgageable interest; the equity holder's position.

DECENTRALIZATION — Dispersion from a center. The movement of people, industry, and business from the city to the suburbs, rural-urban fringe, and/or smaller cities. The movement of business from the central business district. The establishment of plants away from large cities and at some distance from one another; the breaking down of an existing business into smaller units or expanding through establishment of separate units.

DECIDUOUS — Trees which shed their leaves annually.

DECISION TREES — In statistics or decision theory, a method of analyzing problems which involve a sequence of decisions. Alternative actions are represented as "branches" of the tree for each decision to be made.

DECK — An open second-story porch, usually on the roof of a ground floor porch or wing; in modern architecture, may be supported by piers or cantilever.

DECKING — The surfacing material applied to the rafters or floor joists to which the roof cover or floor cover material is applied. Sometimes called sheathing.

DECK ROOF — A nearly flat roof constructed without a fire wall.

DECLINATION — In compass reading, it is the angle formed by the magnetic needle and a geographical meridian.

DECLINING (DECREASING) ANNUITY — A series of periodic (yearly) payments or benefits, the installments of which progressively and systematically decrease. Specifically, in appraising, it refers to a forecast of an annually declining Net Operating Income over the income projection period, implying a systematic decline in gross income, an increase in operating expenses, or a combination of both.

DECLINING ANNUITY METHOD — A valuation technique which utilizes the premise that future income will probably decline progressively and systematically, and reduced the predicted probable income to a present value estimate.

DECLINING BALANCE DEPRECIATION — A method of depreciating an asset by use of a fixed percentage applied to the successive balances remaining after previously computed amounts of depreciation have been deducted. See illustration, page 339.

DECOMPOSITION — The breaking down of complex chemical compounds to form simpler ones. As applied to soils, it refers to the breaking down of soil minerals by solution and chemical change.

DECREMENT — A decrease in value of property, due primarily to the operation of social or economic forces beyond the control of the owner; the amount of such loss. Antonym: increment.

DEDICATED — Property in public use, such as a roadway, which was originally obtained by voluntary gift from the fee owner. Also used to describe land which has been acquired for and dedicated to burial purposes.

DEDICATION — The voluntary giving of private property to some public use by the owner, as the dedication of land for streets, schools, etc., in a development.

DEED — A legal instrument in writing which, when executed and delivered, conveys an estate or interest in real property. See also Administrator's Deed, Bond for Deed, Committee Deed, Executor's Deed, Mortgage Deed, Quitclaim Deed, Trust Deed, Warranty Deed.

DEED DESCRIPTION — A recitation of the legal boundaries of a parcel of land as contained in a deed of conveyance.

DEED IN FEE — A good and sufficient conveyance of a fee simple; free of all incumbrances with the usual covenants of the vendor.

DEED OF RELEASE — A writing duly subscribed and acknowledged by a mortgagee, whereby the mortgaged property is absolved from the lien of the mortgage.

DEED OF TRUST—A sealed instrument in writing, duly executed and delivered, conveying or transferring property to a trustee, usually but not necessarily covering real property. See also Trust Agreement.

DEED RESTRICTION—A limitation which passes with the land regardless of owner, most commonly limiting the type of use or intensity of use of the real estate. See also Restrictive Covenant.

DEFACTO CONTRACT—One which has purported to pass the property from the owner to another—a purchaser in good faith taking from such transferee obtains a good title.

DEFAULT—The failure to fulfill a contractual agreement.

DEFAULT RATIO—The occupancy level at which effective gross income from an income-producing property is insufficient to pay operating expenses plus debt service.

DEFEASANCE—An instrument which defeats the force or operation of some other deed or estate. That which is in the same deed is called a condition, and that which is in another deed is a defeasance.

DEFEASIBLE TITLE—One that is capable of being annulled or made void—not one that is already void, or in absolute nullity.

DEFERRED ANNUITY—An income stream which begins at some future date, i.e., some time removed from date of valuation; e.g., future enhancement of income from a step-up lease.

DEFERRED ASSETS—In accounting, that portion of expense items which is applicable to the period subsequent to the closing date. Deferred charges or deferred expenses preferred usage.

DEFERRED LIABILITY—Liability from transferred real property interests which do not become an obligation to the transferee until sometime after the transfer.

DEFERRED MAINTENANCE—Existing but unfulfilled requirements for repairs and rehabilitation. Contemplates the desirability of immediate expenditures although it does not necessarily denote inadequate maintenance in the past. To some extent it always exists in any operating property.

DEFICIENCY—An inadequacy in the structure or one of its components.

DEFICIENCY JUDGMENT—Judgment granted after a suit to recover a difference between a legally imposed indebtedness and the dollars received from a foreclosure sale of the debtor's assets.

DEFICIT—A falling short in amount, as a deficit in an expense fund; the amount by which the total assets of a business fall short of the total of all liabilities, plus the invested capital.

DEFINITIVE LOAN – A loan, secured by a long term lease, by an entity other than the legal seller to finance the purchase of a fee title. In urban renewal projects, definitive loans are made or guaranteed by the federal government.

DEFLATION – A decrease in the general price level; a period when purchasing power of money is rising.

DEGREE DAY – A unit of fuel consumption; the number of degrees deviation from 65°F, usually totaled over a number of days, e.g., annually or for a heating season. Useful in projecting annual heating or cooling costs.

DEGREES OF FREEDOM – In statistics, the difference between the size of a sample and the number of variables used up in arriving at an unbiased estimate or equation. As the number of degrees of freedom decreases, the related variance and standard deviation increase.

DEMAND – The quantity of an economic good which will be bought at a specified price, in a given market, and at a particular time; that is, market demand. See also Effective Demand, Potential Demand.

DEMISE – A conveyance either in fee for life or for years. Strictly denotes a posthumous grant, and no more.

DEMOLITION GRANT PROGRAM – Established by the Housing and Urban Development Act of 1965, it authorizes federal grants to cities and other municipalities and counties to assist in financing the cost of demolishing structures which under state or local law have been determined to be structurally unsound or unfit for human habitation.

DENSITY – See Forage Density, Height Density, Traffic Density, Use Density, Vegetative Density.

DENSITY ZONING – A system of zoning or land use controls under which residential occupancy is limited by the number of families per unit of land area in one plot, such as an acre, rather than by limiting the number of families permitted to occupy one building.

DEPLETION – A reduction in the value of an asset by reason of the taking away of exhaustible material assets or resources, such as the removal of trees from a forest, the taking of minerals from a mine, the taking of oil from a well, etc.

DEPLETION RATE – The periodical rate or percentage at which a quantity is exhausted; usually in natural resources. Determined by a consideration of the volume of production contemplated periodically, divided into the extent of commercially recoverable reserves; may be expressed in monetary units.

DEPOSIT — An existing quantity of recoverable metallic or nonmetallic natural resources, customarily inferred to be subject to commercial exploitation.

DEPRECIATED COST
1. Cost new less accrued depreciation, as of date of appraisal.
2. Sometimes erroneously used in reference to cost new, less deterioration or physical wear and tear only.

DEPRECIATION — A loss of utility and hence value from any cause. An effect caused by deterioration and/or obsolescence. Deterioration or physical depreciation is evidenced by wear and tear, decay, dry rot, cracks, encrustations, or structural defects. Obsolescence is divisible into two parts, functional and economic. Functional obsolescence may be due to poor plan, mechanical inadequacy or overadequacy, functional inadequacy or overadequacy due to size, style, age, etc. It is evidenced by conditions within the property. Economic and/or locational obsolescence is caused by changes external to the property, such as neighborhood infiltrations of inharmonious groups or property uses, legislation, etc. It is also the actual decline in market value of the improvement to land from time of purchase to the time of resale. See also Accrued Depreciation, Book Depreciation.

DEPRECIATION ACCRUAL RATE — The periodic amount or percentage at which it is judged that loss in property value occurs: the percentage at which amounts are computed to be set aside as accruals for anticipated loss in value due to depreciation.

DEPRECIATION ALLOWANCE — The amount which has been accumulated (presumably out of past operational or other earnings) on books of account to replace an asset; in this usage, more properly an accounting for income tax purposes rather than an appraisal concept.

DEPRECIATION METHODS — Methods used to measure loss in value, either accrued or future, of an improvement through depreciation. In accounting, relates to various methods used to identify recovery of the initial cost of an asset.

DEPRECIATION RECAPTURE — That portion of the gain realized on sale of real property which is attributable to excess depreciation and which is treated as ordinary income rather than capital gain. Excess depreciation deductions resulting from accelerated depreciation during the period of ownership shelters income from taxation at ordinary rates. Thus, the recapture provision is a means of regaining that tax liability albeit deferred.

DEPRECIATION RESERVE — The capital amount which summarizes the annual charges to operations by reason of depreciation. In accounting, the account on the books of a concern wherein the accruals for depreciation are accumulated.

DEPRESSION – The period of a business cycle when production is lowest, unemployment highest, prices lowest, and purchasing power greatly curtailed.

DEPTH CURVE – A graph of depth factors showing the estimated percentage relationships between the front foot value of a given lot and the front foot value of a lot of standard depth as the depth of the given lot varies. Note: Usually the depth of the given lot is plotted on the X-axis (horizontal), and the percentage relationship between the front foot value of the given lot and that of a standard depth on the Y-axis (vertical).

DEPTH FACTOR – A factor (percentage) which represents the relative value of a given depth of a lot with respect to the value of a lot having an adopted standard or unit (100%) depth. Most depth factors are modifications of the "4–3–2–1" rule which affirms that the first quarter of the depth of a standard lot (usually 100 ft.) is worth 40% of the whole, the second quarter of depth is worth 30%, the third quarter is worth 20%, and the fourth (rear) quarter is worth 10%. See also Standard Depth.

DEPTH INFLUENCE – The effect of depth upon the value of a lot or parcel having a given frontage. The increment or decrement of value arising from a depth greater or less than that of the standard lot.

DEPTH TABLE – A table of depth factors containing the estimated percentage relationship between the front foot value of a lot of any given depth and the front foot value of a lot of standard depth. See also Depth Factor, Standard Depth.

DESCENT – A transfer of property at death in the absence of a will; transfer by inheritance.

DESCRIPTION SYSTEM – See Government Survey, Deed Description, Legal Description.

DESCRIPTIVE STATISTICS
1. The branch of the science of statistics that is concerned only with characterizing or describing a set of data (numbers).
2. By extension, the measures used, such as the average, the maximum, or the coefficient of dispersion, to characterize a particular set of data.

DESERT SHRUB – See Types of Range Vegetation, page 349.

DESERT SOIL – See Types of Soil, page 351.

DESIGN – An architectural drawing or draft of the plan, elevations, and sections of a structure. A plan is representative of a horizontal projection; elevation refers to vertical or exterior projections.

DETERIORATION – Impairment of condition; one of the causes of depreciation, reflecting the loss in value brought about by wear and tear, disintegration, use in service, and the action of the elements. Also, synonymous with physical depreciation which may be further classified as curable or incurable depreciation. See also Depreciation, Curable Depreciation, Incurable Depreciation.

DEVELOPMENT COST – Costs incurred in the creation of a property and the subsequent expenditures required to bring it to an efficient status of operation, as distinguished from the costs directly expended upon the construction of the property; may relate to the enterprise as an entirety or, in a limited sense, to the physical property only. In public utility practice, development cost has been accepted to mean the cost or expense incurred in creating a business as distinguished from the physical property.

DEVELOPMENT METHOD – See Anticipated Use Method.

DEVIATION – In statistics, the difference between one of a set of values (or numbers) and the mean of the set. See also Average Deviation, Coefficient of Dispersion, Standard Deviation.

DEVISE – A gift or disposal of real property by last will and testament; the estate so transferred.

DIAGRAM RULES – Full-sized circles of all diameters, representing the top ends of logs, are drawn on large sheets of paper. On these cross sections of the logs the ends or cross sections of the boards which could be sawed from each log are drawn, leaving between each board a space equal to the width of the saw kerf, and squaring off the two ends of each board. The area of boards in square inches is then reduced to boardfeet by the factor 1/12 times length in feet, for logs of standard length. This may be adjusted for logs of all lengths.

DIAMETER-BREAST-HIGH (DBH) – The diameter of a tree at 4½ feet (breast height) above average ground level. The abbreviations, o.b. and i.b., are used to designate whether the diameter refers to the measurement outside or inside the bark.

DIFFERENTIAL ASSESSMENTS – Assessments in a system of law that requires that different classes of property be assessed with different assessment ratios. Usually reserved for systems where the classes are broad and easily divisible, such as classified property tax systems and use value farm land assessment systems. Much the same effect is achieved by partial homestead exemptions, temporary exemptions to encourage rehabilitation, or industrial location and the like.

DIKE – An embankment for restraining the waters of the sea or a river; a levee; a causeway.

DILUVION – The gradual washing away and consequent loss of soil along the banks of streams.

DIMENSION LUMBER – Lumber as it comes from the saw; all yard lumber except timbers, strip, and board, from two inches up to, but not including, five inches in depth, and of any width.

DIMENSION SHINGLES – Shingles cut to a uniform size.

DIMINISHED UTILITY – See Accrued Depreciation.

DIMINISHING ASSETS – Those assets which by exhaustion, lapse of time, etc., are periodically reduced, and the value of which (disregarding fluctuation in market price) must be correspondingly reduced. Such assets include mineral deposits, copyrights, franchises for a limited term, and similar wasting property in which diminution in value cannot be arrested by expenditures (such as maintenance of tangible fixed property). Timber lands are usually included in this category, although they can be maintained at capacity by proper reforestation.

DIMINISHING RETURNS – See Increasing and Decreasing Returns.

DIMINISHING UTILITY – The consumption of each succeeding unit of an economic good yields less satisfaction than the preceding unit. Thus, total utility may be said to increase at a decreasing rate.

DIRECT CAPITALIZATION – The conversion of anticipated net income into present value by dividing the income by an appropriate rate which reflects the prevailing relationship of net income to selling price for comparable properties being sold in the open market; an alternate form of direct capitalization is the use of an appropriate "times earnings" multiplier instead of a rate, i.e., the reciprocal of the appropriate rate. Direct capitalization for land utilizes the Discount Rate, while direct capitalization for land and improvements combined uses an Overall Rate.

DIRECT COMPENSATION – See Just Compensation.

DIRECT COSTS – The costs for direct labor and material devoted specifically to a unit of work. In construction, these costs are directly related to site acquisition and construction of improvements, generally considered to include the following:
1. Land Cost
   a. Purchase price, including broker's commission if paid by the buyer.
   b. All legal and recording charges connected with the purchase of the site.
2. Cost of Building(s) and Improvements on the Land
   a. Construction cost of building and equipment and fixtures, including builder's profit, overhead, performance bond, and

"general conditions" items such as survey and permit fees, fencing, shoring for lateral support of adjacent land or streets, use of equipment, watchmen, contractor's "shack" and/or temporary building for on-the-job fabrication of units and material storage, power line installation, and cost of electric power used in construction.

DIRECT LABOR — Labor costs which are directly connected with a specific product or project as distinguished from indirect labor (overhead, management).

DIRECT REDUCTION MORTGAGE — A loan which is repaid by periodic installments (normally in a constant amount) which include a repayment of part of the principal as well as interest due on the unpaid balance; an amortized loan.

DIRECT SALES COMPARISON APPROACH — That approach in appraisal analysis which is based on the proposition that an informed purchaser would pay no more for a property than the cost of acquiring an existing property with the same utility. This approach is applicable when an active market provides sufficient quantities of reliable data which can be verified from authoritative sources. The direct sales comparison approach is relatively unreliable in an inactive market or in estimating the value of properties for which no real comparable sales data are available. It is also questionable when sales data cannot be verified with principals to the transaction. Also referred to as the Market Comparison or Market Data Approach.

DIRECT STEAM SYSTEM — This heating system uses radiators in the rooms to be heated, the steam or vapor being delivered from boiler to radiators through one of several arrangements of piping. The one-pipe gravity system is widely used for smaller installations. The two-pipe steam or vapor system is used for larger installations.

DIRT TANK — A small reservoir constructed with an earth-filled dam which collects natural runoff to provide livestock water.

DISCLAIMER — A denial or disavowal of any interest in or claim to the subject of the action, such as renunciation of any title, claim, interest, estate, or trust. The owner of a subdivision, the map of which has been filed in a county clerk's office, may disclaim and abandon such subdivision after five years have elapsed by filing an appropriate instrument for record. Thereafter, for the purpose of taxation, the tract is considered as one parcel of land (New York State Law). Also, a statement of limiting conditions in an appraisal report.

DISCOUNT — Money paid at the beginning of a time interval for the use of capital during that interval and commonly deducted from the principal at the time the funds are advanced; reduction of future payments to present worth.

DISCOUNT HOUSE—A retail store which, through self-service and other low overhead methods, can offer merchandise at a price often considerably below the usual or advertised retail price.

DISCOUNT POINT—A charge of $1 per $100 of mortgage funds extended, i.e., a 1% discount. A form of adjusting contract rates (nominal rates) to competitive market rates.

DISCOUNT RATE
1. In appraising, the rate of return on investment in the physical components of land and buildings. It may also be applied to the rate of return on the legal components of leased fee and leasehold interests. Sometimes referred to as Risk Rate or Interest Rate.
2. The annual percentage rate that reflects the competitive rate of return on an investment. Used to distinguish a rate of return on an investment from the rate of interest (interest rate) on borrowed funds, i.e., they are not interchangeable.
3. The charge member banks must pay to the Federal Reserve on their borrowings.

DISCOUNTED CASH-FLOW—Present worth of future annual cash benefits, usually considered in relation to equity investment.

DISCOUNTED CASH-FLOW METHOD—A means of isolating differences in the timing of cash flows by discounting these cash flows to their present values. The two discounted cash-flow methods are the internal-rate-of-return method and the net-present-value method.

DISCOUNTED RATE OF RETURN—Synonym for internal rate of return; often called DCRR in computerized cash-flow analysis.

DISCOUNTING—A concept of time preference which holds that future income or benefits are worth less than the same income or benefits now, and that they decrease in value systematically as the time for their receipt is further deferred into the future. In appraisal analysis, discounting is the arithmetic procedure of applying a specific rate (usually) derived from the market to the anticipated future income stream in order to develop a present worth estimate.

DISCOVERY
1. The process whereby the assessor identifies all taxable property in a jurisdiction and ensures that it is included on the assessment roll.
2. In law, the process by which the lawyers for the opposing sides prepare their cases for trial, through requiring, with court authority, the witnesses for the opposing sides to answer a number of written questions.

DISINTERESTED APPRAISAL—An appraisal in which the appraiser has no interest in the subject property, neither present nor prospective, directly or indirectly.

DISPERSION – In statistics, the degree of scatter of a set of terms or observations, usually measured from a central value such as the mean or the median.

DISPOSABLE INCOME – The income remaining to persons after deducting personal taxes and all other payments to the government.

DISPOSAL FIELD – An area where waste (effluent) from a septic tank is dispersed, draining into the ground through a tile and gravel leaching field system.

DISTEMPER – Composition used for painting walls and murals, in which the pigments are tempered or mixed with size, glue, or the whites or yolks of eggs.

DISTRIBUTED LOAD – An evenly spread weight over an entire surface, or along the length of a girder or beam, measured in pounds or tons per square foot or per lineal foot.

DISTRIBUTION BOX
1. A fuse box; a metal box containing fuses and circuit breakers which permits access to connecting branch circuits.
2. An underground box which receives the waste from the septic tank and distributes it to the laterals of a disposal field.

DISTRIBUTION METHOD – See Abstraction.

DISTRIBUTION PANEL – An insulated board from which electrical connections are made between the main feed circuit and branch distribution circuits.

DISTRIBUTION TILE – Concrete or clay tile laterals leading from a septic tank distribution box, laid with open joints through which effluent drains and seeps into the soil. See also Leaching Trenches.

DISTRICT
1. An area having a common use characteristic such as a retail district, financial district, school district, etc.
2. A unit of local government which has authority to levy taxes and issue bonds to finance schools, parks, etc.

DISTRICT MUTATION – The phenomenon observed frequently in rapidly growing cities whereby the centers of various types of districts, such as the retail district, financial district, etc., move in the direction of city growth.

DITCH – A small surface drain, either man-made or natural; a narrow open excavation.

DIVERSIFIED FARMING – Farming in which there are several sources of farm income.

DIVIDED INTEREST – An interest in a part of a whole property, as a lessee's interest.

DIVIDEND
1. In appraising, synonymous with annual Net Operating Income as defined herein; in Ellwood formulas designated by the symbol, *d*.
2. A distribution to shareholders.

DIVISION FENCE — A cross fence used to divide the land of a ranch into various pastures. See also Fence, Drift Fence, Line Fence, Snow Fence.

DIVISION WALL — An interior load-bearing wall dividing a structure into rooms. A masonry wall, either load-bearing or self-sustaining, which separates two abutting buildings.

DOCK
1. An elevated floor or platform, usually at truck bed or freight car floor height above ground, to facilitate the transfer of goods to or from a vehicle.
2. A structure extending from the shore into the water to permit mooring of vessels; a wharf.
3. The slip or waterway extending between two piers for the reception of ships; such a waterway, closed or open, together with surrounding piers and wharves.
4. An artificial basin for reception of vessels and from which water can be removed; used to repair ships below waterline. A dry dock.

DOG — A metal gripping and fastening implement for binding together timbers or other materials.

DOLPHIN — A post or pile cluster which is used to moor a boat; also, a bumper to protect dock or wharf from a vessel or floating objects.

DOME — A roof or ceiling shaped like a hemisphere or inverted bowl, so constructed as to exert equal, oblique thrust stresses in all directions.

DOMICILE — The locality in which a person or corporation is considered to have its legal residency.

DOOR — In truck terminal valuation, rentals are frequently related to $/door/month and sales comparisons may be made on the basis of $/door. Two cross-dock doors may be referred to as a "double door" unit.

DOOR STOP — A trim piece laid around the inside face of side and top door jambs to prevent damage to a door by reason of swinging too far. See illustration, page 304.

DORMER — A window set upright in a sloping or pitched roof; also, the roofed structure in which this window is set. See illustration, page 306.

DOUBLE-DECLINING BALANCE METHOD OF DEPRECIATION — Spreading the initial cost of a capital asset over time by deducting in each period double the percentage recognized by the straight-line method and applying that double percentage to the undepreciated balance existing at the start of each period. No salvage value is used in this calculation. See illustration, page 339. Also referred to as 200% declining balance.

DOUBLE FLOOR — Wood construction using a subfloor and a finished floor.

DOUBLE FRAMING — A building technique utilizing double joists, trimmers, and other structural members as reinforcement where needed.

DOUBLE-GABLED ROOF — See M Roof or Butterfly Roof.

DOUBLE GLAZING — A double-glass pane hermetically sealed with an air space between the two panes to provide insulation.

DOUBLE HOUSE — A dwelling separated by party walls and designed for use by two families. See also Duplex.

DOUBLE-HUNG WINDOW — A type of window containing two movable sashes which slide vertically. See illustration, page 301.

DOUBLE PITCH — Sloping in two directions, as a gable roof.

DOUBLE PITCH ROOF — A 2-slope roof with the pitch down to a center line; often termed butterfly roof. See illustration, page 300.

DOVETAIL — An interlocking joint commonly used in carpentry, such as drawers or cases.

DOWEL — A pin of wood or metal used to hold or reinforce the juncture of two timbers.

DOWER — That portion of, or interest in, the real estate of a deceased husband which the law gives to his widow for life. The extent varies with statutory provisions.

DOWNSPOUT — A pipe for carrying rain water from roof gutters to the ground or the storm sewer system. See Leader.

DRAINAGE — A system of drains (tiles, pipes, or conduits) designed to remove surface or subsurface water; or to dispose of waste water and sewage. Also, the slopes and courses which afford natural drainage for rainwater.

DRAINAGE DISTRICT — A unit of local government set up to construct and operate a drainage system for the area comprising the district, usually for the purpose of achieving higher and better use of the land. Development and operational costs are levied against the benefited area.

DRAINAGE DITCH – An open water course other than a gutter.

DRAINAGE EASEMENT – See Drainage Right of Way.

DRAIN FIELD – An area containing a system of underground lateral pipes for the purpose of draining septic systems or other types of liquid overflow.

DRAIN TILE – A specially designed pipe used in a drainage system.

DRAINAGE RIGHT OF WAY – The right to flow surface water from one owner's land over the land of one or more adjacent owners. Surface water may or may not be channeled. Also referred to as drainage easement.

DRAW – A natural drainageway on land, usually not of great depth.

DRESS – The process of planing and finishing a wood surface; to cut, trim, and smooth a material.

DRESSED AND MATCHED – Boards which are finished, or dressed, on one or two sides with tongue and groove edges.

DRESSED LUMBER – Lumber machined and surfaced at a mill on all four sides.

DRIFT – Material of any sort deposited in one place after having been moved from another. Glacial drift includes glacial deposits and unstratified till and stratified glacial outwash materials.

DRIFT FENCE – A partial fence, open at both ends to keep stock out of an area in their normal grazing movements. See also Fence, Division Fence, Line Fence, Snow Fence.

DRILL TRACK – A rail track serving industrial property from which individual industry tracks depart to serve plant sites. A track kept open for the movement of locomotives in sorting (classifying) cars or in moving cars to and from yards. It is a track on which a locomotive works and not one on which cars stand. Frequently, it is called a lead track (pronounced "leed").

DRIP

1. A projecting structural member designed to throw off rain water and protect structural parts below; a channel cut on the underside of a sill. See illustration, page 310.
2. The portion of a piping system which conveys condensation from the steam side to the water or return pipes.
3. A species of easement or servitude derived from civil law, by which one engages to permit the falling (or dripping) on one's estate of waters flowing from the roof of a neighbor.

DROP PANEL – In reinforced concrete slab construction, an area of additional slab depth around a column head, normally a mushroom column.

DROP SIDING—A type of tongue and groove weatherboarding applied to the exterior of frame structures. See also Lap Siding.

DROUGHT—Lack of rain; usually used to refer to a relatively long period of time devoid of rainfall and causing crop damage and depletion of moisture in soil.

DROUTHY SOIL—See, Types of Soil, page 351.

DRUMLIN—A long and narrow or oval hill or ridge of unstratified glacial drift, normally compact, and usually having its longer axis parallel to the movement of the ice responsible for its deposition. Such parallel ridges give the land poor drainage, thus creating swampy terrain between drumlins.

DRYER—A facility used to dry or dehydrate farm crops prior to storage or milling.

DRY FARMING—Usually considered to be all phases of land use under semi-arid conditions. Aside from bringing water by irrigation, other methods are used to conserve moisture, such as allowing moisture to accumulate one season for use during the next. This practice would permit a crop only every other season.

DRY ROT—A decay of seasoned wood caused by a fungus.

DRYWALL—Any finish material applied to an interior wall in a dry state as opposed to plaster. May mean plywood, fiber boards, etc., although usually gypsum board.

DRYWALL CONSTRUCTION—Any type of interior wall construction not using plaster as finish material; wood paneling, plywood, plasterboard, or other type of wallboard instead. (Drywall in Boeckh Manual refers to gypsum board.)

DRY WELL—A drainage pit lined or filled with stone to allow liquid effluent or other sanitary wastes or roof run-off to leach or percolate into the surrounding soil.

DUCTS
1. In building construction, pipes used for the transmission and distribution of warm or cooled air from a central unit to the rooms.
2. The space in an underground conduit containing electrical cables or conductors.

DUPLEX—A house containing two separate dwelling units, side by side or one above the other. See also Double House, Flat.

DURABLE CAPITAL GOODS—Goods which can be used over and over again; that is, machinery as distinguished from raw material.

DURABLE GOODS—Consumer goods which are of a durable nature and can be used repeatedly, such as a refrigerator; as distinguished from short-lived goods, such as bread.

DUTCH COLONIAL ARCHITECTURE — A style of home design featuring a gambrel roof and exterior walls of masonry or wood. Porches may be located at the side. It is adaptable to flat sites.

DUTCH DOOR — A door divided horizontally in the middle so that the bottom half remains closed while the top is open.

DUTCHMAN — A piece of wood or other material used to conceal a defect, strengthen a weak part or fill an opening.

EARNING EXPECTANCY — Estimated future net earnings as a function of time; applied to an investment property.

EARNING POWER — The capacity to generate income.

EARNINGS — See Income.

EARNINGS APPROACH — In farm/ranch appraisal, an approach to value based on the annual income stream that a farm/ranch will most likely produce in the future. Applies primarily to commercial operations for the determination of loan value.

EASEMENT — A nonpossessing interest held by one person in land of another person whereby the first person is accorded partial use of such land for a specific purpose. An easement restricts but does not abridge the rights of the fee owner to the use and enjoyment of the easement holder's rights. Easements fall into three broad classifications: surface easements, subsurface easements, and overhead easements.

EAVES — The lower or outer edge of a roof which projects over the side walls of a structure.

ECOLOGY — The pattern of relations between living things and their environments.

ECONOMIC APPROACH — Synonymous with the income approach.

ECONOMIC BASE — The economic activity of a community which enables it to attract income from outside its borders.

ECONOMIC BASE ANALYSIS — A technique of analysis which utilizes the relationship between basic and nonbasic employment as a means of predicting population, income, or other variables having an effect on real estate value or land utilization.

ECONOMIC ENTERPRISE — In agriculture, a business of sufficient resources to provide an accepted standard of living for a family. Often termed an Economic Unit.

ECONOMIC FEASIBILITY — A qualifying term implying the ability of a project or an enterprise to produce a revenue sufficient to pay all expenses and charges, plus a reasonable return to capital on the invested money and recapture of the money invested in the project.

In the case of a service property and a residential property, or under any condition where the revenue produced is not fundamentally involved, the test of economic soundness rests upon the need for and desirability of the property for the particular purpose. An investment project (land and improvement project) is economically feasible if its prospective earning power is sufficient to pay a fair rate of return on its completed cost, including indirect costs; or stated differently, if the estimated value at completion equals or exceeds the estimated cost.

ECONOMIC GOOD – Any obtainable good involving elements of utility and scarcity which create a desire (demand) for the good. An economic good commands a price in market exchange whereas a free good, such as air or sunshine, does not.

ECONOMIC LIFE – The period over which improvements to real estate contribute to the value of the property. This establishes the capital recovery period for improvements in the traditional residual techniques of income capitalization. It is also used in the estimation of accrued depreciation (diminished utility) in the Cost Approach to value estimation. See also Remaining Economic Life.

ECONOMIC OBSOLESCENCE – Impairment of desirability or useful life arising from factors external to the property, such as economic forces or environmental changes which affect supply-demand relationships in the market. Loss in the use and value of a property arising from the factors of economic obsolescence is to be distinguished from loss in value from physical deterioration and functional obsolescence, both of which are inherent in the property. Also referred to as Locational or Environmental Obsolescence.

ECONOMIC RENT – In economics, it is the surplus payment in excess of that necessary to bring the property on the market (or to attract any factor of production into production).

In appraisal practice, the term has traditionally and inappropriately been used as a synonym for "market rental," i.e., the rental income that a property would most probably command on the open market, as of the effective date of the appraisal. See Market Rent.

ECONOMICS – The study of the allocation of scarce resources among competing and relatively unlimited desires in such a way as to maximize human satisfactions.

ECONOMIC SYSTEM – The nature of economic life as a whole, proposed or actual, with particular reference to the ownership and use of property and the extent of government regulation and controls; as capitalism, socialism, communism, etc.

EFFECTIVE AGE – As applied to a structure, the age of a similar structure of equivalent utility, condition, and remaining life expectancy as distinct from chronological age; the years of age indicated by the condition and utility of the structure. If a building has had better than average maintenance, its effective age may be less than the actual age; if there has been inadequate maintenance, it may be greater. A 40-year old building may have an effective age of 20 years due to rehabilitation or modernization.

EFFECTIVE DEMAND — The desire to buy coupled with the ability to pay. When the word "demand" is used in economic writings, effective demand is usually assumed.

EFFECTIVE GROSS INCOME — The estimated Potential Gross Income less Allowance for Vacancy and Income Loss plus Other Income. The anticipated income from all operations of the real estate after allowance for vacancy and income loss.

EFFECTIVE RATE — The actual rate paid on a loan or produced by an investment as distinguished from a nominal rate. It is also an internal rate of return (IRR) to the lender.

EFFECTIVE RATE OF CAPITAL RECOVERY (EFFECTIVE CAPITAL RECOVERY RATE) — The Capital Recovery Rate weighted by the percentage of investment in improvements. It is also the difference between the Overall Rate and the Discount Rate.

EFFECTIVE TAX RATE — The ratio of the annual property tax on a property to the market value of the property; the actual tax rate times assessed value divided by market value; official tax rate times assessment ratio.

EFFICIENCY RATIO — In economics, the ratio of ends produced (output) to means used (input). In land utilization, the ratio existing between the amount of the value product flowing from the site and the labor-capital expense of producing it. Efficiency has reference to the average amount of net product (for example, rent) returned per unit of labor and capital applied.

In appraising, frequently used in expressing the ratio of rentable square feet of office building to gross square footage.

EFFLORESCENCE — A white powder that forms on brick or stone work resulting from a chemical action. It can be washed off with no bad effects. Also, the deposits of soluble salts on the surface of masonry.

EFFLUENT — Liquid sewage after having passed through any stage in its purification.

ELASTIC (ELASTICITY) — In economics, used to describe the responsiveness of prices to changes in supply and/or demand for a good.

ELECTRICAL OUTLET — A point on the wiring system from which current is taken to supply equipment using it.

ELECTRIC HEATING – Any one of several methods of converting electric energy into usable heat.

ELECTRONIC DATA PROCESSING (EDP) – The automatic manipulation of data by an electronic computer system.

ELECTRONIC DATA PROCESSING SYSTEM – The combination of a computer, data base, trained personnel and a program, by means of which a particular data processing function is accomplished.

ELEEMOSYNARY – Of or pertaining to charity; a charitable institution.

ELEVATION

1. A geometrical projection of a vertical plane perpendicular to the horizon, as of the external upright parts of a building (front, side or rear view).
2. Altitude; the distance of a place or point above mean sea level.

ELEVATOR – Applied to a farm storage building in which a commodity, such as wheat, is elevated into a bin.

ELLWOOD – The late L.W. Ellwood, M.A.I., originator of the Ellwood method of mortgage-equity capitalization and author of *Ellwood Tables for Real Estate Appraising and Financing.*

ELLWOOD PREMISE – An extension of basic mortgage-equity analysis involving certain additional assumptions, concerning income flows and the nature of the claims against those income flows. These assumptions include:

1. The purchaser-investor is typically interested in the cash income that the property will produce to support his equity investment.
2. The typical purchaser-investor is sensitive to income taxes and will behave in a manner allowing maximum tax avoidance.
3. The purchaser-investor typically seeks to take maximum possible advantage of leverage to enhance his equity return.
4. The purchaser-investor will typically retain the investment only so long as there is a cash income advantage in doing so.
5. The purchaser-investor typically will anticipate a level income flow over the income projection period, since it is relatively short.
6. The purchaser-investor will have discoverable expectations about the reversion (the most probable resale price of the property) at the end of the income projection period.

EMINENT DOMAIN – The right by which a sovereign government, or some person acting in its name and under its authority, may acquire private property for public or quasi-public use upon payment of reasonable compensation and without consent of the owner. The right or power of the government to take private property for public use upon making just compensation therefor. See also Condemnation.

EMPLOYMENT BASE – The number of gainfully employed persons in a community or city.

ENCLOSURE – Denotes land enclosed with something more than the imaginary boundary line, that there should be some visible or tangible obstruction, such as a fence, hedge, ditch, or something equivalent, for the protection of the premises against encroachment by animals.

ENCROACHMENT – The act of trespassing upon the domain of another. Partial or gradual displacement of an existing use by another use; as locating commercial or industrial improvements in a residential district.

ENCUMBRANCE – An interest or right in real property which may diminish the value of the fee, but does not prevent conveyance of the fee by the owner. Mortgages, taxes and judgments are encumbrances known as liens. Restrictions, easements and reservations are encumbrances, though not liens.

ENERGY AUDIT – An inventory of the physical characteristics of a building which contribute to thermal efficiency, in order to identify appropriate energy conservation measures, estimate the cost of installing such measures, and estimate the dollar savings likely to result from installing such measures.

ENERGY EFFICIENCY – The ability of an appliance or of a building's energy system to produce a given effect with a minimum of effort, expense, or waste in comparison to other buildings or appliances of a similar nature; quantitatively, the ratio of output to energy expended in achieving that output. See Energy Efficiency Ratio.

ENERGY EFFICIENCY RATIO (EER) – A measure of the efficiency of an electric heat pump, air conditioner, or vapor compressor heating or cooling device, expressed as the ratio of output in Btus per hour to the energy input in watts.

ENGINEERING BREAKDOWN METHOD – A method of estimating accrued depreciation under which separate estimates are made for the individual components and then totaled.

ENGLISH ARCHITECTURE – Design using the features of Elizabethan, Tudor, Cotswold, and other English styles; frequently large stone houses with slate shingles on gable roofs, mullioned casement windows, and wainscoted interiors. Exposed timbers constitute the structural frame of authentic Elizabethan houses, although in modern adaptations the half-timbering is purely decorative. There usually is plaster between the half-timbers, although in the original types the spaces were filled with brick nogging.

ENGLISH COTSWOLD ARCHITECTURE – An adaptation of an English country or farm house. The English Cotswold style is characterized by informality relieved by sills, mullions, porches, and chimneys of stone dressed by a hammer. Details are generally heavy. Windows are metal casements. The authentic roof is of variegated slate with irregular shapes, graduated from large sizes at the eaves to smaller at the ridge.

ENGLISH HALF-TIMBERED (Elizabethan) ARCHITECTURE — Rustic, informal, picturesque English houses featuring interesting exterior treatment and ornamentation of half-timber effects, carved wood, stone, and brick. In the original Elizabethan type, the exposed exterior timbers were actually the structural frame of the building. Between the half-timbering there is usually plaster. Roof slopes are steep and project at the ends with barges rather than cornices.

ENGLISH TUDOR ARCHITECTURE — A formal residential architectural style. Exterior walls usually are made of stone or brick laid in a formal pattern. Window and door trim is generally of dressed or cut stone. Windows are usually the casement type. The roof is of slate which is spaced to give the effect of stone.

ENSILAGE — Green fodder, chopped or shredded, preserved in a silo or pit.

ENTREPRENEUR — An employer or developer who assumes the risk and management of a business or enterprise; a promoter, in the sense of one who undertakes to develop.

ENVIRONMENT — The social, physical, political, and economic characteristics of the area surrounding a property which have an effect upon its value.

ENVIRONMENTAL DEFICIENCY — Conditions, circumstances, and influences surrounding and affecting the development of an area which promote blight and deterioration. Examples: overcrowding or improper location of structures on the land; excessive dwelling unit density; conversion of buildings to incompatible uses; obsolete buildings; detrimental land uses; unsafe, congested, poorly designed or otherwise deficient streets; inadequate utilities or community facilities, etc.

ENVIRONMENTAL IMPACT STUDY — An investigation designed to assess the comprehensive and long-range environmental effects of a proposed land use upon society.

ENVIRONMENTAL OBSOLESCENCE — Synonymous with economic obsolescence.

EQUALIZATION — The process by which an appropriate governmental body attempts to ensure that all the property under its jurisdiction is assessed at the same assessment ratio or at the ratio or ratios required by law.

EQUIPMENT – That portion of fixed assets other than real estate; usually qualified as office equipment, automotive equipment, etc., as distinguished from assets which are included under the category of fixtures by virtue of their attachment to real estate, either in a physical sense or by legal interpretation. See Chattels.

EQUITABLE OWNERSHIP – The estate or interest of a person who has a beneficial right in property, the legal ownership of which is in another person: as a beneficiary of a trust has an equitable estate or interest in the trust property.

EQUITY – The net value of a property obtained by subtracting from its total value all liens or other charges against it; the value of the owner's interest in property in excess of all claims and liens.

EQUITY ASSEMBLY – A process of accumulation of cash required for equity investment whether by joint venture, limited partnership, individual or corporate approach.

EQUITY BUILDUP – Increase in the equity investor's share of total property value resulting from gradual debt reduction through periodic repayment of principal on a mortgage loan and/or increase in total property value. In the Ellwood formulation and in mortgage-equity analysis, the effects of equity buildup are incorporated into the overall (composite) rate derived, by explicitly taking into consideration in the derivation of that rate the original loan to value ratio, the amount of mortgage paid off over the holding period and the change in total property value over the holding period. All of these adjustments to the rate are further tempered by the anticipated or projected equity yield rate.

EQUITY CONSTANT – See Equity Dividend Rate.

EQUITY DIVIDEND – Before-Tax Cash Flow (Cash Throw-Off); the residual remaining after deducting annual debt service from Net Operating Income. In the Ellwood formulas, designated by the symbol d_e.

EQUITY DIVIDEND RATE – The ratio of annual Before-Tax Cash Flow (Equity Dividend; Cash Throw-Off to Equity) to the original equity investment. Sometimes called cash on cash.

EQUITY KICKER – An interest in the equity of a property given to the mortgage lender as a condition of obtaining a mortgage on said property.

EQUITY OF REDEMPTION – The right of a mortgagor by absolute deed to redeem the property by paying the debt, even after forfeiture, but before sale under foreclosure or transfer of title, or before this right is barred by statute of limitations.

EQUITY PARTICIPATION — The right of the lender to share in whatever the equity investor–borrower receives, without reference to loan contract terms, i.e., the right has an indefinite term and may endure beyond the maturity of the loan. Equity participation may appear in any one or all of the following forms: Percentage of equity reversion (proceeds from periodic refinancing and/or proceeds of property resale); percentage of equity interest (both annual income and reversionary receipts) that may occur in the future; percentage of tax shelter (a portion of the depreciation associated with the mortgage property). See also Income Participation.

EQUITY PURCHASER — The purchaser of the equity of another in property, who may or may not assume all the indebtedness against the property.

EQUITY RATIO — The ratio of downpayment to total price; the fraction of an investment which is unencumbered by debt.

EQUITY YIELD — The dollar return on equity from all sources, i.e., annual equity dividend including any excess or deficit over original equity investment at termination.

EQUITY YIELD RATE — The annualized rate of return on equity capital including (in addition to the annual dividend) the full effect of any gain or loss from resale at the termination of the investment; that single discount rate which equates the present worth of all future benefits to the equity investment with the cost of that investment, i.e., the internal rate of return (IRR) to the equity investment.

EROSION
1. The wearing away of surface land through natural causes as by running water, winds, or other geological agents.
2. Sheet erosion is the loss of soil, in generally even amounts, over a given surface area, by water.
3. Rill erosion is a term usually applied to loss of soil by heavy rains after field tillage operations. Small channels or streamlets are cut into the soft loose earth as the water races down the slope.
4. Gully erosion is rill erosion which is permitted to continue over a period of time, eroding or cutting away the soft, tilled earth, and into the firm subsoil structure until its depth becomes a barrier between two areas which is not easily crossed with farm tools or normal vehicles or equipment.

ESCALATION CLAUSE — A clause in an agreement providing for adjustment of price based on some event or index. For example, in a lease, this might be the provision to increase rent if operating expenses increase.

ESCARPMENT – A long, precipitous face of rock or land.

ESCHEAT – Reversion of property to the state when the owner dies without leaving a will or heirs.

ESCROW – Money, securities, instruments, or other property or evidences of property deposited by two or more persons with a third person, to be delivered on a certain contingency or on the happening of a certain event. The subject matter of the transaction is the escrow; the terms upon which it is deposited with the third person constitute the escrow agreement; and the third person is the escrow agent.

ESKERS – A ridge of sandy or gravelly material deposited in a stream channel beneath a glacier. These ridges show meandering courses.

ESTABLISHED BUSINESS VALUE – See Going Concern Value.

ESTATE
1. A right or interest in property; it may be fee ownership interest or a lease interest for a period of years. An estate in land is the degree, nature, or extent of interest which a person has in it.
2. The property of a deceased person.

ESTATE IN REVERSION – The residue of an estate left in the grantor, to commence in possession after the termination of some particular estate granted out by the grantor. Not to be confused with Remainder Estate.

ESTIMATE
1. In appraising, an opinion based upon analysis of adequate data by one qualified to develop such an opinion; hence the opinion of an informed person.
2. A preliminary opinion of the cost of doing certain work.

ESTIMATED SELLING PRICE (ESP) – Essentially the equivalent of market value and calculated by regression analysis. Also termed most probable selling price (MPSP) or computer estimated value (CEV).

ESTOPPEL CERTIFICATE – A statement of material facts or conditions upon which another person can rely. The person issuing the certification cannot at a later date deny the facts represented.

ETHNIC GROUP – People of the same race having a common heritage of language, culture, customs.

EVALUATION – As distinct from valuation, the investigation and analysis of any aspect of, or interest in, a parcel of real estate; including but not limited to land utilization studies, supply and demand studies, economic feasibility studies, highest and best use analyses, marketability or investment considerations; such studies may involve specific recommendations to a client, based on the client's own investment objectives and constraints.

EXCEPTION – In contracts, a clause in a deed by which the lessor excepts something out of that which was originally granted by the deed. The exclusion of something from the effect or operation of the deed or contract which would otherwise be included.

EXCESS CONDEMNATION – The policy on the part of the condemnor of taking, by right of eminent domain, more property than is physically necessary for the public improvement. See also Condemnation.

EXCESS FRONTAGE TABLE – A table of factors designed to reflect the decrease in unit front foot value of a parcel of (usually residential) land attributable to an excess of frontage, in one ownership, over and above the typical or standard lot frontage in the area.

EXCESS INCOME – That part of the contract rental income which is in excess of the market rental at the time of the appraisal. This might be temporarily due to such a factor as favorable location; or it might be more permanent because of a fortuitous lease or unusual management. In the income approach, it is usually treated separately from the market rental and capitalized at a higher rate and possibly for a shorter income projection term. Synonym: surplus income.

EXCESS (SURPLUS) LAND – The area or frontage (or both) in excess of a normal or standard site for the neighborhood or market.

EXCESS RENT – The amount by which contract rent exceeds market rent. See Excess Income, Percentage Lease.

EXCESS VALUE – Value over and above market value which is ascribable to lease which guarantees contract rental income in excess of market rental at the time of the appraisal.

EXCHANGE VALUE – The value, in terms of money, of a commodity to persons generally; as opposed to use value to a specific person.

EXCLUSIVE AGENCY LISTING – A contract to sell property as an agent, according to the terms of which a single agent is hired to sell the property but the seller retains the right to sell through his own efforts without paying a commission. The term is also applied to the property so listed.

EXCLUSIVE RIGHT TO SELL LISTING – A contract to sell property as an agent, according to the terms of which the listing broker is entitled to receive the commission regardless of who sells the property – owner included.

EXCLUSIVE ZONING – A system of zoning under which all uses of land and buildings are excluded, except those specifically permitted.

EXECUTION SALE – A legal procedure to permit the enforcement of a payment judgment. Property is sold to obtain the dollars adjudged to be paid.

EXECUTOR – An individual or trust institution designated in a will and appointed by a court to settle the estate of the testator.

EXECUTOR'S DEED – A transfer of real estate wherein the grantor is the executor of the granting estate.

EXEMPTION – See Tax Exemption.

EXPECTED VALUE – An event weighted by the probability of its occurrence. The sum of a series of possible events each weighted by their probability of occurrence.

EXPENSE RATIO – The ratio of expenses to gross income; the fraction of gross income consumed by expenses; normally, in appraisal practice, the ratio of stabilized expenses to projected effective gross income.

EXPENSES – See Operating Expenses.

EXPERT – An expert is one who, by reason of education, experience, or study is presumed to have special knowledge of (or skill in) a field.

EXPERT TESTIMONY – Testimony of persons who are skilled in some art, science, profession, or business, which skill or knowledge is not common to others, and which has come to such experts by reason of special study and experience in such art, science, profession, or business. (Culver v. Prudential Ins. Co., 6 W.W. Harr. 582,179 A. 400.)

EXPERT WITNESS – One qualified to render expert testimony.

EXPONENT – A power to which a number is raised; it is the number of times a number is to be multiplied by itself. In compounding and discounting, n (the number of time periods involved) is the exponent. Exponents are additive.

EXPRESSWAY – A highway with full or partial control of access and with important crossroads separated in grade from the pavements for through traffic of all types. Expressways are generally divided highways. Some streets may be left as crossings at grade to be eliminated at a later time. In some instances the term has been incorrectly applied to named highways not having expressway characteristics.

EXPROPRIATION – A Canadian and British term representing the act of a sovereign in reclaiming its inherent ownership in real estate which in law was never given up. It is similar to the taking of private property under the law of eminent domain in the United States.

EXTENSIVE FARMING – The use of comparatively small amounts of labor and working capital per acre of land.

EXTERIOR FINISH – The outside finish of a structure. It includes such items as roof and wall covering, gutters, door and window frames. Generally, the protective outer cover.

EXTERIOR FIXTURE – An outside item, such as areaway, canopy, marquee, platform, loading dock, which is permanently attached to and part of the building structure.

EXTERIOR WALL – Any outer wall (except a common wall) serving as a vertical enclosure of a building.

EXTERNAL OBSOLESCENCE – See Locational and Economic Obsolescence.

EXTRAPOLATION – The calculation or estimation of a quantity beyond the range of data upon which the calculation or estimate is based; projections into the future or the unknown presuming a continuation of observed trends, patterns, or relationships.

FACADE – The principal exterior face of a structure, usually the front face or front elevation of a building.

FACE
1. The most important side of a structure; the front or facade.
2. The exposed surface of an object, such as the earth, structure, wall, panel.

FACE BRICK – A better grade of brick which is used in the exterior wall of a building, frequently only on the front or principal side.

FACED WALL – A wall, usually masonry, the exterior face of which is of a different material, and with the two materials so bonded that they serve as a single load-bearing unit.

FACE VALUE – Par value of bonds, stocks, mortgages, and similar securities as set forth in the documents themselves.

FACTOR
1. One of the elements which contributes to bringing about a given result; for example, land as a contribution to the value of an improved property.
2. One of two or more numbers which, when multiplied together, produce a given number; that is, 2 and 5 are factors of 10; also, a divisor.
3. Arithmetically, the reciprocal of a rate. For example, in the Inwood or level annuity table, the factors contained in the table are the reciprocals of the respective annual constant. A multiplier or coefficient. See Amortization Factor, Level Annuity Factor, Reversion Factor, Sinking Fund Factor, Gross-Income Multiplier.

FACTORS IN PRODUCTION – The factors in the production of wealth, income, or services which can be sold for money. The factors are:

(1) labor, (2) management (coordination), (3) capital, (4) land (or natural resources). Of the gross income from any enterprise, labor has the first claim. The costs of labor are wages, salaries, and cost of benefits, such as health insurance, unemployment insurance, etc. After labor are the costs of coordination, (entrepreneurial incentive together with those services necessary to coordinate the offices of the other three factors and weld them into a productive unit) and the costs of capital, by which is meant payment for the use of capital, interest on and amortization of the investment in buildings, equipment, furnishings, etc., but not land. Then last, and least in the order of preference, is the claim of land to the residual portion of the gross income.

FACTORY AND SHOP LUMBER – Lumber intended to be cut up for use in further manufacture. It is graded on the basis of the percentage of the area which will produce a limited number of cuttings of a specified or a given minimum size and quality.

FAIR CASH VALUE – Used synonymously with Market Value.

FAIR HOUSING LAWS – Federal, state, and local laws guaranteeing persons the right to buy, sell, lease, hold, and convey property without being subjected to discrimination on the basis of race, color, religion, sex, or national origin. Major federal legislation dealing with fair housing would include the Civil Rights Act of 1866; Executive Order 11063; Title VI of the Civil Rights Act of 1964; and Title VIII of the Civil Rights Act of 1968.

FAIR MARKET VALUE – A legal term. Synonym: market value.

FAIR RENTAL – See Market Rent.

FAIR VALUE
  1. Value that is reasonable and consistent with all of the known facts. Synonym: market value.
  2. A term of legal significance and applicable in public utility rate-making practice, designating the base upon which a reasonable return could be established in connection with which service rates and charges, with equal justice to the public and to the public utility, may be predicated or analyzed.

FAIRWAY
  1. The unobstructed, navigable channel in a river or harbor for the passage of vessels; the usual course taken by ships.
  2. The part of a golf course lying between tees and putting greens where the grass is kept close mown.

FALLING GROUND – The condition, slope, and configuration of the ground on which trees will land after they are felled. This must be considered in making a mill-cut cruise of redwood timber because of the size and brittleness of the timber.

FALLOW
1. Land ordinarily used for crops which is allowed to lie idle during the growing season.
2. The tilling of land without sowing it for a season.

FAMILY ROOM — An informal living room, usually the center of family activities, as distinguished from the more formal living room. Synonym: family living room.

FAN WINDOW — See Circlehead Window.

FARM — A tract of rural land devoted to agriculture. Also, a tract of land or water used for industrial purposes as tank farm, oyster farm.

FARM BUDGET — The plan for the financial organization and operation of a farm for a specified period of time, including a detailed statement of the anticipated gross income, expenses, and net income.

FARM CAPITAL EARNINGS — Compensation for farm capital. It is derived by deducting the value of the operator's labor from net farm income. If it is expressed as a percentage, it should be designated as percent earnings of farm capital.

FARM CREDIT ADMINISTRATION — An independent agency of the executive branch of the government, the general purpose of which is to provide a comprehensive credit system for agriculture, including long term, intermediate, and short term credit to farmers and to farmers' organizations.

FARM EXPENSES — The sum of the annual cash operating expenses, value of unpaid family labor, decrease in farm inventory, depreciation, and the value of living from the farm furnished to hired laborers.

FARM FAMILY EARNINGS — The compensation, including the value of family living from the farm, for operator's labor and management and for labor of unpaid members of the operator's family. It is derived by deducting an interest charge for the use of farm capital from net family farm income.

FARM FAMILY LABOR UNPAID — The labor used in conducting the farm business which is furnished by the members of the farm family, other than the operator, for which no direct wage is paid. Its value is determined on the basis of the amount of additional labor the operator would have to hire at current wages to carry on the same size business had the family labor not been available.

FARM FAMILY NET INCOME — The compensation, including the value of family living from the farm, for farm capital, labor, management of the operator, and labor of unpaid members of the operator's family. It is derived by deducting farm expenses, exclusive of unpaid family labor, from gross farm income.

FARM INCOME — The sum of the annual receipts from sales, miscellaneous farm receipts, increase in farm inventory, and the value of living from the farm furnished to the operator, the operator's family, and hired laborers.

FARM LABOR AND MANAGEMENT WAGE — The name applied to a measure of overall success as derived from farm account or survey records. Theoretically, it represents the residue of income left to pay the farm operator for his labor and management after all outlays are deducted for operating costs, including taxes and insurance, and with approximate deductions for recapture of and return on invested capital.

FARM LAND — Land devoted to agricultural production; usually used to refer to the land comprising a farm. Such land includes both tillable and untillable areas as well as any woodlots.

FARM LAYOUT — Indication of the location of farm buildings, field arrangement, field shapes and sizes, travel routes, obstructions in various fields and all other important land features.

FARM MANAGEMENT — The science of the organization and operation of farms. It considers the effectiveness of different sized operating units in relation to various combinations of productive resources, enterprises, and operating practices; programs of adjustment for farm areas; and the impact of public policies and programs on economic activities of farms.

FARM NET INCOME — The compensation, including the value of family living from the farm, for farm capital, and for labor and management of the operator. It is derived by deducting farm expenses from gross farm income.

FARM OPERATOR'S EARNINGS — The compensation, including the value of family living from the farm, for operator's labor and management. It is derived by deducting an interest charge for the use of farm capital from net farm income.

FARM OPERATOR'S LABOR — The farmer's estimate of what would have to be paid to another person in cash and in kind to do the labor the farmer normally performs.

FARM OPERATOR'S MANAGEMENT — The farmer's estimate of the charge (fee for management) in cash for the management services performed.

FARM POND — A man-made earthen storage reservoir for farm water supply, usually used for watering livestock, but may be used for household plumbing if the pond is in suitable location. The pond is made by constructing a small dam across a natural drainageway.

FARM PRODUCTION – Productivity of a specific unit, usually measured by percent of tillable land or per acre yield of various crops grown.

FARM SIZE – Total acres in unit measured by acres of cropland or number of livestock units.

FARMSTEAD – The site and location of the farm buildings; the focal point of the farm operations.

FARM-TO-MARKET ROAD – A road outside the primary state highway system which connects farms with towns or primary highways.

FARROWING HOUSE – A building used for housing hogs when they are giving birth.

FASCIA – A long flat member or band; the horizontal division of an architrave. The finishing board used to conceal the ends of the rafters. See illustration, page 306.

FEASIBILITY – A real estate project is "feasible" when analysis indicates that there is a reasonable likelihood of satisfying explicit objectives and when a selected course of action is tested for fit to a context of specific constraints and limited resources. The context defines the problem. Feasibility of a real estate project is normally related to its probable economic potential.

FEASIBILITY SURVEY
1. An analysis of the cost-benefit ratio of an economic endeavor.
2. A survey of an urban area using federal funds to determine if it is practicable to undertake an urban renewal project, or projects, within that area.

FEDERAL HOME LOAN BANK SYSTEM – A system of 12 regional banks created under the authority of the Federal Home Loan Bank Act of 1932 to provide a source of credit for the banks' member home-financing and thrift institutions. Every federal savings and loan association is required to become a member of its regional federal home loan bank.

FEDERAL HOME LOAN MORTGAGE CORPORATION (FHLMC) – A government agency operating in the secondary market in conventional residential mortgages. Created by Congress in 1970.

FEDERAL HOUSING ADMINISTRATION (FHA) – A unit of the United States Department of Housing and Urban Development which insures private lending institutions against loss on loans secured by residential mortgages and on loans advanced for repairs, alterations, and improvements which may be secured by collateral.

FEDERAL LAND BANK – A bank administered by the Farm Credit Administration. Its primary purpose is to provide long term, first mortgage loans to farmers, and (with certain limitations) to livestock corporations. There are 12 federal land banks, one in each farm credit district.

FEE
1. The form of remuneration received by professional people such as doctors, lawyers, appraisers, etc.
2. An estate of inheritance of real property; that is, an estate in fee. See also Fee Simple, Fee Tail.

FEE SIMPLE—An absolute fee; a fee without limitations to any particular class of heirs or restrictions, but subject to the limitations of eminent domain, escheat, police power, and taxation. An inheritable estate.

FEE TAIL—An estate of inheritance limited to some particular class of heirs of the person to whom it is granted. Estates in fee tail have been abolished in most states, converting them to fee simple estates.

FEED BUNK—A trough constructed of wood or concrete for the purpose of holding feed for direct consumption by livestock and poultry.

FEEDER—A prefabricated container from which animals or birds self-feed.

FEEDER CATTLE—A market classification for cattle on feed, usually yearlings to mature cattle, which have not reached a finished or prime condition for slaughter.

FEEDLOT—An enclosed area where feeder cattle are finished for the market. The usual equipment includes feed/hay bunks or self-feeders, watering facilities, some paving and adjacent shelter.

FELT—A nonwoven fabric of wool, fur, hair, or vegetable fibers matted together by heat, moisture, and pressure.

FELT PAPER—Paper which is used for sheathing on walls and roofs and which serves as a barrier against heat, cold, and dampness. When used on certain types of roofs, such as flat roof, it is covered with tar or asphalt and surfaced with gravel.

FENCE—A wall-like barrier around a lot, yard or field, usually of wood or steel wire, but may be of brick, stone, or other material. See also Division Fence, Drift Fence, Line Fence, Snow Fence.

FENESTRATION—The design and disposition or arrangement of windows or other openings in a building wall.

FIBERBOARD—A prefabricated building material composed of wood or other plant fibers compressed and bonded into a sheet.

FIBERGLASS—Finespun filaments of glass made into yarn, used in batts as insulation; or it may be added to gypsum or concrete products to increase tensile strength.

FIDUCIARY — The relationship between a person charged with the duty of acting for the benefit of another, as between guardian and ward. The person so charged.

FIELD — In computer terminology, the formation of a unit of information from a group of characters in a word. On a punched card, a field is one or more columns assigned to a particular usage.

FIELD BOX — In agriculture, a unit of measure applicable to harvested fruit crops. The quantity varies according to variety and locality. Sometimes called field lug.

FIELD CROP — In agriculture, an annual crop which is planted and harvested by mechanical means.

FIELD TILE
  1. Porous tile laid around the foundation of a building to drain off excess water in the ground and to prevent its seepage through the foundation.
  2. System of drain tiles placed far enough below surface or ground to drain subsoil of a field.

FILL — Use of material, or the material used, to equalize or raise topography to a desired grade. In highway construction, the use of stones and earth to fill low sections of the right of way to control its grade.

FILL SLOPE — That portion of a roadway between the outer edge of a road shoulder and the toe of the slope at a different elevation.

FILTERING — Movement of people of one income group into homes that have recently dropped in price and that were previously occupied by persons in the next higher income group.

FINAL RECONCILIATION — The application of the process of evaluating alternative conclusions and selecting from the indications of value derived from each of the approaches utilized in the appraisal problem to arrive at a final estimate of value. Appraisers weigh the relative significance, applicability, and defensibility of the indication of value derived from each approach, and place most weight and reliance on the one which, in their professional judgment, best approximates the value being sought in the appraisal. Appraisers reconcile the facts, trends, and observations developed in their analyses and review their conclusions and the probable validity and reliability of those conclusions.

FINAL VALUE ESTIMATE — The appraiser's opinion or conclusion resulting from the application of appraisal analysis, including reconciliation of findings, to the appraisal problem at hand. The resultant conclusion derived from an analysis of the indications developed in the approaches to value as utilized in the appraisal. This estimate will reflect the definition of value sought. For market value, the final estimate is that value which most nearly represents what the typical, informed, rational purchaser would pay for the subject property if it were available for sale on the open market as of the date of the appraisal, given all the data utilized by appraisers in their analyses.

FINANCIAL CORPORATION—A corporation engaged primarily in some form of banking activities, such as bank, trust company, insurance company, or savings and loan association.

FINANCIAL MANAGEMENT RATE OF RETURN (FMRR)—One of a number of modified forms of internal rate of return specifically derived from the assumption that the primary goal of the investor is to maximize his long-run wealth position. The model therefore is based upon the terminal value rate of return concept, which is a specialized version of the geometric rate of return. It is specialized because the structure of the model has been modified to include as many of the unique characteristics of the real estate market as possible. The FMRR model is designed to overcome the deficiencies of the IRR model by (1) avoiding the possibility of nonunique or nonexistent solution, and (2) making explicit those assumptions implicit in the use of the internal rate of return regarding the discounting of outflows and the reinvestment of inflows.

FINANCIAL STATEMENT—The listing of assets and liabilities of any entity.

FINANCIAL STRUCTURE—The character and extent of distributed ownership and control of the assets of a corporation. Particularly the evidence thereof, such as the setup of bonds, preferred stock, and common stock under qualified rights.

FINANCING COSTS—The cost of acquiring capital to finance a project.

FINANCING STATEMENT—An instrument conveying a security interest in chattels and equipment, recorded in chattel records and indexed in land records.

FINE SANDY LOAM—See Types of Soil, page 351.

FINE TEXTURED SOIL—See Types of Soil, page 351.

FINISH FLOOR—The top flooring, usually made of hardwoods (such as oak) laid over the subfloor. Linoleum, terrazzo, and tile are also used.

FINISH HARDWARE—See Hardware.

FIREBACK—See Chimney Back.

FIREBRICK—A brick made of fire clay which is capable of resisting high temperatures; used to line heating chambers and fireplaces.

FIRE CUT—A diagonal cut across a horizontal, wood-supporting member at the end which is framed into a masonry wall. The cut is made from the top to bottom of the member and is slanted from the interior toward the outside wall. Its purpose is to make it possible for the member, in the event of failure from fire or other cause, to collapse without causing the wall to collapse with it. See illustration, page 306.

FIRE DOORS AND WALLS—Doors and walls constructed of fire resistive materials designed to prevent the spread of fires.

FIREPROOF CONSTRUCTION—Designed to withstand a complete burnout of the contents of the structure, without impairment of its structural integrity.

FIREPROOFING—The use of incombustible materials to protect structural components of a building so it can withstand a complete burnout of contents without losing structural integrity.

FIRE RESISTIVE CONSTRUCTION—Not combustible at ordinary fire temperatures; capable of withstanding ordinary fire conditions for at least one hour without serious damage to the structure. Used interchangeably with Fireproof Construction and preferred terminology.

FIRE RETARDING MATERIAL—Materials which tend to inhibit combustion.

FIRE STOPS—The use of incombustible material to block air spaces through which flames could travel within a structure.

FIRE WALL—A brick or other incombustible wall built between buildings, or parts of a building, as a fire stop.

FIRST BOTTOM—The normal plane of a stream, part of which may be flooded at intervals. See also Second Bottom, Flood Plain.

FIRST MORTGAGE—A mortgage which has priority as a lien over all other mortgages on a property.

FISCAL YEAR—Any 12 months selected as an accounting period. It may or may not coincide with the calendar year.

FIXED ASSETS—Assets not readily convertible into cash. This term is synonymous with capital assets in undertakings in which capital is employed for the purpose of producing revenue; but it may also refer to tangible assets in undertakings where there is no proprietary accountability as hospitals, religious and charitable organizations, and educational institutions. "Fixed assets" denotes a fixity of purpose or intent to continue use or possession. It does not refer to the immobility of an asset which is the distinctive characteristic of fixtures. See also Capital Assets.

FIXED CAPITAL—Capital invested in property that has come to a stationary form and that may be used many times in production. Assets which are considered permanent in character, as land; ordinarily, but not necessarily tangible assets.

FIXED CAPITAL GOODS—See Durable Capital Goods.

FIXED EXPENSES (CHARGES)—Those expenses that do not vary with occupancy (e.g., ad valorem taxes and fire insurance) and that have to be paid whether the property is occupied or vacant. Fixed expenses are not necessarily or absolutely fixed in amount, and tend to vary from year to year.

FIXED LIABILITIES—Long term debts; debts payable more than one year hence as distinguished from current liabilities.

FIXED RATE MORTGAGE (FRM)—The standard mortgage form which carries an interest rate that does not vary over the life of the loan.

FIXED WINDOW—A window which does not open, as in a fixed bay window, a fixed bow window, or a picture window. See illustration, page 301.

FIXTURE
1. A tangible thing, which previously was personal property, and which has been attached to or installed in land or a structure thereon in such a way as to become a part of the real property. The legal interpretation of what constitutes a fixture varies among states.
2. Any nonportable lighting device which is more or less permanently built in or attached securely to the walls and/or ceiling.
3. The permanent parts of a plumbing system such as toilets, bathtubs, etc.

FLAGSTONE—A flat, irregular slab of stone used for paving; usually sandstone or shale which can be split into slabs. Used for walks, patios, terraces, planter boxes.

FLANGE—A projecting edge, ridge, rim, collar, etc., on an object for attaching it to another object, for keeping it in place. The projecting horizontal portions of an I-beam are flanges.

FLANK—The side of a building, or of an arch.

FLASHING—The strips of sheet metal, copper, lead, or tin used to cover and protect structural angles and joints, to prevent water seepage of leaks. See illustration, page 308.

FLAT—A multiple-family residential structure containing a limited number of units, each unit of which usually has a separate outside entrance. See also Apartment.

FLAT COAT—Used to designate the first coat of paint applied to a finished surface.

FLAT COST—Used in the building trades to indicate only the cost of labor and material.

FLAT ROOF—A roof having a slope just sufficient to provide for proper drainage; one where the pitch does not exceed 1 to 20 degrees. See illustration, page 300.

FLAT SLAB CONSTRUCTION—A method of construction in which a concrete floor slab is supported only by columns. Requires a thicker slab than when beams are used.

FLEXIBLE CONDUIT—A conduit made of flexible material such as fabric or spiral metal strip.

FLEXIBLE LOAN INSURANCE PLAN (FLIP)—One form of alternative mortgage instrument. It is a graduated payment mortgage that combines the unique elements of graduated payments for the home buyer, level payments for the lender, and conventional underwriting. The FLIP mortgage program utilizes a portion of the down payment of the home buyer which is deposited in a pledged, interest-bearing savings account and serves as cash collateral for the lender and as a source of supplemental payments for the borrower during the first few years of the loan. The lender withdraws predetermined amounts from the savings account and adds them to the borrower's reduced payment to make a full, normal mortgage payment. The supplemental payment decreases each year and vanishes entirely at the end of the supplemental period, when the savings account is liquidated.

FLIGHT PATTERN—The zone of approach or departure of aircraft from airport runways.

FLITCH BEAM—A beam composed of two timber beams between which has been placed or sandwiched an iron plate and all three securely bolted together.

FLOAT—A valve-like device, such as a hollow ball, which, through its buoyancy, automatically regulates the supply, outlet, and level of a liquid, as in a toilet tank.

FLOAT FINISH—The surface of concrete finished by a continuous spreading of the material with a flat board.

FLOATING CAPITAL—Capital invested in current assets, such as inventory and receivables.

FLOATING FOUNDATION—A colloquial expression; proper term is mat, raft, or rigid foundation. Mat or raft foundations consist of concrete slabs usually from 4 to 8 feet in thickness, covering the entire foundation area. Reinforcing bars are closely spaced at right angles to each other above the bottom and below the top of the concrete slab. It is preferred that the concrete be poured over the entire foundation area in one continuous operation. Columns and perimeter walls are superimposed on the slab for erection of the superstructure. Rigid foundations are more complicated foundations dealing with the science of displacement and trusses. Raft, mat, or rigid foundations are used when bearing power of the soil is so low that spread footings cannot be used, and where piles cannot be used advantageously or are not necessary.

FLOATING RATE — A variable interest rate charged for the use of borrowed money. It is determined by charging a specific percentage above a fluctuating base rate, usually the prime rate of major commercial banks.

FLOATING ZONE — Used to describe a provision in a zoning ordinance which permits the planned development of a tract of land, usually on the basis of binding, agreed-upon controls, for some use not permitted in the zone in which the land is located.

Ordinarily, such development requires approval of a regulatory body but does not entail an exception, variance, or change of zone.

FLOOD IRRIGATION — An irrigation method where water is applied directly to the land surface.

FLOOD PLAIN — The nearly flat surfaces along the courses of rivers and streams which are subject to overflow and flooding.

FLOOR
1. The lower horizontal surface of a room or building; the portion on which one walks.
2. The different stories of a structure such as ground floor, first floor, etc.
3. The horizontal structure dividing the building into stories.

FLOOR AREA — Total horizontal surface of a specific floor, or the total area of all floors in a multi-story building, computed from the outside building dimensions of each floor. Balcony and mezzanine floor areas are computed separately and added to the total floor area.

FLOOR-AREA RATIO — The relationship between the floor area of a building and the square-foot area of the plot on which it stands. In planning and zoning, it is often expressed as a decimal; for instance, 0.25 indicates that the floor area of a building is 25% of the total land area.

FLOOR FURNACE — A metal, box-like, warm-air furnace installed directly underneath the floor and with its grilled upper surface flush with the finished floor of the room.

FLOOR JOISTS—Horizontal framing lumber to which flooring is attached. See illustration, pages 304–306.

FLOOR LOAD—As commonly used, the live weight-supporting capabilities of a floor, measured in pounds per square foot; the weight, stated in pounds per square foot, which may safely be placed upon the floor of a building if uniformly distributed. This is also known as the live load. The weight of the building itself, including equipment, such as boilers, machinery, etc., is known as the dead load and is not included as a part of the floor load capacity.

FLOOR LOAN—That part of a total loan that will be disbursed when the physical improvements are complete. The balance of the loan is disbursed when the other requirements of the lender are met, such as rent roll achievement. See Ceiling Loan.

FLOOR OF FOREST—The dead vegetative matter on the ground in a forest, including litter and unincorporated humus. In fire control it is termed duff. See also Litter.

FLOWAGE EASEMENT—The perpetual right, power, privilege, and easement to overflow, flood, and submerge the lands affected; reserving, however, to the fee owner of the lands all such rights and privileges as may be used and enjoyed without interfering with or abridging the rights granted in the flowage easement. It may be either permanent or occasional.

FLOW LINE—The profile of the low point of a drainage channel or structure. It is measured at the low point of the inside of the water course.

FLUE
1. The smoke passage in a chimney.
2. Any duct or pipe for the passage of air, gases, smoke, etc.

FLUE LINING—The tile or pipe inside a chimney.

FLUME—An open artificial channel to carry water such as one by which logs can be transported. It may or may not be supported on a trestle at points in its course.

FLUORESCENT LIGHTING—Lighting fixtures consisting of glass tubes which have an inside coating of fluorescent materials which, when subjected to a stream of electrons from the cathode, are capable of producing light.

FLUSH SIDING—A level siding of tongue and groove boards laid flush on the sidewalls.

FODDER—Coarse food for horses, cattle, or sheep.

FOOTING—A flange-like part at the base of a foundation wall which ties or locks the foundation into the ground thus preventing shifting and settling. Footings also assist in distributing the load of the superstructure over a greater area. See illustration, page 305.

FORAGE – All browse and herbaceous food that is available to livestock or game animals. Forage may be either used for grazing or harvested for feeding.

FORAGE-ACRE – A theoretical acre totally covered with vegetation, all of which is properly usable by livestock. The forage-acre factor times the number of surface acres of a type indicates the total forage-acres in a plot.

FORAGE-ACRE FACTOR – The factor obtained by multiplying the weighted-use factor by the forage density of the vegetation. This is a forage index expressing the part of a range that is covered with available vegetation which can be eaten entirely by livestock without damage to the range. See also Weighted-use Factor.

FORAGE CROP – A member of the grass family, such as corn or grain sorghum; often it is harvested and stored in silos as a reserve food supply for livestock.

FORAGE DENSITY – The part of the total vegetative density which is within the reach of livestock, generally within a reach of 4 feet for sheep and 5 feet for cattle.

FORBS – Any herb other than grass.

FORCED PRICE – The price paid in a forced sale or purchase; that is, a sale in which there was not allowed a reasonable time to find a purchaser, or in which the purchaser was forced to buy.

FORCED SALE
1. The act of offering and transferring property, and for a valuable consideration, under conditions of compulsion.
2. Frequently a sale at public auction made by virtue of a court order.

FORECASTING – Making an estimate of a future happening or condition. Forecasting is based on an analysis of trends in the recent past, tempered with analytical judgment concerning the probable extent to which these trends will continue into the future.

FORECLOSURE – The legal process by which a mortgagee, in case of default by the mortgagor, forces sale of the property mortgaged in order to recover all or part of a loan.

FORESHORE – The land (in its natural condition) between mean high and mean low water along a shore.

FOREST – A large tract of land covered with trees.

FOREST, MATURE—A forest which has reached its age of maximum utilization. The meaning differs with the objects of forest management.

FOREST PERMIT—The permit issued by the U.S. Forest Service to a stock raiser which permits the grazing of a specified number of head on a national forest for a certain time or season.

FORFEITURE—The means by which the property of the citizen inures to the benefit of the state through the violation of law and occurring in the United States only in case of seizure for taxes.

FORM CLASS—In forestry, the relationship between diameter outside bark, breast high, and diameter inside bark at top of the first 16′ log. The relationship provides a percentage of taper or form. For example, if D.B.H. is 24″ and top diameter is 12″, the form class is $12'' \div 24'' = .5 \times 100$, or Form Class 50.

FORMICA—A trade name for a plastic material used primarily for the top of counter areas, but also used for wall covering, as a veneer for plywood panels, or as a wallboard where a fire-resistive material is desirable. Similar and competitive materials are produced under other trade names.

FORMS—Temporary panels, usually of wood, plywood, or steel, which control the shape of poured concrete until it hardens.

FORMULA RULES—Formulas used to derive the board-foot contents of the log from its diameter and length, allowing for waste in saw kerf and waste in slabs, and reduction of residual volume to board feet. Extreme care must be exercised in using formulas. See Humboldt Rule, Log Rules, Scribner Rule, Spaulding Rule.

FOUNDATION—That upon which anything is built; that part of a structure upon which the building is erected; usually that part of a building which is below the surface of the ground and on which the superstructure rests.

4-3-2-1 RULE—See Depth Factor.

FOYER—The lobby of a theatre or hotel; entrance hall of a house.

FRACTIONAL APPRAISAL
1. An appraisal of one of the component parts of a property, for example, the land regardless of the building, or the building regardless of the land; and the appraisal of a lessee's or a lessor's interest.
2. An appraisal of a unit in itself without regard to the effect of its separation from the whole.

FRACTIONAL INTEREST—See Divided Interest.

FRACTIONAL PROPERTY — A part of the whole, for example, improvements considered separately from the land upon which they are situated.

FRACTIONAL QUARTER — Theoretically, a section of land contains 640 acres. However, due to the convergence of lines and surveying errors not all sections contain this exact amount. To avoid small errors in all sections all shortages or surpluses have been assigned to the north and west sections in each township. Hence, remaining quarter sections are described as fractional sections.

FRACTIONAL RATE — See Split Rate.

FRAME (Wood) CONSTRUCTION — Walls and partitions formed by wood framing of studs or posts and girts, supporting wood roof and floor decks; may be enclosed by wood, metal, or composition siding or shingles; also, may be veneered with brick or stone facing.

FRAMING — The system of structural members which provide lateral, longitudinal, transverse, and vertical support for a building. See, illustration, pages 304–306 and 308–310.

FRAMING LINE — The outside vertical plane of exterior wall framing.

FRANCHISE — A privilege or right conferred by grant upon an individual or group of individuals. Usually, an exclusive privilege or right to furnish public services or sell a particular product in a certain community.

FREE BORD — An allowance of land outside the fence, which may be claimed by the owner. An allowance, in some places, two and a half feet wide outside the boundary or enclosure.

FREE GOOD — Any useful thing, external to man and so plentiful that it is available without any effort, as climate, fresh air, sunshine.

FREEHOLD
1. An estate of inheritance, an estate for life, or an estate during the life of a third person.
2. In appraising, the unencumbered property; that is free of mortgage.

FREE SWITCHING — An absence of charge by a railroad for handling freight in certain switching districts or in areas where reciprocal switching is provided. The rail tariff includes the charge for switching cars to and from sidings designated as entitled to free switching even though the siding is not on the railroad performing the line haul. In effect, every siding designated as entitled to free switching is on every railroad serving the area which enjoys the free switching tariff.

FREE SWITCHING LIMITS — The specified boundaries within which a railroad will switch, without further charge, carload freight on which it receives a line haul, to or from private spur tracks or its own team tracks; also competitive traffic on which the line haul carrier absorbs the switching charge of the switching line.

FREEWAY—A multiple-lane highway with full control of access and with all intersecting roads separated in grade from the pavements for through traffic. See also Expressway, Toll Road, Turnpike, Superhighway.

FRENCH ARCHITECTURE—Any of several styles originating in France. Most common is the small formal house, perfectly balanced, with a steep roof hipped at the ends, plastered walls on the first story, and with dormer windows provided for the second-floor rooms. The French farmhouse style is informal, of stone, painted brick, or plaster. Sometimes half-timbering is used as an accent. Norman French architecture is large in scale, and usually distinguished by a round tower.

FRENCH CURVE—A stencil-like draftsman's device used for drawing curves other than circles or arcs. Synonymn: irregular curve.

FRENCH DOORS OR WINDOWS—A pair of glazed doors hinged at the jamb, functioning as both doors and windows.

FREON—A trademark name for a group of refrigerants which are used in air conditioning systems. They have nontoxic and nonflammable properties.

FREQUENCY DISTRIBUTION—The arrangement of data into groups according to their number of repetitions.

FRESCO—A mural painting method using watercolors on freshly plastered walls.

FRIABLE—Easily crumbled by the fingers; nonplastic.

FRIEZE—A horizontal trim piece immediately below the cornice soffit. See illustration, page 000.

FRONT—The primary face of a structure, particularly that which contains the principal entrance. Synonymn: facade.

FRONTAGE ROAD—A local street paralleling a limited access highway and built to service abutting properties and to gather and control vehicles entering or leaving the major traffic artery. It is also referred to as a service road.

FRONT ELEVATION—The front view of a building.

FRONT FOOT—A land measure being one foot in width along the frontage of a property.

FRONT FOOT COST—Cost of a parcel of real estate expressed in terms of front foot units.

FRONT MONEY
1. Cash outlay required to launch a project.
2. Money required to be expended prior to the availability of financing.
3. In connection with FHA rental housing projects, this is a cash outlay by the sponsor equal to the difference between the mortgage amount and the FHA estimate of replacement cost for on-site improvements. On FHA rental housing projects, front money, also known as "over and above" money, must be deposited by the project sponsor with the lender at the time the loan is approved for insurance and must be the first money disbursed, before insured advances are made, during construction.

FULL CUT LUMBER — Lumber which is cut to full dimension.

FUNCTIONAL CURABLE OBSOLESCENCE — Functional obsolescence which may be corrected or cured when the cost of replacing the outmoded or unacceptable component is at least offset by the anticipated increase in utility, and hence ultimately in value, resulting from the replacement.

FUNCTIONAL INCURABLE OBSOLESCENCE — Functional obsolescence that results from structural deficiencies or superadequacies that the prudent purchaser or owner would not be justified in replacing, adding or removing, because the cost of effecting a cure would be greater than the anticipated increase in utility resulting from the replacement, addition, or removal.

FUNCTIONAL OBSOLESCENCE — Impairment of functional capacity or efficiency. Functional obsolescence reflects the loss in value brought about by such factors as defects, deficiencies, or superadequacies, that affect the property item itself or its relation with other items comprising a larger property. The inability of a structure to perform adequately the function for which it is currently employed.

FUNCTIONAL REPLACEMENT — The replacement of real property, either lands or facilities or both, acquired as a result of a transportation-related project, with lands or facilities or both which will provide equivalent utility.

FUNCTIONAL UTILITY — The sum of the attractiveness and usefulness of the property. It is the ability of the property to perform the function for which it is intended, in terms of current market tastes and standards. Elements of functional utility in a residence include architecture, design and layout, traffic pattern, sizes and types of rooms, and performance standards.

FUNCTIONAL UTILITY VALUE — The marketable measure of the ability to provide usefulness, service, or profit.

FUNCTION OF THE APPRAISAL — The reason for which the appraisal is made or is intended to be used. Relates to the character of the decision to be based on the appraisal, e.g., price at which to buy or sell, amount of mortgage to be made. Not the same as Purpose.

FUNCTIONS OF MANAGEMENT — As proper valuation methods usually assume competent management, the function of management is therefore not ordinarily a factor of value, but one of its attributes.

FUNGIBLE — In law, goods of such kind or nature that one specimen, part, or unit such as money, food, and the like, may be used in place of another in the satisfaction of an obligation. Because of its characteristic of uniqueness (particularly in regard to location), real estate is a prime example of a nonfungible good.

FURLONG — A linear measure. See Measures, page 271.

FURNITURE AND FIXTURES — An accounting term used to designate movable properties with limiting qualifications, such as office furniture and fixtures. Strictly speaking, the word "fixtures" is improper; however, it is strongly entrenched by long usage, primarily by accountants. The term should be clarified when used. See Fixture.

FURRING — The strips of wood or metal applied to a rough wall or other surface to provide a level fastening surface for application of a finish material or to form an air space.

FURRING STRIP — Small (usually 1" X 2") strips of wood fastened to walls or ceilings to provide (1) a level surface for the application of lath for plaster or other finish material, or (2) a breather or air space between an outside masonry wall and the plaster. See illustration, pages 305–306.

FUSE — A protective device which controls the flow of electricity through a circuit, so constructed that it melts when the circuit is overloaded thus stopping the flow of electricity.

FUSE BOX — The container which houses the fuses controlling the electric circuits of a structure.

FUTURE DEPRECIATION — That loss from present value which presumably will occur in the future.

FUTURE WORTH OF ONE — See Amount of One.

FUTURE WORTH OF ONE PER PERIOD — See Amount of One Per Period.

GABLE — The end of a building, generally triangular in shape; the vertical plane which lies above the eaves and between the slope of a ridged roof.

GABLE DORMER — See illustration, page 306.

GABLE ROOF — A ridged roof, the ends of which form a gable. See illustration, page 300.

GALLERY
1. A covered walk or corridor, extending from an upper story of a building and running along either the exterior or interior wall.
2. The highest balcony in a theatre.
3. A room for art exhibitions.

GALLONS PER MINUTE — A measurement of flow. See Measures, page 274.

GAMBREL ROOF — A ridged roof, the side of which has two slopes, with the lower slope being the steeper. See illustration, page 300.

GAP LOAN — Development financing for income producing property frequently involves some arrangement under which certain requirements must be met by the developer or by the property before the total loan will be disbursed by the permanent lender. This may take the form of a "leasing hold back." The developer, in order to secure the equivalent of these withheld funds to complete development prior to final disbursement, may secure a loan elsewhere, generally on an interim basis and generally approximating the amount of the "hold back." This is commonly referred to as a "gap" loan although it may continue for an extended period if, for example, the requirements for complete disbursement of the first mortgage are not met as contemplated. "Gap loan" may also be applied to secondary financing providing funds to meet any deficiency between the total of the available first mortgage plus equity and the total cost of development.

GARBAGE DISPOSAL — An electrical appliance, usually installed in a sink, which reduces garbage to small particles which may be disposed of by washing down the drain.

GARDEN APARTMENTS — Used to distinguish an apartment development of two or three story walk-up structures in a garden-like setting. Such apartments are customarily a suburban or rural–urban fringe development.

GARRET — See Attic.

GATHERING PENS — A corral or pen usually constructed on the range at some distance from ranch headquarters to facilitate the gathering of herds at shipping time, for branding and other purposes.

GENERAL BENEFITS — The benefits which accrue to the community at large, to the area adjacent to the improvement, or to other property similarly situated as that taken but which property is not taken. See also, Benefits, Special Benefits, Set-off Rule.

GENERAL OVERHEAD COSTS – See Indirect Construction Costs.

GENESIS OF SOIL – Mode of origin of the soil, referring particularly to the processes responsible for the development of the solum from the unconsolidated parent material.

GEOCODE – A code used to locate or identify a point such as the center of a parcel of real estate, geographically. Usually expressed in coordinates relative to some standard point of reference.

GEODETIC SYSTEM – The United States Coast and Geodetic Survey System. The skeleton of the system consists of a network of bench marks covering the entire country. Each bench mark is located by its latitude and longitude. The system was initiated to identify tracts of land owned by the federal government but gradually has been extended throughout the nation.

GEOGRAPHICAL SEQUENCE – A method for filing appraisal data by location. In assessing, the property record cards are filed according to lot number, then by blocks, and finally by subdivisions.

GEOMETRIC (MEAN) AVERAGE – The nth root of the product of n items. Its characteristics are: dependent on size of all values; less affected by extreme values than arithmetic average; smaller than the arithmetic average. It is particularly useful in the computation of index numbers, although difficult to compute and cannot be calculated when there are negative values or one value is zero.

GEOMETRIC PROGRESSION – A sequence of items in which the ratio of any item to the preceding item is a constant, as 2, 4, 16, 64, 256.

GEORGIAN ARCHITECTURE – A formal colonial style adapted from English design of the eighteenth century; characterized by simple lines, balanced window openings, doors and chimneys, and first-floor windows extending to the ground.

GEORGIAN COLONIAL ARCHITECTURE – Most formal of the colonial types of residential architecture. Balanced openings and chimneys predominate. Ceilings are usually higher than in the other colonial designs. Wings, dropped to follow the contour of the ground, are kept simple in detail; but porches at front or side are rather elaborate.

GIFT TAX – A graduated tax imposed by the federal government since 1932 and by some states on transfers of property by gift during the donor's lifetime. Gifts, under this law, may include irrevocable living trusts.

GINGERBREAD WORK – A term used to describe the excessive use of ornamentation in architecture, especially of a house.

GIRDER – Principal horizontal structural member or beam which supports lesser beams, joists, or walls. See illustration, page 305.

GIRT—A horizontal, framing member extending between columns or studs to stiffen framework and/or to carry the siding material.

GLA—See Gross Leasable Area.

GLACIAL SOIL—See Types of Soil, page 351.

GLASS—A hard, brittle, generally transparent or translucent substance produced by fusion. Common varieties such as window glass, are produced by the fusion of mutually dissolved silica, soda, and lime.

GLASS BLOCK—A hollow building block made of translucent glass, admitting light yet affording privacy with sound insulating qualities; not intended for use in a load-bearing wall.

GLASS-WOOL INSULATION—Material made of glass fibers, usually in the form of blankets of equal thickness wrapped in a heavy asphalt-treated or vapor-barrier paper. See also Mineral Wool.

GLAZE—To fit, furnish, or cover with glass; to produce a vitreous or glossy surface.

GLAZED BRICK—A dress brick, one having a glossy surface made of vitreous material.

GLAZED FACING TILE—A hollow clay tile having one or two faces finished with a glazed surface.

GLEAN—The gathering (either by livestock or handpicking) of grain or other produce left in fields by combines.

GOING CONCERN VALUE
1. The value existing in a proven property operation, considered as an entity with business established, as distinct from the value of real estate only, ready to operate but without a going business.
2. Includes consideration of the efficiency of plant, the know-how of management, and the sufficiency of capital.
3. It is an excess of value over cost which arises as a consequence of a complete and well-assembled operation production mechanism; it is the value of an efficient layout and operational control system resulting in the most desirable synchronization of the merchandising, production, or distribution activities of the enterprise, and includes goodwill. Synonym: value in use.

GOING VALUE—See Going Concern Value.

GOOD—In economics, any material or immaterial thing which satisfies human desire and is external to humans. Goods are considered in two categories: free goods and economic goods.

GOODWILL—An intangible, salable asset arising from the reputation of the business and its relation with its customers as distinguished from the value of the physical plant and its stock.

GOODWILL VALUE

1. The advantage which a business has developed due to intangible values applicable to the specific business concern itself, such as name, certain types of patents, and trademarks, or similar rights or benefits. Primarily, these are of an intangible nature which may not freely be enjoyed by competitors.
2. That part of the value of a going enterprise which is in excess of the capital investment and is an ingredient of going concern value.

GORE — A small triangular piece of land.

GOVERNMENT LOTS — Those land areas which, because of location or size, could not be divided into sections and quarters under government survey. Such tracts usually lie along the edge of rivers or lakes and extend from the waterline to the first section boundary.

GOVERNMENT SURVEY — A ground survey authorized by the Continental Congress in 1785 and by subsequent Congressional acts, encountered in Florida, Alabama, Mississippi and all States (except Texas) north of the Ohio or west of the Mississippi Rivers. The land is divided into townships approximately six miles square, each township normally containing 36 sections and each section normally containing 640 acres. See Legal Description. See also illustration, page 294.

GRADE

1. The slope of a surface, such as a lot or road, with the vertical rise or fall expressed as a percentage of horizontal distance; e.g., a 3% upgrade means a rise of three feet per one hundred feet of horizontal distance.
2. Frequently used to denote the level or elevation of a lot. For instance, rough grade means the level, slope, or general elevation of the land surface on which will be placed topsoil for landscaping; finish grade denotes the final level, slope or elevation of a lot.
3. Sometimes used in the sense of "on or at the same level;" e.g., a crossing at street grade; a lot at street grade.
4. Also, to reduce a parcel of land to a practical level for development.
5. A letter, number, or word denoting the quality of construction materials.

GRADE BEAM — A horizontal load-bearing foundation member but end-supported like a standard beam; not ground-supported like the foundation wall.

GRADE SEPARATION — A structure used to separate vertically two intersecting roadways, thus permitting traffic on the one road to cross traffic on the other road without interference.

GRADED TAX—A local tax designed so as to impose progressively heavier burden upon land values and a decreasing burden on improvements. The differential is achieved by varying either the assessment or the tax rate.

GRADIENT—The rate of the rise or fall of land, e.g., the degree of inclination of a road.

GRADUATED LEASE—A lease which provides for a certain rent for an initial period, followed by an increase or decrease in rent during a stated following period or periods.

GRADUATED PAYMENT MORTGAGE (GPM)—Another form of alternative mortgage instrument. A mortgage specifically designed to provide borrowers with an advantage over the traditional fixed payment mortgage by matching mortgage payments to projected increases in income. With the GPM, the monthly payments start out at a low level and gradually increase until they rise to the level at which the standard conventional mortgage would have been written. Since payments in the early years of the loan are not sufficient to amortize the mortgage, the homeowner, in effect, is borrowing the difference between the payments and the current interest due.

GRAIN—The arrangement or direction of the fibers in wood; the resulting appearance or surface markings.

GRAIN ELEVATOR
1. A special-purpose structure designed for the handling and/or storage of grains. There are two basic types: rural elevators and terminal elevators. Rural elevators receive the grains grown locally for storage until shipped to terminal elevators which are equipped to prepare grains for the market or for long-term storage.
2. A piece of mechanical equipment found on grain farms which has replaced the scoop shovel for loading and unloading grain from trucks or wagons to storage bins.

GRAND LIST—In New England, the tax roll or assessment list of a community.

GRANT—The act of transferring property or an interest in property to another.

GRANTEE—A person to whom property is transferred by deed or to whom property rights are granted by a trust instrument or other document.

GRANT-IN-AID—The allowable contribution made by local parties in cash or its equivalent as a part of the local share of an urban renewal project.

GRANTOR—A person who transfers property by deed, or grants property rights through a trust instrument or other document.

GRANULAR STRUCTURE—Soil aggregates varying in size up to two centimeters in diameter, of medium consistency, and more or less subangular or rounded in shape. Coarse granular implies aggregates close to maximum size. Fine granular is applied to aggregates under five millimeters in diameter.

GRAPH—A line which presents statistical data in visual form. A system of coordinates for plotting data.

GRASSES—Plants with hollow, jointed stems and leaves in two rows on the stems. Veins in the leaves are parallel.

GRASSLAND—See Types of Range Vegetation, page 349.

GRAZING CAPACITY—The maximum stocking rate possible without inducing damage to vegetation or related resources. See also Capacity.

GRAZING FEE—Charge, usually on a month or season basis, for grazing of livestock.

GRAZING LICENSE OR PERMIT—Official written permission to graze a specified number, kind, and class of livestock for a specific period on a defined allotment.

GRAZING PERIOD—The length of time that livestock are grazed on a specific area.

GRAZING SEASON—A period of grazing to obtain optimum use of the forage resource. On public lands, an established period for which grazing permits are issued.

GRAZING UNIT—An area of rangeland, public or private, which is grazed as an entity.

GREASEWOOD—See Types of Range Vegetation, page 349.

GREAT SOIL GROUPS—Soil classification: A group of soils having common internal soil characteristics; includes one or more families of soils. See, also Natural Land Classification.

GREENLINING—Sometimes used to describe a policy on the part of a lender, group of lenders, or other organizations to affirmatively seek out loans in specific neighborhoods.

GREEN LUMBER—Lumber, the moisture content of which is greater than air- or kiln-dried lumber; unseasoned lumber.

GREEN MANURE CROP—Any crop grown and plowed under for the purpose of improving the soil, especially by the addition of organic matter.

GRID — A grating of crossed bars; a pattern composed of equal areas made by parallel lines intersecting at right angles. The plan layout for a building.

GRIDIRON — A term used to describe the rectangular street pattern of cities or subdivision developments.

GRILLAGE — A system of beams, laid crosswise to form a foundation to evenly distribute imposed loads.

GROIN — A structure usually of piling, sometimes with a stone apron at the end, placed on a beach to act as breakwater. In architecture, the curved line or edge formed by the intersection of two vaulted or arched surfaces.

GROSS AREA — The total floor areas of a building, except those of unenclosed areas, measured from the exterior of the walls; superstructure floor area plus substructure or basement area.

GROSS INCOME — The scheduled income from the operation of the business or the management of the property, customarily stated on an annual basis. See Effective Gross Income, Potential Gross Income.

GROSS INCOME MULTIPLIER (GIM) — The relationship (ratio) between sales price (value) and either Potential Gross Income or Effective Gross Income in income-producing properties. These relationships are not be intermingled, i.e., there must must be consistency in the method of computing multipliers used for analysis. It is used to estimate value as a multiple of annual gross income (potential or effective).

GROSS INCOME (RENT) MULTIPLIER ANALYSIS — That approach in appraisal analysis which is based upon the proposition that an informed purchaser would pay no more for a property than the cost of obtaining a return (in income or amenities) of the same amount and embodying the same risk as that involved in the subject property. This approach is applicable when sufficient numbers of comparable properties are rented at the time of sale. The gross income (rent) multiplier approach is not applicable when few or no comparable properties are rented in the competitive market. This approach also is questionable in market situations in which market rentals and sales prices do not bear a constant relationship to each other.

GROSS LEASABLE AREA (GLA) — The denominate common to all shopping center and office building operations. Typically, the dollar values per unit of gross leasable area are on an annual basis. See Standard Area Measures, page 295.

GROSS LEASE — A lease which provides that the lessor is obligated to pay all or a major part of the property charges, but at least real estate taxes, insurance, and structural repairs. Precise definition may be subject to local real estate market practice.

GROSS NATIONAL PRODUCT—The money value of all final goods and services produced by a nation's economy before deduction of depreciation and allowances for consumption of durable capital goods.

GROSS RENT MULTIPLIER (GRM)—The relationship (ratio) between sales price (value) and monthly rental income for single family residential properties.

GROSS SALES—The total amount of sales as shown by invoices, before deducting returns, allowances, etc.

GROUND AREA—The area computed from the exterior dimensions of the ground floor.

GROUND BEAM—A horizontal member of iron, steel, or stone located on or near the ground, used to support the superstructure and distribute its load.

GROUND COVERAGE—The percentage of ground area covered by ground floor building improvements.

GROUND FLOOR—The floor of a building which is approximately level with the ground.

GROUND LEASE—A lease which grants the right of use and occupancy of land.

GROUND RENT—Rent paid for the right to use and occupy land; that portion of the total rent which is allocated to the underlying land.

GROUND WATER—All water beneath the surface of the ground or in the subsoil which has seeped down; or water from springs or wells.

GROUNDS—The strips of wood placed around wall opening to indicate finish level for plaster or concrete.

GROUT—A thin, fluid mortar used to fill small joints and cavities in masonry work.

GROVE—A planting of uniformly spaced fruit or nut-bearing trees, but more commonly applied to citrus plantings. The term may also apply to plantings of walnuts or other specialty nut crops.

GROYNE—See Groin.

GUARANTEED TITLE—A title, the validity of which is insured by an abstract, title, or indemnity company.

GUIDE MERIDIAN—See Meridian.

GUMBO SOIL—See Types of Soil, page 351.

GUNITE — A trade term for a cement-like compound which is dispensed from a gun under pneumatic pressure.

GUTTER
1. A channel running the length of a building which carries off rainwater, usually by means of downspouts.
2. The ridge formed by the edge of a street and a raised sidewalk or a depressed ridge in a road's shoulder which is a control for the flowage of storm water.

GYPSUM — A common mineral, hydrated calcium sulphate; in form, colorless crystals or masses which are easily crumbled. It is an ingredient of plaster of Paris and Keene's cement.

GYPSUM BLOCKS — Building material which, because of its friable nature, is not suitable for load-bearing walls.

GYPSUM SHEATHING BOARDS — A prefabrication material composed of set gypsum covered with water-repellent paper. It takes the place of sheathing and sheathing paper.

GYPSUM WALLBOARD — A type of wallboard used as substitute for plaster in drywall construction. It is a prefabricated sheet composed of a gypsum core covered by a type of paper to which paint or wallpaper can be applied.

H BEAM — An H-shaped steel structural member, frequently used as a column.

HABENDUM CLAUSE — A clause in a real estate document which specifies the extent of the interest (e.g., life or fee) to be conveyed.

HABITABLE ROOM — A room designated to be used for living, sleeping, eating, or cooking, excluding bathrooms, toilet compartments, closets, halls, storage, and similar spaces.

HALF SHRUB — See Types of Range Vegetation, page 349.

HALF-TIMBERED — House construction where timber wall framing is exposed, the space in between being filled with masonry or lath and plaster; simulated half-timbering involves boards applied on plaster walls. Half-timbering is a distinguishing characteristic of the Elizabethan style of architecture.

HALL
1. A room at the entrance of a building or a passage providing access to various parts of a building.
2. A large room used for public gatherings.

HAND — A linear measure of four inches.

HAND MOVE SPRINKLER — Portable irrigation sprinkler system generally constructed from aluminum pipe and moved by hand for each irrigation setting.

HARD FINISH — The final smooth finished coat of plaster which is applied to rough plastering.

HARDPAN — See Types of Soil, page 351.

HARDWARE
1. The metal fittings of a building; that is, hinges, locks, lifts, doorknobs, etc. Also known as builders' hardware or finish hardware.
2. The physical equipment making up a computer system.

HARDWOOD — Lumber cut from broad-leaved trees, such as oak, mahogany, walnut, birch, and which is used for interior finishes and flooring. Refers to the type of tree, not to the actual hardness of the wood.

HARMONIOUS — Used to describe a pleasing arrangement of architectural masses or detail in a building; the appropriateness with which a structure blends or harmonizes with other structures in its neighborhood; a neighborhood of compatible people.

HATCHWAY — A lifting or sliding door in the ceiling which gives access to the attic; or in a floor, to the cellar. Synonym: scuttle.

HAY — Meadow grasses which are cut and cured for livestock feed.

HAYMOW — That part of a barn where hay or straw is stored.

HEAD
1. The difference between the height of the surface of a free liquid above a given level as the water behind a dam and that below it.
2. The source of a river or stream.
3. The pressure of a confined body of steam or other gaseous material per unit of area.
4. The topmost framing member of a window or door.

HEADER — In masonry, a brick or building stone laid across the thickness of a wall with one end toward face of wall. In carpentry, a wood beam set at right angles to joists to provide a seat or support, a wood lintel.

HEAD JAMB — A piece of finish material across the underside of the top of a door or window opening. See illustration, pages 304–310.

HEAD ROOM — The distance between the top of a finished floor and the lowest part of the floor structure above.

HEADWAY — The time passage between automobiles traveling in the same direction past a given place.

HEATING SYSTEM — Any device or system for heating a building; usually a furnace or boiler used to generate steam, hot water, or hot air. A burner or air device using coal, oil, gas, or electricity to heat water or air which is then circulated through the system. Types of heating systems are: warm air, hot water, direct steam, radiant, electric.

HEAT PUMP—A reverse cycle refrigeration unit which can be used for heating or cooling.

HEAVY INDUSTRY—Used to distinguish those industries which physically are of an extensive or complex nature and usually require large tracts of land. In this category would be steel mills, refineries, foundries, packing plants. "Heavy industry" also refers to those industrial operations which produce hazards and/or nuisances, such as objectionable fumes, pollution, noise, and vibration.

HEAVY SOIL—See Types of Soil, page 351.

HEAVY STEEL FRAME—A building having framing members of heavy steel, such as beams, girders, columns, which have the capacity to carry heavy loads, absorb shocks and vibrations.

HECTARE—A French unit of land use measurement. See Measures, page 273.

HEDGE ROW PLANTING—Planting of trees or vines within rows, but with less than normal spacing between the plants in each row, for the purpose of increasing production or decreasing the cost of production. Hedge row planting is usually introduced to allow greater mechanized operation of harvesting, pruning or other cultural operations. The economic life of the tree or vine may be affected by such planting.

HEDGING—In agriculture, the act of trimming or mechanically pruning permanent plantings, such as orchards or groves.

HEEL—In construction, refers to that part of a framing member which rests on the wall plate.

HEIGHT DENSITY—A zoning regulation designed to control the use or occupancy within a given area by designating the maximum height of structures.

HEIR—A person who inherits property, real and/or personal. Also, the person designated by law to inherit the estate of one who died intestate.

HEREDITAMENTS—Every sort of inheritable property, such as real, personal, corporeal, and incorporeal.

HETEROGENEOUS—In real estate, used to describe an area or neighborhood composed of diversified types of property uses and/or occupants of dissimilar cultural, social, or economic backgrounds. Antonymn: homogeneous.

HIGHEST AND BEST USE—That reasonable and probable use that supports the highest present value, as defined, as of the effective date of the appraisal.

Alternatively, that use, from among reasonably probable and legal alternative uses, found to be physically possible, appropriately supported, financially feasible, and which results in highest land value.

The definition immediately above applies specifically to the highest and best use of land. It is to be recognized that in cases where a site has existing improvements on it, the highest and best use may very well be determined to be different from the existing use. The existing use will continue, however, unless and until land value in its highest and best use exceeds the total value of the property in its existing use. See Interim Use.

Implied within these definitions is recognition of the contribution of that specific use to community environment or to community development goals in addition to wealth maximization of individual property owners. Also implied is that the determination of highest and best use results from the appraiser's judgment and analytical skill, i.e., that the use determined from analysis represents an opinion, not a fact to be found. In appraisal practice, the concept of highest and best use represents the premise upon which value is based. In the context of most probable selling price (market value) another appropriate term to reflect highest and best use would be most probable use. In the context of investment value an alternative term would be most profitable use. See Most Probable Use, Most Profitable Use.

HIGH-RISE APARTMENT BUILDING — An indefinite term which has come into use since World War II; probably in an attempt to distinguish the modern elevator apartment from its prewar counterpart. The term of reference usually applied has to do with height, but this standard varies among cities and different sections of the country.

HIGH WATER LINE — The point on the shore to which the tide normally rises. It will vary with seasons, time, wind, and other causes. See also Mean High Water Line.

HIGHWAY CAPACITY — The numerical capacity of a roadway to accept traffic. It is controlled by the types of vehicles using it, number and width of travel lanes, allowable speed, relation to road curvature and topography, and the limitations of access and development controls of adjacent real estate.

HIGHWAY EASEMENT — A right granted, or taken, for the construction, maintenance and operation of a highway. Ordinarily, in the case of a public thoroughfare, the abutting landholders are assumed to own the fee to the center line of the right of way.

HIGHWAY FRONTAGE — Land which is adjacent to and abuts a highway right of way.

HIGHWAY HOTEL — Designates the highway motel, usually of two or more stories, offering services comparable to those of a hotel.

HIGHWAY LINE—The outside limits of a highway right of way; not to be confused with the limits of actual construction such as curbs, shoulders or slopes. Also referred to as Right of Way Line.

HILLY LAND—Uneven land with dominant slopes varying between 16% and 30%.

HIP—The inclined ridge formed by the intersection of two sloping roof surfaces, whose eave lines are not parallel.

HIP-ROOF—A roof whose sides and ends both slope. Distinguished from a pyramid roof in that the end slopes are connected by a ridge, the length of which is commonly referred to as a "run" while all slopes of a pyramid roof meet so that virtually no ridge remains. See illustration, page 300.

HISTOGRAM—A set of vertical bars whose areas are proportional to the frequencies represented. See also Frequency Distribution.

HISTORICAL COST—The actual or first cost of a property at the time it was originally constructed and placed in service. It should not be confused with original cost, the latter term more properly being used to designate the actual cost to the present owner, who may have purchased at a price more or less than the historical or first costs. In an assembled property, such as a public utility, the historical cost as of any date means the first cost as defined, plus all subsequent additions and betterments less deductions.

HISTORIC DISTRICT—An area created by zoning in a municipality to retain and preserve the historic quality.

HISTORIC PRESERVATION—The preservation of historic sites and districts by regulation and/or rehabilitation.

HISTORIC SITE—A parcel which is distinguished because of an important historic event which occurred on or near the site.

HISTORY OF THE FARM—Indication of past and present owners, crop and/or livestock units grown; a recent chronological order of ownership indicating direct or tenant operation.

HOG FACTORY—In agriculture, a hog feeding facility where hogs are grown from farrowing to slaughter size in confinement under controlled conditions.

HOGWALLOWS—Describes the surface microrelief of a body of soil containing a series of rounded low mounds with diameters up to 40 feet and variable heights up to about three feet.

HOLD HARMLESS AGREEMENT—A legally binding agreement in which the liability of one party is assumed by another party to the agreement.

HOLDING PERIOD—The term of ownership for an investment.

HOLDING PERIOD YIELD — The total yield on an investment, particularly a bond held for less than full term, including the gains or losses from resale as well as regular earnings; the sum of all current yield and deferred yield; sometimes a contraction for the holding period yield rate; analogous to the equity yield rate and internal rate of return.

HOLDOVER TENANT — A tenant who remains in possession of leased real estate after the lease has expired. In many states, the lease is automatically renewed if the lessor accepts another rent payment after the expiration of a lease.

HOLLOW-NEWEL STAIR — A circular stairway having a wellhole in the middle.

HOLLOW WALL — A wall, usually of masonry, consisting of two vertical components with air space between.

HOMESTEAD — The fixed residence or dwelling place of the head of a family, including the principal house, buildings, and land about it.

HOMESTEAD EXEMPTION
1. A lawful withdrawal of a property occupied by the head of a family from attachment by the occupant's creditors or forced sale for general debts.
2. A release from assessment or property tax, or the application of a lower tax rate granted by law to the head of a family, on property designated as the family homestead.

HOMOGENEOUS — In real estate, used to describe an area or neighborhood in which the property types and uses are similar and the inhabitants have compatible cultural, social, and economic interests. Antonymn: heterogeneous.

HOOD — A canopy over a casement window to afford protection; a projecting part of a fireplace over the hearth; a cap on a chimney to eliminate down draft; a canopy over a cooking appliance, usually ventilated, to control and disperse heat or offensive odors.

HOPPER WINDOW — See Hospital Window.

HOPPER — A draft-preventer used on sides of hospital windows.

HORIZON — A layer of soil approximately parallel to the land surface with more or less well-defined characteristics which have been produced through soil-building processes. See also A Horizon, B Horizon, C Horizon, D Horizon.

HOSKOLD — H.E. Hoskold, English mining engineer and former Chief of the Argentine Government Division of Mines and Geology; originator of Hoskold method for valuation of coal mines, timber land and other real estate with depleting assets, author of Hoskold Tables, first published in 1877.

HOSKOLD FACTOR—A multiplier obtained by calculation or from special tables which is used to capitalize income produced by a wasting asset. The Hoskold factor provides for recapture by actual or hypothetical contributions to a sinking fund which grows with compound interest at a "safe rate." In addition, the Hoskold factor provides for "return on" the investment at a higher "speculative rate."

HOSPITAL WINDOW—A window with a lower section hinged at the bottom and opening inward and with draft-preventers or hoppers at the sides.

HOTEL—Typically, an inner city facility offering lodging accommodations, as well as a wide range of other services such as restaurants, convention facilities, meeting rooms, recreational facilities, commercial shops, and the like.

HOT-WATER SYSTEM—A heating system consisting basically of a boiler, radiators, expansion tank, and interconnecting piping. The system is filled with water which circulates from the boiler through the pipes and radiators where its heat is liberated, the water returning to the boiler. Such heating units are classified as gravity or forced circulation systems, either of one or two pipes, and with open or closed expansion tanks.

HOUR-INCH—A flow of miner's-inch for one hour, being 1/50th of a cubic foot per second in southern California, Idaho, Kansas, Nebraska, and New Mexico; and 1/40th of a cubic foot per second in northern California, Arizona, Montana, and Oregon. See Measures, page 274.

HOUSE—A general all-inclusive term used to designate a building which is used as a residence. In construction, they are distinguished as single, double, duplex, townhouse, row house, split-level, ranch.

HOUSE SEWER—The drain pipe system or pipes which connect with the main sewer in the street. See Lateral.

HOUSING AND URBAN DEVELOPMENT, DEPARTMENT OF—The federal department which is responsible for the major programs of housing and urban development, such as urban renewal, low rent public housing, mortgage insurance, metropolitan planning, etc. It is the twelfth department in the President's cabinet. It was created in 1965 and replaced the Housing and Home Finance Agency.

HUMBOLDT RULE (OR SCALE)—The Humboldt Log Rule is the Spaulding Rule less 30%. This rule was developed for use with old growth redwood to take care of the large amount of invisible defect. It is difficult to "scale out" defect in redwood logs. As a consequence, a blanket 30% deduction is made. In some areas where the amount of defect is small, a large overrun is found. The Humboldt Log Rule has been used at times to scale Douglas fir, but this practice is not recommended, as it is possible to scale out the defect in fir logs. See also Log Rules.

HUMMOCKS—Low mounds in swamp soils formed by the wind or by pasturing.

HUMUS—The well-decomposed, more or less stable part of the organic matter of the soil. Humus tends to keep the soil soft and granular and to increase its capacity for holding water and plant food.

HUNDRED PERCENT LOCATION—The term is usually used to refer to the location in the central business district which commands the highest land value. It may also refer to the site which is best adapted to meet the requirements of a specific user.

HUTCH—Housing for domestic rabbit production.

HYDRAULIC CEMENT—A cement which hardens under water.

HYDROELECTRIC PLANT—A plant, including engines, dynamos, etc., with the building or buildings, designed to generate and distribute electrical power derived from the energy of falling water.

HYDROGRAPH—A chart which shows the quantity of flow of water in a stream at intervals during a period of time.

HYDROPONICS—The science of growing plants in liquid mineral solutions where all plant nutrients are artificially introduced.

HYPOTHESIS—A statement in inferential statistics the truth of which one is interested in determining. The usual procedure is to state what one chooses to accept in the absence of sufficient evidence to the contrary (this statement is called the null hypothesis), specify the relationship or statement to be proved (termed the alternative hypothesis), and analyze the available data to determine whether the null hypothesis can be rejected (and hence the alternative hypothesis accepted) at some confidence level.

I BEAM—A steel beam resembling the letter I in cross section.

IGNEOUS ROCK—A rock produced through the cooling of melted mineral material; also known as fire rock.

ILLIQUIDITY—Describes assets which are not readily converted into cash.

ILLUVIATION—The process whereby soil materials from an upper horizon are deposited in the horizon below.

IMMATURE SOIL—See Types of Soil, page 351.

IMPERVIOUS SOIL—See Types of Soil, page 351.

IMPORTANT LAND FEATURES — Relating to soil types, topography, road location. Basically, an outline indicating all pertinent features upon the land.

IMPROVED LAND
1. Land which has been developed for some use by the erection of buildings and other improvements pertinent thereto. See also Improvements-on-Land.
2. Land which has been prepared for development as distinguished from raw land. This implies such things as grading, draining, and installation of utilities or access.

IMPROVEMENTS — Broadly, buildings or other more or less permanent structures or developments located upon or attached to land. Not a significant or informative term without qualification. See also Improvements-on-Land, Improvements-to-land.

IMPROVEMENTS-ON-LAND — Structures erected permanently on a site for its utilization, such as buildings, fences, driveways, retaining walls.

IMPROVEMENTS-TO-LAND — Usually additions to land to make property usable, such as curbs, sidewalks, street lights, sewers, drains, fills.

IMPUTED INCOME — The equivalent of income attributable to owner-occupied income properties due to rents saved or not paid by the user. From these savings in what would otherwise have to be paid as rent, funds are generated to support ownership. Sometimes used to refer to income allocated to land and/or buildings in the physical residual techniques.

INADEQUATE IMPROVEMENT — See Underimprovement.

INCINERATOR — A device for burning waste material and rubbish.

INCOME — Money or other benefits, generally assumed to be received periodically. Technically, earnings applying to the operation of a firm rendering service as distinguished from one selling commodities. Profits apply to manufacturing and mercantile concerns. Income, while frequently used by corporations to refer to net earnings, more particularly applies to the compensation or profits received by an individual. See also, Cash Flow, Excess Income, Potential Gross Income, Net Operating Income, Operating Income, Stabilized Income.

INCOME APPROACH — That procedure in appraisal analysis which converts anticipated benefits (dollar income or amenities) to be derived from the ownership of property into a value estimate. The income approach is widely applied in appraising income-producing properties. Anticipated future income and/or reversions are discounted to a present worth figure through the capitalization process.

INCOME MULTIPLIER—A factor which is the reciprocal of the Overall Rate (sometimes called "net income multiplier").

INCOME PARTICIPATION—The right of the mortgagee to share in some portion of future income to be generated by the property, usually over the maturity term of the underlying mortgage. See also Equity Participation.

INCOME PREMISE—The underlying assumptions as to the pattern of the future income expectancy which represents the basis of income capitalization in the appraisal process. The income premise may be based on the assumption that, while future income installments may fluctuate, their equivalent is assumed to be: (a) a level yearly income of a certain amount; (b) a series of future incomes graduating upwards or downwards or in both directions as per the series assumed in the appraisal for valuation purposes.

INCOME PROPERTY—A type of property the primary purpose of which is to produce monetary income.

INCOME RISK—The risk inherent in any future income projection reflecting the degree of assurance that the income will be achieved, and reflected in the rate necessary to attract capital.

INCOME TAX LIABILITY—An obligation to the federal, state and/or local government based upon an individual or corporation's marginal tax rate and taxable income generated. More specifically, in income-producing properties, it is Net Operating Income less deductible items, e.g., interest on debt and depreciation, times the appropriate marginal tax rate.

INCREASING AND DECREASING (DIMINISHING) RETURNS—A valuation principle which states that when successive increments of one or more factors of production are added to fixed amounts of the other factors there is a resulting enhancement of income (in dollars, benefits, or amenities), initially at an increasing rate to a point of maximum return and then decreasing until eventually the increment to value becomes increasingly less than the value of the added factor (or factors). The Principle of Increasing and Decreasing Returns is sometimes known as the Principle of Diminishing Returns or the Principle of Variable Proportions.

INCREASING ANNUITY—A forecast of annual amounts of Net Operating Income over the income projection period, normally implying a systematic annual increase in gross as well as net (operating) income.

INCREMENT UNEARNED—See Unearned Increment.

INCUBATOR BUILDING—Typically, an older industrial property that has been subdivided into low rent space for fledgling business or manufacturing firms which have limited operating capital.

INCUMBRANCE – See Encumbrance.

INCURABLE DEPRECIATION – Elements of physical deterioration or functional obsolescence which either cannot be corrected; or, if possible to correct, cannot be corrected except at a cost in excess of their contribution to the value of the property.

INDENTURE – A deed involving two or more parties with reciprocal and paralleling rights and obligations to each party.

INDEPENDENT APPRAISAL – One in which the conclusion of value is reached independently of, and without collaboration with, another appraiser, although not necessarily without consultation.

INDEX NUMBER – A device for measuring differences in the magnitude of a group of related variables in comparison with a base period, the value of which is typically 100. The most common types of index numbers are those which show the change in prices of specific commodities or group averages over a period of time.

INDIRECT COST – That cost in the development of a property which would not be included in a general contract for construction or for land acquisition, including:
1. Fees (architectural, engineering, consulting, or legal).
2. Financing costs.
3. Insurance and taxes during construction.
4. Interest on land cost during construction and on construction loans.
5. Owner's overhead during construction.
6. Title changes, surveys, or feasibility studies.
7. Loss of reasonable return on investment until anticipated occupancy is developed.

INDIRECT LIGHTING – Reflected or diffused lighting obtained by directing the light against the ceiling, against the walls, or some other surface.

INDUSTRIAL PARK – A controlled, park-like development, designed to accommodate specific types of industry, and providing the required appurtenances therefor, such as public utilities, streets, railroad sidings, water and sewage facilities, etc.

INDUSTRIAL PROPERTY – Land or land and improvements adaptable for industrial use. Ideally, a combination of land, improvements, and machinery which has been integrated into a functioning unit intended for the assembling, processing, and manufacturing of finished or partially finished products from raw materials or fabricated parts, such as factories; or a similar combination intended for rendering service, such as laundries, dry cleaners, storage warehouses; or for the production of natural resources, such as oil wells.

Industrial improvements may be classified as:

General Purpose — readily adapted to alternate uses or users.

Special Purpose — adaptable to alternative uses or users only with difficulty and considerable expense.

Single Purpose — infrequently possible and rarely practical or feasible to adapt to alternative uses or users.

INDUSTRIAL SIDING — A spur track alongside an industry to which a railroad delivers and removes freight cars.

INDUSTRIAL TAX EXEMPTION — An exemption from local property taxes, usually granted for a definite period of years, used to attract new industries to the community or to encourage the expansion of existing industry.

INFERENTIAL STATISTICS
1. The branch of statistical studies concerned with making predictions about the values of a large number of observations of a variable on the basis of a small number of observations of that variable and related facts.
2. By extension, the statistics calculated in such predictions.

INFILTRATION
1. The gradual displacement of the present uses or residents by shifts in the economic, social, and physical forces creating the environment.
2. (AIR) The flow of air into a building through cracks around doors, windows, and other openings in the building envelope.

INFLATION — A disproportionately large and relatively sudden increase in the general price level. Inflation may occur when the quantity of money or deposit currency in circulation is large compared with the quantity of goods and services offered, or when, because of a loss of confidence in the national money on the part of the public, a general and widespread attempt to convert money into commodities is precipitated. A normal increase in the price level after a period of depression is not generally regarded as inflation.

INHARMONIOUS — The opposite of Harmonious.

INHERITANCE TAX — A tax on the right to receive property by inheritance; to be distinguished from an estate tax.

INLAID PARQUET — See Parquet Floor.

IN LIEU TAX — A substitute for property taxes as in the case of public utilities or public housing where taxes are usually based on gross earnings. May apply also to other government owned tax-exempt properties and occasionally to voluntary payments by non-governmental tax exempt property. Also referred to as in lieu payments and payments in lieu of taxes.

IN PERSONAM – Against a person, not against a thing.

IN REM – Against a thing, not against a person.

INSIDE LOT – A lot sufficiently removed from a street intersection as to be unaffected by any corner influence.

INSIDE TRIM – See Interior Trim.

INSTALLMENT CONTRACT – A type of purchase with the payment made in prescribed installments. If default occurs, the payments are usually forfeited in total. When used in connection with the sale of real property, title is not normally transferred until completion of payments under the contract.

INSTITUTIONAL PROPERTY – Property of a public character owned and operated by nonprofit organizations or the government, such as hospitals, orphanages, private and public educational facilities, correctional facilities, museums, etc. The term is frequently extended to include properties of private operations such as banks, insurance companies, etc.

INSTRUMENT – In relation to real estate, refers to a formal legal document, such as a contract, deed, lease, will.

INSTRUMENTALITIES – Often applied to agencies of the federal government whose obligations are not the direct obligation of the federal government. However, there is an implied support; for example, Federal Land Bank bonds.

INSULATING BOARD OR FIBERBOARD – A building board made of compressed plant fibers, such as wood, cane or corn stalks; usually formed by a felting process, dried and pressed to specified thickness.

INSULATION – Any material used to reduce the transfer of heat, cold, or sound. Also, the nonconductive covering of electrical wires.

INSURABLE (INTEREST) VALUE – Used conventionally to designate the amount of insurance which may be or should be carried on destructible portions of a property to indemnify the owner in the event of loss.

INSURANCE – The act or business of insuring property, life, or the individual against loss or harm arising from certain specified contingencies, such as fire, death, theft, etc.

INTANGIBLE ASSETS – Items of property, such as franchises, trademarks, patents, copyrights, and goodwill; also such deferred items as development or organization expense. May be used synonymously with intangible property.

INTANGIBLE PROPERTY – See Intangible Assets.

INTANGIBLE VALUE—A value not imputable to any part of the physical property, such as the excess value attributable to a favorable lease, or the value attributable to goodwill.

INTENSITY—Intensity of land use is a reflection of the input of labor and capital per unit of land area. Relates to the extent of physical development rather than to the maximum economic potential (highest and best use) of the land.

INTENSIVE FARMING—The use of comparatively large amounts of labor and working capital per acre of land, generally implying maximum productivity.

INTERCEPT—Graphically, the point at which a line, such as the regression line, intercepts the axis upon which the dependent variable is represented; the value of the predicted variable when the value of the predictor variable in the model is zero; the coefficient a or b_0.

INTERCHANGE—A sytem of underpasses and overpasses for routing traffic on and off highways without interfering with through traffic, and for linking two or more highways.

INTERCHANGE RAMP—A travelway for traffic to change from one roadway to another.

INTEREST—Money paid for, or earned by, the use of capital; return on capital as distinguished from return of capital. In mortgage-equity work, the term "interest" is reserved for the return on a mortgage loan. In effect, interest represents rent for the use of capital.

INTEREST ONLY LOAN—A non-amortizing loan for which the lender receives only interest during the term of the loan and recovers principal in a lump sum at the end of the term; a "straight" loan.

INTEREST RATE—The rate of return on investment irrespective of, and independent of, any capital recovery received or demanded by the investor. Specifically, the rate on borrowed money. See also Discount Rate, Risk Rate.

INTEREST RISK—The risk that future rates of discount will be higher and that the present worth of a given income stream will decline in the future. A preferable term is "Money Market Risk."

INTERIM USE—That existing and relatively temporary use where the transition to highest and best use is deferred. A building or other improvement may have a number of years of remaining life yet may not enhance the value of the land which has a higher use, except as an interim-use taxpayer while the land is in transition.

INTERIOR, DEPARTMENT OF THE—A major administrative unit of the federal government with a secretary of cabinet rank, created March 3, 1849. Among the more important of its somewhat miscellaneous subsidiary units are the United States Fish and Wildlife Service, the Bureau of Mines, the Reclamation Bureau, the National Park Service, the Bureau of Land Management, and the Bonneville Power Administration.

INTERIOR LOT — See Inside Lot.

INTERIOR TRIM — The finish on the interior of a building; usually refers to such items as casing, molding, baseboard, etc.

INTER-JURISDICTIONAL EQUALIZATION — The adjustment of an assessment base, through the application of multipliers or factors to each individual assessment comprising the base, to a common level of assessment for all assessment or taxing jurisdictions within a state or county. Inter-jurisdictional equalization may also embrace the adjustment of individual assessments and the ordering of reassessments.

INTERNAL RATE OF RETURN (IRR) — The annualized rate of return on capital which is generated or is capable of being generated within an investment during the period of ownership. It may be the effective mortgage interest rate on a mortgage loan; it may be the Discount Rate on total property investment; or it may be the Equity Yield Rate on an equity investment. It is that rate which discounts all returns to equal the original investment. The IRR is generally considered to be the result of calculation rather than a specified or desired (given) rate of return.

INTERPOLATION — The calculation or estimation of a quantity within the range of data upon which the calculation or estimate is based; the process of approximating an intermediate value which falls between tabular entries in a set of tables.

INTERSECTION — The point at which two lines cross each other; the crossing at grade of two streets.

INTERSTATE HIGHWAY SYSTEM — A network of limited access divided highways within the United States and the District of Columbia which connect the principal metropolitan areas and industrial centers; serve the national defense, and connect with principal intercontinental routes extending into the Dominion of Canada and the Republic of Mexico.

INTESTATE — The circumstance of dying without leaving a valid will.

IN-TOWN MOTEL — Used to describe motels located within or in close proximity to the central business district of cities. "In-town motels" afford the advantages of motel-type accommodations but also may provide certain hotel services, such as valet and room service.

INTRACTABILITY — The characteristic of a soil which is difficult to work.

INTRINSIC VALUE—The amount of money which is equivalent to the worth inherent in the thing itself; for example, the intrinsic value of a bronze medal. Applies to the value of tangible assets only as separated from the intangible assets, but assuming the existence of the latter in a property. Strictly a misuse of the word value, since value depends upon extrinsic things; that is, the attitude of persons toward the thing valuable. Should never be used in the looser sense as simply adding emphasis to the value estimated for the whole.

INVENTORY APPROACH TO VALUE—Synonymous to cost approach, although approached frequently by purchasers assigning separate values in use to buildings and land.

INVENTORY VALUE—Book value. Cost of a building less any calculated depreciation allowed between date of purchase and date of valuation. Figures are generally accountant-oriented and used in financial statements.

INVERSE CONDEMNATION—A legal process by which an owner may claim damages for loss in value of the property and receive compensation when proposed condemnation action has not been instituted by the condemning body.

INVESTED CAPITAL—The original capital (equity) invested in an enterprise plus accumulated profits therefrom which are not withdrawn but allowed to remain and hence augment the initial investment.

INVESTMENT—Monies placed in a property normally with the expectation of producing a profit, assuming a reasonable degree of safety and ultimate recovery of principal; especially for long term use, as opposed to speculation.

INVESTMENT ANALYSIS—A process by which the attractiveness of an investment is determined by analyzing a number of ratios which reflect the relationship between acquisition price and anticipated future benefits from the investment. These ratios (multipliers, financial ratios, profitability) may be tested against similar ratios for alternative investment opportunities or against specific investor criteria.

INVESTMENT PROPERTY—Property which is within itself a business enterprise consisting of all tangible and intangible assets assembled and developed as a single unit of utility for lease or rental (in whole or in part) to others for profit. A type of real property which is normally purchased in expectation of annual net income and/or capital gain.

INVESTMENT TRUST—An investment type of company that raises its capital through the sale of its own stock, and invests the money received almost exclusively in the stocks and bonds of other companies, mainly common stocks. Such companies purchase stock as an investment, rather than as a means of controlling the policies of the companies in which they invest. Investment trusts are of two kinds: closed-end and open-end. Open-end are those not having a fixed number of shares and are continuously selling new shares and redeeming those offered for purchase. In contrast, closed-end trusts have a fixed number of shares, and such shares are traded on the open market in the same manner as stocks and bonds, rather than being sold and redeemed by the trust. See also Real Estate Investment Trust.

INVESTMENT VALUE—Value to a particular investor based upon individual investment requirements, as distinguished from the concept of market value, which is impersonal and detached.

INVESTMENT YIELD—The return produced by both income and resale expressed as a periodic rate. It is the rate at which both income and reversion are discounted to equal the cost of the investment.

INWOOD—William Inwood, 1771–1843. English architect, mathematician and compiler of "Tables for the Purchasing of Estates and for the Renewal of Leases Held under Corporate Bodies," first published in 1811.

INWOOD ANNUITY—A contraction of "Inwood annuity capitalization" or "Inwood annuity tables;" the name Inwood is popularly used to identify the traditional technique of using present worth factors (Inwood coefficients) from standard compound interest tables to capitalize, or discount to present worth, a stream of level income; an annuity which can be capitalized with an Inwood factor (coefficient).

INWOOD FACTOR—A factor which reflects the present worth of one dollar per period for a given number of periods discounted at a given discount rate, obtained from standard compound interest tables or by calculation; one of the classic six functions of one dollar. Synonym: Inwood coefficient.

IRREGULAR CURVE—See French Curve.

IRRIGATION—The artificial application of water to the soil for full crop production when the rainfall is not sufficient at the time of need, or in arid regions.

IRRIGATION DISTRICT—An agency established by local government and having authority to set up and operate an irrigation system for the district; and with power to levy taxes to finance its operations.

ISLAND—In highway construction, the defined land area between opposing travelways for their control or for the safety of pedestrians.

ISLAND ZONING—A planning and zoning concept which refers to the placement of a property or a small group of properties in a permitted use category which is not in conformity with the zone classification and general tenor of the neighborhood; substantially the equivalent of the legal concept of spot zoning.

ISOHYETAL LINE — An imaginary line connecting those places on the surface of the earth where the quantity of annual rainfall is about the same. It delineates the zones of different rainfall.

ITALIAN ARCHITECTURE — A style which varies from a completely balanced design to an informal composition with formal treatment and openings. Typical details include high window openings which are completely framed, often with circular heads. Roofs are covered with S-shaped red tile.

ITERATION — A process involving repetitive computations: a mathematical process of solving for an unknown quantity by trial and error, starting with a trial quantity and approaching the solution with a series of repetitive calculations until the error is negligible.

ITERATIVE ROUTINE — A computer subroutine for establishing a repeated calculation to derive a required value through repeated approximations. See Loop.

J FACTOR — An income adjustment factor used in the Ellwood method of mortgage-equity analysis in which, assuming a stable overall rate, income and value changes are projected corresponding to selected equity yield rates.

JACK RAFTER — A short roof rafter which extends from another structural framing member and not necessarily from the top of the exterior wall.

JACK STUD — An auxiliary, vertical supporting member in a frame wall or partition over a door, window or archway opening.

JALOUSIES — Adjustable glass louvers in doors or windows to regulate light and air or exclude rain.

JAMB — The side framing or finish of a doorway or window.

JERRY-BUILT — To be cheaply or poorly constructed.

JETTY — A pier or structure composed of stones, piles, etc., projecting into a body of water to protect a harbor. In construction, term is used to refer to projecting parts of a structure, such as a bay window, balcony.

JOINT — The point or place where two objects or surfaces join or meet. The space occupied by mortar or bonding material between units in a masonry wall. See also Butt Joint, Lap Joint.

JOINT PROBABILITY — The probability that two or more events will both occur.

JOINT TENANCY — Refers to the situation in which two or more individuals own inseparable interests in a parcel of real property, i.e., an individual does not own a particular part of a property, but a proportionate share of the entire property. The ownership interests of each individual expire with the individual's demise and cannot be transferred through a will, except in the case of the last survivor (the right of survivorship).

JOINT VENTURE — Joint ventures are in many ways like partnerships and are treated as such for tax purposes. The main distinction between a joint venture and a partnership is that the joint venture is a special association for a specific enterprise or project, such as constructing a building or large-scale land development, with no intention on the part of the associates to enter into a continuing partnership relationship or to assume partnership obligations and liabilities. Joint ventures cannot represent their associates and incur liabilities on their part as freely and broadly as may partners.

JOIST
1. Lumber of rectangular cross section, two inches up to, but not including, 5 inches thick, and 4 or more inches wide, graded with respect to its strength in bending when loaded either on the narrow face, the joist, or on the wide face, the plank.
2. Any of the small horizontal timbers or beams ranged in parallel, supporting a floor. See illustration, pages 304–306.

JUDGMENT — The ability to formulate an opinion, estimate, or conclusion with respect to the data or evidence presented. In appraising, the ability to render an estimate of value, usually depending on the knowledge, experience, and analytical ability of the appraiser.

JUDGMENT SAMPLING — A sample selected according to someone's personal judgment. While such samples may be biased, they are often less costly than probability samples and in certain instances may be superior, e.g., in small-scale surveys; in "pilot studies"; or in constructing index numbers.

JUNCTION BOX — A box in the electrical system where one main circuit is connected to another or where the smaller circuits join the main circuit.

JUNIOR LIEN — A lien placed on the property after a previous lien has been made and recorded or a lien made secondary to another by agreement.

JUNK VALUE — See Salvage Value.

JURISDICTION — Power, authority, control. The extent or range of such power, authority, or control. The physical territory over which such power, authority, or control is exercised.

JUST COMPENSATION—In condemnation, the amount of the loss for which a property owner has established a claim to compensation. It is the payment of the market value of the real estate which was taken.

JUSTICE, DEPARTMENT OF—A major administrative unit of the federal government, created June 22, 1870, the head of which, the attorney general, has cabinet rank. The department has certain supervisory powers over federal prosecuting agencies and provides representation in courts in cases in which the federal government is a party.

K FACTOR—A measure of heat transmission, used to rate insulating value of materials.

KALAMEIN—Trade name for galvanized sheet steel cladding of solid core wood doors.

KAME—A short irregular ridge, hill, or hillock of stratified glacial drift. Most kames are hilly and are interspersed with depressions, having no surface drainage.

KEENE'S CEMENT—A white, hard-finished plaster which sets quickly, producing an extremely durable wall; used for bathrooms and kitchens. It is made of plaster of Paris soaked in a solution of borax or alum and cream of tartar.

KEYSTONE—A wedge-shaped or trapezoidal structural piece forming the top center unit of a masonry arch. See illustration, page 303.

KICKER—A colloquialism referring to additional payments made to a lender over and above debt service. See Equity Participation.

KICK PLATE—A metal strip placed at the lower edge of a door to protect the finish.

KILN—An oven-like chamber used to bake, harden, or dry an object; a kiln in which green lumber is dried or bricks baked.

KILO—One thousand; used as a prefix, as kilogram, 1,000 grams.

KILOGRAM—One thousand grams which is 2.204 pounds avoirdupois weight.

KILOMETER—A metric linear unit of 1,000 meters. See Metric System, pages 272–277.

KILOVOLT—One thousand volts.

KILOWATT—One thousand watts.

KILOWATT HOUR (KWh)—A common unit of electrical energy consumption. One KWh is the total energy consumed when 1,000 watts are drawn for one hour.

KING POST – The vertical member at the center of a triangular truss.

KIP – A unit of weight equal to 1,000 pounds used to express dead-weight load.

KITE WINDER – A triangular-shaped (kite) step in a circular stairway at the angle where the direction of the stairway changes.

KNEE – A brace placed diagonally at the juncture of a post and beam to provide rigidity.

KNOB INSULATOR – A porcelain knob to which electric wires may be fastened. It is used in a single line, open wiring system. Rarely used in building today but used on pasture fences which are charged by a low voltage current to further confine animals to the pasture.

KNOCK DOWN – The term is used to refer to prepared construction materials which are delivered to the building site unassembled but complete and ready to be assembled and installed, such as a window.

KNOT – A defect in lumber caused by cutting through a limb at the juncture with the bole or through one embedded in a tree.

L & H HARDWARE – Door hinges and latches in "L" and "H" patterns, designed to create a colonial atmosphere.

LACUSTRINE SOIL – See Types of Soil, page 351.

LAISSEZ-FAIRE, LAISSEZ-PASSER – Let things proceed without interference. The expression was first used by French economic writers and later developed by Adam Smith into the economic concept of free trade, in opposition to basic concepts of mercantilism. Also, used to convey the concept that an individual is most productive when allowed to follow his own self-interest without external restrictions.

LALLY COLUMN – A column made of steel, usually filled with concrete, used to support beams and girders.

LAMBING GROUND – A specific point or area used in connection with sheep raising. The place where the ewes are held for grazing at lambing time. Usually it has good protection and water.

LAMELLA ROOF STRUCTURE – An arched roof-framing structure identified by the diamond-shaped arrangements of the planking with which it is formed.

LAMINATE – To build up with layers of wood, held together to form a single unit. A layer is known as a lamination or ply. The process used to produce plywood and laminated beams.

LAMINATED FLOOR – A floor deck made by gluing or spiking 2 × 4's or planks together.

LAMINATED WOOD — Wood made by lamination in which the fibers or grains of the plies used run parallel, the whole assembly being bonded together by glue or some other bonding material. In contrast, in making plywood the grain of the plies are assembled crosswise, only the fibers of the exterior plies being parallel.

LAND

1. In an economic sense, one of the major factors of production consisting sometimes of a free good, but usually of a material economic good which is supplied by nature without the aid of man. Land may include not only the earth's surface, both land and water, but also anything that is attached to the earth's surface. Thus, all natural resources in their original state, such as mineral deposits, wildlife, timber, and fish, are land within the technical meaning of the term; so also are sources of energy, outside of man himself, such as water, coal deposits, and the natural fertility of the soil.

2. In a legal sense the solid part of the surface of the earth, as distinguished from water; any ground, soil or earth whatsoever, regarded as the subject of ownership, and everything annexed to it, whether by nature, such as trees, and everything in or on it, such as minerals and running water, or annexed to it by man, such as buildings and fences.

3. Property rights in land are established on the theory that the rights in fee simple ownership in land normally include the wedge-shaped area downward from the earth's surface to the center of the earth (sub-surface rights) and the area upward from the earth's surface out into space (supra-surface or air rights). The latter is limited by Acts of Congress concerning public use of navigable air space which is considered in the public domain.

LAND/BUILDING RATIO — The proportion of land area to gross building area.

LAND CLASSIFICATION

1. The classification of specific bodies of land according to their characteristics or their capabilities for use.

2. The classification of soils into groups which have common features of position in the landscape, texture, drainage, slope, erosion, and a narrow range in rating. It includes the two rural factors of soil type and topography. See also Great Soil Groups.

LAND CONTRACT — Sometimes called "contract for deed." A contract given to a purchaser of real estate who pays a small portion of the purchase price when the contract is signed, but agrees to pay additional sums, at intervals and in amounts specified in the contract, until the total purchase price is paid and the seller gives a deed. This type of instrument is used primarily to protect the seller's interest in the unpaid balance of the purchase price since the time required to exercise foreclosure proceeding is less than in a mortgage foreclosure.

LAND COURT—A court that exercises jurisdiction over issues related to real property and interests in real property.

LAND ECONOMICS—The science that concerns land from the standpoint of its ability to meet the needs or desires of mankind.

LAND GRANT—See Land Patent.

LAND IMPROVEMENTS—Physical changes in, or construction of a more or less permanent nature attached to or appurtenant to land of such character as to increase its utility and/or value. Not a wholly informative term. See also Improvements-on-land, Improvements-to-land.

LANDING
1. The floor at the head or foot of a flight of stairs; a platform between the flights of stairs to break the rise or change the direction of their course.
2. A place or platform where goods or persons are landed as from a boat.

LANDLOCKED PARCEL—A parcel of land without access to any type of road or highway. This situation usually arises in the partial taking of land for highway purposes.

LANDOWNER'S ROYALTY—That interest in unsevered oil and gas which is retained or reserved to the landowner on the occasion of the landowner's alienation of an interest in the real property involved.

LAND PATENT—The legal document used by the federal government in conveying title to land to an individual.

LAND RECLAMATION—Making land capable of more intensive use by changing its character, environment, or both, through operations, such as drainage, provision of water, etc.

LAND RESIDUAL TECHNIQUE—A valuation technique which presumes that income can be split between land and improvements and that the residual to land can then be capitalized into value. Typically, the building is valued independently of the land, and the annual return on the building value (return on investment and provision for capital recapture) is deducted from the anticipated Net Operating Income to the property (land and building). The residual amount is said to be attributable to the land and is capitalized at the appropriate Risk (Discount) Rate to indicate the land value. For new structures, the value assigned to the building is cost, which assumes no accrued depreciation and construction at a proper current cost. If reasonably new and subject to minimal depreciation which can be satisfactorily estimated, the assigned value is the depreciated value as of the date of appraisal.

In the case of an old structure it is preferable to assume the construction cost and rental income for a hypothetical new and proper structure as the basis for estimating the net income attributable to the land.

LANDSCAPE

1. In general, a view of rural scenery, more or less extensive.
2. The natural or man-made elements which characterize one area of land from another.
3. To improve the landscape by modifying its features to obtain beautiful or advantageous effects.
4. The natural setting for a structure.

LANDSCAPING—The act of modifying an area or tract of land by the addition of improvements such as trees, shrubs, lawns, paths, gardens. The items which constitute the above.

LAND-SERVICE ROAD—A road which is used primarily to give access to land.

LAND SURVEYING—The location and identification of a parcel of land in the field by a professional surveyor or engineer.

LAND TRUST—An unincorporated association for holding real property by putting the title in one or more trustees for the benefit of the members whose interests are evidenced by land-trust certificates.

LAND USE CAPABILITIES—Based on: (1) soils, (2) relief or slope, and (3) the amount of top soil which remains. Usually determined by soil classifications indicating the various limitations on land use, e.g., guides to crop rotations, cropping practices, and recommendations to erosion control.

LAND USE MAP—An overall map of a community or section of a community which reveals the character of the land uses therein and the extent and density of each use.

LAND USE PLANNING—The development of plans for the uses of land which over a long term are considered to best serve the general welfare, together with the formulation of ways and means of achieving such uses.

LAND USE REGULATION—Broadly, any legal restriction, such as zoning ordinances which control the uses to which land may be put. A land use regulation may include such controls as those established by restrictive covenants or by redevelopment or urban renewal plans approved by local governing bodies.

LAND UTILIZATION AND MARKETABILITY STUDY (LUMS) — An analysis of demand for various uses of urban renewal land which have been approved by the local public agency in charge of the renewal program. The study evaluates the total demand for various implicit or explicit reuses in the appropriate market area. Specific demand is then allocated from the total market demand, net of that already, or likely to be allocated to areas competitive with the urban renewal land under study.

LAND VALUE MAP — An assessment map which depicts the value of land by location and expressed, depending upon the type of land involved, as value per square foot, per acre, etc.

LAP JOINT — The contact of two pieces of timber, wallpaper or other material by overlapping one on the other. See Butt Joint.

LAP SIDING — The siding used for finishing the exterior surface of a house or other structure. Also referred to as Ship Lap Siding.

LARGER PARCEL — In condemnation, that portion of a property which has unity of ownership, contiguity, and unity of use. These are the three conditions which must be present to establish the larger parcel for the purpose of considering the extent of severance damage in most states. However, in federal cases and in some state cases, the matter of contiguity is sometimes subordinated to that of unitary use. In Baetjer v. U.S. (143 Fed. 2d 391) the court held: "Integrated use, not physical contiguity, is the test of whether land condemned is part of a single tract warranting an award of severance damage."

LATERAL — Of or pertaining to the side. Anything situated at, proceeding from, or directed to a side. A lateral part or extension as any line which branches off or extends from a main line, such as the laterals of a septic system or of a central sewer line. Also used to describe an irrigation distribution ditch or pipe.

LATH — Any material used as a base for plaster including wood lath, gypsum lath, wire, and metal lath.

LATITUDE — The degree distance north or south from the equator of a point on the earth's surface as measured on the meridian through that point.

LATTICE — Any openwork panel of crossed strips, rods, or bars of wood or metal, forming a screen.

LAUNDROMAT — A commercial enterprise which provides on its premises automatic laundry equipment which is rented to customers who do their own laundering.

LAVATORY — A place where washing is done; a wash bowl. Also, a room fitted with a wash bowl and toilet facilities.

LAY OF THE LAND—An expression which indicates topographic factors.

LAYOUT—An arrangement or plan, e.g., the plan or sketch of the details of a room or the arrangement of partitions and areas constituting a floor plan of a building. A working plan for completion of a project, as for a construction job or an appraisal.

LEACH LINE—In sewage disposal, a loose tile or perforated pipeline used to distribute sewage effluent through the soil.

LEACHING—Removal of material from the soil by taking it into solution.

LEACHING TRENCHES—Trenches which carry waste liquids from sewers, constructed in gravelly or sandy soils which permit the liquids to percolate into surrounding soils, or dug in firm ground to the required depth and filled with broken stones, tile, gravel, and sand through which liquids leach.

LEADER—A pipe-like length of metal which carries rain water from the gutter to the ground or other place of disposal. Sometimes called a "downspout" or a "rain leader."

LEAN-TO—A small structure with a single pitched roof, usually erected against an outside wall of a larger structure.

LEAN-TO ROOF—A sloping roof supported on one side by the wall of an adjacent building. See illustration, page 300.

LEASE—A written document by which the rights of use and occupancy of land and/or structures are transferred by the owner to another person or entity for a specified period of time in return for a specified rental.

LEASE INTEREST—One of the dividend interests resulting from separation of the bundle of rights by a lease, i.e., the leased fee estate or the leasehold estate.

LEASEBACK—See Sale-Leaseback.

LEASED FEE—A property held in fee with the right of use and occupancy conveyed by lease to others. A property consisting of the right to receive ground rentals over a period of time, plus the right of ultimate repossession at the termination of the lease.

LEASED FEE ESTATE—The ownership interest of the owner or landlord.

LEASEHOLD—A property held under tenure of lease. The right of use and occupancy of real property by virtue of a lease agreement.
   The right of a lessee to use and enjoy real estate for a stated term and upon certain conditions, such as the payment of rent.

LEASEHOLD IMPROVEMENTS – The improvements and/or additions to leased property which have been made by the lessee.

LEASEHOLD ESTATE – A non-freehold estate, the tenant's or lessee's interest. An estate in property created by a lease.

LEASEHOLD VALUE – The value of a leasehold interest; the right to the use, enjoyment, and profit existing by virtue of the rights granted under a lease instrument. The value of a leasehold interest is the present (discounted) worth of the rent saving, when contractual rent at the time of appraisal is less than the current market rent. If land is improved by the lessee, then the value of the leasehold interest is the present value of the saving in ground rent, if any, in addition to the value (not cost) of the improvements of the lessee. If the contractual rent is greater than the currently established market rent, the present worth of the difference is subtracted from the value of the improvements.

LEAVES – The sliding, hinged, or detachable parts of a folding door, window, shutters, or table top.

LEDGER – See Ribbon Board.

LEGAL ACCESS – The right of an adjacent owner who abuts a highway to legally use it for property ingress and egress. See also Access Rights.

LEGAL DESCRIPTION – A statement containing a designation by which land is identified according to a system set up by law or approved by law. See also Geodetic System, Metes and Bounds, Public Land System, Recorded Map. See also U.S. Public Survey Diagram, page 294.

LEGAL OWNER – The owner of title; term used to distinguish the title owner from other interests, such as beneficial or possessory interests.

LENDER PARTICIPATION – The requirement of mortgage lenders that they share in the income and/or ownership of a real estate venture as a condition of the loan.

LESSEE – One who possesses the right to use or occupy a property under lease agreement; a tenant.

LESSEE'S INTEREST – The market value of the property less the value of the lessor's interest.

LESSOR – One who holds title to and conveys the right to use and occupy a property under lease agreement; a landlord.

LESSOR'S INTEREST – The present (discounted) value of the contract (lease) rents in addition to the present (discounted) value of the reversion; a leased fee.

LEVEE—An embankment preventing the overflowing of a river; one of the small continuous ridges surrounding irrigated fields.

LEVEL ANNUITY—A forecast of constant annual amounts of Net Operating Income over the income projection period.

LEVERAGE—The use of fixed cost funds to acquire an income-producing asset in the expectation of a higher rate of return on the equity investment as a result; produced by trading on equity. The extent of leverage may be determined by the relationship between the effective cost of debt and the overall rate on the property.

LICENSE—A formal agreement from a lawful source which allows a business or profession to be conducted. A franchise is a license.

LICENSEE—The person or corporate body to whom a license or franchise to conduct a business or profession is granted.

LIEN—A charge against property whereby the property is made the security for the payment of a debt.

LIFE—The period of existence or duration of a property, usually the period of anticipated physical or economic utility. See also Economic Life, Physical Life, Remaining Economic Life, Useful Life.

LIFE ANNUITY—An annuity which continues only during the lifetime of the recipient as distinguished from an annuity certain which continues for a specified period of time.

LIFE-CYCLE COST—The total costs of owning, operating, and maintaining a building or capital equipment over its useful life, including its fuel and energy costs.

LIFE-CYCLE COSTING—The analysis of the cost of an investment over its economic or useful life, often related to building energy costs. Life-cycle costs are determined on the basis of the discounted present value of aggregate future payments or benefits derived from current investments. Life-cycle costing makes apparent the trade-offs between additional dollars invested today and reduced costs in the future.

LIFE ESTATE—An ownership interest with the right of use or enjoyment limited to the owner's own life or the lifetime of another. See also Life Interest, Life Tenant.

LIFE INTEREST—An estate in real property which continues only during the life of the owner or some other designated person.

LIFE TENANT—One who owns an estate in real property for their own life or for another person's life or for an indefinite period limited by a lifetime.

LIFT SLAB—A construction system in which the floor and roof slabs are cast one on top of the other at ground level and are then jacked into position and fastened to the columns.

LIGHT — A window pane; a section of a window sash or a single pane of glass.

LIGHTERAGE — The transfer of freight between railroad terminal and various points by means of barges, floats, or lighters.

LIGHTERAGE LIMITS — The points in a harbor beyond which the railroad companies will not deliver merchandise by lighter as part of the service included in the freight rate.

LIGHTERAGE PIER — A structure, such as a dock, wharf, or quay, on which there are railroad tracks connected with railroad yards, making possible the direct transfer of freight between the railroad cars and lighters, barges, or floats.

LIGHT INDUSTRY — Used to describe those industries the physical plant requirements of which are not so extensive as those of heavy industry and the productive operations of which are not objectionable. See also Heavy Industry.

LIGHT TEXTURED SOIL — See Types of Soil, page 351.

LIGHT WELL
1. A well-like open area within a building which provides a degree of light and ventilation to inside rooms.
2. The open subsurface space around a basement window to provide light and air. Synonyms: areaway, window well.

LIME — One of the ingredients used in making plaster, mortar, and cement. It is prepared by burning limestone. The term is also used to designate any calcium compounds used to improve lime-deficient soils.

LIMEN — See Threshold.

LIMESTONE — Rocks composed essentially of calcium carbonate used extensively for building purposes and from which lime is made. It is a sedimentary deposit in the earth originating from an accumulation of the calcareous remains of organisms, such as shells.

LIMING — The act of applying ground limestone to an agricultural field.

LIMITED ACCESS HIGHWAY — See Controlled Access Highway.

LIMITED PARTNERSHIP — This form of partnership has two classes of partners: The general partners, who manage the affairs of the partnership; and the limited partners, who invest money as silent partners, with no real voice in the management, and no personal liability beyond their investment.

LIMITING CONDITION — A statement in the appraisal that the appraisal is subject to consummation (or elimination) of situations prior to the effective date of the appraisal (or completion of transaction) which items, if not done, invalidate the value conclusion.

LINE FENCE — A fence on the boundaries or perimeter of a property such as a farm or ranch.

LINE-OF-SIGHT EASEMENT — A right which prohibits the use of lands within the easement area in any way that obstructs the view of some distant area or object.

LINING — A layer of material on the inside of something. The term is used to designate the covering on the interior of a building in contrast to the covering on the exterior, the latter being the casing.

LINKAGES — Time and distance relationships between a particular use, e.g., residential, and supporting facilities as schools, shopping and employment. These uses are interrelated and they must be provided through either public or private market action.

Transfer costs can be regarded as linkages with other parcels of real estate.

LINOLEUM — A floor covering made by coating burlap on canvas with a material composed of powdered cork, powdered wood, linseed oil, pigments, and rosins which is smoked and glazed under pressure and cured by baking.

LINTEL — A piece of wood, stone, or steel placed horizontally across the top of door and window openings to support the walls immediately above the openings. See illustration, page 303.

LIQUID ASSETS — Assets which are immediately convertible into cash and therefore are immediately available for liquidating indebtedness. Synonym: quick assets.

LIQUIDATION PRICE — A forced price if there is not allowed a reasonable time to find a purchaser.

LIS PENDENS — Notice of a suit pending.

LISTING — A written contract between an owner and a broker under which the broker attempts to sell the real estate of the owner. The broker earns a specified commission when a sales contract is signed.

LISTING CONTRACT — A written agreement between an owner and a broker, employing the broker to sell the owner's real estate.

LITER (LITRE) — 61.02 cubic inches, which is slightly more than 1 quart U.S. liquid measure (1.0567 liquid quart).

LITTER — The uppermost layer of the organic debris, composed of freshly fallen or slightly decomposed organic materials. Commonly it is designated by the letter *L*.

LITTORAL — Pertaining to the shore. Sometimes that area between high and low water levels.

LITTORAL RIGHTS — The right of an owner of land which has a contiguous shore line to its use and enjoyment without change in position by artificial interference. Not to be confused with riparian rights and water rights.

LIVABILITY — The suitability of property as a place of abode. The ability of a residential property to meet the needs and desires of the typical occupant. See also Functional Utility.

LIVE — An adjective to describe a conductor or circuit when it carries a current or has a voltage on it.

LIVE LOAD — Any moving or variable superimposed load, expressed in pounds per square foot of floor and roof areas for various types of building occupancy, e.g., weight of people, merchandise, or stock on a floor; snow load or wind pressure on a roof. Consult local building code requirements. See also Dead Load, Floor Load, Total Load.

LIVESTOCK SHARE RENT — A form of rent similar to crop share rent. Usually, the landlord and tenant are equal owners in the livestock and equally divide the proceeds from sales.

LIVING TRUST — A trust which becomes effective during the lifetime of its creator; opposed to a trust under will.

LOAD
1. The weight supported by a structural part or member.
2. The power delivered by a motor, transformer, generator, power station.
3. The electrical current carried through a circuit.

LOAD-BEARING WALL — See Bearing Wall.

LOADING CHUTE — Inclined chute associated with holding pens or corrals permitting livestock to walk from ground level to dock height for loading onto trucks or rail cars.

LOAFING SHED — Open shed generally associated with feed bunks which provides livestock shelter.

LOAM — See Types of Soil, page 351.

LOAN CONSTANT — See Mortgage Constant.

LOAN-TO-VALUE RATIO — The ratio of mortgage loan to the value of security pledged. It is usually expressed as a percentage. Institutional lenders operate under various state laws which generally prescribe maximum loan ratios.

LOBBY — An inside or internal entrance way to a theatre, public building, hotel, or office building.

LOCAL GOVERNMENT — Any division of government less than a state government and which has jurisdiction over that division, as a county and a municipality, and in some states, districts, townships, authorities.

LOCAL HOUSING AUTHORITY (LHA)—A governmental entity or public body authorized to engage in the development or operation of low-rent housing. A LHA is usually an independent corporate body initially authorized to function in a locality by the governing body of the locality pursuant to state or territorial law or, in the case of the District of Columbia, by Act of Congress. In a few states municipalities are vested with this power and, in turn, create agencies with limited powers to act in their behalf.

LOCAL PUBLIC AGENCY (LPA)—An official body empowered to contract with the federal government for assistance in carrying out urban renewal projects. It may be a state, county, municipality, or other governmental entity or public body, or two or more such entities, authorized to undertake the project for which federal assistance is sought.

LOCATION—An economic characteristic of real estate composed of immobility, constant change, dependence, and elements of special distribution. Location is an economic concept, even though a location can be described in physical and legal terms.

LOCATIONAL (EXTRINSIC) OBSOLESCENCE—That loss in value experienced by a structure as a result of negative environmental forces outside the boundaries of the property. Also known as environmental obsolescence or economic obsolescence.

LOCATION ANALYSIS—A thorough study of a location in terms of a specific use, environment, time and anticipated pattern of change.

LODGING—The falling down or falling over of crops, particularly small grain and hay, due to excessive vegetative growth and/or rain and wind.

LOESS—See Types of Soil, page 351.

LOFT—An attic-like space below the roof of a house or barn; any of the upper stories of a warehouse or factory.

LOFT BUILDING—A multistoried building of open-floor design used for small light manufacturing, warehousing, and sometimes for offices.

LOG—To cut and deliver logs; also, tree segments suitable for lumber. Logs are classified as butt, peeler, or saw.

LOGARITHM—A mathematical device for substituting the labor of long multiplication and division by the simpler and speedier processes of addition and subtraction.

LOG DECK—A storage area for logs.

LOG RULES—Tables showing the calculated amount of lumber which can be sawed from logs of given length and diameter. See Diagram Rules, Formula Rules.

A board foot is a piece of lumber one inch thick and one foot square. There are not 12 board feet in one solid cubic foot in the tree or log, because a portion is lost in slab and saw kerf. The lumber recovery usually is about eight board feet per cubic foot of wood (12 board feet).

Ordinarily, there is an overrun when timber estimates are based upon log rules because of the premise that only one-inch boards will be cut. When thicker boards are cut from the log there is less saw kerf wastage.

Log rules provide a means of measuring the actual board foot volume in the log by allowing for waste in slabs and sawdust. There are several different log rules but only three are in common use in the redwood region. See also Humboldt Rule, Scribner Rule, Spaulding Rule.

LOG SCALE—The measurement of felled trees (length of tree or log to a top fixed diameter in relation to the diameter at the larger end) reflected in volume tables.

LONGITUDE—The degree distance east or west on the earth's surface as measured by the angle between the meridian of a particular place and a prime meridian as that of Greenwich, England.

LONGITUDINAL—Of or pertaining to longitude or length; extending in the direction of the length; running lengthwise.

LONG–LIVED ITEMS—Those basic structural components which in the normal course of events have economic lives as long as the economic life of the entire structure.

LONG–TERM LEASE—Generally considered to be a lease agreement extending for 10 years or more. Its terms and provisions are customarily set forth in detail in legally correct and complete form. Under such leases the tenant may desire, or be required, to do extensive remodeling; or if the property leased is land, to construct a building or other improvements.

LOOP—A group of instructions repeated one or more times in a calculation until a prescribed condition is satisfied. See Iterative Routine.

LOSS OF ACCESS—The depriving of an abutting owner of inherent rights of ingress and egress to the abutting highway or street.

LOT—A distinct portion or piece of land; a piece of land forming a part of a district, community, city block, etc. The smaller portion into which a city block or subdivision is divided, described by reference to a recorded plat or by definite boundaries. Also, a piece of land in one ownership, whether platted or unplatted.

LOT AND BLOCK DESCRIPTION—See Recorded Map.

LOT LINE—The boundary line of a plot of ground as legally described in the title to the property.

LOUVER (LOUVRE)—Slats or fins over an opening, pitched so as to keep out rain or snow. A finned sunshade on a building. The diffusion grill on fluorescent light fixtures.

LOWER LOW WATER—The lower of the two low waters of any tidal day. Over a considerable period of time the mean value of the lower low waters is used as the plane of reference (charts datum) for hydrographic work on the coasts of the United States.

LOW FREQUENCY—An electric current which has a small number of cycles per second.

LOW WATER LINE—The point on the shore to which the tide ebbs. It will vary with seasons, time, wind, and other causes. See also Mean Low Water Line.

LUMBER—The product of the saw and planing mill; it receives no further processing by sawing, resawing, passing lengthwise through a standard planing mill, or crosscutting to length. Lumber is classified as veneer when the thickness is not in excess of ¼ inch and is to be used for veneering. Other lumber is classified as boards, clear, dimension, factory and shop, green, joist, plank, scantling, strip, structural, timber, and yard.

LUMINOUS CEILING—A suspended ceiling of translucent materials, above which is installed a system of fluorescent tubes, making the entire ceiling the source of light; a practice which greatly reduces glare and shadows.

M ROOF—A type of roof which is made up of two double-pitch roofs. This type of construction has two advantages: it utilizes shorter material for rafters and reduces the elevation of the building. See illustration, page 300.

MAI—Member Appraisal Institute; a professional designation conferred by the American Institute of Real Estate Appraisers of the National Association of Realtors; conferral of the designation denotes competence in the field of real estate valuation and evaluation, limited only by the depth and breadth of the individual appraiser's training, skills and experience. The designation is conferred on candidates who have met the Institute's requirements of experience, education, and extensive examinations on appraisal procedures and who have pledged themselves to adhere to the Code of Professional Ethics and Standards of Professional Conduct of AIREA.

MBM—In forestry, an abbreviation for thousand boardfoot measurement.

MACHINE SHED—A farm building used for the storage of farm machinery. It generally has an open wall on one side.

MADE-LAND—Ground which is formed by filling in natural or artificial pits with rubbish or other material. The creation of additional land along a shore by extending the shore line farther into the water; usually the fill is dredged sand.

MAGNESITE FLOORING—A composition flooring made of calcined magnesite and magnesium-chloride solution with a filler of sawdust, wood flour, ground silica, or quartz. It is used to cover concrete floors on which it is floated in a layer about 1½ inches in thickness.

MAIN—A large pipe or conduit; the main line or conduit which carries the larger load to or from branch lines.

MAIN CIRCUIT—An electric circuit which carries a heavy electrical load to the branch circuits of the distribution system.

MAINTENANCE—The act of keeping, or the expenditures required to keep a property in condition to perform efficiently the service for which it is used. Such expenditures do not extend the useful life of the property. In contrast with betterment, it is upkeep of a fixed asset which preserves its value, but does not increase the book value. See also Deferred Maintenance, Replacement.

MAINTENANCE RESERVE—An amount reserved to cover costs of maintenance. Its object is to spread equitably over operations the individual costs of maintenance, although these costs may actually be incurred at irregular intervals and in unequal amounts.

MALL—Originally, a shaded walk. The term has been adopted to designate an area in a retail section or center designed for pedestrian use only.

MANAGEMENT—The act of directing or conducting affairs. One of the elements of overhead or undistributed construction costs. See also Farm Management, Property Management.

MANAGEMENT FEE—As an item of expense, the sum paid or the amount equivalent to the value of management service.

MANAGEMENT PROGRAM—Definite aims in directing and/or conducting the management of a property together with the manner or means by which such aims could be achieved.

MANIFOLD—Having many different parts, elements, features as the juncture of many small pipes with a larger pipe or main.

MANSARD ROOF—A roof with two slopes or pitches on each of the four sides, the lower slopes steeper than the upper. Convenient for adding another story to a building. See illustration, page 300.

MANTISSA—In floating point arithmetic, the mantissa designates the fractional part of a number. See also Characteristic.

MARGINAL—Situated on the border or edge. In economics, marginal refers to supplying goods at a rate merely covering the cost of production. In real estate, marginal applies to any property earning an income which is sufficient to cover only operating costs.

MARGINAL LAND—That which barely pays the cost of working or using. Land whereon the costs of labor, coordination (management), and capital approximately equal the gross income. See also Factors in Production.

MARGINAL PROBABILITY—The probability of the occurrence of a single event, determined as the sum of the joint probabilities involving that event.

MARGINAL UTILITY—At any given point of consumption, the addition to total utility by the last unit of a good. In general, the greater the number of items, the less the marginal utility; that is, the greater the amount of an item or product, the less the value of each item comprising the amount.

MARGINAL UTILITY SCHOOL—A school of economic thought developed primarily through the writings of Karl Menger, W.S. Jevons, and Leon Walras who explained the relationship between desirability and price by reference to the marginal utility concept; that is, the added amount of satisfaction from an additional unit of a good.

MARINA—A boat basin offering dockage and other services for small craft.

MARINE SOIL—See Types of Soil, page 351.

MARKET—A set of arrangements for bringing buyers and sellers together through the price mechanism. The real estate market reflects attitudes and opinions in the minds of buyers and sellers and their actions in the market create market data.

MARKETABILITY—State of being salable.

MARKETABILITY STUDY—A study to determine to what extent a particular piece of property can be marketed or sold under current or anticipated market conditions. It is inclusive of a market study (analysis) of the general class of property being considered.

MARKETABLE TITLE—A title not subject to such reasonable doubt as would create a just apprehension of invalidity in the mind of a reasonable, prudent, and intelligent person; one for which a person of reasonable prudence and intelligence, guided by competent legal advice, would be willing to accept and pay fair value.

MARKET ANALYSIS—A dynamic process involving the projection and analysis of the components of demand.

MARKET AREA – That geographic area or political jurisdiction within which alternative similar properties are effectively competitive with the subject property in the minds of probable potential purchasers.

MARKET DATA APPROACH – Traditionally, an appraisal procedure in which the market value estimate is predicated upon prices paid in actual market transactions and current listings, the former fixing the lower limit of value in a static or advancing market (price wise), and fixing the higher limit of value in a declining market; and the latter fixing the higher limit in any market. It is a process of analyzing sales of similar recently sold properties in order to derive an indication of the most probable sales price of the property being appraised. The reliability of this technique is dependent upon (a) the availability of comparable sales data, (b) the verification of the sales data, (c) the degree of comparability or extent of adjustment necessary for time differences, and (d) the absence of non-typical conditions affecting the sales price.

In essence, all approaches to value (particularly when the purpose of the appraisal is to establish market value) are market data approaches since the data inputs are presumably market derived. See Direct Sales Comparison Approach.

MARKET PRICE – The amount actually paid, or to be paid, for a property in a particular transaction.

Differs from market value in that it is an accomplished or historic fact, whereas market value is and remains an estimate until proved. Market price involves no assumption of prudent conduct by the parties, of absence of undue stimulus or of any other condition basic to the market value concept.

MARKET RENT – The rental income that a property would most probably command on the open market as indicated by current rentals being paid for comparable space (as of the effective date of the appraisal). This is preferred terminology to the term "Economic Rent" which has traditionally been used in appraisal analysis.

MARKET RENTAL RISK – The risk that rents will change significantly while the property is subject to a fixed-rental long-term lease.

MARKET STUDY – The comparison of market analysis projections with the supply of space for a specified activity in an effort to identify market opportunities.

MARKET SURVEY – See Market Study.

MARKET VALUE – The most probable price in terms of money which a property should bring in competitive and open market under all conditions requisite to a fair sale, the buyer and seller, each acting prudently, knowledgeably and assuming the price is not affected by undue stimulus.

Implicit in this definition is the consummation of a sale as of a specified date and the passing of title from seller to buyer under conditions whereby:

1. buyer and seller are typically motivated.
2. both parties are well informed or well advised, and each acting in what they consider their own best interest.
3. a reasonable time is allowed for exposure in the open market.
4. payment is made in cash or its equivalent.
5. financing, if any, is on terms generally available in the community at the specified date and typical for the property type in its locale.
6. the price represents a normal consideration for the property sold unaffected by special financing amounts and/or terms, services, fees, costs, or credits incurred in the transaction.

Numerous definitions of Market Value have been devised over the years by professional organizations, government bodies, courts, et cetera.

The Supreme Courts of most states have handed down definitions of Market Value for use in the state courts. These definitions are subject to frequent change.

Persons performing appraisal services which may be subject to litigation are cautioned to seek the exact definition of Market Value in the jurisdiction in which the services are being performed. See Most Probable Sales (Selling) Price.

MARQUEE – A permanent hood which projects over an entrance to a building and is not supported by posts or columns.

MASONRY

1. Anything constructed of stone, brick, tile, cement, concrete, and similar materials.
2. The work done by a mason who works in stone, brick, cement, tile, or concrete.

MASONRY WALL – A wall of stone, brick, tile, cement block, concrete, etc.

MASS APPRAISING – The process of valuing a universe of properties as of a given date, in a uniform order, utilizing standard methodology, employing a common reference for data, and allowing for statistical testing.

MASSACHUSETTS TRUST – A form of business organization which is neither a corporation nor a partnership, conducting its business through a trustee or trustees who hold legal title to the property of the business. Capital contributions are made to the trustees by the beneficiaries whose equitable title and interests in the property of the trust are evidenced by trust certificates. The earnings of the trust are paid to them, as dividends are paid to stockholders. The beneficiaries may enjoy limited liability, but the control and management of the trust rests solely with the trustees.

MASTER PLAN – A comprehensive, long-range plan officially recognized as a guide for the physical growth and development of a community, together with the basic regulatory and administrative controls needed to attain the physical objectives. Basic components of the plan for physical development are: land use plan, thoroughfare plan, community facilities plan, and public improvements program. Synonyms: city plan, general plan, comprehensive community plan.

MASTIC – An adhesive material used to cement two surfaces together; also an elastic caulking compound.

MAT FOUNDATION – See Floating Foundation.

MATCHED BOARDS – See Tongue and Groove.

MEADOW – See Types of Range Vegetation, page 349.

MEAN – A measure of central tendency of data; a calculated average. See also Arithmetic Average, Geometric Average, Median, Mode, Moving Average, Weighted Average.

MEAN DEVIATION – See Average Deviation.

MEAN HIGH WATER LINE – The point on the shore which is the mean distance between tide rises, as ascertained through a long series of observations of the rise and fall of tides. This line, as of an established date, is often the seaward boundary line of privately owned upland. See also Mean Low Water Line, Ordinary High Water Mark.

MEAN LOW WATER LINE – The point on the shore which is the mean distance between tide ebbs, as ascertained through a long series of observations of the rise and fall of tides.

MEANDER – A winding course.

MEANDER LINE – A line designed to point out the curves and lines of the bank or shore; a survey line to establish the bank or shoreline of a stream or lake.

MECHANIC'S LIEN – Lien given by statute to those who perform labor, services or furnish materials in the improvement of real property.

MEDIAN – The value of the middle item where an odd number of items are arranged (arrayed) according to size; or the arithmetic average of the two central items if there is an even number of items. It is a positional average and is not affected by the size of extreme values. See illustration, page 316.

MEDIAN STRIP — In highway construction, a section or strip down the center of the highway dividing opposing lanes of traffic. It may be a narrow concrete buffer, or a wider landscaped strip.

MEDIUM TEXTURED SOIL — See Types of Soil, page 351.

MEETING RAIL — Same as Check Rail.

MELLOW — See Types of Soil, page 351.

MEMBRANE — A thin sheet or film of waterproof material used to prevent the movement of moisture through a floor or wall.

MERCANTILISM — A political and economic theory of the 16th and 17th centuries, that precious metals are the most important form of wealth and that maintaining an excess of exports over imports is the best way to increase their supply at home. Achievement of this goal implies the need for governmental control of exports, imports, wages, and prices. It was the effect of mercantilism which led Adam Smith to develop his theory of free trade.

MERGE LINE — When a parcel extends from one street to another street in the rear, the merge line is that which divides the parcel into two parts, in such a manner that the highest total value (of the two parts) will be developed, if each is considered a separate lot valued on the basis of the front foot unit value modified by the depth factor for the depth to the merge line.

MERGER — The absorption through the vesting of control of two or more corporations in a single one by the issuing of stock in the controlling corporation in place of a majority of stock in the others, usually without the dissolution of the individual companies. The act of creating common land ownerships for adjacent ownerships that were formerly owned separately. See also Consolidation, Assemblage.

MERIDIAN
1. A great circle of the earth passing through the poles and any given point on the earth's surface.
2. In government survey, the true north and south lines which run from a base line, at which point they are 24 miles apart. More commonly referred to as guide meridians. See also Base Line, Range, Standard Parallels.

MESQUITE — See Types of Range Vegetation, page 349.

METAL CLAD BUILDING — A building sheathed in metal.

METAL LATH — A sheet of metal slit at intervals; when expanded the grille-like panel forms a base for plaster.

METAL VALLEY — See Flashing.

METAMORPHIC ROCK – A rock the constitution of which has undergone pronounced alteration. Such changes are generally effected by the combined actions of pressure, heat, and water. Frequently, it results in a more compact and crystalline condition of the rock.

METES AND BOUNDS – A description of a parcel of land by reference to the courses (bearings, that is, the angles east or west of due north or due south) and distances (usually in feet or chains) of each straight line which forms its boundary, with one of the corners tied to an established point; that is, the bearing and distance from an established point, such as a section corner, or to the intersection of the center lines of two roads, etc.

If one part of the boundary is on a curve, this part is described by showing the number of degrees of the central angle subtended by the curve (arc), the length of the radius, and the length along the curve.

METROPOLITAN AREA PLAN – An extension and adaptation of the fundamentals of general community planning to embrace an entire metropolitan area, or group of municipalities and suburban neighborhoods.

METROPOLITAN SHOPPING CENTER – A tract of land improved with a coordinated group of retail buildings with a full variety of types of stores, one or more department stores, parking facilities, under single ownership or control, and catering to an entire metropolitan area.

MEZZANINE – An intermediary floor having less area than the regular floors. In a theatre, a shallow balcony between the main floor and the first balcony.

MICRORELIEF – Surface irregularity. A term used by farm appraisers to describe slight land surface irregularity, such as smooth channels, hogwallows, low hummocks, high hummocks, and dunes.

MIDDLE RAIL – The center horizontal structural member. See illustration, page 304.

MILK HOUSE – A building associated with dairies used exclusively for the storage of milk.

MILK PARLOR – A building associated with dairies used exclusively for milking cows.

MILL CONSTRUCTION – Slow burning; substantial self-supporting brick or other masonry walls carrying wood roof and floor decks much thicker than in ordinary joist construction, supported by heavy timber framing; avoidance of corners, projections, and small section members which ignite easily; separation of stories by incombustible fire stops and elevator hatches, and encasement of stairways by incombustible partitions.

In Standard Mill Construction relatively thick plank flooring is laid directly on heavy timber beams 8 feet to 11 feet o.c., which in turn are supported (usually) by wood posts.

"Mill Construction with Laminated Floors" consists of the same general construction except that the plank flooring is laid on edge and supported by girders 12 to 18 feet on center.

In Semi-mill Construction, plank floors are laid on heavy beams 4 to 19 feet o.c., which in turn are supported by heavy girders. The beams are either set on the girders or are carried by metal hangers. See also Slow-burning Construction.

MILL-CUT ESTIMATE — See Will-Cut Cruise.

MILLWORK — Generally all building materials made of finished wood and manufactured in millwork plants and planing mills are included under the term millwork; for example, doors, window and door frames, sash, blinds, porch work, mantels, panel work, stairways, and special woodwork. It does not include finish dressed four sides, or siding, or partition, which are items of yard lumber.

MINERAL RIGHTS — See Subsurface Rights.

MINERAL WOOL — Insulation material made by blasting molten slag or rock with steam. Such materials are known as rock wool, glass wool, etc.

MINER'S INCH — A flow of 1/50th or 1/40th of a cubic foot per second. See Measures, page 274.

MINIMUM LOT — A zoning regulation establishing the minimum acceptable size of lots which can be developed in an area or community.

MINIMUM RENTAL — The base (fixed) payment in a percentage lease.

MISCELLANEOUS VALUES — Numerous descriptive terms have been applied to the term value in attempting to add to or take from the basic concept of Market Value.

Among these adjectives are: Actual Cash, Amenity, Antique, Appraised, Assemblage, Capitalized, Caprice, Cash, Commercial, Comparative, Condemnation, Conservative, Depreciated, Economic, Equitable, Face, Fair, Fair Market, Forced Sale, Full, Improved, Inheritance, Intangible, Intrinsic, Junk, Liquidation, Loan, Long Term, Mortgage Loan, Net, Nuisance, Occupancy, Physical, Plottage, Potential, Present, Real, Remainder, Salvage, Scarcity, Scrap, Sentimental, Speculative, Stabilized, True, Upset, Warranted.

These terms, for the most part, are used in an attempt to modify market value to serve the specific need of an occasion. As such, they are usually incorrect and can be the cause of unethical practice and serious misunderstanding.

MISPLACED IMPROVEMENT – Improvements (on land) of a type which do not conform to the most profitable use-type for the site.

A structure which is out of place or which does not conform to its environs in the matter of architectural design, age, or type; e.g., a "contemporary" dwelling among a group of "Victorian" mansions; or a newer ranch type single-family dwelling among 30-year-old duplexes or two flats.

While the improvement may be architecturally, functionally, and physically acceptable in a proper location, it may be subject to environmental (locational) obsolescence by reason of being misplaced. Whether environmental obsolescence affects value adversely is revealed by market action.

MISSION ARCHITECTURE – Design following the characteristics of early California missions, generally Spanish in style.

MOBILE HOME – A house trailer; a complete livable dwelling unit equipped with wheels so that it may be towed from place to place by a truck or automobile, depending on its size and the highway regulations of the states through which it will travel.

MOBILE HOME PARK – See Trailer Park.

MOBILITY – In real estate, the ease with which people can move from one location to another.

MODE – The most frequent value in an array of numbers. It is a positional average, the typical value; and its value is independent of extreme items. It is the most descriptive average and may be easily approximated by observation where there are a small number of items; however, if the number of items is too small, none of the values may be repeated and thus no mode exists. See illustration, page 317.

MODERN ARCHITECTURE – Contemporary, functional design, intended to combine esthetic quality and utility in a home.

MODERN COLONIAL (NEW ENGLAND) ARCHITECTURE – A residential style usually having two full stories; dormers may be added to a third floor space. Windows are divided into small panes. The houses are typically simple in design, and have good functional utility.

MODERN ENGLISH ARCHITECTURE – A style having many features of the earlier English styles, including steep roof slopes of variegated and graduated slate or red tile, and absence of cornices or eaves. Windows are of the casement type, made of wood or metal. Rooms and spaces are arranged informally. It is especially suitable for sloping ground.

MODERN GEORGIAN ARCHITECTURE – Stately, symmetrical, perfectly scaled houses which are modern counterparts of the houses built in England during the reign of the four Georges. They are extremely conventional in character.

MODERNIZATION—The process of taking corrective measures to bring a property into conformity with changes in style, whether exterior or interior or additions necessary to meet standards of current demand. It normally involves replacing parts of the structure or mechanical equipment with modern replacements of the same kind and hence seldom includes capital improvements.

MODIFIED INTERNAL RATE OF RETURN (MIRR)—An internal rate of return (IRR) concept which holds that all negative cash flows up to the first positive cash flow are part of investment capital, but successive cash flows are the result of the investment beyond time period zero. All subsequent cash flows beyond the first positive cash flow whether negative or positive are discounted using standard discounting procedures. In other words, all subsequent cash flows are discounted at a rate such that they exactly equal the adjusted capital outlay. That rate is the modified internal rate of return.

MODULE—A standard measure, of any size, used in construction and design, adopted to allow repetition in design and use, and saving in material and labor costs.

MOISTURE BARRIER—The insulation material placed in a wall, floor or other parts of a structure to form a barrier against the passage of vapor or moisture in order to prevent condensation within such walls or floor.

MOISTURE EQUIVALENT—The amount of water retained (in percentage) by a soil against a force of 1,000 times that of gravity. This arbitrarily determined moisture percentage has been correlated with other soil properties, such as moisture-holding capacity, wilting percentage, texture, etc.

MOLDING—A finishing piece, usually a long, narrow strip of plain or curved wood used to cover a joint, e.g., formed by the ceiling and the wall; may be ornamented.

MONEY—Any generally accepted medium of exchange and unit of account. In common usage, the term refers to currency; that is, minted coins and paper money issued by a government for legal exchange or tender.

MONITOR—A raised structure on a roof having windows or louvers for ventilating or lighting the building, as a factory or warehouse.

MONITOR ROOF—A type of framing which includes an elevated central section. It is generally encountered in industrial buildings and provides better lighting and ventilation.

MONOLITHIC — One piece. Monolithic concrete is poured in a continuous process so there are no separations or joints due to different setting times.

MONOPOLY — In the broadest sense, a market in which one person or a group controls the supply of a good and thus is able to control its price.

MONOPOLY PROPERTY — A property used by an enterprise, which through franchise, license, zoning regulation, etc., has the exclusive right to carry on that enterprise.

MONTEREY ARCHITECTURE — The two-story style adapted from the architecture prevalent in the early Spanish era in California. Usually, it is characterized by a balcony across the entire front of the building.

MONUMENT — A stone or other fixed object used to establish real estate boundaries.

MONUMENTS DESCRIPTION — A method of property description by reference to natural or man-made objects in the field.

MOP BOARD — See Baseboard.

MORAINE — A mass of material deposited by a glacier commonly at the front (terminal moraine) or along the sides (lateral moraine) of the glacier. Usually, it consists of a more or less irregular ridge deposited as the ice melted along the rim of the glacier at a rate about equal to its forward flow.

MORTAR — A pasty substance of lime and/or cement mixed with sand and water which hardens when exposed to the air; used as a bonding material in brick and stone work.

MORTGAGE — A legal document pledging a described property for the performance of the repayment of a loan under certain terms and conditions. See also Amortized Mortgage.

MORTGAGE BANKER — Those who make mortgage loans on their own behalf with their own funds, usually in the expectation of reselling the loans to lenders at a profit and servicing them.

MORTGAGE BROKER — One who places mortgages (finds appropriate borrowers or willing lenders) for a fee which is usually a percentage of the amount of the loan.

MORTGAGE COEFFICIENT — A multiplier used in the Ellwood formula to compute an overall rate "R_o." The mortgage coefficient is a function of the terms of the mortgage loan, the projected period of ownership and the equity-yield rate. The mortgage coefficient is designated by the symbol C in the Ellwood formulas and may be found for a selected range or mortgage terms, projection periods and yield rates in the Ellwood Tables.

MORTGAGE CONSTANT—The total annual payments of principal and interest (annual debt service) on a mortgage with level-payment amortization schedule, expressed as a percentage of the initial principal amount of the loan.

MORTGAGE CORRESPONDENT—One who acts as an agent for national lenders and makes loan commitments for them in terms of standards of acceptability established by lender. A mortgage correspondent also frequently services the loans for the lender for an additional fee.

MORTGAGE DEED—A deed by way of mortgage which has the effect of a mortgage on the property conveyed and imposes a lien on the granted estate.

MORTGAGEE—The party who advances the funds for a mortgage loan and in whose favor the property serving as security is mortgaged; the lender.

MORTGAGE–EQUITY—Capitalization and investment analysis procedures which recognize the influence of mortgage terms and equity requirements in the valuation of income properties.

MORTGAGE NOTE—A document or clause in a document in which the borrower agrees to become personally responsible to repay a debt.

MORTGAGE REQUIREMENT—The installment or periodic level payment required for debt service (interest plus principal) on a direct reduction loan; the installment for amortization and interest, also called the partial payment; when annualized (12 × monthly payment, 4 × quarterly payment, etc.) it is the same as the annual constant; one of the classic six functions of one dollar.

MORTGAGE RISK RATING—The process of thoroughly analyzing the major factors of risk undertaken in the making of a mortgage in accordance with the risk involved in the loan transaction or in connection with insurance of the mortgage. It serves as a basis for the classification of mortgages in accordance with their quality as investments.

MORTGAGE VALUE—Value for mortgage purposes, usually market value.

MORTGAGOR—One who gives a mortgage as security for a loan; the borrower.

MORTISE—A notch or hole cut in a piece of wood or other material to receive a projecting part (called the tenon) of another piece of material for the purpose of joining the two.

MOSAIC—A decoration in which small pieces of glass, stone, ceramic or other material are laid in mortar or mastic to form a design.

MOST APPROPRIATE USE—A planning and zoning concept applicable to that use of land which: (1) will promote the greatest good for the greatest number; (2) is in the best interests of the community as a whole. It may or may not be the highest and best use. Likewise, it may or may not be a present use or it may be a future use.

MOST PROBABLE SALES (SELLING) PRICE—That price at which a property would most probably sell if exposed to the market for a reasonable time, under market conditions prevailing as of the date of the appraisal. See also Market Value.

MOST PROBABLE USE—Highest and best use in the context of market value.

MOST PROFITABLE USE—Highest and best use in the context of investment value.

MOTEL—In general, a building or group of buildings located on or near highways which are designed to serve the needs of travelers and offer as a minimum only lodging and parking. However, they may afford any number of other services and amenities, such as telephone, food and beverage, recreational areas, service station, shops. See also Highway Hotel, In-town Motel, Resort Motel.

MOTEL-HOTEL—A term used to designate motels, the services and operations of which most closely approximate those of a hotel.

MOULDED BASE—A two-member base consisting of a common base with moulding above, or a three-member base consisting of a common base, base mould above, and a shoe mould below. See Sanitary Base. See illustration, page 307.

MOVING AVERAGE—In statistics, successive arithmetic averages or arithmetic means developed by eliminating the first item in each averaged group and adding the next quantity in the series, thereby arriving at the succeeding average or mean; used to reduce fluctuations in a graph or curve designed to reflect a pattern or trend.

MUCK—See Types of Soil, page 351.

MULLION—Thin vertical bars of wood, lead, or stone which divide multiple windows, panes of glass, wall panels, screens, etc. Not to be confused with muntin.

MULTICOLLINEARITY—The phenomenon of two or more variables being correlated. If the two correlated variables are both independent variables (obviously if they are correlated they are not truly independent in the relationship sense) used to predict the value of some other dependent variable, then modeling problems will arise. If the multicollinearity is perfect, the MRA algorithms simply will not work; if the multicollinearity is serious but imperfect, the coefficients generated by the algorithm will be individually meaningless (although the model as a whole may still be useful).

MULTIFAMILY HOUSING (FHA Section 207) — A section of Title 11 of the National Housing Act under which the FHA insures mortgages, including advances made during construction, on multifamily rental housing projects of eight or more units.

MULTILEG INTERSECTION — A road intersection with five or more travel routes.

MULTIPLE REGRESSION ANALYSIS — Measuring the simultaneous influence of a number of independent variables on one dependent variable.

MULTIPLE USE — Harmonious use of range for more than one of the following purposes: grazing of livestock, wildlife production, recreation, watershed, and timber production. Not necessarily the combination of uses that will yield the highest economic return or greatest unit output. Not synonymous with Highest and Best Use.

MULTIPLIER — A figure which, times the income, produces an estimate of value. It is called a gross income multiplier when gross income is used, and a net income multiplier when net income is used. May be monthly or annual.

MUNTIN — Slender horizontal bars of wood or metal dividing lights in a window or panels in a door. See illustration, page 310.

NATIONAL ECONOMY — The economic life of a nation. The term implies that the economic life of a nation forms a unified whole.

NATIONAL INCOME — The total net earnings ascribable to the various factors employed in the production of goods and services in a nation during a particular period.

NATIONAL WEALTH — The total money value at any particular time of all the material economic goods possessed by members of a given nation.

NATIVE PLANTS — Plants native to an area and not introduced as a result of man's activities.

NATURAL FEATURES — Those features or elements of man's physical environment which are the result of natural causes rather than those created or erected by man. These would include such features as rivers, plains, hills, valleys, minerals, etc.

NATURAL LAND CLASSIFICATION — A classification of soils into groups which have common features of position in landscape, texture, drainage, slope, erosion, and a narrow range in rating. It includes the two rural factors of soil type and topography. See Great Soil Groups.

NATURAL RESOURCE PROPERTY — A property involving primarily recoverable or adaptable resources of nature which may be or are susceptible to being commercially exploited. Property containing deposits of valuable material laid down by nature, such as rock, sand, gravel, or clay; oil, gas, coal; and metallic minerals. The enterprise utilizing these resources is known as an extractive industry.

NATURAL RESOURCES—Wealth supplied by nature. Mineral deposits, soil fertility, timber, potential water power, and fish and wildlife are included in the concept. See also, Natural Resource Property.

NATURAL SEASONING—The seasoning or drying of lumber by stacking to permit free circulation of air around each timber.

NAVIGABLE WATERS—Those waters, either fresh or salt, which form in ordinary conditions, by themselves or by uniting with other waters, a continued highway over which commerce may be carried on with other states or foreign countries.

NEGATIVE LEVERAGE—The magnification of financial losses resulting from borrowing when the cost of capital exceeds the return on capital; reverse leverage; negative leverage magnifies loss, whereas positive leverage magnifies profits.

NEIGHBORHOOD—A portion of a larger community, or an entire community, in which there is a homogenous grouping of inhabitants, buildings, or business enterprises. Inhabitants of a neighborhood usually have a more than casual community of interest. Neighborhood boundaries may consist of well-defined natural or man-made barriers or they may be more or less well-defined by a distinct change in land use or in the character of the inhabitants.

NEIGHBORHOOD ANALYSIS—The objective analysis of observable and/or quantifiable data indicating discernible patterns of urban growth, structure, and change that may detract from or enhance property values.

NEIGHBORHOOD LIFE CYCLE—The life of a neighborhood, usually involving the following stages, varying only in intensity and duration: development and growth; stability; transition and decline. This pattern may be followed by renewal and rehabilitation, at which point the cycle is repeated.

NEIGHBORHOOD SHOPPING CENTER—A tract of land improved with a coordinated group of retail buildings providing a limited variety of convenience goods and service facilities, free parking, under single ownership or control, and catering to a limited trade area (neighborhood), usually consisting of from 10 to 30 stores.

NET CASH PROCEEDS OF RESALE—The net reversionary interest (before taxes) to the equity position, i.e., net of sales commissions and mortgage debt outstanding at the time of resale. See also After-Tax Net Cash Proceeds of Resale.

NET EARNINGS — See Net Operating Income.

NET GROUND LEASE — The lease of unimproved land with the lessee agreeing to accept and pay the owner's expenses, such as the ad valorem taxes, assessments, and all expenses for any improvements created by the lessee.

NET INCOME MULTIPLIER — The relationship between price or value and net income expressed as a factor: the reciprocal of the overall rate.

NET INCOME RATIO — The ratio of net income to effective gross income; the fraction of gross income which remains after deducting all expenses except depreciation and debt service; the complement of the expense ratio.

NET LEASE — A lease where, in addition to the rental stipulated, the lessee assumes payment of all property charges, such as taxes, insurance, assessments, and maintenance. In some areas, the degree of "netness" is expressed as a "net, net" or "net, net, net" lease. These latter terms are considered synonymous with "net" lease and their use is redundant.

NET OPERATING INCOME (NOI) — Annual net income remaining after deducting all fixed and operating expenses but before deducting financial charges such as recapture or debt service; same as annual dividend. In mortgage-equity formulas, designated by the symbol d. Sometimes referred to as Net Income Before Recapture (NIBR) or Net Income Before Depreciation (NIBD).

NET PRESENT VALUE (NPV) — The difference, if any, between the cost of an investment and the discounted present value of all anticipated future benefits to that investment. Generally, where NPV is positive, the proposal (investment) is acceptable; where NPV is zero, the proposal is marginally acceptable; and where NPV is negative, the proposal is unacceptable.

NET SALES — The gross sales less returns and allowances including freights, trade discounts, etc.

NET SALES AREAS — As applied to department or retail store, the area available for sale of merchandise, excluding storage, equipment, rest rooms, etc.; the actual floor area used for merchandising.

NET SPENDABLE INCOME — Cash throw-off less income tax liability; more appropriately referred to as after-tax cash flow.

NET WORTH — The measure of the equity capital reflected upon the balance sheet of a business as of a certain date and represented by the outstanding capital stock plus the surplus and undivided profits; properly, the excess of the value of the assets over the liabilities.

NEUTRAL SOIL — See Types of Soil, page 351.

NEWEL—The vertical post at the top and bottom of a stairway or at a landing turn, which supports the handrail. It is also used to designate the post about which a circular stairway winds.

NEW ENGLAND COLONIAL (SALT BOX) ARCHITECTURE—A type of comfortable dwelling developed by New England carpenters who attempted to imitate in wood some of the classic motifs of the Georgian houses of brick and stone. They are generally of clapboard exterior, are painted white, and have shingle roofs, and have excellent proportions. Exterior openings are often treated with moldings of refined detail.

NIBD—Net income before depreciation. See Net Operating Income.

NIBR—Net income before recapture. See Net Operating Income.

NOGGING
1. Brick filling in the spaces of a frame wall.
2. Pieces of wood inserted in a masonry wall to receive nails.

NOMINAL INTEREST RATE—A stated or contract rate; an interest rate (usually an annual rate) which does not necessarily correspond to the true or effective rate of growth at compound interest (e.g., a true or effective periodic interest rate of 1% monthly may be called a nominal annual interest rate of 12%, even though true or effective growth with monthly compounding would amount to slightly more than 12.68% per annum). See Effective Interest Rate.

NOMOGRAM—A diagram, chart or arrangement or scales used for the graphic solution of problems with fixed numerical relationships.

NONBASIC ACTIVITIES—In economic base analysis, those activities with outputs mainly consumed within the subject area (community).

NONBASIC CROPS—Agricultural products which are entitled to government support but which are not basic to the areas in which they are grown. They include oats, barley, rye, certain dairy products, honey, wool, etc. See also Basic Crops.

NONBEARING PARTITION—A partition wall which is used to divide space and does not carry overhead partitions or joists.

NONBEARING WALL—A self-supporting wall which carries no vertical load.

NONCONFORMING BUILDING—A building, or portion thereof, which was lawfully erected or altered and maintained, but which, because of a subsequent change of a zoning ordinance, no longer conforms to the use, height, or area regulations of the zone in which it is located. See also Nonconforming Use.

NONCONFORMING USE—A use which was lawfully established and maintained but which, because of a subsequent change of a zoning ordinance, no longer conforms to the use regulations of the zone in which it is located. A nonconforming building, or nonconforming portion of the building, shall be deemed to constitute a nonconforming use of the land upon which it is located. Such uses preclude additions or changes without municipal approval.

NONCONFORMITY – Used to describe a property which does not conform as to usage or harmonize as to physical attributes with neighboring properties.

NONDURABLE GOODS – Short-lived consumer goods, such as food, clothing, etc.

NONOPERATING INCOME – The income which a business concern receives from sources other than the business operation, e.g., from earnings on investments or from capital gains.

NONRECOURSE LOAN – A loan in which the lender waives any personal liability of the borrower.

NONRECURRING EXPENSE – An expense occasioned by some condition that is not regularly repeated in the ordinary course of business operations, e.g., a loss by fire or theft.

NORMAL CURVE – In statistics, a symmetrical, bell-shaped curve that portrays the distribution of a population of certain types of measurements or the frequency distribution of all possible means of large samples that might be drawn from almost any kind of population.

NORMAL DISTRIBUTION – In statistics, a continuous distribution usually represented by the Normal Curve.

NOSING – The rounded projecting edge of a stair tread or landing.

NOXIOUS WEEDS – Unwanted plants which due to their vigorous growth or propagation are considered agricultural hazards. Chemical eradication is usually necessary.

NUISANCES – Annoying, unpleasant, or obnoxious things or practices.

NUISANCE VALUE – The price which probably would be paid for the avoidance of, or as a relief from, an objectionable condition.

NULL HYPOTHESIS – In statistics, a statement that there is no difference between two comparable and calculated statistics and then proceeding to test that hypothesis against evidence found in samples.

NURSE CROP – A crop planted primarily for the purpose of sheltering less vigorous seedlings. An example is planting barley and alfalfa to establish an alfalfa stand.

NUTRIENTS – Elements essential to plant growth and in soil development. A factor in soil analysis.

OAKUM—Loose fiber obtained from untwisting and picking apart hemp or rope, used for caulking joints.

OBJECTIVE OPINION—Describes an opinion free of bias, prejudice, or personal feelings. An opinion formulated after the consideration of definite facts and observable conditions as opposed to a subjective opinion (one existing in the mind).

OBSERVED CONDITION—The condition of a property ascertained by a detailed inspection. A physical condition.

OBSERVED CONDITION METHOD—A method of estimating accrued depreciation which considers and estimates separately the deductions for physical deterioration, functional obsolescence and economic obsolescence. The several estimates are then added to provide a lump-sum deduction from reproduction cost new.

OBSERVED DEPRECIATION—The loss in utility and value of a property, as compared with a new property or one capable of rendering maximum benefits, the estimate of which is based upon direct inspection, detailed estimates of accrued deterioration, studies of functional deficiencies, and other observable conditions affecting the property and its desirability.

OBSOLESCENCE—One of the causes of depreciation. It is the impairment of desirability and usefulness brought about by new inventions, current changes in design, and improved processes for production, or from external influencing factors, which make a property less desirable and valuable for a continued use. Obsolescence may be either economic or functional. See also Depreciation, Economic (Locational) Obsolescence, Functional Obsolescence.

OBSOLETE—The state of being no longer useful or desirable, for reasons other than physical deterioration.

OCCUPANCY—State of being in possession.

OCCUPANCY, COST OF—The total costs included in the occupancy of a given property as distinguished from the cost of conducting a business therein. For a tenant: the rent, plus such items as heat, utilities, janitor service, and taxes not included in the rent, in addition to amortization of the tenant's cost of alterations over the term of the lease. For an owner-occupant: the latter items plus a charge equivalent to the fair rental value.

OCCUPANCY RATES—The relationship which exists between the income received from rental units of a property and the income to be received if all units were occupied. It is derived by multiplying the number of units by the number of days rented and dividing by the number of rentable units multiplied by the days of the year.

OCCUPATIONAL SAFETY AND HEALTH ACT (OSHA)—An act imposing federal safety standards on employers.

OFF-LINE—Pertaining to peripheral equipment or devices not subject to the direct control of the central processing unit.

OFFSET—A ledge formed by a difference in the thickness of a wall. See also Set-back, Set-off.

ON CENTER—The distance from the center of one structural member to the center of a similar member, such as spacing studs, joists, girders. Abbreviated, O.C.

ON-LINE—Pertaining to equipment or devices under direct control of the central processing unit.

OPEN BEAM CONSTRUCTION—Frame construction in which the ceiling and ceiling joists are eliminated, leaving the beams and deck of the roof exposed and treating them as an element of the interior finish of the room. In this type of construction, the structural members of the roof are usually heavier and may be on wider centers.

OPEN-END MORTGAGE—A mortgage which permits the mortgagor to borrow additional sums, usually on the condition that a stated ratio of assets to the debt must be maintained, or for other specified terms.

OPEN OCCUPANCY—A residential rental property the occupancy of which is not restricted by race, color, or religion. Used generally to refer to residential developments which have been constructed with the aid of government funds. All property by law is "open occupancy" under the U.S. Constitution.

OPEN PLANNING—House design wherein a minimum use is made of partitions between the different activity areas, as between living room, dining room, kitchen, and family room.

OPEN SPACE RATIO—The ratio, expressed as a percentage, of the site area to the floor area of the building in an apartment project as established by zoning area.

OPEN STEEL CONSTRUCTION—Unwrapped, i.e., without fireproofing, rigidly connected steel frame which carries all loads directly to foundation and footings.

In the case of a multi-story structure, the exterior walls are carried on this framework, usually at each level.

OPEN WEB JOIST—Lightweight, prefabricated metal, parallel chord trusses.

OPERATING EXPENSE RATIO—The ratio of annual operating expenses to annual effective gross income usually expressed as a percentage.

OPERATING EXPENSES—Generally denotes all expenses necessary to maintain the production of income from operation of a property; the difference between effective gross income and Net Operating

Income (NOI). Also used to denote a category of expense exclusive of fixed expense, debt service, depreciation allowance and reserves for replacements.

OPERATING INCOME — Income derived from the general operation of a business. Not synonymous with net profit, but rather indicates a stage in the profit-and-loss account where all direct costs of operation and all direct income from operation have been taken into the account and nothing else. See also Net Operating Income.

OPERATING PROFIT — Profit arising from the regular operation of an enterprise engaged in performing services, excluding income from other sources and excluding expenses other than those of direct operation.

OPERATING STANDARDS — Standards of performance. They are standards based upon analyses of comparable properties and are called comparative standards. Derived from analysis of the experience of operating expenses of a number of comparable properties.

OPERATING STATEMENT — An accounting in writing of the gross income, annual expenses, and resulting Net Operating Income of an investment in real estate during a specified period. A section of the profit-and-loss account of an enterprise whose main source of revenue is the performance of services.

OPERATIVE PROPERTY (OPERATING PROPERTY) — Any property which may be reasonably necessary for use in the operation and conduct of the particular kind or kinds of business in which such property is employed.

OPINION OF TITLE — A certificate pertaining to title in real property from an attorney or a title insurance company.

OPTIMUM USE — See Highest and Best Use.

OPTION — An agreement which permits one to buy, sell, or lease real property for a stipulated period of time in accordance with specified terms. A unilateral right to exercise a privilege.

ORCHARD — A planting of uniformly spaced fruit or nut bearing trees. Spacing will normally be arranged to allow the highest production from a specific variety of tree and for ease of equipment operation. Certain crops will require plantings of more than one variety for proper pollination.

ORDINARY ANNUITY — An annuity or stream of income with payments made at the end of specified time intervals (in arrears) as distinguished from an annuity with payments made at the beginning of each time interval (in advance).

ORDINARY HIGH WATER MARK — The point on the bank or shore up to which the presence and action of the water is so continuous as to leave a distinct mark by erosion, destruction of terrestrial vegetation, or other easily recognized characteristics. See also Mean High Water Line.

ORDINARY INCOME — Income which is subject to income taxes at the regular rate for the taxpayer as distinguished from capital gains income which may be taxable at a lower rate.

ORDINATE — The distance along the vertical axis of a curve, diagram, or chart. See also Abscissa.

ORGANIC MATTER — The more or less decomposed material of the soil derived from organic sources, usually from plant remains.

ORGANIC SOIL — See Types of Soil, page 351.

ORGANIZATION COST — The cost incurred in the formation of the functional phases of an enterprise; that is, other than the promotional expense, obtaining of capital, construction of the property, and acquiring of the business.

ORIEL WINDOW — A window projecting from the outer face of a wall, especially an upper story, and supported by brackets or a cantilever. Not to be confused with bay window which is at first floor level and generally supported by a foundation.

ORIENTATION — Placing or positioning a structure on its lot with regard to exposure to the sun, prevailing winds, privacy, and protection from noise.

ORIGINAL COST — The actual cost of a property to its present owner; not necessarily the "first" cost at the time it was originally constructed and placed in service. See also Historical Cost.

OUTDOOR LIVING — Refers to the best utilization of porches, patios, terraces, lawns, gardens, and rooms which open into the yard or have extensive glass areas which tend to "bring the outdoors in."

OVERAGE INCOME — Rental income over and above a guaranteed minimum payable under the terms of a lease which requires additional rent under prescribed conditions such as the achievement of a particular level of profit or retail sales volume by the tenant; commonly used in connection with additional rent paid under a percentage clause in a lease.

OVERALL RATE — The direct ratio between Annual Net Operating Income (NOI) and Value or Sales Price. Denoted by the symbol R_0 or the formula d/V in the Ellwood formulation.

OVERGRAZING — The overstocking or overuse of a range until the better forage is gone, the secondary species decline in vigor until they too are gone, and in time a change of forage occurs both in kind and quality.

OVERHANG—A type of roof in which the rafters and roofing extend beyond the exterior walls of a structure; used to protect against precipitation and direct sunlight.

OVERHEAD—In general, the expenses of direction and administration necessary to conduct a business of any kind.

OVERHEAD EASEMENT—The right to use the space at a designated distance above the surface of the land; as for power lines, avigation, and air rights.

OVERHEAD IRRIGATION—Sprinkler irrigation installed with tall rises permitting water to be delivered above the crop. Frequently installed in orchards, groves and vineyards.

OVERIMPROVEMENT—An improvement which is not the most profitable for the site on which it is placed because of its excessive size or cost, and consequent inability to develop the maximum possible land value. May be temporary or permanent.

An overimprovement typically reflects environmental obsolescence, although a substantial market may exist for such property among a group which takes personal pride in owning the most expensive home in the block and is willing to pay a price commensurate with cost.

OVERPASS—A grade separation where one highway passes over another highway or railroad to avoid surface intersections and resulting traffic congestion. It is accomplished by bridging one traffic route over the other.

OVERRIDING ROYALTY—That interest in unsevered oil and gas which the lessee retains on the occasion of executing a sublease or assignment.

OVERRUN—The amount of lumber actually sawed from logs which is in excess of estimated volume. Usually, it is expressed in terms of percentage.

OVERSTOCKING—Placing a number of animals on a given area that will result in overuse at the end of a planned grazing period. Not to be confused with overgrazing, because an area may be overstocked for a short period but the animals may be removed before the area is overutilized. However, continued overstocking will lead to overgrazing.

OVERSTORY—That portion of a forest which contains the tallest trees, or the top canopy.

PACKAGE MORTGAGE—A mortgage which covers personalty as well as realty.

PALATABILITY—The relish that an animal shows for a particular species, plant, or plant part.

PANEL – A section of a surface, as a wall or ceiling, which is either raised or recessed, and usually enclosed in a frame-like border. The term is also used to refer to prefabricated construction materials, such as gypsum board, plywood, fibreboard, plasterboard, and the like.

PANEL BOARD – A panel to which are attached electrical meters and control equipment for electrical service distribution.

PANEL HEATING – A radiant heating system; one in which the pipes or coils are embedded in the walls or ceiling and serve as heating panels.

PANEL WALL – A prefabricated section of wall erected in one piece. See Curtain Wall.

PARAMETER
1. A variable that may assume any of a given set of values.
2. A statistic that characterizes a population. Usually parameters are unknown and must be inferred.

PARAPET – A low wall or railing constructed along the edge of a roof, balcony, bridge, or terrace for protection; or to control water on a roof resulting from rain or artificial flooding; or for insulation against heat-producing sun rays.

PARCEL – A piece of land, regardless of size, in one ownership. See also Larger Parcel, Remainder.

PARCEL IDENTIFIER – A code number which serves as an abbreviation of, or replacement for, a parcel's legal description. The purpose of a parcel identifier is to facilitate the storage and use of land data in an information system. Parcel identifiers may be based on geocodes, government surveys, or tax maps.

PARENT MATERIAL – The unconsolidated mass from which the soil profile develops.

PARENT ROCK – The rock from which parent materials of soils are found.

PARGING – A thin coating of mortar applied to masonry wall. Used on the exterior face of below-grade walls as waterproofing or used to smooth a rough masonry wall.

PARITY – The state of being equivalent. Used in this sense to refer to federal price policies for agricultural products; that is, policies designed to bring farm income into parity with the income of other sectors of the national economy.

PARKING AREA – The area of a facility, such as shopping area, industrial plant, supermarket, used to park automobiles of customers and/or employees.

PARKING GARAGE—A commercial facility where automobiles may be parked for a fee; may be either a public or private enterprise.

PARKWAY—An arterial highway for noncommercial traffic, with full or partial control of access, and usually located within a park or a ribbon of park-like development.

PARQUET FLOOR—A floor laid in rectangular or square patterns, not in long strips, often prefinished, thin, fabricated wood blocks.

PARTIAL INTEREST—Same as fractional interest; rights in real estate which may be divided or undivided but which amount to less than the whole. See Divided Interest.

PARTIAL PAYMENT—That factor used to identify the periodic level payment required to amortize a given investment at a specified discount (interest) rate over a specified period of time; provides for both return on and return of investment over the period specified. It is the reciprocal of the level annuity or Inwood factor. The partial payment, when expressed on an annual basis, is the Mortgage (Annual) Constant.

PARTIAL TAKING—The taking of only a part of a property for public use under the power of eminent domain and for which compensation must be paid, taking into consideration the damages and/or special benefits to the remainder property.

PARTICIPATION—See Equity Participation, Income Participation.

PARTICIPATION MORTGAGE—A mortgage held by more than one lender.

PARTITION—A dividing wall between rooms or areas.

PARTNERSHIP—An association of two or more persons for the conduct of an enterprise other than in corporate form. The rights, duties, responsibilities of the people so associated may be covered by a partnership agreement or, if not, they are determined by law.

PARTY WALL—A common wall erected along the dividing line between adjoining properties and in which the respective owners have common rights of use.

PASTURE—Land devoted to the production of tame or native forage which is harvested directly by livestock.

PATIO—A courtyard; an open paved area used for outdoor living and which may or may not be partially or entirely surrounded by rooms or other parts of a house.

PAY-BACK PERIOD—The time required for complete recovery of an investment; often used with the concept that all income is considered a return of capital until the entire investment is recaptured and that income received after complete pay-back is considered profit.

PEAT SOIL—See Types of Soil, page 351.

PEDALFERS SOIL—See Types of Soil, page 351.

PEDESTRIAN OVERPASS—A structural grade separation, such as a bridge, which permits pedestrian traffic to pass over a highway.

PEDESTRIAN UNDERPASS—A structural grade separation, such as a tunnel, which permits pedestrian traffic to pass under a highway.

PEDESTRIAN WALKWAY—A continuous way designated for pedestrians and separated from the through lanes for motor vehicles by space or barrier.

PEDOCAL SOIL—See Types of Soil, page 351.

PEELER LOG—A log suitable for the manufacture of rotary cut veneer.

PENNSYLVANIA FARMHOUSE COLONIAL ARCHITECTURE—A regional variation of the colonial, especially adapted for flat ground. It is informal in character. The main section and its higher roof line dominate the design. The exterior stone walls may be whitewashed or plastered. Details are simple. The roof is either of slate or wood shingles.

PENSTOCK—A conduit for conveying water to a power plant; a sluice-like device to control the flow of water.

PENTHOUSE—A building on the roof of a structure to house elevator machinery, ventilating equipment, etc. A separate dwelling unit or apartment on the roof of an apartment or other building. Also, any roof-like shelter or overhanging part, as to shelter a door.

PERCENTAGE LEASE—A lease which provides that the rental shall be based on a percentage of income (gross or net) from the sale of specified merchandise or services. Often it includes a guaranteed minimum and occasionally a maximum rental regardless of business volume.

PERCENTAGE RENT—Rental income received in accordance with the terms of a percentage clause in a lease, usually with a guaranteed minimum. See Percentage Lease.

PERCH—A unit of measure found in old deeds, usually accepted as being equivalent to 16½ feet.

PERCOLATION—The seepage of water through soil; the ability of soil to absorb water or other liquid as effluent from a septic system.

PERCOLATION TEST—The test made by hydraulic engineers and others to determine the percolation rate of the soil. These tests are used by health departments and others in their determination of the amount of land area necessary to have an operational septic system.

PERENNIAL FORB – See Types of Range Vegetation, page 349.

PERFORMANCE BOND – A bond to guarantee specific completion of an undertaking in accordance with an agreement, such as that supplied by a contractor guaranteeing the completion of a building or a road. Also the bond supplied by a subdivider to the municipality guaranteeing proper completion, road construction, and utility installations.

PERFORMANCE STANDARDS – Tests given to a prospective use of land to determine whether the proposed use will be in harmony with the purposes of applicable zoning. In an industrial area performance standards would include the test of smoke control, noise levels, off-street parking and loading, expansion room for future utilization, and similar factors.

PERIMETER – The total length of the periphery of a given area, e.g., equals the distance around the outside of a building.

PERIODIC GROWTH – Growth which occurs in increments at regular intervals such as financial growth at compound interest as distinguished from continuous growth as it occurs in nature.

PERMEABILITY – A term used when discussing the behavior of water in soil. A soil easily permeated by water would be friable, deep, and without dense or compacted horizons which would restrict free movement of water.

PERPETUITY – The state of being continued forever; for example, an ordinary annuity which extends into the future without termination.

PERSONAL PROPERTY – Generally, movable items; that is, those not permanently affixed to and a part of real estate. In deciding whether or not a thing is personal property or real estate, usually there must be considered (1) the manner in which it is annexed; (2) the intention of the party who made the annexation (that is, to leave permanently or to remove at some time); (3) the purpose for which the premises are used. Generally, and with exceptions, items remain personal property if they can be removed without serious injury either to the real estate or to the item itself.

PERSONALTY – Personal, rather than real property. That which is movable. See Personal Property.

pH – A notation to designate the degree of acidity or alkalinity. Technically, the common logarithm of the reciprocal of the hydrogen ion concentration (grams per liter) of a system.

PHASE SOIL – See Types of Soil, page 351.

PHYSICAL ASSETS – Assets which have a physical existence; as land, buildings, machinery, equipment, etc.

PHYSICAL CURABLE DETERIORATION — Physical deterioration which the prudent buyer would anticipate correcting upon purchase of the property. The cost of effecting the correction or cure would be no more than the anticipated addition to utility, and hence ultimately to value, associated with the cure. Curable physical deterioration is frequently termed "deferred maintenance" or rehabilitation, because these terms reflect the type of activity typically associated with correcting the condition.

PHYSICAL DESCRIPTION — A statement of the description of physical (tangible) attributes of a property including, but not limited to, elevation, contour, size, shape, subsoil conditions, and natural growth on land, and size, shape, design, materials used in construction, equipment, condition, and layout of buildings.

PHYSICAL DETERIORATION — A reduction in utility resulting from an impairment of physical condition. For purposes of appraisal analysis, it is most common and convenient to divide physical deterioration into curable and incurable components.

PHYSICAL INCURABLE DETERIORATION — Physical deterioration which in terms of market conditions as of the date of the appraisal is not feasible or economically justified to correct. The cost of correcting the condition or effecting a cure is estimated to be greater than the anticipated increase in utility, and hence ultimately in value, of the property that will result from correcting or curing the condition. For purposes of appraisal analysis, incurable physical deterioration may be divided into short-lived and long-lived elements.

PHYSICAL POSSESSION — The state or condition of being in occupancy.

PHYSIOCRATS — A group of French statesmen and philosophers who, about the middle of the 18th century, made the first systematic attempt to form an economic science on a broad basis. They particularly emphasized land as a source of wealth.

PICTURE WINDOW — A large window, usually a fixed pane, plate or insulating glass, with ventilation provided by smaller windows alongside; sometimes divided into small panes; designed to command an interesting view or vista, or allow more light into the interior of the home.

PIER
1. A quay or wharf structure which extends seaward from the shore, at an angle, and which provides a landing place on each side for vessels to receive and discharge passengers and cargo.
2. A square column.
3. A support at the point where two abutting bridge spans meet.

PIERHEAD LINE — See Bulkhead Line.

PIG PARLOR — A farm building especially designed and used for the breeding and raising of hogs and swine.

PILASTER — An upright architectural member, rectangular in plan, structurally a pier, but architecturally treated as a column.

PILE — A wood timber; a steel or hollow steel tube filled with concrete having the shape of a post, either round or square, which is driven into the ground to serve as support for the foundation of a building, pier, or other structure.

PILINGS — Columns extending below the ground to bear the loads of a structure when the surface soil cannot. They may extend down to bearing soil or support the load by skin friction. Sheet piling is used to form bulkheads or retaining walls. Also used to support docks or piers.

PINON-JUNIPER — See Types of Range Vegetation, page 349.

PIPELINE — A conduit of connected pipes for transmission of liquids or gases.

PIPELINE EASEMENT — The right to construct, operate, and maintain a pipeline for the transmission of liquids, gases, or anything which may be transmitted in such a line, over the lands of others within prescribed geographical limits. The wording of the easement will determine the extent of the rights granted.

PITCH — The slope or incline of a roof, expressed in inches of rise per foot of length, or by the ratio of the rise to the span.

PIVOT SPRINKLER — An automatic irrigation system designed so a mechanically moved mainline rotates around a pivot point. A 1320-ft. system installed on a quarter section irrigates a circle containing approximately 128 acres.

PLAN — A horizontal cross section of a structure at any level showing room arrangement, location of doors, windows, etc. Also may show the site surrounding the building and objects thereon.

PLANK — A piece of unfinished lumber 2 to 4 inches thick and at least 8 inches wide.

PLANNED UNIT DEVELOPMENT (PUD) — A type of land development which may be at variance with traditional zoning and lot layout. May be residential, commercial or industrial. Buildings are clustered and/or set on smaller lots than usual. Result is a development with an overall density the same or slightly greater than is typical of conventional developments and zoning, but containing large open park-like areas with buildings concentrated in a few areas. Individual properties are owned in fee with either joint ownership of the open areas or, if local law requires, with open areas deeded to the city.

PLANT—A very broad term which may include land, buildings, machinery, equipment, furniture, etc.; also applied to a portion of an assembled property, such as a power plant, or to the fixed property of an enterprise, such as an educational plant.

PLANTATION—In forestry, an area planted to forest seedlings or seeded by broadcast methods. Also known as tree farms.

PLANTING EASEMENT—An area of land, the use and control of which is obtained by easement rights, for establishing and maintaining plant growth for safety and beautification.

PLASTER—A mixture of lime, sand, and water, used as a finished surface for walls and ceilings.

PLASTER GROUND—A narrow strip of wood or metal around the perimeter of a room at the base, and sometimes at chair rail or picture mould height, and around openings; used as a nailing strip for trim and as a plane to "plaster to." See illustration, page 310.

PLASTER OF PARIS—Calcined gypsum; that is, gypsum which has been converted to a fine white powder by action of heat.

PLASTIC—Synthetic substances which may be molded or shaped by heat.

PLAT

1. A plan, map, or chart of a city, town, section, or subdivision indicating the location and boundaries of individual properties.
2. A map or sketch of an individual property showing property lines which may include features such as soils, building locations, vegetation, topography, etc.

PLAT BOOK—A record showing the location, size, and name of owner of each plot of land in a stated area.

PLATE—A horizontal structural member laid across the top of a row of studs, serving as the frame for interior partitions, and exterior walls.

The purpose of a plate is (1) to provide lateral rigidity for the wall by "tying" the studs together, and (2) to serve as a support for upper story floor joists, ceiling joists, and as the lower support for rafters. Often called a top plate. See illustration, pages 305–306.

PLATE GLASS—A high quality glass which has been ground and polished on both sides.

PLINTH OR PLINTH BOX—Usually a square block of trim material placed upright on either side of the bottom of a door opening at the floor line, or at the base of a column. The lower end of the door casing, and the end of the baseboard are butted against it. See illustration, page 304.

PLOTTAGE – The process of assembling two or more sites under a single ownership such that there is an increment derived from greater utility. See also Plottage Value.

PLOTTAGE VALUE – An increment of value as a consequence of the combining of two or more sites so as to develop one site having a greater utility than the aggregate of each when separately considered, or the value of an existing site of abnormal size or special shape which has greater utility than average lots of more conventional smaller size.

PLY – A term to denote the number of thicknesses or layers as 3-ply; for roofing felt, veneers, etc.

PLYWOOD – An assembled product constructed of three or more layers of veneer joined with glue and usually laid with the grain of adjoining plies at right angles. Almost always an odd number of plies are used to give balanced construction.

PODZOL – See Types of Soil, page 351.

POINT – One percent – a percentage point; used in connection with a discount from or a share of a principal amount deducted at the time funds are advanced. "Points" may represent payment for services rendered in connection with a loan or they may represent additional interest to the lender payable in advance. See Discount Point.

POINTING – The process of removing deteriorated mortar from masonry and replacing it with new mortar, also the final patching, filling or finishing of mortar joints in new masonry work.

POLE CONSTRUCTION – A construction method frequently used in farm outbuildings where poles or timbers are installed at intervals for structural support. The method does not use continuous foundations.

POLE LINE EASEMENT – An easement for the construction, maintenance and operation of a pole line, usually for the transmission of electric power.

POLICE POWER – The right of government to limit the exercise of property rights in real estate, without compensation, provided the limitation is not specific to one parcel. The limitation is to serve the interest of public health, public safety, public morals and the general welfare.

POROSITY – See Soil Porosity.

PORT AUTHORITY – A commission or other agency, usually created by special legislative act and enjoying a legal entity, which is given power to coordinate land, air and water traffic in and about a port. Its power may extend to the construction and maintenance of bridges, tunnels, and other structures essential to the development of the port area. In the United States, because of federal control over navigable waters and because the area of a port may affect the territory of more than one state, the concurrence of Congress and of the legislatures of all states affected is necessary to the creation of such an authority; e.g., the Port of New York Authority.

POSSESSORY INTEREST—Basically, the right to possession and use of property. However, in practice it is used to distinguish the interest of a lessee in government-owned property from the interest of a lessee in privately-owned land.

POSSIBLE CAPACITY—The maximum number of vehicles that can pass a given point on a lane or roadway during one hour under prevailing roadway and traffic conditions.

POST—A vertical structure member carrying stresses in compression, used where strength in bending is not a requisite.

POSTERIOR DISTRIBUTION—In Bayesian analysis, a decision-making distribution which represents the decision-maker's uncertainty about the unknown value of the population mean after taking into account sample evidence.

POSTS AND TIMBERS (PIER)—Lumber of square or approximately square cross section, 5 × 5 inches and larger, graded primarily for use as posts or columns carrying longitudinal load but adapted for miscellaneous uses in which strength in bending is not especially important.

POSTSTRESSED CONCRETE—A method of giving concrete tensile strength after the concrete has hardened by putting reinforcing cables in metal sheaths which are placed in the wet concrete; the cables are stressed after the concrete sets and the sheathing filled with grout. After the grout sets, the cables are released and the stress is transmitted to the concrete.

POTENTIAL DEMAND—The desire or need for real estate. Potential demand represents the quantity of real estate of a particular type that would be taken off the market by being purchased.

POTENTIAL GROSS INCOME—The income that a property will produce with 100% occupancy. The potential gross income is generally derived by multiplying the rental value per unit times the number of units in the building.

POTENTIAL VALUE—The value which is expected to develop if and when stated probabilities become actualities.

POWER FEED WIRING—The main electric power line entering a building from a utility or private source; supplies electric power to machinery and equipment through main bus ducts or heavy wiring in conduit; does not include branch feed lines or controls from main line to machinery.

POWER PLANT — A plant, including engines, dynamos, etc., within the structure or buildings, for the generation of power derived either from coal, gas, oil or water. The power so created may be for an industry's own operations or for commercial distribution to other users. See also Hydroelectric Plant, Water Power Plant.

PRACTICAL CAPACITY — The maximum number of vehicles that can pass a given point on a roadway or lane during one hour without the traffic density being so great as to cause unreasonable delays, hazards, or driving restrictions under prevailing roadway and traffic conditions.

PRAIRIE — An extensive tract of level or rolling land that was originally treeless and grass covered. A prairie is usually characterized by a deep, fertile soil.

PRAIRIE SOILS — See Types of Soil, page 351.

PRECAST CONCRETE — Concrete structural components which are not formed and poured in place in the structure, but are cast separately, either at a separate location or on site.

PREDICTION — Forecasting the future with an implied degree of accuracy or precision.

PRE-ENGINEERED BUILDING — A building constructed of pre-designed, manufactured, and assembled units such as wall, framing, floor and roof panels erected at the construction site.

PREFABRICATION — The manufacturing and assembling of construction materials and parts into component structural units, such as wall, floor, and roof panels, which are later erected at the construction site.

PRESCRIPTION — Title obtained in law by long possession. Occupancy for the period prescribed by the Code of Civil Procedure as sufficient to bar an action for the recovery of the property gives title by prescription.

PRESENT OPERATOR — Reference to individual cropping the land, either direct operation or tenant farmed.

PRESENT VALUE — The current monetary value. Sometimes it is used synonymously, and inadvisedly, with the term present worth. It is the today's cash lump sum which represents the current value of the right to collect future payments. It is the discounted value of aggregate future payments.

PRESENT WORTH OF FUTURE COLLECTIONS (BENEFITS, RECEIPTS) — The present value of money to be collected at a specified future time when discounted from that time to the present date at a specified rate of discount.

PRESENT WORTH OF ONE – The reversion factor which is used to discount a single future payment to a present worth figure, given the appropriate discount rate and the discount period.

PRESTRESSED CONCRETE – A method of giving concrete tensile strength by stressing the reinforcements in the concrete before it sets and releasing the reinforcements after the concrete has hardened.

PRICE – The quantity of one thing which is exchanged for another; the amount of money paid, asked, or offered where sale is contemplated; the money consideration which is expected or given in exchange for commodities or services. Price is sometimes value expressed in terms of money. In real estate valuation a distinction is made between price and value because price may be justified or not, while value is properly a justified price.

In economic theory, the basic device by which allocation of resources occurs in the competitive market.

PRICE LEVEL – The average of prices, usually at wholesale, of a selected list of representative commodities at a stated time, usually expressed as an index number. Comparison of the average of one year with that of any other year shows the change in the price level.

PRICE SUPPORTS – Various governmental programs designed to maintain market prices from falling below a certain minimum level, such as those for agriculture which are supported either by outright subsidies or purchases at higher than market prices, etc.

PRIMARY SOIL – See Types of Soil, page 351.

PRIME COST – The cost of direct labor and materials in any project.

PRIME RATE – The interest rate (or discount rate) which a commercial bank charges for short term loans to borrowers with highest credit ratings; the minimum obtainable interest rate in commercial banking at a particular point in time; often the basis for "floating rates" such as "prime plus 2," meaning the prevailing prime rate plus two percentage points.

PRINCIPAL – A capital sum invested; payment which represents partial or full repayment of capital loaned or invested as distinguished from payment of interest; the unrecovered capital remaining in a loan or investment (principal balance).

PRINCIPAL MERIDIANS – Boundary lines indicating the rectangular survey system of the continental United States. Farm land description is by rectangular survey.

PRINCIPAL RISK – The risk that principal or capital investment will be worth less (especially as a reversion) than anticipated or forecast.

Includes the risk of total capital loss, especially of a highly leveraged equity investment.

PRIOR DISTRIBUTION – In Bayesian analysis, a decision-making distribution which represents the decision-maker's uncertainty about the unknown value of the population mean before a sample of the population is taken.

PROBABILITY – A number between 0 and 1, inclusive, representing the chance or likelihood that an event will occur.

PROCESSOR – The hardware that performs the actual arithmetical and logical operations of the computer system, using programs and data stored in the memory.

PRODUCTION – See Factors in Production.

PRODUCTIVITY
1. The capacity of a soil to produce crops under the environment where it occurs and under a specified system of management.
2. The amount of goods produced by labor, or other factors of production, per unit of time.
3. The net value of the services provided by space. Productivity is a direct function of use.

PROFESSIONAL APPRAISER – One who, properly qualified, estimates value. To be considered a competent appraiser or an expert in the field of real estate valuation, one should have
1. the ability to assemble and competently evaluate an adequate and pertinent data program;
2. the necessary background and experience, particularly with respect to the property type under appraisement;
3. the essential personal characteristics of unquestioned integrity, sound judgment, and willingness to work;
4. a thorough familiarity with the stimuli motivating market reaction; and
5. a thorough familiarity with techniques and methods of presentation.

PROFILE, SOIL – See Soil Profile.

PROFIT
1. As used in theoretical economics, the residual share of the product of enterprise accruing to the entrepreneur after all payments for capital (interest), for land (rent), and for labor including management (wages). Synonym: pure profit.
2. As used in accounting, a broad term indicating an increase in wealth resulting from the operation of an enterprise. The term gross profit usually indicates the difference between the selling price and the cost price, such items as selling expenses and operating expenses being customarily deducted from the gross prof-

its in order to arrive at the net profit or net income. See also Operating Profit.

3. The excess of proceeds over cost in an incidental transaction; that is, profit on sale of real estate (or investment).

PROFITABILITY INDEX — The relationship (ratio) of the present worth of all future benefits to an investment to the present worth (cost) of the capital outlay.

PROFIT AND LOSS STATEMENT — A statement prepared from the books and records of a going enterprise conducted for profit, which assembles all the income and expenses, or profits and losses applicable to a stated period, the balance of the items indicating the net profit or loss.

PROGRAM — A set of instructions for the solution of a problem or the manipulation of data.

PROGRAMMER — One who prepares sequences of instructions for a computer.

PROJECTION — A mechanical process of extrapolation or extending the experience of the past into the future by means of a mechanical formula. May be a simple straight line projection or one based on a more complex formula. In either event, projection is based on the presumption that the same conditions and rates of change that have prevailed in the past will continue in precisely the same way in the future.

PROJECTION PERIOD — The period of time over which expected Net Operating Income is projected for purposes of analysis and valuation; a presumed period of ownership.

PROPER STOCKING — Placing a number of animals on a given area that will result in proper use at the end of the planned grazing period. Continued proper stocking will lead to proper grazing.

PROPERTY — Any object that may be lawfully acquired or owned which may normally, but not necessarily, have value.

A group of rights inhering in a party's relation to the physical thing, as the right to possess, use, and dispose of it.

Property is a bundle of rights which, collectively, is designated as the fee simple.

The right to the future benefits of economic goods — material and nonmaterial — as determined by law. Although, technically, the term means a right or interest in things rather than the things themselves, common usage makes it applicable to the things rather than to the right or interest.

PROPERTY BRIEF — A description of a property for sale, with complete details and pictures, in a form suitable for presentation to a prospect.

PROPERTY DESCRIPTION – Unequivocal identification of the real estate being described.

PROPERTY LINE – The division boundary between two parcels of land or between a property and a travelway, such as a street or alley.

PROPERTY RESIDUAL TECHNIQUE – A capitalization technique in which the Net Operating Income is considered attributable to the property as a whole rather than divided into land and building components. In annuity capitalization, this technique involves computation of the present worth of an income stream to which is added the present worth of a reversion at its assumed termination.

PROPERTY TAX – In general, a tax levied on any kind of property; that is, both real and personal.

PROPRIETARY LEASE – The lease given to tenant-shareholders in a cooperative apartment corporation. In such ventures each tenant is required to purchase so many shares of stock before obtaining possession of an apartment, and each month thereafter makes a payment to the corporation covering his pro rata share of the operating expenses and debt servicing charges.

PROSCENIUM – The stage in front of the curtain, sometimes including the curtain and the framework which supports it; the arch or opening which separates the stage from the auditorium.

PROXIMITY DAMAGE – An element of severance damages caused by the proximity of the remainder to the improvement being constructed, such as a highway. It may also arise from proximity to an objectionable site or improvement, dirt, dust, noise, or vibration.

PRUNING – A practice of selectively cutting or removing branches or twigs from a tree, shrub or vine.

PUBLIC DOMAIN LAND – Land owned by the federal government.

PUBLIC GOOD – An economic good furnished by government, as a recreation park, public education, museums, etc. Not to be confused with free good.

PUBLIC HOUSING ADMINISTRATION – A unit of the United States Department of Housing and Urban Development which administers legislation providing for loans and subsidies to local housing authorities to encourage the creation of low-rental dwelling units.

PUBLIC LANDS – Lands owned by the government; public domain. In the United States the federal government has title to vast tracts included in Indian reservations, national parks and forests, and grazing lands.

PUBLIC LAND SYSTEM – A description of a parcel of land by reference to its position in the Public Land Survey, such as the NE1/4 of the SW1/4 of Section 4, in Township 5 South, Range 7 West, Mt. Diablo Base and Meridian. See also Government Survey.

PUBLIC ROADS, BUREAU OF (FEDERAL HIGHWAY ADMINIS-TRATION) — A unit of the Department of Transportation of the United States government which administers federal grants-in-aid to the states for the construction and maintenance of major highways, and cooperates with the Departments of Agriculture and the Interior in the construction of roads in national forests, national parks, and elsewhere.

PUBLIC UTILITY PROPERTY — A property devoted to the production of commodities or service of general community consumption, usually having status as a monopoly or quasi-monopoly with or without benefit of franchise and ordinarily under some form of governmental regulation and control.

PULPWOOD — A forest product used in the pulp and paper industry.

PURCHASE AND LEASEBACK — See Sale-Leaseback.

PURCHASE MONEY — It is the common understanding that it means money paid for the land or the debt created by a purchase.

PURCHASE-MONEY MORTGAGE — A mortgage given by a purchaser of real property to the seller in part payment of the purchase price.

PURCHASING POWER — The ability and willingness to pay for an economic good.

PURCHASING POWER RISK — The risk that future dollars received will have less purchasing power as a result of inflation. This risk is rarely accounted for in specific terms in appraisal analysis, on the assumption that income receipts and expenses will move approximately proportionately and in the same direction.

PURLIN — A structural member laid horizontally supporting roof rafters or roof deck; also used in mansard roof construction as a base or support for the rafters in the upper slope of a gambrel or mansard roof. See illustration, page 306.

PURPOSE OF THE APPRAISAL — The type of value being sought. Not the same as Function.

PYLON — A gateway. A marking post or tower in an airport; a post or other marker for guiding aviators over a prescribed course of flight.

PYRAMID ROOF — A roof which resembles a pyramid with four sides and four ridges. Usually comes to a point in the center. Church steeples and many small garages have pyramid roofs. See illustration, page 300.

PYRAMID ZONING — A zoning ordinance in which the uses permitted in each more restricted zone are permitted in the less restricted zone classifications.

QUADRATIC MEAN – See Standard Deviation.

QUANTITY-SURVEY METHOD – A method of construction cost or reproduction cost estimating. In its strictest application it is a repetition of the contractor's original procedure of estimating the quantity and grade of each type of material used in the structure, estimating labor hours required, and applying unit costs to the material and labor quantities, with additional allowance for such items of indirect costs as overhead costs, labor insurance, and contractor's profit. The quantity survey, although still an estimate, is the most accurate and provable method. However, it is time-consuming to prepare and its general use is confined to contractors and in the valuation of public utility and special-purpose properties.

QUARRY TILE – A hard-burned, unglazed ceramic tile.

QUARTER – In public land survey, it is a division of a section containing 640 acres, the quarter being 160 acres.

QUARTILE – The item dividing a frequency distribution into four groups equal in number. There are three quartile points with the second quartile making the median.

QUAY – A landing place, built parallel to navigable water, for use in loading or unloading vessels.

QUEEN POST – Either of two vertical members of a triangular truss, each being equidistant from the apex.

QUESTION OF FACT – Questions arising from evidence given in court which are frequently in opposition or contrast to law, and which must be decided by jury. Such questions are based on absolute reality; that is, events, actions, conditions, or occurrences that actually took place, or physical objects or appearances as they actually exist or existed, as distinguished from mere supposition of evidence or opinions.

QUESTION OF LAW – Questions arising from evidence given in court which deal with the letter of the law, and which must be determined by the court. Such questions are based on interpretation of legal principle, conceived law, and established rules of duty.

QUICK ASSETS – See Liquid Assets.

QUITCLAIM DEED – A form of conveyance whereby whatever interest the grantor possesses in the property described in the deed is conveyed to the grantee without warranty of title.

QUOTIENT – The answer or result obtained by division, i.e., by dividing one number (numerator) by another (denominator).

RM – Residential Member; a professional designation conferred by the American Institute of Real Estate Appraisers of the National Association of Realtors. See also MAI.

RABBET—A cut or groove made on the edge or surface of a board or other timber so as to receive the end or edge of another board similarly cut.

RACEWAY—A slim metal conduit carrying electric or telephone wires with convenience outlets at frequent intervals; a plug-in strip.

RADIAL HIGHWAY—Traffic artery leading to and from an urban center to less densely developed, suburban, or rural areas.

RADIANT HEATING—Method of steam, electric, or hot water heating consisting of pipes which are concealed in floors, ceilings, or walls. Synonym: concealed heating, panel heating.

RADIANT HEATING SYSTEM—The warming of floors or other surfaces by means of hot air or hot water, usually the latter. Here pipes are embedded in the floor slab or in side walls with the air or water distributed by forced circulation. Lower temperatures are used.

RADIATION—The emission of rays of heat or light. The principle of radiation is applied in heating systems through use of radiators, convectors, etc.

RADIATOR—Accurately applied only to the type of exposed fixture which heats by means of a combination of radiation and convection effects. The common cast-iron radiator is an example. The several types of finned heating elements, such as baseboard heating, which are concealed within walls or in cabinets, are called convectors.

RAFTER—Structural members (joists or beams) which shape and form the support for the roof deck (or sheathing) and the roof covering. See illustration, pages 305–306.

RAFT FOUNDATION—See Floating Foundation.

RAIL—The cross or horizontal piece of a door, window sash, or panel. The top horizontal member of a balustrade.

RAILROAD GRADE CROSSING—A common area of intersection of a traffic artery and a railroad which includes their intersections at the same grade elevation.

RAILROAD SIDING AGREEMENT—A contract between a railroad and another, usually an adjacent industry, for the construction and maintenance of a sidetrack. It may be located on either party's land. See also Industrial Siding.

RAKE—A board or molding placed along the sloping sides of a frame gable to cover the ends of the siding.

RAMP—An inclined walk or roadway. In highway construction, the term refers to the roadway used to enter or leave a controlled access highway.

RANCH
1. An establishment for the raising of livestock under range conditions where forage grasses are the main source of feed.
2. Also used interchangeably with farm, homestead, etc., to describe a rural property.

RANCH IMPROVEMENTS — Any or all of the following: places of habitation, fences, water developments, and corrals.

RANCH STYLE HOUSE — A one-story house which is usually rambling, low to the ground, with low pitched gable roof or roofs, and in which the room plan is open with respect to the interior layout. It may have a basement.

RANCH UNIT — A term used in the public domain states to describe an entire operating unit. It is the combination of fee owned land and either or both of Taylor Grazing Act permit land and Forest Service permit land.

RANDOM — Without uniformity of dimension or design; e.g., masonry wall with stones placed irregularly, not in a straight course; random flooring.

RANDOM ACCESS — Direct or immediate access to any memory location, regardless of the location last accessed.

RANDOM SAMPLE
1. In statistics, selection by chance of a number of observations from a universe; that is, the selection of items from an entire aggregate of items at stated intervals.
2. In forestry, a sample chosen in such a way that each individual tree or stem in the population has an equal or independent chance of being included.

RANDOM SHINGLES — Shingles of different widths.

RANDOM VARIATIONS — These include such unusual disturbances as wars, disasters, strikes, fads, or other nonrecurring factors. Synonymns: accidental variations, residual variations.

RANGE
1. An extensive stretch of grazing land, land producing native forage plants.
2. One of a series of government survey lines which extend due north and south at six-mile intervals and which are numbered east or west from the principal meridian. These form the east and west boundaries of townships.
3. The region or area over which something is found, is distributed, or occurs.
4. The difference between the smallest and largest items in a statistical distribution.

RANGE CAPACITY—The grazing capacity of grassland that will typically maintain a satisfactory grass cover expressed as the number of acres of grass needed to carry one animal unit per grazing season or for a specified period.

RANGE CAPACITY FORMULA

$$\text{Range Capacity} = \frac{\text{Density} \times \text{Use Factor} \times \text{Surface Acres}}{\text{Forage Acre Requirement}}$$

RANGE INVENTORY—An itemized list of resources of a management area such as range sites, range condition classes, range condition trends, range use, estimated proper stocking rates, physical developments, and natural conditions such as water barriers, etc.

RANGE MANAGEMENT—The planning and directing of range use to obtain sustained maximum animal production consistent with perpetration of the natural resources. See also Multiple Use.

RANGE SITE—An area of land having a combination of edaphic, climatic, topographic, and natural biotic factors that is significantly different from adjacent areas. These environmental areas are considered as units for purposes of discussion, investigation, and management. Changes from one site to another represent significant differences in potential forage production and/or differences in management requirements for proper land use.

RANGE STATES—Generally considered as the seventeen western states. In these states the major portion of land is used for the production of livestock from range.

RANGE SURVEY—The science of range reconnaissance, or survey, the aim of which is to assemble data which leads to an estimate of grazing capacity. It is divided into two phases: (1) the mapping of grazing types of cover together with such culture and topography as may influence grazing value; and (2) the analysis of the vegetation as to density and species composition for the purpose of determining its livestock grazing capacity.

RANGE UTILIZATION—The degree to which animals have consumed the total current herbage production of a range area, expressed in percentage by weight.

RANGE VEGETATION TYPES—For description of basic types of vegetative cover commonly used in the classification of western grazing lands, see pages 349–350.

RATE—A ratio of one quantity to another, e.g., the ratio of NOI to sales price (or value) is the overall rate; in appraisal work, a capitalization rate is the reciprocal of a capitalization factor.

RATE BASE—The total amount of fair value upon which a public utility is permitted to earn a fair return under the law.

RATE OF INTEREST—The rate on borrowed money; the lending or borrowing rate.

RATE OF RETURN—The current year's annual net income from the operation of an enterprise related to the capital invested, or the appraised value or some other selected capital sum, or the net yield during investment life, giving effect to a finite period of economic life (of buildings), or to limiting time factors (such as the interval to maturity of a bond).

RATE SURCHARGE—The difference between the Capitalization Rate and the Discount Rate; the increment or loading which is added to a basic return on capital to provide for recapture or to compensate for the risk of future loss in capital value.

RATIO—The relation between two similar magnitudes in respect to the number of times the first contains the second, either integrally or fractionally, as the ratio of 3 to 4 may be written 3:4 or 3/4.

RAW MATERIAL—Nonfabricated material used in processing or manufacturing, during the course of which its nature or form is changed. Thus, iron is a raw material used in the production of steel, and steel is a raw material used in the manufacture of automobiles.

REAL ESTATE—The physical land and appurtenances, including structures affixed thereto. In some states, by statute, this term is synonymous with real property. See Real Property.

REAL ESTATE ANALYST—A real estate consultant whose concern often focuses upon investment alternatives, long range effects on investment desirability and specific application to a client's overall business operations and policies. While valuation may be considered by the analyst, it is not necessarily the prime objective. See CRE and SREA. See also Counseling.

REAL ESTATE INVESTMENT TRUST (REIT)—An assembly method which is essentially designed to provide for investment in real estate what the mutual fund has provided for investment in securities. The real estate investment trust provides small investors with a means of combining their funds with those of others, and protects them from the double taxation that would be levied against an ordinary corporation or trust.

REAL ESTATE MARKET—A commercial activity designed to facilitate the exchange of rights in realty, set prices for mutually advantageous exchanges, allocate space among competing alternative uses, determine the pattern of land and space use, and adjust supply to demand.

REAL PROPERTY—The interests, benefits, and rights inherent in the ownership of the physical real estate. It is the bundle of rights with which the ownership of real estate is endowed. In some states, this term, as defined by statute, is synonymous with real estate. Does not include personal property.

REALTOR®—An active member of a local real estate board which, in turn, is a member of the National Association of Realtors.

REALTIST—A member of the National Association of Real Estate Brokers.

REALTY—See Real Estate.

REASSESSMENT—The process of revaluing all the property within a taxing jurisdiction to assign new assessed values. See also Revaluation.

RECAPTURE OF PURCHASE CAPITAL—Recovery by an owner of money invested in real estate generally by a combination of mortgage amortization, annual dividend, and the resale of the equity. The recapture of the mortgage component occurs according to the terms of the periodic installment contract (mortgage) without regard to fluctuations in market value.

RECAPTURE RATE—The annual amount which can be recaptured (or allocated for future recapture), divided by the amount of the original investment.

RECEIVER—A person appointed by a court to exercise control over and administer a property or business when, in the interest of justice, it appears necessary to the court that a qualified and impartial person assume such authority.

RECENT SOIL—See Types of Soil, page 351.

RECESSION—A mild form of depression; a mild slackening in economic activity, not of sufficent strength to create a major change in the business cycle.

RECIPROCAL—Any number divided into 1, e.g., the reciprocal of 2 is ½ or .5; the reciprocal of .2 is $1/.2$ or 5. In appraising, the reciprocal of a rate $(1/R)$ is a factor and, conversely, the reciprocal of a factor $(1/F)$ is a rate.

RECLAMATION—Any method for bringing waste natural resources into productive use. Thus, desert land may be reclaimed through irrigation, forest lands may be restored by artificial planting and seeding, and fields, if not too badly eroded, may be restored through proper methods of cultivation.

RECLAMATION, BUREAU OF—A principal bureau of the United States Department of the Interior. It is engaged in irrigation projects, supplying water to arid sections of 17 western states, and in related activities, such as construction of dams and reservoirs, power plants, transmission lines, canals, tunnels, and aqueducts.

Major projects of the bureau include the Colorado-Big Thompson, the Missouri Basin, the Central Valley, and the Columbia River projects.

RECONCILIATION – The process by which the appraiser evaluates, chooses and selects from among two or more alternative conclusions or indications to reach a single answer (final value estimate). Preferable terminology to the traditional term "correlation." See also Final Reconciliation.

RECONDITIONING – See Rehabilitation.

RECONSTRUCTED OPERATING STATEMENT – A statement usually prepared by an appraiser from figures obtained from numerous sources including an auditor's statement which, in the appraiser's opinion, reflects the probable future Net Operating Income and is in keeping with the quantity and quality of services anticipated in the stabilized income estimated by the appraiser.

RECORDED MAP – A description of a parcel of land by reference to a map which has been filed in the office of the county recorder, e.g., as per map recorded in Book 56 at page 20 of Maps, Records of Blank County, California.

RECORDED PLAT – See Plat.

RECORDING – The entering or recording of a copy of certain legal instruments or documents, as a deed, in a government office provided for this purpose; thus making a public record of the document for the protection of all concerned and giving constructive notice to the public at large.

REDEVELOPMENT – The development or improvement of cleared or undeveloped land in an urban renewal area. In technical usage, this term includes erection of buildings and other development and improvement of the land, by private or public redevelopers to whom the land has been made available, but it does not include site or project improvements installed by a local public agency in preparing the land for disposition by sale or lease.

REDLINING – The reluctance of lenders, investors, or insurers to make loans, invest, or issue insurance on usual terms in a particular geographic area because of some feature or characteristic in the area which is perceived as adversely affecting the utility or security and hence the value of individual parcels of property in the area.

REFINED DEATH RATE – See Death Rate.

REGRESSION – The measurement of the closeness with which two or more variables are associated.

REHABILITATION – The restoration of a property to satisfactory condition without changing the plan, form, or style of a structure. In urban renewal, the restoration to good condition of deteriorated structures, neighborhoods, and public facilities. Neighborhood rehabilitation encompasses structural rehabilitation, and in addition may extend to street improvements and a provision of such amenities as parks and playgrounds.

REINFORCED CONCRETE—Concrete which is strengthened by iron or steel bars, rods, or mesh embedded in it.

REINFORCED CONCRETE CONSTRUCTION—Construction using reinforced concrete for the foundation, frame, floor, roof, or other structural members.

REINFORCEMENT—A system of steel rods or mesh for absorbing tensile and shearing stresses in concrete work, complementing the inherent compressive qualities of concrete.

REINFORCING—Strengthening. Steel rods or mesh are imbedded in concrete to increase the strength in tension. See Reinforced Concrete. Frequently asbestos and glass fibers are used as reinforcement for plaster.

REINVESTMENT RATE—An obtainable rate of return for capital recaptured from a prior investment.

RELICTION—The gradual recession of water from the usual watermark. See also Accretion.

RELIEF—The configuration (irregularities) of a land surface; the topography of the land.

RELIEF MAP—A topographical map; one representing the relief of an area, usually by generalized contour lines.

RELINQUISHMENT—The conveyance by a state transportation agency of a portion of a transportation facility to another governmental agency for transportation use.

RELOCATION—The process by which a federal agency, state or local public agency fulfills the statutory requirements for providing relocation services, moving cost payments and related expenses to individuals, families and businesses displaced from urban renewal areas or because of other federal or federally assisted programs.

RELOCATION PAYMENT—The cash amount paid by a federal agency, state or local public agency to individuals, families and businesses for their reasonable moving and related expenses resulting from their displacement from urban renewal areas or because of other federal or federally assisted programs.

RELOCATION PLAN—The program of governmental agencies for effecting relocation of occupants of an urban renewal area who will be displaced by project activities or by other governmental action.

REMAINDER

1. A future possessory interest in real estate that is given to a third party and matures upon the termination of a limited or determinable fee. For example, A gives B a life estate in A's farm for B's lifetime. A also gives C an interest in the farm upon B's demise. C's interest is a remainder interest. If the farm were to revert to A, the future interest would be a reversionary interest.
2. Property remaining in possession of the owner after a partial taking in eminent domain.

REMAINDERMAN — The person who is entitled to an estate after the prior estate or interest has expired.

REMAINING ECONOMIC LIFE — The number of years remaining in the economic life of the structure or structural component, as of the date of the appraisal.

In part a function of the attitudes and reactions of typical buyers in the market, and in part a function of the market reactions to competitive properties on the market.

REMNANT — A remaining part of land, after a partial taking, that is so small or irregular, to have little economic utility or value.

REMODELING — Changing the plan, form, or style of a structure to correct functional or economic deficiencies.

RENEWAL — As related to property, a replacement of a part or item of property.

RENT — The amount paid for the use of land and/or improvements, or for the use of capital good. For the various types of rent, see Cash Rent, Contract Rent, Crop Share Rent, Dead Rent, Ground Rent, Livestock Share Rent, Market Rent, Percentage Rent, Share Cropping Rent.

RENTABLE AREA — See Gross Rentable Area, Standard Area Measures, pages 295–296.

RENTAL VALUE — The monetary amount reasonably expectable for the right to the agreed use of real estate. It may be expressed as an amount per month or other period of time; per dollar of sales; or per room, per front foot, or other unit of property. Usually, it is established by competitive conditions.

REPAIRS — Current expenditures on the general upkeep to maintain property of any kind as nearly as possible in its original condition and efficiency, without the renewal of any substantial part thereof (i.e., replacement), or change in either the form or material of the building; generally all necessary repairs are undertaken within the period of about one year. This may include renewal of small parts of any unit of a plant. See also Cost of Repairs, Maintenance.

REPLACEMENT — The substitution of a capital asset which has become exhausted or inadequate with one of fundamentally the same type or utility. If the cost of the substitution is greater than the value of the asset replaced, the difference is a betterment. Minor replacements are in the nature of repairs; that is, expenditures for articles or labor which do not increase the original value of that which is replaced. The ordinary use of replacement suggests improvement. An expenditure which is made to extend the remaining life of an item of property, such as the heating system. See also Replacement Cost.

REPLACEMENT COST — The cost of construction at current prices of a building having utility equivalent to the building being appraised but built with modern materials and according to current standards, design and layout. The use of the replacement cost concept presumably eliminates all functional obsolescence, and the only depreciation to be measured is physical deterioration and economic obsolescence.

REPLACEMENT COST LESS DEPRECIATION — The cost of replacement new at current prices less a deduction for depreciation. The deduction for depreciation is the total loss in value arising from physical, functional, and economic causes. It may be greater or less than that indicated by use of age-life guides; for example, the straight line method. See illustration, pages 337–340.

REPRODUCTION COST — The cost of construction at current prices of an exact duplicate or replica using the same materials, construction standards, design, layout, and quality of workmanship, embodying all the deficiencies, superadequacies and obsolescence of the subject building.

REPRODUCTION COST LESS DEPRECIATION — The cost of reproduction new at current prices less a deduction for depreciation. Since the reproduction cost estimate embodies functional obsolescence. The deduction for depreciation requires the measurement of functional obsolescence for valuation purposes. A measure of functional obsolescence may be estimated by comparing reproduction cost new to replacement cost.

RES — Residential Evaluation Specialist. A professional designation conferred by the International Association of Assessing officers upon residential real property appraisers employed in the assessment field.

RESERVE — Appropriation from surplus, allocated to deferred or anticipated contingencies. In business, the amounts of past or current contributions carried in credit accounts created for the purpose of accumulating funds to retire indebtedness or losses payable or expected to accrue in the future. Also, in natural resource properties, the extent of proven or unproven but commercially available resources not required or involved in current operations.

RESERVE FOR DEPLETION—An amount set up before determining net worth to offset the depletion of some asset, such as a mineral deposit, which is carried in the accounts at the value placed upon it before the depletion occurred.

RESERVE FOR DEPRECIATION—An amount reserved before determining net worth to offset depreciation of fixed assets carried at values which were assigned before they had suffered the depreciation for which the reserve is provided. Also referred to as provision for depreciation and allowance for depreciation. See Book Value.

RESERVE FOR REPLACEMENTS—An allowance in the annual operating statement to provide for the replacement of shorter life items (e.g., stoves, refrigerators, carpeting, air-conditioning units), which is necessary in order to sustain a projected level of income.

RESERVOIR—A natural or artificial place, as a lake, pond, or tank, where water is collected and stored to supply water for a community, irrigation, or power plant. The water above a dam used to control the flow of a stream.

RESIDENCE—Any property used as a dwelling. In law, the legal domicile. The presumed motivation is for the owner's occupancy rather than investment income.

RESIDENTIAL BUILDING RATE—The rate of housing starts per 1,000 population, used to determine the level of residential construction in a community.

RESIDENTIAL PROPERTY—A property consisting of a vacant or improved parcel of land devoted to or available for use primarily as a place of abode, such as single-family homes, apartment-hotels, hotels, motels, rooming houses, etc.

RESIDENTIAL SQUARE—Park-like city square, usually cooperatively owned by the occupants of the row houses or town houses which abut on the square.

RESIDUAL—The quantity left over at the end of a process; remainder; commonly used in connection with capitalization techniques (e.g., building residual technique, land residual technique) which develop the value of a property component based upon residual income attributable thereto; sometimes used as a synonym for reversion, i.e., remainder value which reverts to the owner at the end of a lease.

RESIDUAL PROCESS—A technique of the income approach used to estimate the value of the land and/or the building, as indicated by the capitalization of the residual net income attributable to it. See also Building Residual Technique, Land Residual Technique, Property Residual Technique.

RESIDUAL SOIL—See Types of Soil, page 351.

RESORT MOTEL—A motel operation in a recreational or resort area, offering the customary advantages of a motel plus varying degrees of hotel-type services; and with guests staying for periods usually longer than overnight as in the typical motel. A resort motel may be a part of a planned resort area including such facilities as a marina, tennis courts, golf course, etc.

RESORT PROPERTY—The types of property located in resort areas or devoted to recreational use; either public or private. Summer homes, hotels, motels, etc., are types of resort property.

RESTRICTIVE COVENANT—A private agreement restricting the use and occupancy of real estate which is a part of the conveyance and is binding on all subsequent purchasers. Such covenants may have to do with control of lot size, set-back and/or placement of buildings, architecture, cost of improvements.

RETAINING WALL—A sloping or vertical structural support for confining or restricting movement of adjoining mobile material (earth or water).

RETROFIT—A modification in the design, construction, material, or equipment of an existing building in order to reduce energy use.

REUSE APPRAISAL—An appraisal under the provisions of the National Housing Act of 1949, as amended, to estimate the resale value of either vacant land or (in some instances) improved property in an urban renewal project area, subject to the restrictions and controls set forth in the Urban Renewal Plan for the project area. Among others, the Plan will specify land use, density or floor area ratios, coverage, and height. The appraisal is the basis on which disposal prices are established for resale purposes.

REVALUATION—The mass appraisal of all property within an assessment jurisdiction to obtain equalization of assessed values. Also for reappraisal of a former assignment.

REVALUATION LEASE—A type of lease which provides for the periodic revaluation of the leased property and re-establishment of its rental based upon a revised estimate of the market value of the leased property.

REVENUE STAMPS (DOCUMENTARY STAMPS)—Adhesive stamps issued by the state government, which must be purchased and affixed, in amounts provided by law, to documents or instruments representing original issues, sales, and transfers of stocks and bonds; and deeds of conveyances (may provide an indication of sales price).

REVERSE ANNUITY MORTGAGE (RAM)—An alternative mortgage instrument which enables the homeowner (particularly elderly) to realize the value of their home equities in the form of an annuity-like income flow for life (or a predetermined fixed period). This income would presumably make it possible for elderly homeowners, especially those with low incomes, to remain in their homes for their lifetimes.

REVERSE LEVERAGE—See Negative Leverage.

REVERSION—The return of rights in real estate to the grantor, such as the return of the full use of real estate to a lessor at the expiration of a lease; the estate returned or due to be returned; in mortgage-equity analyses synonymous with proceeds of resale at end of the ownership projection period.

REVERSIONARY RIGHT—The right to repossess and resume the full and sole use and proprietorship of real property which temporarily has been alienated by lease, easement, etc. According to the terms of the controlling instrument, the reversionary right becomes effective at a stated time or under certain conditions, such as the termination of leasehold, abandonment of a right of way, or at the end of the estimated economic life of the improvements.

REVERSION FACTOR—That factor (present worth of one) which is used to discount a single future payment to a present worth figure, given the appropriate discount rate and discount period. See Basic Formulas, pages 334–335.

REVERTER CLAUSE—A clause providing that title reverts to grantor upon violation of restriction set forth in deed. Effect of such reverter would affect marketability of title of mortgagee and thus the value of the property.

RIBBON BOARD—A board used as a horizontal structural member which is "let into" outside wall studs, on which upper story floor joists rest while being spiked to the studs in balloon framing; also called a ledger or ledger board. See illustration, page 305.

RIBBON DEVELOPMENT—See Roadside Development.

RIDGE—The top horizontal edge or peak of a roof.

RIDGE BOARD—The horizontal structural member at the top of a roof, against which the upper ends of the rafters are butted. See illustration, page 306.

RIGHT OF ACCESS—See Access Right.

RIGHT OF ENTRY—The right to enter and begin construction of a project upon land which is in the process of being acquired.

RIGHT OF IMMEDIATE POSSESSION — The right to occupy property after preliminary steps for acquisition have been taken and before final settlement.

RIGHT OF WAY — The privilege which one person, or persons particularly described, may have of passing over the land of another in some particular line. Usually, an easement over the land of another. Used to describe a strip of land used for railroad and highway purposes, for pipe or pole lines, and for private or public passageways.

RIGHTS — A claim to title to, or interest in, anything whatsoever which is enforceable by law. See also Abutter's Access, Air, Avigation, Flowage, Littoral, Reversionary, Riparian, Squatter's, Subsurface, Surface, Water Rights.

RIGID CONDUIT — A rigid pipe used as a protective cover for electrical wiring.

RIGID FOUNDATION — See Floating Foundation.

RIPARIAN — Pertaining to the bank of the river or other body of water.

RIPARIAN RIGHTS
1. The right of owners of land bordering on a stream to have the natural flow of the stream wash their land. The right to use the water which passes over and along their land provided they use it so as not to injure other riparian owners. This right of use is a property right and is part of an owner's estate in the land.
2. The common law doctrine of riparian rights has been superseded by the doctrine of beneficial use in some states.
3. It is a right of an owner of land abutting a body of water to make use of the water area for piers, boat houses, for fishing, boating, and navigation, and the right of access for such purposes, which right is limited by public need if on a navigable stream.
4. The right of owners to the use and enjoyment of water which flows across or along their land. See also Water Rights, Beneficial Use, Accretion.

RIPRAP — A foundation or wall of stones or rocks loosely placed together without order; especially used in deep water to prevent scour on the sides of bulkheads and similar construction, and at the bends of a river to prevent erosion during seasons of fast flowing water. May also be wood or concrete beams laid in regular patterns.

RISER — The vertical part of a stair step back of the tread.

RISK — The possibility of loss. The term is used to describe the chance of loss on an investment or from a particular hazard, such as fire, earthquake or wind.

RISK FACTOR—The portion of any given return or rate of return from capital invested in an enterprise that is assumed to cover the risks pertinent to the particular investment; as distinguished from and in excess of the return or rate obtainable from funds invested upon conditions of virtual certainty of the safety of principal.

RISK PREMIUM—In risk or security analysis, the return over and above the risk free rate.

RISK RATE—The annual rate of return on capital which is commensurate with the risk assumed by the investor; the rate of interest or yield necessary to attract capital.

RIVER BED—That part between the banks worn by the regular flow of the water.

ROADSIDE DEVELOPMENT—The term applies to those ribbon-like residential, commercial, and industrial developments which occupy the frontage properties abutting on highways leading from urban communities.

ROCK—Mineral matter of various compositions, consolidated or unconsolidated, found in nature. See also Igneous Rock, Metamorphic Rock, Sedimentary Rock.

ROCK WOOL—See Mineral Wool.

ROLL—See Tax Roll.

ROLLOVER (RENEWABLE) MORTGAGE—A mortgage, the terms (interest rate) of which are reviewed and adjusted periodically and according to contract. Technically, the outstanding principal balance is due at the renewal date; however, lenders may offer to extend for a second renewal period at going market rates or even renew the entire amount of the mortgage at the then current market rate. Typically, only the interest rate is adjusted, and monthly payments are computed on the basis of the remaining term for the following renewal period.

ROLL ROOFING—A roofing material made of compressed fibers saturated with asphalt, supplied in rolls.

ROOF—The top portion of a structure. Types of roofs include double-pitch or butterfly, flat, gable, gambrel, hip, lean-to, M, mansard, pyramid, sawtooth, semicircular, single-pitch. See illustrations, page 300.

ROOF PITCH—The slope or inclination of a roof. It is usually expressed in inches as a five inch pitch, or sometimes a 5-in-12 or 5-to-12 pitch, each of which means that for every 12 inches of horizontal distance, the roof slope rises 5 inches.

ROOFER—A piece of lumber, usually one inch (nominal) thick, laid fastened to the rafters; used to enclose the top of a building frame and to serve as base for roof covering; sometimes called roof sheathing. See illustration, page 306.

ROOM — An interior subdivision of a structure, usually accompanied by descriptive term signifying use, such as living room, bedroom. Rooms are customarily designated as being of three types. See Bathroom, Habitable Room, Utility Room.

ROOM COUNT — There is no accepted national standard. FHA counts as one-half room an alcove opening off the living room, and does not count dining space within the kitchen. Most generally accepted method is to consider as separate rooms only those which are effectively divided, excluding bathrooms.

ROOT-MEAN-SQUARE AVERAGE — See Standard Deviation.

ROOT STOCK — That part of the tree or vine which includes the root system and which may differ in type from the crown and trunk of the plant. A plant will be budded or grafted to a differing root stock in order to provide a root system more resistant to disease or nematodes, or for rapid growth encouragement. The life span of the tree or vine will be dependent upon the type of root stock.

ROTARY INTERCHANGE — A multiple intersection of highways in which the traffic interchange for entrance and exit is controlled in a circular traffic flow.

ROTATION — The growing of two or more different crops on the same parcel of land in different years, to maintain or enhance the fertility and productivity of the soil.

ROTUNDA — A circular building or room, covered by a dome.

ROUGHAGE — Plant materials containing a low proportion of nutrients per unit of weight and usually bulky and coarse, high in fiber, and low in total digestible nutrients. Roughage may be classified as either dry or green.

ROUGH HARDWARE — Metal ware such as nails, screws and bolts which are "buried" in the construction and are rarely exposed to view.

ROUND TIMBER — Timber used in the original round form, such as poles, piling, and mine timbers. See also Lumber, Timber.

ROW CROP — Farm crops planted in rows which permit cultivation during growth. They are generally vegetables or produce used for human consumption, although some seed crops are planted in rows.

ROW HOUSES — A series of individual houses, having architectural unity and a common wall between each unit, e.g., townhouses, maisonettes.

ROW STORES — See Strip Development.

ROYALTY—In real estate usage, it is the money paid to an owner of realty for the right of depleting the property of its natural resource, such as oil, gas, minerals, stone, builders' sand and gravel, and timber. Usually, the royalty payment is a stated part of the amount extracted, as one-sixth or one-eighth of the oil and gas removed, or five cents per ton of sand and gravel taken away, or a given price per cubic yard of material extracted. The royalty payment is a combination of (1) rent and (2) depreciation (depletion charge). See also Landowner's Royalty, Overriding Royalty.

RUBBLE—Field stone.

RUBBLEWORK—Masonry built of rubble or roughly dressed stones laid in irregular courses.

RURAL—Pertaining to the country, as distinguished from the city or the town; in contrast to urban or suburban.

RURAL-URBAN FRINGE—A term devised to describe those areas lying outside but adjacent to cities where the land use is in transition from rural to urban.

RURBAN
1. Neither rural nor urban, but having characteristics of both.
2. In some sections, used to denote the characteristics of land or an area (a) beyond the limits of cities or thickly settled communities, (b) on an all-weather road, (c) having available many of the usual urban utility services, and (d) generally divided into small tracts or country estates.
3. In other sections, used to denote the characteristics of an area in a state of active transition from farm use to suburban development.

SRA—Senior Residential Appraiser: a professional designation conferred by the Society of Real Estate Appraisers. See SREA.

SREA—Senior Real Estate Analyst: a professional designation (subject to certification every 5 years) conferred by the Society of Real Estate Appraisers. Professional membership in the Society is awarded after extensive examination of an applicant's qualifications, education, experience and local standing. Members are pledged to maintain a high level of trust and integrity in their practice and adhere to a specified code of ethics and standards of professional practice.

SRPA—Senior Real Property Appraiser: a professional designation conferred by the Society of Real Estate Appraisers. See SREA.

SAFE RATE—The rate obtainable on an investment with maximum safety and minimum risk; the prevailing interest rate on insured savings accounts or government savings bonds.

SAGEBRUSH – See Types of Range Vegetation, page 349.

SALE BARN – A livestock auction shed located at auction sales yards. Livestock offered for sale are exhibited as they are sold.

SALE CONTRACT – A basic, written document signed by buyer and seller agreeing to the transfer of ownership interests in real estate.

SALE-LEASEBACK – A financing device in which real property is sold by its owner-user who simultaneously enters into a lease with the buyer such that the owner-user has continuing use of the property. The sale-leaseback carries with it the same essential advantages and disadvantages to lessor and lessee that leasing in general provides.

SALE PRICE – The price at which a property actually sold.

SALES-ASSESSMENT RATIO – The ratio derived by dividing the selling price by the assessed value.

SALES-RATIO ANALYSIS – Study of the relationship between assessed values, sales prices and the deviations resulting from differences between the two. The purpose of such an analysis is to determine the efficiency and fairness of assessing activities of a particular jurisdiction.

SALES VALUE – An incorrect term for sale price.

SALINE SOIL – See Types of Soil, page 351.

SALT BOX ARCHITECTURE – See New England Colonial (Salt Box) Architecture.

SALTBUSH – See Types of Range Vegetation, page 349.

SALVAGE VALUE – The price expectable for the whole (that is, a house) or a part of the whole (that is, a plumbing fixture) for removal from the premises, usually for use elsewhere.

SAMPLE – In statistics, a limited or finite number of observations selected from a universe and from which qualified quantitative generalization can be drawn with respect to the universe.

SAMPLING ERROR – The difference between a sample statistic and the same characteristic which would have been found had the entire population been tested.

SAND – Small rock or mineral fragments having diameters ranging from 1 to 0.005 mm.: coarse sand, 1 to 0.05; sand, 0.50 to 0.25; fine sand, 0.25 to 0.10; very fine sand, 0.100 to 0.005. The term is also applied to soils containing 90% or more of all grades combined.

SANDWICH BEAM – See Flitch Beam.

SANDWICH LEASE – A lease in which the "sandwich leaseholder" is the lessee from one party and the lessor to another (the owner of a sandwich lease is neither the fee owner nor the user of the property); a leaseholder in a chain of leases excluding the ultimate sub-lessee.

SANDWICH LEASEHOLDER — Lessor under a sandwich lease (see above).

SANDWICH PANEL — A core of insulation covered on both sides with such materials as concrete, metal, or asbestos.

SANDY LOAM — See Types of Soil, page 351.

SANITARY BASE — A three-member base consisting of a common baseboard, base mould above, and a shoe mould which is "let up" behind the common base.

    This differs from the others in that the shoe mould is fastened to the floor and the common base is nailed to the studs above it, whereas in the case of common and moulded bases the common baseboard rests directly on the floor. See illustration, page 307.

SANITARY SEWER — A sewer carrying only sewage, not storm water rainfall.

SASH — The framework which holds the glass in a window or door.

SATELLITE CITIES — Subordinate communities in a metropolitan area, having vital economic ties with the central city.

SATISFACTORY RATE OF RETURN — The interest rate, risk rate, or yield rate which is considered sufficient to attract capital and satisfy the investor; it may or may not be the same as the internal rate of return developed or capable of being developed within a particular investment or portfolio.

SATURATION ZONE — The lower ground water zone. The area below the aeration zone serving as a reservoir for ground water which feeds wells, streams, and springs.

SAW LOG — A log large enough to permit the production of sawed lumber or other sawed products. Its size and quality vary with the utilization practices of the region.

SAW-TOOTH ROOF — The series of single-pitch roofs usually found on factory buildings, garages, or similar structures. Allows abundant light and ventilation. See illustration, page 300.

SCALE
1. The estimated sound contents in terms of a given log rule of a log or group of logs. Also, to estimate the sound contents of a log or group of logs.
2. A measured length on maps and other engineered plans which relates map measurements to actual measurements. For example, one inch on a map equalling one foot of physical length.

SCANTLING LUMBER — Yard lumber 2 inches thick and less than 8 inches wide.

SCARCITY — Limitations on the available supply of an economic good relative to the desire for it.

SCARCITY VALUE — Value caused by a demand for a good, the supply of which cannot be increased. Antique furniture is an example.

SCATTER DIAGRAM — A chart with data points plotted according to coordinates representing two variables.

SCENIC EASEMENT — A restriction imposed upon the use of the property of the grantor for the purpose of preserving the natural state of scenic and historical attractiveness of adjacent lands of the grantee, usually the city, county, state, or federal government. In the grant, the grantor agrees to refrain from the erection of any advertising structure or any new structure, or the alteration of any existing structure without the consent of the grantee.

SCRAP VALUE — The price expectable for a part of a property for sale and removal from the premises for the reclamation of the value of the basic material itself, such as copper.

SCRATCH COAT — The first coat of plaster, which is scratched or scored to provide a bond for the second coat.

SCR BRICK — A larger than average brick, designed for use in a one-story wall where a single layer of such bricks is sufficient.

SCRIBNER RULE (OR SCALE) — The Scribner Log Rule is a diagram rule that assumes one-inch boards at least 4 inches wide and a one-fourth inch saw kerf. This rule does not take into account the taper of logs. It gives a large overrun for small logs, and for logs longer than 16 feet. It is not recommended for logs less than 12 inches in diameter. The Scribner Rule, oldest diagram rule (1846) now in general use, is used on all national forest timber scales. It is also more generally used on fir and pine timber.

SCULPTURE — Decorative features carved from wood, stone, marble, or other similar materials.

SCULPTURING — Regrading land to provide privacy, restrict sound and increase aesthetic appeal.

SCUTTLE — A framed opening in a ceiling or roof, fitted with a lid or cover.

SECONDARY LOCATION — A term of relativity, signifying the locations surrounding or adjacent to the prime location; second-best locations; locations which gain enhancement from proximity to a prime location.

SECONDARY MORTGAGE MARKET — The market in home mortgages. Transactions in the secondary market are the purchases and sales of such mortgages after their origination by lenders. FNMA, commercial savings banks, insurance companies, and savings and loan associations, for example, are often buyers in the secondary market. Mortgage companies in particular and commercial banks to some extent are interested in the resale of mortgages. The ability of this secondary market to absorb mortgage loans into investment portfolios has a direct relationship to the amount of new mortgage loans made.

SECONDARY SOILS – See Types of Soil, page 351.

SECOND BOTTOM – The first terrace level of a stream valley lying above the flood plain rarely or never flooded. See also First Bottom, Flood Plain.

SECOND FOOT – A measurement term indicating a flow of one cubic foot of water per second, or 449 gallons per minute. See Measures, page 274.

SECOND GROWTH – Forest growth which comes up after removal of the old stand by cutting, fire, or other causes. It is the smaller trees left after lumbering, or the trees available for a second logging operation.

SECTION – In public lands survey, one of the 36 sections, each a mile square, into which each township is divided. In architecture, a drawing depicting a view of a cross section of a building, showing the details of that particular portion of the building.

SECULAR TREND – The long-time growth or decline occurring within the data. Ordinarily, the period covered should include not less than ten years.

SEDIMENTARY PEAT – That which is made up of finely divided plant and possibly some animal remains. See also Peat Soil; Types of Soil, page 351.

SEDIMENTARY ROCK – A rock composed of particles deposited from suspension in water. The chief groups of sedimentary rocks are: (1) conglomerates (from gravel); (2) sandstones (from sands); (3) shales (from clays); and (4) limestones (from calcium carbonate deposits). There are many intermediate types.

SELECT LUMBER – Lumber, such as flooring, which is "selected" for length, color, grain, and relative absence of imperfections; very close to "clear" grade and usually contains a substantial quantity of it.

SELF-SUPPORTING WALLS – Walls which support their own weight, but do not carry the weight of the floors above or below, the roof, or the live load.

SEMICIRCULAR ROOF – A curved roof often used on farm barns. See illustration, page 300.

SENTIMENTAL VALUE—An emotional relationship between a person (usually the owner) and a property. Not related to market value.

SEPTIC SYSTEM—A private sewage system usually consisting of a septic tank, distribution box, and septic field, together with connecting pipes and laterals.

SEPTIC TANK—A tank in which sewage is held until decomposition of the organic matter by natural bacterial action has taken place, dissolving most of the solids into liquids and gases which flow or are released into the septic field.

SEQUENTIAL—Operations performed one after another.

SERVICE INDUSTRY—An industry based upon the sale of a service, such as utility companies, as compared to the sale of a product.

SERVICE LINE—A pipeline which connects a public water or gas main with a property.

SERVICE PROPERTY—See Special-Purpose Property.

SERVICE ROAD—See Frontage Road.

SERVICE STATION—A commercial enterprise designed for the special purpose of providing services and products for automobiles and trucks. Referred to as filling stations, gasoline stations or gasoline service stations.

SERVICES
1. The term is used in economics to describe the contribution of persons or business organizations which render a service, as a teacher or laundry, rather than the production of goods.
2. The contributions of a community provided by local government, as police and fire protection, water and sewer systems, etc.

SET-BACK—The term refers to zoning regulations which designate the distance a building must be set-back from the front property line; or the height at which the upper floors of a building are recessed, set-back, from the face of a lower structure. In tall buildings there may be more than one set-back.

SET-BACK LINE—A line outside the right of way, established by public authority or private restriction, on the highway side of which the erection of buildings or other permanent improvements is controlled.

SET-OFF—A reduction in the thickness of a wall; a flat or sloping ledge or projection below a thinner part of a wall. Also, used to describe a sunken panel or recess of any kind in a wall.

SET-OFF RULE—In eminent domain, the rule with respect to setting off special benefits. The federal courts and those of some states allow set-off of benefits against both the value of the land taken and the damages to the residue. In other jurisdictions the rule allows the setting off of benefits against only the damages to the residue. It is a moot question in some jurisdictions whether benefits which exceed the value of the land taken and damages may be off-set against the property being appraised.

SEVERANCE DAMAGES—It is the diminution of the market value of the remainder area, in the case of a partial taking, which arises (a) by reason of the taking (severance), and/or (b) the construction of the improvement in the manner proposed.

SEWER—An underground system of pipes or conduits which carry sewage and/or rainfall water from the point of reception to the point of disposal. See also Combination Sewer, Sanitary Sewer, Septic System, Storm Sewer.

SEWER LINE EASEMENT—An easement for the construction, maintenance and operation of a sewage disposal line.

SHARE CROPPER—A tenant farmer who, in addition to land and living quarters, receives seed, stock, and implements from the owner and in payment therefor shares the crops produced.

SHARE CROPPING RENT—A compromise between renting and wage payments. Ordinarily, the tenant contributes labor only and is managed and financed by the owner.

SHEATHING—The first tight covering applied to the outside of a building; in frame construction, applied to studs or rafters to serve as a base to which outside covering is fastened. See illustration, pages 304–306 and 308–310.

SHEATHING LINE—The outside vertical plane of exterior wall sheathing.

SHEET PILING—Planking or steel shafts driven close together vertically, to form a temporary wall around an excavation.

SHED ROOF—See Lean-to Roof.

SHELTER BELT—A band or row of trees or large shrubs which is planted in a manner to afford protection for farm buildings against blizzards, snowstorms, and prevailing winds in open plains country.

SHINGLES—A roof or wall surfacing material composed of thin small sheets of various types of waterproof material, such as asphalt, wood, slate, or tile.

SHOE OR SOLE—A structural member laid horizontally on the rough flooring, which serves as a base for interior partition framing. Used extensively in platform-type construction. See illustration, page 305.

Also used as a base for bearing partitions on top of an "I" beam or steel beam where studs are "let down" to their support. See illustration, page 306.

SHOPPING CENTER—A tract of land improved with a coordinated group of retail buildings having a variety of types of stores, free parking and under single real estate ownership or control. Generally there are three widely recognized types: Regional, Community, and Neighborhood.

SHORE LINE—The land between high and low tide.

SHORING—Temporary structural columns, beams, and bracing, used to support loads during construction.

SHORT-LIVED ITEMS—Those components or elements of a structure or items of equipment whose remaining economic lives are shorter or are expected to be shorter than the remaining economic life of the entire structure.

SHORT-TERM LEASE—An indefinite term, but customary usage implies a contract period of any term under ten years.

SHOULDER—The boundary land along the outer edge of a paved highway which may or may not be paved. Its function is to accommodate stopped vehicles.

SIDE—The longitudinal walls of a structure.

SIDE DITCH—An open water course, possible paved, for the control and removal of storm water from the paved surface of the adjacent highway.

SIDE JAMB—A piece of finish material laid vertically on the interior sides of a door or window opening, which actually shapes the opening. See illustration, pages 304 and 308–310.

SIDING

1. Finish lumber used on exterior walls, such as bevel siding, boards and battens, shingles.
2. A railroad track auxiliary to the main track used for meeting or passing trains, storage of cars, loading or unloading, and other designated purposes with connection at both ends to the main track.

SIGHT LINE—A line or area of unimpeded visibility, usually used to indicate the distance from which an existing business property or potential commercial site is visible to approaching (vehicular) traffic.

SIGHT LINE EASEMENT—An easement granted for the protection of a sight line, which usually prohibits construction or natural growth which might obstruct visibility of a property to approaching (vehicular) traffic.

SILAGE – See Ensilage.

SILL

1. Framing lumber placed atop and around a foundation to serve as a level base on which to support exterior wall studs and the ends of floor joists.

   See illustration pages 304 and 306 for Box Sill used in platform wall framing, and common sill used in balloon wall framing.

2. The lowest piece on which a window or exterior door stands, usually slanted down slightly from the horizontal to provide for rain water runoff. See illustration, pages 304 and 308–310.

SILO – A tall cylindrical building in which fermenting green fodder is preserved as ensilage.

SILT – Small mineral soil grains, the particles of which range in diameter from 0.050 to 0.002 mm. The individual grains cannot be detected by feel. See also Loam, page 154, Types of Soil, page 351.

SILT CLAY LOAM – See Types of Soil, page 351.

SILT LOAM – See Types of Soil, page 351.

SIMPLE INTEREST – Interest paid only on the original principal, not on interest accrued.

SIMULATION – The use of an experimental model designed to approximate actual conditions.

SINGLE FAMILY HOUSE – A basic term used to designate all types of dwellings designed for occupancy by one family.

SINGLE PITCH ROOF – A single plane roof pitched more than 20 degrees. See illustration, page 300.

SINKING FUND – A fund in which periodic deposits of equal amounts of money are made for the purpose of ultimately paying a debt, or replacing assets. Usually it is a fund in which is placed equal annual or monthly deposits which, with compound interest thereon, will accumulate to a predetermined amount at the end of a stated period of time.

SINKING FUND FACTOR – A multiplier used to compute periodic contributions to a sinking fund which will grow with compound interest at a selected rate for a specified period of time; the amortization rate; the amount per period which will grow to one dollar at a given rate in a given period of time; one of the classic six functions of one dollar.

SINKING FUND METHOD – A process by which provision is made for recovery of the value or cost of an asset by means of a sinking fund.

SINKING FUND TABLE—A tabulation of amounts which, if invested annually in a compound interest-bearing account at a stated rate, accumulate a desired amount at a specified date in the future.

SIPHON—A bent tube for carrying water from an irrigation ditch to the field.

SITE—A parcel of land which is improved to the extent that it is ready for use for the purpose for which it is intended.

SITE ANALYSIS—The identification and analysis of the characteristics that create, enhance or detract from the utility and marketability of a site.

SITE DEVELOPMENT COST—Those direct and indirect costs which have to do with preparing a site for use, as clearing, grading, installing public utilities, etc.

SIX FUNCTIONS OF ONE DOLLAR—The six related compound interest functions shown in standard compound interest tables and used in the mathematics of finance. The six functions are called: Amount of $1; amount of $1 per period; sinking fund factor; present worth of $1; present worth of $1 per period; partial payment. See illustration, page 333–336.

SKELETON STEEL CONSTRUCTION—See Steel Construction.

SKEWNESS—The degree of deviation from symmetry in a distribution.

SKIN—Any covering, outer coating, or surface layer. In construction, used to indicate the covering of a structure.

SKIN WALL—External wall covering of aluminum, porcelain enamel, steel, or other material.

SKYLIGHT—A glassed opening in a roof.

SLAB—Any broad, flat, relatively thin piece of wood, stone, or other solid material. Has been adopted to describe a floor or foundation of concrete, either on the ground or supported.

SLASH—Branches, bark, tops, chunks, cull logs, uprooted stumps, and broken or uprooted trees left on the ground after logging. Also, large accumulation of debris after wind or fire. See also Slashing.

SLASHING—Forest area which has been logged off and upon which the limbs and tops remain, or which is deep in debris as the result of fire or wind.

SLEEPER—A timber laid horizontally, as on the ground, to support something above it. A strip of wood anchored to a concrete floor or nailed to subflooring and to which the finished floor is nailed.

SLIDING WINDOW—See Traverse Window.

SLIP—Navigable water space between two piers, generally for small boat storage.

SLOPE—The inclination or deviation of a surface from the horizontal; the grade. The degree of inclination usually expressed as a percentage. In highway usage it refers to the graded area beyond the shoulder area which extends to natural and undistributed ground. Slopes are classified as:

0%– 2%—nearly level and/or gently undulating
3%– 8%—gently sloping and/or undulating
9%–15%—moderately sloping and/or rolling
16%–30%—strongly sloping and/or hilly
31%–45%—steep
Over 45%—very steep

SLOPE EASEMENT—An easement acquired to permit the cuts or fills of highway construction.

SLOW-BURNING CONSTRUCTION—Mill construction; so called because its structural members will char under ordinary fire temperatures for some time before failure.

SLUM AREA—Slum areas usually are characterized by a coincidence of overcrowding in old, obsolete, deteriorated structures which lack natural light, ventilation, and sanitary facilities, as well as other modern conveniences. See also Blighted Area.

SNOW FENCE—A portable slat fence which is placed along the course of a highway or road at strategic points to keep off drifting snow.

SOD—Vegetation which grows so as to form a mat; synonymous with "turf."

SOFFIT—The undersurface of a building member, as an arch, cornice, overhang, or stairway. See illustration, page 305.

SOFTWARE—Programs and routines associated with a computer system as distinct from the equipment (hardware) itself.

SOFTWOOD—Wood from conifers, as redwood, cedar, pine, fir, etc.

SOFTWOODS—In forestry, applied usually to conifers or evergreens; no relationship to the hardness of the wood.

SOIL—The natural medium for the growth of plants on the surface of the earth. A natural body in which plants grow. It is composed of organic and mineral materials. For description of various types of soil, see pages 351–354.

SOIL AGGREGATE—A single mass or cluster of soil consisting of many soil particles held together, such as a clod, prism, crumb or granule. See also Granular Structure.

SOIL BANK – A program administered by Commodity Stabilization Service of the Department of Agriculture in which farmers contract to divert land from production of unneeded crops to conservation uses, and for which they receive an annual rent (payment).

SOIL CAPABILITY – The relative suitability of soils for crops, grazing, and other purposes. There are eight such capability classes. All of the soils in each class may have limitations and may present management problems of the same relative degree, but of different kinds. Productivity may vary widely among soils of one capability class.

SOIL CONSERVATION – The methods and techniques used to prevent soil depletion and to restore its productivity. It includes the use of chemical or organic fertilizers to replace elements lost through usage or leaching; adaption of proper tillage methods and crop rotation to prevent breakdown of soil structure; and use of terracing or contour cultivation to reduce erosion of topsoil.

SOIL CONSERVATION SERVICE – A division of the Department of Agriculture concerned with the department's conservation program with respect to obtaining a better balanced agriculture through physical adjustments in the use of land, to conserving natural resources, and to reducing flood hazards. It cooperates with local soil conservation districts by providing technical assistance.

SOIL EROSION – The wearing or carrying away of the topsoil by running water or wind. See also Erosion.

SOIL FERTILITY – The quality which enables a soil to provide the proper compounds, in the proper amounts, and in the proper balance for the growth of specified plants when other factors, such as light, temperatures, and the physical condition of the soil, are favorable. An expression of the relative amounts of available soil nutrients.

SOIL FUMIGATION – The practice of chemically treating the soil, usually prior to planting, for the purpose of destroying soil-borne diseases, fungus, nematodes or noxious grasses and weeds. Such chemicals may be sprayed or drilled into the soil. If introduction is in a gaseous form, retention is normally accomplished by covering the ground with plastic sheets.

SOIL GENESIS – Mode of origin of the soil, referring particularly to the processes responsible for the development of the solum from the unconsolidated parent material.

SOIL MAP – A map designed to portray the distribution and location of soil types, phases, and complexes as well as other selected cultural and physical features.

SOIL PHASE—A subdivision of soil type covering departures from the typical characteristics. For example, these may be such factors as deep phase, shallow phase, poorly drained phase. See also Phase Soil, page 353.

SOIL POROSITY—The degree to which the soil mass is permeated with pores or cavities. It is expressed as the percentage of the whole volume of the soil which is unoccupied by solid particles.

SOIL PRODUCTIVITY—The capacity of a soil to produce crops under the environment where it occurs and under a specified system of management.

SOIL PROFILE—A vertical section of the soil through all its horizons and extending into the parent material.

SOIL PROFILE GROUP—A grouping of soils based upon certain profile characteristics. Alluvial soil profile groups are differentiated by progressive increases in compaction and fine clay accumulations in the subsoils. Primary soil profile groups are differentiated on the basis of the nature and composition of the underlying parent material.

SOIL SAMPLE—A vertical cross-section of the soil profile which is usually taken from the top 6 to 18 inches of the soil.

SOIL SERIES—A grouping of soils having the same character of profile; the same general range in color, structure, consistence, sequence of horizons, and the same conditions of relief and drainage; and of common or similar origin (parent material) and mode of formation.

SOIL STRUCTURE—The arrangement of the individual particles in the soil and the size and shape of the aggregates. The following are the principal types of soil structure: columnar, adobe, granular, buckshot, crumb, lumpy, cloddy, puddled, nutlike, massive.

SOIL SURVEY REPORT—A written report with a soil map, describing the areas surveyed, the characteristics and capabilities for use of the soil types and phases shown on the map, and the principal factors responsible for soil development.

SOIL TEXTURE—The relative proportion of the various size groups of individual soil grains.

SOIL TYPE—A soil which, throughout its full extent, has relatively uniform texture in addition to the soil series characteristics. For description of various types, see pages 351–354.

SOLAR DESIGN
  1. Active. A building design which uses solar collectors outside the building envelope to gather energy for space and/or water heating.

2. Passive. A building design which takes into account the position and intensity of the sun to provide interior heating.

SOLID SET—A sprinkler irrigation system with permanently installed laterals and sprinklers.

SOLUM—The upper part of the soil profile, above the parent material, in which the processes of soil formation are taking place. In mature soil this includes the A and B horizons (which see) and the character of the material may be, and usually is, greatly unlike that of the parent material beneath. Living roots and life processes are largely confined to the solum.

SONIC—Anything pertaining to or of sound; also, denotes a speed approximately that at which sound waves travel.

SOUND VALUE—Used synonymously with depreciated cost for fire insurance purposes.

SOUTHERN COLONIAL ARCHITECTURE—Style of design similar to both Georgian and modern colonial, but is distinguished by the use of two-story columns which form a porch across the long facade or at the side.

SPAN—The horizontal clear distance between supports, as those of a bridge, or between columns of a structure.

SPANDREL—A triangular space formed by an arch, any horizontal construction member above it, and any vertical member or another arch beside it. Used to designate any horizontal space lying between two structural features of a building, as that between the top of windows on one floor and the windows on the floor above.

SPANDREL BEAM—A beam which lies in the same vertical plane as the exterior wall.

SPANISH ARCHITECTURE—A residential architectural style characterized by its heavy tile roof and walls of adobe or stucco. Featuring an enclosed patio, it is designed for outdoor living.

SPAULDING RULE (or scale)—The Spaulding Rule is the statute log rule of California. It was constructed by N.W. Spaulding in 1878 from diagrams of logs measuring 10 to 96 inches in diameter. An 11/32-inch saw kerf and one-inch lumber was assumed.

The size of the slab was varied according to the size of the log. This error of construction gives an overrun for large logs. The table is prepared for logs from 12 to 24 feet long. Longer logs are scaled by doubling the value in the table. By doing this, the taper in logs is ignored. This feature is the most serious defect in the rule. There is considerable overrun when the modern band saw is used because of the large saw kerf used in the Spaulding Rule.

The Spaulding Rule is used throughout the redwood region either in its original form or as the Humboldt Rule.

SPECIAL ASSESSMENT—A charge made by government against real estate to defray the cost of making a public improvement adjacent to the property which, while of general community benefit, is of special benefit to the property so assessed.

SPECIAL BENEFITS—Those benefits which accrue directly and solely to the advantage of the property remaining after a partial taking. See also Benefits, General Benefits, Set-off Rule.

SPECIAL-PURPOSE PROPERTY—A property devoted to or available for utilization for a special purpose, such as a clubhouse, a church property, a public museum, a public school, and so on. It also includes other buildings having value, such as hospitals, theatres, breweries, etc., which cannot be converted to other uses without large capital investment.

SPECIFIC HEAT—The quantity of heat required to raise the temperature of one pound of any substance 1°F, expressed in B.T.U.'s.

SPECIFICATIONS—Written instructions to the builder containing all the information pertaining to dimensions, materials, workmanship, style, fabrication, colors, and finishes which supplement the details appearing on the working drawings.

SPECULATIVE VALUE—See Potential Value.

SPECULATOR—One who speculates; that is, one who buys any commodity, including real estate, in the expectancy of selling in a higher market.

SPEED-CHANGE LANE—An auxiliary travel lane designed and constructed to permit the acceleration and deceleration of vehicles entering and leaving travelways of varying average vehicle speeds.

SPENDABLE INCOME—Income which remains after payment of all expenses, debt service and income taxes; after-tax cash flow.

SPLIT-LEVEL HOUSE—A house, the living areas of which are on two or more levels, with the levels being at heights less than a single story.

SPLIT RATE CAPITALIZATION—A capitalization process denoting the application of different rates to portions of total net income presumed to be earned by fractional parts of an improved property, e.g., one rate applied to earnings attributed to land and another applied to net income attributed to the building; commonly known as "Split Rates."

SPOT CLEARANCE—Demolition activities which involve removal of single structures or comparatively small groups of structures from areas where a substantial proportion of existing structures will be retained.

SPOT ZONING—An exception to the general zoning rules. Said exception permits specific, usually small, parcels of land to become spot zoned to a use different from that of the surrounding area. See Zoning Variance.

SPREADER DAM—A dam built across a gully in order that the accumulated run-off will be diverted onto the flats on either side.

SPRINKLER SYSTEM—A fire protection system installed in buildings. It consists of an overhead system of pipes, containing pressurized water, and fitted with valves (sprinkler heads) which open automatically at certain temperatures.

SPUR TRACK—Any segment of track which turns out from another track, generally connected at only one end to such other track for the purpose of serving an industrial site or plant, for which there is no regular train service. The term applies equally to trackage of the railroad company in this same category, being used also for siding purposes.

SQUARE—In roofing, a finished roof area of 100 square feet.

SQUARE FOOT COST

1. The result obtained by the division of the actual or estimated cost of a building by its gross floor area, or by the division of the actual or estimated cost of land improvement by its square foot area.
2. The unit (in terms of money) which, multiplied by the number of square feet in a building or land improvement, results in the actual or estimated cost.

SQUARE FOOT METHOD—One of the methods of estimating construction, reproduction, or replacement costs of a building by multiplying the square foot floor area by an appropriate square foot construction cost figure.

SQUARE MEASURE—See Measures, page 271.

SQUATTER'S RIGHTS—The rights to occupancy of land created by virtue of long and undisturbed use, but without legal title or arrangement; in the nature of right at common law.

STABILIZED EXPENSE—Projected expense which is subject to change but which has been adjusted to express the equivalent stable annual expense.

STABILIZED INCOME—Projected income which is subject to change but which has been adjusted to express the equivalent stable annual income.

STABILIZED VALUE

1. A value estimate which excludes from consideration an abnormal relation of supply and demand, such as during boom peri-

ods when cost and sale price may exceed the long term value, or during depression periods when cost and sale price may be less than the long term value.

2. A value estimate which excludes from consideration any transitory condition which may cause excessive cost of construction, such as a bonus or premium for material, the abnormal inefficiency of labor, the cost of delay; and, which may cause an excessive sale price, such as a premium for possession made possible by a temporary shortage of supply.

STACK — A vertical waste or vent pipe.

STAGING — A temporary scaffolding to support workmen and materials during construction.

STAINLESS STEEL — An alloy of steel, containing a larger percentage of chromium to which may be added nickel, copper, or other alloys. It is a hard, corrosion resisting steel which retains a polish.

STAIR LANDING — A platform between flights of stairs.

STAIRS — A flight of steps from one level or floor to another.

STAIRWAY — The flights of stairs and the landings which form a continuous passage in a building from one floor to another.

STANDARD AREA MEASURES — See Measures, pages 295–296.

STANDARD CONSOLIDATED AREA (SCA) — Two groupings of standard metropolitan statistical areas (SMSAs) as designated by the Office of Management and Budget (OMB). These groups would include, for example, the New York–Northeast New Jersey SCA and the Chicago–Northwest SCA.

STANDARD CUBIC CONTENT — See Cubic Content.

STANDARD DEPTH

1. The depth of the typical neighborhood or community lot, usually applied to lots in particular use categories such as central business lots, outlying commercial lots, and lots in different-priced residential neighborhoods.
2. The assumed depth of the typical neighborhood or community lot for use in mass appraising.
    These assumed standard depths may bear little recognizable relationship to community wide conditions.

STANDARD DEVIATION — A statistical measure of the extent of absolute dispersion, variability, or scatter in a frequency distribution, obtained by extracting the square root of the arithmetic mean of the squares of the deviations from the arithmetic mean of the frequency distribution. Synonymns: quadratic mean, root-mean-square average.

STANDARD ERROR—In statistics, a measure of the distribution of an estimate of a parameter.

STANDARD ERROR OF THE ESTIMATE—In statistics, an estimate of the variation likely to be encountered in making predictions based on a regression equation.

STANDARD METROPOLITAN STATISTICAL AREA (SMSA)—As established by the Bureau of the Census for the 1950 census, it is an area which includes a central city of a minimum population of 50,000 or two contiguous cities having a combined population of 50,000; and the county or counties in which they are located, but may include all or part of adjacent counties if they are economically integrated with the central city.

STANDARD OF LIVING—The minimum of the necessities or luxuries of life to which a person or a group may be accustomed or to which they aspire.

STANDARD PARALLELS—The east and west lines, running parallel to and at 24-mile intervals north and south of a base line, establishing the north or south boundary lines of the townships. Because the government survey was a rectangular survey, the necessary corrections for the curvature of the earth were made on these lines in establishing the corners of the townships. Synonym: correction lines.

STAND-BY COMMITMENT—A commitment by a lender to provide a loan on real estate at some date in the future. Used by borrowers who get interim financing, say for construction, from a lender who does not want the permanent loan.

STAND CRUISE—The estimate of lumber in the standing forest which is based upon a particular log rule or volume table, and from which estimate no deduction is made for breakage or other waste in the woods.

STANDING TIMBER—Timber still on the stump; that is, in the tree.

STARTER COURSE—The first, or under course on which and from which wall or roof shingles are laid, necessary to provide watertight joints at first or lowest shingle course.

STARTING INCOME—The level of income which prevails as of the date of valuation as distinguished from stabilized or projected income, which may or may not be equal to starting income.

STATISTICAL INFERENCE—The whole process of reasoning from the specific to the general.

STATISTICAL TABLE—A systematic arrangement of numerical data presented in columns or rows for the purpose of comparison. See also Arrangement of Data.

STATISTICS – The art or science dealing with the collection, classification, and use of numerical data relating to a subject. The data themselves.

STATUTORY LAW – Law created by legislative enactment.

STEEL CONSTRUCTION – A rigidly connected frame of steel or reinforced concrete carrying all external and internal loads and stresses to the foundations; enclosing walls are supported by this frame, usually at floor levels. If frame is steel without fireproofing, it is known as unprotected metal construction.

STEEP LAND – Used to describe land, the topography of which has slopes ranging from 30% to 45%.

STEP LEASE – A lease under which rent payments are increased or decreased at fixed intervals.

STEP-WISE REGRESSION ANALYSIS – A form of multiple regression analysis in which the independent variables enter the model and leave it, if appropriate, one by one according to their ability to improve the equation's power to predict the value of the dependent variable.

STILE
1. The structural members of a parallel or glazed door; in this usage synonymous with Rail. See illustration, page 304.
2. The outside or perimeter members of a window, except the meeting or check rail in a double hung window; in this use, synonymous with Rail. See illustration, page 310.

STOCK
1. The aggregate of goods kept on hand by a commercial firm or merchant.
2. Livestock, as cattle, sheep, horses; animals kept or raised on a farm or ranch.
3. The shares of a company or corporation.

STOCK DRIVEWAY – A corridor of government-owned land set aside for the use of stock raisers in an area to enable the movement of herds between seasonal pastures or from range to shipping point.

STOCKING RATE – Actual number of animals expressed in either animal units or cows on a specific area at a specific time.

STOCK TRAIL – A trail through grazing land to enable the greater use of the range, either in rough or steep areas or through areas too heavily wooded to enable passage.

STOOL – The base or support of wood at the bottom of a window, as the shelf-like piece inside and extending across the lower part of a window opening.

STORES—Raw materials held for use in manufacture, as distinguished from manufactured stock; sundry supplies for repairs, and so on, required in operations. The contents of a storeroom maintained to provide the current requirements for consumption. Not to be confused with merchandise stock.

STORIE INDEX—A classification of soils developed by Earl Storie (University of California) in which the physical characteristics of the soil (profile development, texture, slope, drainage, erosion, and fertility) are expressions of their ability to produce; a rating derived by multiplying the following factors:

Factor A: that portion of the index rating concerned with the character of profile, expressed as a percentage, with most favorable condition rated 100%.

Factor B: that portion of the index rating which evaluates the surface texture of the soil.

Factor C: that portion of the index rating which takes into account the dominant slope of the land.

Factor X: that portion of the index rating dealing with the less permanent conditions of the soil, such as drainage, alkali, nutrient level, acidity, erosion, microrelief.

STORM SEWER—A sewer normally carrying only rainwater, but sometimes also carrying industrial waters.

STORY—A horizontal division of a building; that portion between one floor and the floor above or below.

STRAIGHT LINE METHOD—A method of estimating the periodic amount of capital recapture or depreciation. Assumes an equal amount of capital is recaptured each period. This method divides the total capital to be recovered by the number of periods over which it is to be recaptured. Can be used in either the Direct Capitalization Method to estimate future capital recovery or to estimate accrued depreciation in the Cost Approach.

STRAIGHT LINE RECAPTURE—The recovery of capital invested in a wasting asset in equal periodic increments over the remaining economic life of the asset; typically applicable in straight capitalization, its use implies that income attributable to the asset declines annually to the extent that the annual recapture increment reduces the return requirement on the declining capital investment.

STRATIFICATION—The division of the market for urban real estate into many sub-markets.

STRATIFIED—Composed of, or arranged in, strata or layers, such as stratified alluvium. Those layers in soils which are produced by the process of soil formation are called horizons, while those inherited from the parent material are called strata.

STRATIFIED RANDOM SAMPLE—A statistical sample in which the population is divided into fairly uniform groups or strata and then a random sample is drawn from each selected stratum.

STREAM—A body of water flowing in a channel or bed; a river or brook; any flow of water, as from a faucet. The term, because of the flow characteristic, has been adopted to describe the flow of income from a property, as the income stream.

STREET—The distance between property lines. It includes sidewalks and parkways. Commonly referred to as a trafficway.

STREET IMPROVEMENTS—The facilities, as paving, curbs, sidewalks, sewers, provided and usually maintained by local government.

STRENGTH IN COMPRESSION—The ability of a construction item to withstand an external force which tends to shorten it to the point of deformation.

STRESS—The action within a structural member when any outside force is acting against it; any force or all forces that act on a structural member at the same time.

STRESSED SKIN—A design in which frame and skin or sheathing are joined so that the skin may aid in resisting strains.

STRETCHER—A brick or other masonry unit laid lengthwise in a wall. See illustration, page 302.

STRINGER—A long heavy, horizontal timber which supports a floor; the inclined member supporting the treads and risers of a stair. See illustration, page 306.

STRIP DEVELOPMENT—The term is used to designate the type of commercial development wherein the main thoroughfares of a city are bordered by an almost continuous row or strip of retail stores and allied service establishments. Also, refers to any shopping area consisting of a row of stores.

STRIP LUMBER—Yard lumber less than 2 inches thick and less than 8 inches wide.

STRUCTURAL LUMBER—Lumber that is 2 or more inches thick and 4 or more inches wide.

STRUCTURE—An edifice or building; an improvement.

STRUT—Any piece of wood fixed between two other pieces or members, designed to receive pressure or weight in the direction of its length.

STUBBLE—The basal portion of herbaceous plants remaining after the top portion has been harvested either artificially or by grazing animals.

STUCCO—A cement plaster used as an exterior wall surface finish; usually applied over a metal or wood lath base.

STUD—A vertical wood or metal framing member to which horizontal boards or laths are nailed, as the supporting elements in walls and partitions.

STUMPAGE—In a general sense, the standing timber, usually with reference to its value.

SUBBASE—The lowest part of a structural base consisting of two or more horizontal members, as the base of a column; a baseboard. Also, the bed of crushed rock or gravel used to provide a stable base under a slab or roadway.

SUBDIVISION—A tract of land which has been divided into blocks or plots with suitable streets, roadways, open areas, and other appropriate facilities for development as residential, commercial, or industrial sites.

SUBFLOOR—A floor laid on top of the floor joists underneath the finish floor.

SUBJECTIVE—Describes (or denotes) opinions, attitudes, and thoughts existing or formulated in the mind. In appraising, subjective is used to designate the opinions and attitudes of people which motivate their actions with respect to real estate transactions. Their collective actions or reactions with respect to any class of property is indicative of the market and the value of that type of property.

SUBJECTIVE PROBABILITY—An evaluation by a decision-maker of the relative "likelihood" of unknown events.

SUBJECTIVE VALUE—The importance which a commodity is considered to possess with reference to the satisfaction of desires by an individual. It is also called personal value. The measure of the subjective value of a property is the amount which might be paid by a specific person for possession. Usually, this depends upon the amount of estimated benefits expectable such as net income. See Investment Value.

SUBLEASE—An agreement conveying the right of use and occupancy of a property in which the lessor is the lessee in a prior lease.

Usually considered synonymous with Sandwich Lease, except that often a sublease involves the subletting of but a portion of the premises included in the prime lease.

SUBLESSEE—One who enjoys the benefits, rights, and obligations of a sublease.

SUBMARGINAL LAND—Land from which the receipts are inadequate to pay the cost of production, even if the land were free. It may also refer to the average physical quality of the land with reference to the area's average quality.

SUBMETROPOLITAN SHOPPING CENTER—A tract of land improved with a coordinated group of retail buildings with a full variety of types of stores, one or more department stores, free parking, under single ownership or control, and catering to a large portion of a metropolitan area.

SUBORDINATION AGREEMENT—A contractual arrangement in which a party having an interest in real estate, such as a lessee, grants a prior claim on the assets of the real estate to a mortgagee.

SUBSIDENCE—The sinking of the upper part of the ground due to a number of causes, as lowering of the water table during a long period of drought or the removal of minerals, such as coal. Where severe enough it can cause the structural damage to buildings.

SUBSOIL—The term usually refers to the B horizon of soils; but cannot be designated accurately since it depends on the type of soil profile. Common usage describes it as that part below plow depth or below the solum.

SUBSTITUTION, PRINCIPLE OF—A valuation principle that states that a prudent purchaser would pay no more for real property than the cost of acquiring an equally desirable substitute on the open market. The Principle of Substitution presumes that the purchaser will consider the alternatives available and will act rationally or prudently on the basis of the information about those alternatives, and that reasonable time is available for the decision. Substitution may assume the form of the purchase of an existing property, with the same utility, or of acquiring an investment which will produce an income stream of the same size with the same risk as that involved in the property in question.

SUBSURFACE EASEMENT—The right to use the land at a designated distance below the surface of the land; as for pipelines, electric and telephone circuits and cables, storage facilities, etc.

SUBSURFACE RIGHTS

1. This is the right to the use and profits derived from the underground portion of a designated property. Usually, it refers to the right to extract oil, gas, other hydrocarbon substances, coal, and minerals as designated in the grant. Usually, the grant includes a right of way over designated portions of the surface.
2. Also, it refers to the right to construct and maintain tunnels, subways, subcellars, pipelines, sewers, etc.

SUBURBAN—Pertaining to the area adjacent to a city; comprising residential communities with their related commercial and industrial developments and which are economically and socially allied to the city.

SUM OF YEARS' DIGITS METHOD—A depreciation process by which an asset is assumed to lose its value in a manner in which the rate of depreciation is very rapid in early years and more gradual in late years. This method is a variation of the weighted rate method, which in turn is similar to the straight line method. See illustration, page 338.

SUMMATION APPROACH—The addition of the estimated value of the improvements and the contributory value of site improvements to the estimated value of the site, as of the date of the appraisal. See Cost Approach, Reproduction Cost Approach.

SUMP PUMP—An automatic electric pump installed in a basement or other low area to empty the sump, a pit serving as a drain.

SUPERADEQUACY—A greater capacity or quality in a structure or one of its components than the prudent purchaser or owner would include or would pay for in the particular type of structure under current market conditions.

SUPERHIGHWAY—A general term referring to any type of limited access highway designed to provide for high-speed through traffic, usually an expressway, freeway, or toll road.

SUPERMARKET—A large retail store built on one level and in which goods are conveniently and conspicuously displayed so that customers may select what they want without the help of a clerk. Purchases are paid for at a checkout counter. The most common types of merchandise sold are food products and household supplies; but a wide variety of consumer goods can be offered. Most supermarkets are units of large chain store corporations.

SUPERSESSION—Transition of use, e.g., agricultural to residential, parking lot to skyscraper, loft building to parking lot, etc.; the sudden or gradual economic death and rebirth of property.

SUPERSTRUCTURE—Part of a structure above the ground or above the top of foundation walls.

SUPPLEMENTAL FEEDING—Supplying concentrates or harvested feed to correct deficiencies of the range diet.

SUPPLEMENTAL PASTURE—An artificial pasture to quantitatively or qualitatively augment range forage, particularly during emergency situations. Supplemental pastures may be provided by annual grasses and/or legumes or by aftermath of meadows, grainfields, etc.

SUPPLY—The quantity of real estate of a particular type that will be made available at given price levels. Supply consists of the existing stock in the particular sub-market in question, new construction, and conversion of existing structures from other uses.

SUPPLY AND DEMAND, PRINCIPLE OF—A valuation principle which states that market value is determined by the interaction of the forces of supply and demand in the appropriate market as of the date of the appraisal.

SURFACE EASEMENT—The right to use only the surface of the land; as for easements of access, flowage, or for rights of way.

SURFACE WATER—That water which spreads over the surface of the ground, or stands in swamps, or percolates through or under the soil.

SURPLUS INCOME—See Excess Income.

SURPLUS PRODUCTIVITY—The net income that remains after the proper costs of labor, organization, and capital have been paid, which surplus is imputable to the land and tends to fix the value thereof.

SURPLUS PROFITS—The amount by which the net income of a business exceeds a reasonable return upon its appraised capital requirements.

SURVEY—The process of scientifically ascertaining the quantity and/or location of a piece of land; it may include physical features affecting it, such as grades, contours, structures. A statement of the courses, distances, and quantity of land.

SWEAT EQUITY—That contribution to a development in forms other than cash. Most generally, this contribution is in the form of labor or services by the equity position.

SWITCHING—See Free Switching.

SYNDICATE—A combination of individuals formed to carry out some project requiring large sources of capital which individually none could undertake.

SYNDICATION—A grouping of persons or legal entities who combine to carry through some financial transaction or who undertake some common venture in a very flexible business arrangement. A common structure or form is the limited partnership.

SYNERGISM—The situation that occurs when the total effect is greater than the sum of independent action designed or developed to create that effect. In real estate, the reference is most often made to multiuse properties where the value of the total development is greater than the sum of the individual parts.

TAIL RACE—A channel or flume through which the mill tail (water from a mill after generating power) flows.

TALUS—A slope; a sloping mass of rocky fragments at the foot of a cliff.

TANGIBLE PROPERTY—Property that, by its nature, is perceptible by the senses. Generally the land, fixed improvements, furnishings, merchandise, cash, and other items of working capital used in carrying on an enterprise.

TANGIBLE VALUE—The value assigned to the physical portion of property, such as land, building, machinery, furnishings, merchandise, cash, and other items which are perceptible by the senses.

TAX—A compulsory contribution exacted of persons, corporations, and other organizations by the government, according to the law, for the general support of the government and for the maintenance of public services.

TAXABLE INCOME—Income subject to income tax; for income-producing property it is Net Operating Income Less Depreciation and Interest on Debt.

TAXABLE VALUE—See Assessed Value.

TAXATION—A system for raising revenues. Assessments upon property for federal, state, and municipal purposes; one of the four constitutional limitations on property.

TAX BASE—The unit of value to which the tax rate is applied to determine the tax due. For property taxes, the tax base is the assessed valuation; for income taxes, the net taxable income.

TAX BOOK—See Tax Roll.

TAX DEED—The deed conveying title to property purchased at a tax sale; absolute title, with waiver of all prior claims and liens, may or may not be conveyed, depending on the law of the state concerned.

TAX DISTRICT—A political subdivision, comprising one or more assessment districts, over which a governmental unit has authority to levy a tax.

TAX EXEMPTION—Total exemption or freedom from tax such as is granted educational, charitable, religious, and similar non-profit organizations. Exemptions may also be partial, such as the ad valorem tax exemption granted by some states on homesteads.

TAX FREE CASH—The amount by which annual depreciation charges for a specific property exceed annual mortgage amortization (principal repayment) for the same property.

TAX LEVY—In property taxes, the total revenue which is to be realized by the tax.

TAX LIEN—A lien which automatically attaches to property in the amount of property taxes unpaid on the property.

TAX MAP—A map, drawn to scale, depicting the boundaries of individual lots and parcels and showing their location within an assessment jurisdiction. Synonyms: Assessment Map, Cadastral Map.

TAX PARTICIPATION—A provision in a lease which obligates the lessee to assume all or a part of the property taxes.

TAXPAYER—An interim improvement which allegedly does not represent the ultimate most profitable use of the land, usually a one-story commercial building.

TAX RATE—The ratio of the tax to the tax base. The rate to be applied to the assessed value to determine the amount of tax. The rate is obtained by dividing the amount of the tax levy by the total assessed value of the tax district; usually expressed in dollars per hundred of assessed value.

TAX ROLL—The official list of each taxpayer subject to a property tax, together with the amount of the assessment and the amount of taxes due. Synonym: tax book.

TAX SALE—The sale of a taxpayer's property to collect delinquent taxes from the proceeds of the sale when the taxpayer has failed to redeem it within the statutory period.

TAX SHELTER—The various features of an investment which offer relief from income taxes or opportunities to claim allowable deductions from taxable income; the money saved by a taxpayer as a result of reductions in taxable income without corresponding reductions in actual income.

TAX STOP—A clause in a lease which limits the landlord's tax obligation through the lessee's assumption of taxes in excess of some established level.

TAX TITLE—See Tax Deed.

TAYLOR PERMIT—The permit issued to a stock raiser under the terms of the Taylor Grazing Act (federal) which defines the use of the public domain by private parties for grazing purposes.

t–DISTRIBUTION—A symmetric but nonnormal distribution. In the case of small samples (fewer than 30 degrees of freedom) the sample standard deviation may be a rather inaccurate estimator of the standard deviation of the population. In such cases, greater accuracy in the estimation of the population standard deviation might be implied, and therefore, the t–Distribution (which is flatter than the normal and thus associates a lower probability to any given interval) is employed.

TDN—Total digestible nutrients in a feed. It is that portion of livestock feed which is digested and used by the animal for maintenance, growth and production.

TEAM TRACK—A track on which a railroad spots cars for loading and unloading by shippers. It is a track open to use by the public as distinct from the private nature of an industrial siding. Driveways are alongside team tracks to accomodate vehicles. In a team yard the tracks are spaced far enough apart to permit driveways between.

TEMPERA—A process of painting, in transparent colors on plastered walls or panels, in which powdered pigment and parchment size is mixed with water and gum arabic or egg, either the white or yolk. The ground is a hard surface of the fine thin plaster called gesso.

TENANCY
1. Nature of tenure.
2. The holding of property by any form of title.
3. A lease or right to occupy for years; for a definite period, as one year and six months; at will, being ended at any time by land lord; at sufferance, when tenant remains after expiration of the lease; or for life, the right to occupy for one's life.

TENANCY AT SUFFERANCE—An interest in real estate which exists when a person, who formerly had an estate in land, wrongfully continues in possession of the real estate after the termination of such estate.

TENANCY AT WILL—An estate in real estate which may be cancelled at will by either landlord or tenant and which has no fixed term.

TENANCY BY THE ENTIRETY—Tenancy by a husband and wife in such a manner that, except through joint action, neither has a disposable interest in the property during the lifetime of the other. Upon death of either, the property passes to the survivor.

TENANCY IN COMMON—The holding of property by two or more persons each of whom has an undivided interest which, upon the death of one, passes to the heirs and not to the survivor or survivors.

TENANCY IN SEVERALTY—An ownership interest in real estate by one owner.

TENANT—In general, one who holds or possesses real property. Common usage of the term has tended to narrow the concept to a person who occupies and uses the property of another under a lease; more correctly such a person is a lessee, not a tenant.

TENANT CHANGES—The regular or periodic changes in fixed improvements necessary to meet the varied requirements of continuing or succeeding tenants.

TENANT FARMER—A lessee of a farm; the rental usually is either in crops or cash, or a combination thereof.

TENANTS' IMPROVEMENTS
1. Fixed improvements to land or structure installed and paid for by a tenant or lessee.

2. The original installation of tenant space finish in a construction project, such items being subject to periodic later changes for succeeding tenants.

TENDON – The wires and cables used in reinforcing prestressed and post-stressed concrete.

TENEMENT – Any house or dwelling to live in; any portion of a house or building occupied by a tenant. In a legal sense, tenement originally implied any type of property, such as land, houses, rents, an office, a franchise which may be held of another. See also Tenement House.

TENEMENT HOUSE – An obsolete apartment house, especially in a slum area.

TENURE – The holding or possession of anything. The right to possession and use of property; the period of that possession and use.

TERMINAL
1. That point in a computer system by which data can either enter or leave the system.
2. In transportation, that point at which people or goods can either enter or leave the system.

TERNEPLATE – A tin plate of inferior quality in which the tin is alloyed with a large percentage of lead; used as a roofing material.

TERRA COTTA – A hard, usually unglazed, earthenware of fine quality which has been hard burned and molded; used for architectural decorations, such as facing material.

TERRACE
1. A broad surface channel or embankment constructed across sloping lands, on or approximately on contour lines at specific intervals, for control of run-off or soil erosion.
2. A flat or undulating plain, commonly rather narrow and usually with a steep front, bordering a river, a lake, or the sea. Many streams are bordered by a series of terraces at different levels, indicating the flood planes at successive periods. Although many older terraces have become more or less hilly through dissection by streams, they are still regarded as terraces.
3. An elevated level surface of earth with a vertical or sloping front and/or sides faced by masonry or turf; especially a series of such levels rising one above another.
4. A finished but unroofed outdoor area adjacent to, and accessible from within, a house (or other structure), usually at grade or slightly elevated.

TERRAZZO – A floor material made of small fragments of colored stone or marble, embedded in cement, and polished in place to a high glaze.

THEORY—A statement setting forth an apparent relationship among observed facts which has been substantiated to a degree.

THERM—A unit of heat measure equal to 100,000 Btu's. See Btu.

THERMAL—Of, or pertaining to, heat or temperature.

THERMOSTAT—A device, electrically operated, actuated by thermal conduction or convection, which automatically functions to establish and maintain a desired temperature.

THREAD OF THE STREAM—The center line between the banks of the stream.

THRESHOLD—A strip of wood, stone, or metal placed beneath a door.

TIDAL BASIN—A dock or basin, without water gates, in which the water level changes.

TIDE—The alternate rising and falling of the surface of the ocean. The tide ebbs and flows twice in each lunar day of 24 hours and 51 minutes, so that six hours and 13 minutes elapse between high and low tide. The inflow, or rising of the water is called the flood tide or high tide; the reflux is called the ebb tide. Slack tide is the period between changes of the tide movement.

TIE—A timber, rod, chain, clip, wire, etc., which holds two or more structural members together, e.g., wall ties which secure brick veneer to the structural backing.

TIE BEAM—Any structural members used to hold two separated members together. It is sometimes referred to as a collar tie.

TIER—A row of townships, running east and west, lying between any two consecutive township lines, comprising an area six miles wide.

TILE—Originally used to describe only a molded and burned clay or cement material used for flooring, facing walls, and trim; includes tiles made of many different materials, as asphalt, plastics, vinyl, fiberglass; and used for a number of other purposes, as field tile, sewer tile, ceiling and acoustical tile.

TILL—A deposit of earth, sand, gravel, and boulders transported by glaciers. Till is unstratified.

TILLABLE LAND—Land suitable for growing annual crops which require plowing, harrowing, planting, cultivating, and harvesting as distinguished from land on a farm not so adapted, as marsh or swamp land, wood lots.

TILL PLAIN—A level or undulating land surface covered by glacial till.

TILTH—The physical condition of a soil in respect to its fitness for the growth of a specified plant.

TILT-UP CONSTRUCTION—A method of construction where concrete wall sections are cast horizontally and tilted or lifted into position.

TIMBER—Loosely applied to forest stands or their products. Wood in forms suitable for heavy construction, specifically, sawed lumber 4 by 4 inches or more in breadth and thickness.

TIMBER CRUISING—See Cruise.

TIME SERIES—A statistical device for presenting data graphically. The analysis of the time series consists of the description and measurement of the various changes or movements as they appear in the series during a period of time. These changes or movements may be classified as: cyclical movement, random variations, seasonal variation, secular trend.

TIME-SERIES CHART—A graphic representation of statistical data in which the independent variable, plotted along the horizontal axis, is time, and the values of the dependent variable, plotted along the vertical axis, are shown at various intervals of time, these values being connected by straight lines to form a continuous curve extending over the entire period covered by the chart. Synonym: temporal distribution.

TITLE—The union of all elements which constitute proof of ownership. See also Abstract of Title.

TITLE I (URA)—The portion of the Housing Act of 1949, as amended, which contains most of the basic legislative provisions pertaining to the urban renewal program. Title I authorizes most of the federal financial and technical aids for communities participating in the program. Through the amending Housing Act of 1954, it sets out the workable program prerequisites, and adds the concept of rehabilitating blighted areas as well as redeveloping slum areas.

TITLE COMPANY—A corporation organized for the purpose of issuing or insuring title to real property.

TITLE OPINION—An analysis and interpretation of a title search concerning present ownership, encumbrances, clouds on title, and other infirmities.

TITLE INSURANCE—Insurance against financial loss resulting from claims arising out of defects in the title to real property, which are existent but undisclosed at the time the policy is issued by the title company. See also Torrens System.

TITLE SEARCH—An investigation of public records to abstract the nature of instruments relating to the status of the title to ownership of a specific piece of real estate. It may include liens, encumbrances, easements, and other conditions affecting the quality of the title of ownership.

TOBACCO BARN — A farm building, usually of simple frame construction designed with hinged side panels which may be opened to provide necessary ventilation for curing of the tobacco. It may also be used for grading and packing for market.

TOLL ROAD — A highway for which use a toll charge is collected.

TONGUE AND GROOVE — A method of joining two pieces of board wherein one has a tongue cut in the edge and the other board has a groove cut to receive the corresponding tongue. Used to modify any material prepared for joining in this fashion, as tongue and groove lumber.

TOPOGRAPHIC MAP — A map charting the topography of an area of the earth's surface, using contour lines, tinting, or shading.

TOPOGRAPHY — The relief features or surface configurations of an area, as hills, valleys, slopes, lakes, rivers. Surface gradations are classified as: compound slope, gently sloping land, hilly land, hog-wallows, hummocks, rolling land, steep land, undulating land, very steep land.

TOP RAIL — The horizontal member forming the top of a panelled door or a window; also designated "top stile." See illustration, pages 304 and 310.

TOPSOIL — A general term applied to the surface portion of the soil, including the average plow depth of the A horizon where this is deeper than plow depth. See also Horizon.

TORRENS SYSTEM — A system of land registration used in some jurisdictions in which the sovereign governmental authority issues title certificates covering the ownership of land which tend to serve as title insurance.

TOTAL LOAD — Dead load plus live load. This is the total weight which must be compensated for in design.

TOWN HOUSE — Formerly referred to a residence in town, the term now is used to describe those residential developments which permit single-family construction on high cost land by use of row houses.

TOWNSHIP — The area included between two township lines and two range lines, normally containing 36 sections of approximately 640 acres each.

TOWNSHIP LINES — Survey lines, running east and west, at six mile intervals north and south of a base line, and forming the north and south boundaries of townships.

TOWNSHIP ROAD — A rural road outside the primary state highway system and the county road system, under the jurisdiction of a township.

TRACT HOUSE – A house in a large residential development where the houses are mass produced and highly similar in style, materials, and prices.

TRADE AREA – Generally used to refer to the area adjacent to a retail or service property from which it draws or should draw its trade (customers). The size of the trade area is dependent upon the size of the facility, its accessibility, and the scope of the merchandise or services offered, and the competitive effectiveness of other facilities. See also Market Survey.

TRADING ON EQUITY – The use of borrowed funds in an effort to increase the rate of return on the equity investment. This is the derivation of the term leverage.

TRAFFIC – The movement of people, vehicles, etc., along a way or past a point; the people and vehicles so moving along the way.

TRAFFIC COUNT – A count of the number of people and/or vehicles moving past a location during a period of time. Traffic counts are used to determine the volume of vehicular traffic past a proposed service station site; the number of pedestrians passing a retail location as a measure of its potential sales volume. Counts may be made to determine the composition of the traffic, as the number of men or women, private automobiles in contrast to number of trucks, buses, etc. They may be made to reflect traffic conditions on certain days of the week or year, and at certain hours of the day.

TRAFFIC DENSITY – The number of vehicles occupying a unit length of the moving lanes of roadway at a given instant. Usually expressed in vehicles per mile.

TRAFFIC SURVEY – A survey made to obtain information, such as data on the quantity and composition, origin and destination, purpose of trip, means of transportation; and usually in relation to some specific time as of a certain day of the week.

TRAILER – A mobile home, a house trailer.

TRAILER PARK – Any site having facilities suitable for parking two or more mobile homes more or less permanently. Such parks vary as to the extent and adequacy of the facilities provided. In general, the minimum facilities would be: parking space for the mobile home, sewer and water connections, electrical service, streets, bathing and laundry facilities.

TRANSFERABLE DEVELOPMENT RIGHTS (TDR) – A method of land use regulation which recognizes the separability of rights in land and its transferability to other sectors of the community. Most generally involved with the preservation of agricultural land, although it may include as well historic sites, open space, and protection of scenic features.

TRANSIENT HOUSING STUDY—A supply to demand analysis of transient housing needs and potentials of a community or specific area on both a qualitative and quantitative basis.

TRANSITION—District or neighborhood use changes, such as farm to residential, residential to business. Also, ethnic or economic changes.

TRANSPORTED SOIL—See Types of Soil, page 351.

TRAVELED WAY—That portion of a roadway which is designed for the movement of vehicles. It excludes shoulders, acceleration and deceleration lanes, and other auxiliary lanes.

TRAVERSE WINDOW—A type of window containing two movable sashes set in separate grooves, permitting the windows to slide past each other horizontally. Synonym: sliding window. See illustration, page 301.

TREAD—The horizontal width of a step between risers in a stairway.

TRELLISING—A support system for grape or other vine type crops. Such a system will usually consist of wires or thin ropes extended above the vine between anchor posts.

TREND—An arrangement of statistical data in accordance with its time of occurrence. A series of related changes which may be identified and projected into a probable future pattern. See also Moving Average.

TRIM—The visible finishing work of the interior of a building, including any ornamental parts of either wood, metal or plastic used for covering joints between jambs and plaster around windows and doors. The term may also include hardware.

TRIMMER—The beam or floor joist which supports the end of a header in floor framing.

TRUSS—Any of various structural frames based on the geometric rigidity of the triangle and composed of members subject only to longitudinal compression and tension; rigid under anticipated loads, spans large area without interior support, i.e., Bowstring, Cambered, Flat Roof, Sawtooth, Scissors and Triangular.

TRUST—A fiduciary relationship, and instrument thereof, which places the legal title to and control of property in the hands of a trustee for the benefit of another person. A trust may be temporary, conditional, or permanent.

TRUST AGREEMENT—A written agreement between settler and trustee setting forth the terms of a trust. See also Deed of Trust.

TRUST DEED—A deed which establishes a trust. It generally is an instrument which conveys legal title to property to a trustee and states the trustee's authority and the conditions binding upon the trustee in dealing with the property held in trust. Frequently trust deeds are used to secure lenders against loss. In this respect they are similar to mortgages.

TRUSTEE – A person who controls legal title to property under a trust agreement.

TRUST INSTRUMENT – Any writing – will, trust agreement, declaration of trust, deed of trust, or order of court – under which a trust is created.

TUCK POINTING – The finishing of joints along the center lines with a narrow parallel ridge of fine putty or fine lime mortar. In existing brick or masonry work, the raking out of deteriorated mortar joints to an appropriate depth and refilling with new mortar.

TURNPIKE – A controlled access highway for the use of which tolls are usually paid.

TYPE OF FARMING – Various patterns of land use, also known as agricultural enterprise, e.g., dairy, truck crop, beef/sheep ranch, feed lot, poultry, vineyard, orchard, nuts, grain, cotton, etc.

TYPE SOILS – A group of soils having genetic horizons similar as to differentiating characteristics, including texture and arrangement in soil profile, and developed from a particular type of parent material.

TYPICAL OPERATOR CONCEPT – Productive capacity of the farm/ranch is based on typical operators in the area utilizing similar management inputs. Basically, utilized in the earnings approach.

UNBALANCED IMPROVEMENT – An improvement which is not the highest-best use for the site on which it is placed; may be an over- or underimprovement.

UNDERFLOOR WIRING SYSTEM – A system composed of ducts and/or raceways built into the floor to house the electrical wiring.

UNDERIMPROVEMENT – An improvement which is inadequate to develop the highest and best use of a site: usually a structure which is of lesser cost, quality, and size than typical neighborhood properties.

UNDERPASS – A passageway under a street, highway, or railroad right of way. In rural areas, a passageway under a highway for animals and farm equipment. Also a grade separation where one traveled way passes under an intersecting traveled way or railroad right of way.

UNDERPINNING – An expression applied to timbers, steel, or other props temporarily supporting a foundation during construction;

also to permanent supports added to increase load-bearing capacity of a foundation or wall.

UNDERSTOCKING – Placing a number of animals on a given area that will result in underuse at the end of the planned grazing period.

UNDERSTORY
1. That portion of a forest which is under or below the overstory or top canopy.
2. Plants growing beneath the canopy of another plant. Usually refers to grasses, forbs, and low shrubs under a tree or brush canopy.

UNDULATING LAND – Land on compound slopes of 3 to 8%.

UNEARNED INCREMENT – An increase in the value of property, not anticipated by the owner, due primarily to the operation of social or economic forces rather than to the personal efforts, intelligence, skill, or initiative of the owner; usually, but not necessarily, applied to land. This concept was developed by Henry George who believed that increases in the value of property ought not to accrue to the owners since they were due to social forces and hence "unearned." By contrast, however, he did not agree that losses were also due to social forces and that owners ought then to be compensated. Unearned increment, therefore, may be said to be a misnomer because the increment usually is a reward for the risk taken in such ventures.

UNECONOMIC – Applicable to any action or process which does not add to the total sum of useful goods and services; or, which produces goods or services less effectively or at a greater cost than is warranted by existing technical knowledge or by the potential for reasonable profit.

UNIFORMITY – As used in assessment practice, uniformity denotes assessed values which have the same relationship to market value, or some other value standard, as do all other assessments within the tax district; implies the equalization of the tax burden.

UNIMPROVED LAND – Vacant land or land lacking in essential appurtenant improvements required to serve a useful purpose.

UNIT – A single thing; any standard of quantity by which other quantities of the same kind may be measured and expressed. Not significant or informative without qualification.

UNIT COST – The price or cost of one of a number of similar items or units of property which, when multiplied by the total number, will determine the price or cost of the whole; usually expressed as cost per square foot or cubic foot. Synonym: unit price.

UNIT-IN-PLACE METHOD – A method of estimating construction costs which involves estimating the unit cost of component section of the structure installed or "in place." The unit includes both materials and labor.

UNIT RULE – The need to determine what constitutes the larger parcel, the complete unit, affected by a partial taking, in order to estimate severance damages and/or special benefits to the remainder. The test of unity considers three factors: physical location, use, and ownership. See also Unity of Title, Unity of Use.

UNIT VALUE
1. Market value of the whole reduced to a unit of measurement. For example:
   a. Fifty acres of meadow with a market value of $10,000 reflects a unit value of $200 per acre.
   b. A 100 front-foot lot with a market value of $10,000 reflects a unit value of $100 per front foot.

   In this usage, it is essential that the whole be comprised of similar units. For instance, a unit value of a combination of pasture and timberland cannot be established without reference to the proportionate value which each contributes to the market value of the whole.
2. In the assessment of public utilities, railroads, and other properties spanning several assessment or taxation districts, such properties are often appraised by a "unit valuation method." That is, the operating property of the utility, etc., is appraised as a unit or on the basis of the business enterprise as a whole. Three techniques are used in unit valuation: a cost approach (sometimes limited to book costs); a market approach (the stock and debt approach); and an income approach (where it is important to distinguish between the capitalization rate used in valuation and the rate of return the utility is allowed to receive on its invested capital). The unit value is then apportioned and allocated among the state and local governments involved. See also Central Assessment.

UNITED STATES PUBLIC LAND DESCRIPTIONS – See Government Survey, Public Land System.

UNITS OF COMPARISON – The reduction of properties to appropriate units in terms of which comparisons of otherwise not directly comparable properties can be made. These units of comparison can then be applied to individual properties to formulate estimates of value, income, cost, etc. Ideally, they should represent units in terms of which properties are in fact sold, rented, built, or valued.

UNITY, DOCTRINE OF – In an economic sense, the only supportable concept of value is market value. Each of the indications of value arrived at by the separate approaches must be supported by market data of one kind or another; and the indications of value by each of the approaches should be substantially the same.

UNITY OF TITLE—The rule, both in federal and state courts, is that a parcel to be considered a part of the remainder property must be held by the condemnee under the same quality of ownership as that from which the taking occurs. (McIntyre v. Board of County rel. Wirt v. Superior Court, 10 Wash. 2d 362, 116 P. 2d 752 [1941]; United States v. Honolulu Plantation Co., 182 F. 2d 172 [CA9, 1950].)

UNITY OF USE—The rule is that a parcel in order to be part of the remainder must be devoted to the same use as the parcel from which the taking is made. Traditionally, and in most states, the rule also requires that the parcels have unity of physical location. The federal rule holds that unity of use or operation carries greater weight than physical location (City of Stockton v. Marengo, 137 Cal. App. 760, 31 P. 2d 467 [1934]; Baetjer v. United States, 143 F. 2d 391 [CA 1, 1944].)

UNIVERSE—In statistics, the entire body of possible data. Used particularly to distinguish between all the data and a sample obtained from all the data.

UPLAND

1. Parcel abutting one with riparian rights, i.e., refers to owner once removed from a water right by a riparian owner.
2. Land above the surface of a body of water or above a high mean water line.

UPLAND SOIL—See Types of Soil, page 351.

UPSET PRICE—A term of legal significance used to designate an amount representing the minimum bid at which a property may be sold.

URBAN LAND ECONOMICS—The study of the allocation of urban space among alternative uses.

URBAN RENEWAL—The controlled process of redevelopment within urban areas. Although it is often used to refer to Title I and other public projects, it also encompasses private redevelopment efforts.

URBAN RENEWAL AREA—A blighted, deteriorated, or deteriorating area, or an open land area, which is approved by Department of Housing and Urban Development as appropriate for an urban renewal project.

URBAN RENEWAL PLAN—A plan, developed by a locality and approved by its governing body, which guides and controls undertakings in a special urban renewal project area.

URBAN RENEWAL PROJECT—The name given to the specific activities undertaken by a local public agency in an urban renewal area to prevent and eliminate slums and blight. The project may involve slum clearance and redevelopment or rehabilitation or conservation, or a combination thereof.

URBAN SPACE—Urban real estate which is distinguished by the fact that its value stems directly from its location. Its function is to serve as a locus for some human activity or human enjoyment. Urban space includes both land (or site) and space in buildings.

USE DENSITY—The number of buildings in a particular use per unit of area; sometimes represented by a percentage of land coverage or density of coverage. See Floor-Area Ratio.

USE FACTOR (PALATABILITY)—An index to the grazing use that is made of a forage species, based upon a system of range management that will maintain the more economically important forage species for an indefinite time. It is expressed as the percentage of the current year's weight production, within reach of stock, that is consumed. See also Weighted-use Factor.

USEFUL LIFE—The period of time over which the structure may reasonably be expected to perform the function for which it was designed or intended.

USE/USER VALUE—The value of a property designed to fit the specific requirements of the user. Such value often applies to the classification of "special purpose" property. Special purpose property, however, may be viewed on a continuum from a tract home to a property that has no counterpart anywhere. At one end of the continuum, then, use/user value coincides with the concept of market value, whereas at the other end of the continuum it coincides with the concept of value in use.

USE VALUE ASSESSMENT—An assessment based on the value of property as currently used rather than on market value in which alternative uses would be contemplated. Use value assessments are encountered where such legislation has been enacted to, among other things, preserve farmland, timberland, and/or other open space land on the fringes of urban areas.

USUFRUCT—The right of using and enjoying the fruits or profits of something belonging to another.

UTILITIES—Usually refers to services rendered by public utility companies, such as telephone, electricity, gas, water, etc.

UTILITY—In general economic theory, the capacity of an economic good to satisfy human desires or needs.

UTILITY ROOM—A ground-floor room, other than a habitable room, in a basementless house designed or used for laundry or heating equipment, or related purposes.

VACANCY – Rental property or any unit thereof which is unrented. See Allowance for Vacancy and Income Loss. See also Effective Gross Income.

VACANCY RATE – See Allowance for Vacancy and Income Loss.

VACANT LAND – See Unimproved Land.

VALLEY

1. The line of intersection of two sloping roofs.
2. The lowland lying between two hills.

VALLEY FLASHING – Pieces of lead, tin or sheet metal used along the valley of a roof to make the roof intersection waterproof.

VALUATION – The act or process of estimating value. The amount of estimated value.

VALUATION PRINCIPLES – Economic principles concerning value which are applicable in the valuation of real property. Significant ones include: anticipation, supply and demand, change, substitution, highest and best use, increasing and decreasing returns, competition, contribution, conformity.

VALUATOR – One who estimates value: a valuer. A competent valuator is one who possesses ability to discover, classify, and rate the separate influences which combine to create, sustain, or destroy value, and is therefore skilled in the technique of valuation. See also Appraiser.

VALUE

1. The quantity of one thing which can be obtained in exchange for another.
2. The ratio of exchange of one commodity for another, e.g., one bushel of wheat in terms of a given number of bushels of corn; thus, the value of one thing may be expressed in terms of another. Money is the common denominator by which real property value is usually measured.
3. It is the power of acquiring commodities in exchange, generally with a comparison of utilities – the utility of the commodity acquired in the exchange (property).
4. Value also depends upon the relation of an object to unsatisfied needs; i.e., scarcity or supply and demand.
5. Value is the present worth of future benefits arising out of ownership to typical users or investors.
6. The verb "value": The act or process of estimating value. See Valuation.

VALUE AFTER THE TAKING – In condemnation proceedings, in the case of a partial taking, it is the market value of the remainder of the larger parcel considered as a new larger parcel.

VALUE BEFORE THE TAKING—In condemnation proceedings, it is the market value of the whole property affected by the taking. See also Larger Parcel.

VALUE FOR OTHER USE (VOU)—Used in connection with corridor valuation, particularly in relationship to value of railroad corridors. Also termed liquidation value.

VALUE IN EXCHANGE—The amount of goods and services or purchasing power which an informed purchaser would offer in exchange for an economic good under given market conditions. Value in exchange is relative, as there must be a comparison with other economic good or goods, and alternatives available from which the potential purchaser may make a choice.

VALUE IN PLACE—That amount a prudent purchaser would pay for an item (equipment and/or fixtures) in place for use as it contributes to the whole.

VALUE IN USE—A value concept which is based upon the productivity of an economic good to its owner-user. Value in use may be a valid substitute for market value when the current use is so specialized that it has no demonstrable market and when the use is economic and likely to continue.

VALVE—A device for regulating the flow of liquids or gases in a pipe.

VAPOR BARRIER—Material used to retard the passage of vapor or moisture into walls and floors thus preventing condensation within them, as foil-surfaced insulation placed in walls, or paints applied to outside foundation walls.

VARA—A Spanish and Portuguese unit of linear and square measure sometimes used in California, Florida, New Mexico, and in Mexico and other countries under Spanish influence; varying in length from 32.993 inches to 33.87 inches.

VARIABLE—A quantity that may take any one of a specified set of values.

VARIABLE ANNUITY
1. A determinable income stream which varies in amount per period.
2. In an appraisal context, a forecast of annual amounts of Net Operating Income over the income projection period, implying the income stream may vary from year to year but determinable in amount and direction.

VARIABLE EXPENSES—Those expenses, usually computed on an annual basis, which vary with occupancy or other factors and which must be stabilized and estimated from market experience. Variable expenses may depend upon the type of property involved, the climate, and the terms of the landlord-tenant relationship.

VARIABLE RATE MORTGAGE (VRM)—An alternative mortgage instrument carrying an interest rate that varies with changes in market rates in general, such as the prime rate or the bond market rate.

VARIANCE—In statistics, a measure of the degree of spread among a set of values; a measure of the tendency of individual values to vary from the mean value.

VARIATE—The specific value of a variable; loosely, a variable.

VAULT
1. A continuous length of arched ceiling.
2. A room especially designed for secure storage.

VEGETATION—Plants collectively; the community of plants in a region as distinct from the kinds composing it.

VEGETATIVE DENSITY—The density of vegetative cover of range land is the estimated percentage of the ground covered, being the area that would be represented by the projection of all herbaceous plants and all the current year's growth of shrubby plants onto the ground surface viewed from directly above. See also Forage Density.

VENEER—A layer of material covering a base of another substance for ornamental or protective purposes such as walnut veneer on less valuable wood; or brick exterior finish over less expensive construction or cheaper backing material.

VENEERED CONSTRUCTION—A method of construction in which a layer of facing material is applied to the external surface of steel, reinforced concrete, or frame walls, e.g., face brick veneer over frame construction.

VENT—A small opening to allow the passage of air through any space in a building, as for ventilation of an attic, unexcavated area under a first-floor construction, in the soffits of an overhang.

VENTILATION—The circulation of air in a room or building; a process of changing the air of a room by either natural or artificial means.

VENT PIPE—A small pipe extending from plumbing fixtures to a vent stack through the roof allowing sewer gases to escape to the outside air.

VERIFICATION OF DATA—The confirmation or authentication of transactions data with the buyer or the seller, or an authorized agent of either, especially data concerning sales price, date, terms of sale and financing, and motivating forces. May also refer to income and expense data, cost data, etc.

VESTIBULE—A small entrance hall to a building or to a room.

VETERANS ADMINISTRATION—An independent establishment of the United States government to which is entrusted the execution of all laws enacted for the benefit of war veterans. Such benefits include special compensation and allowances, pensions, vocational rehabilitation, education, insurance, loans, and hospitalization and medical care.

VICINAGE—The vicinity, region, or area near or about a particular place.

VIEW

1. A drawing representing a particular viewpoint, as a front view, a side view.
2. The scene or prospect as viewed from a site or property.

VIRGIN FOREST—A mature or overmature forest.

VISUAL RIGHTS—The right to clear vegetation and restrict structures at intersections. Where enabling legislation has been enacted, the right to prohibit the erection of advertising media along the highway rights of way.

VITAL STATISTICS—Statistics having to do with births, marriages, deaths, health, diseases, and other related human factors.

VITRIFIED TILE—Pipes made of clay, baked hard and then glazed to make them impervious to water, used particularly for underground drainage.

VOLT—A unit of electromotive force. Residences are usually wired either with 110 volt or 110/220 volt circuits. Factories and large commercial properties, in addition to the 110/220 circuits, may include 440 volt power circuits.

WAGES —Pay given for labor, usually manual or mechanical, at short stated intervals, as distinguished from a salary or fee. More broadly, that share of return which goes as a reward to labor for service, as distinguished from the renumeration received by capital in its various forms.

WAINSCOT—Wooden lining of an interior wall, usually in panels; the lower part of an interior wall when the surface is a different material or separated by a molding and differently decorated from the upper portion. Also known as a dado.

WALL—A vertical structure of stone, brick, wood, or other similar material, serving to enclose, divide, support, protect; as one of the vertical enclosing sides of a building or room. Also, a solid masonry fence or retaining wall.

WALL-BEARING—A wall which supports any vertical load in addition to its own weight, as a wall-bearing partition.

WALL-BEARING CONSTRUCTION—Roof and floors carried directly by exterior walls of plain or pilastered brick or other masonry;

posts or columns used only when length of interior span requires intermediate support for roof or floors.

WALLBOARD — Any of the artificially prepared sheet materials or panels which are used as a covering for walls or ceilings as a substitute for plaster finish, or as a base for plaster.

WALL FURNACE — A small, gas-fired, hot-air furnace that fits between the studs of a wall. This type of furnace has no ducts, but makes use of a small fan to circulate the room air through the furnace and to distribute the heated air.

WALL PANEL — A nonbearing or curtain wall between the columns or piers of a structure which is supported by girders or beams of the structural frame at each story height.

WALL TILE — A ceramic or plastic tile used as a finish material for interior walls or a wainscoting.

WAREHOUSE PROPERTY — A property or structure designed and used for storage of wares, goods and merchandise. Such properties are usually classified as industrial.

WAREHOUSING OF MORTGAGES — An arrangement whereby an originator-mortgagee obtains short-term interim credit secured by mortgages for the purpose of bridging the gap between the completion of construction and eventual sale of the mortgage on the property to an investor-mortgagee. This arrangement is characterized by lender and borrower relationship, an outright lending of funds, plus an agreement whereby the lender collects interest on the amount of the loan.

WARM AIR SYSTEM — A heating system in which furnace-heated air moves to living space through a single register or a series of ducts, circulated by natural convection (gravity system) or by a fan or blower in the ductwork (forced system).

WARRANTED PRICE — Amount justified in exchange. The fixing of a warranted price presupposes a prospective exchange of property; e.g., of real estate for money. Warranted refers to that which is justified or fair. As the price which is warranted can vary according to whether it is one which a seller should accept or a buyer should pay, and according to the circumstances of either or both of these parties, there can be no determination of that which is warranted except in connection with definite assumptions as to related matters or with definite limiting conditions. Thus the term warranted price, by itself, without a statement of the underlying assumptions or limiting conditions, lacks meaning. A warranted price in consideration of the seller's peculiar circumstances might be different from a warranted price which a buyer should pay in view of prospective benefits obtainable through purchase.

WARRANTED VALUE — Erroneously used in place of warranted price.

WARRANTY DEED—A deed conveying to the grantee title to the property free and clear of all encumbrances, except those specifically set forth in the document.

WASHFOUNTAIN—See Bradley Fountain.

WASTE—See Types of Range Vegetation, page 349.

WASTE PIPE—The vertical plumbing line into which fixtures within a structure empty and through which waste is carried to the sewer lines.

WASTING ASSETS—See Diminishing Assets.

WATER—See Ground Water, Irrigation, Surface Water.

WATERFRONT PROPERTY—Land abutting on a body of water; the part of a community so abutting. In real estate, the term is used to distinguish property so located from property in general.

WATER-HOLDING CAPACITY—The amount of water that soil will hold against the pull of gravity with free drainage, expressed as a percent of the dry weight of the soil.

WATER LEVEL—The surface level of any body of water. See also Water Table.

WATER LINE EASEMENT—The same as Sewer Line Easement except that a water supply is to be transmitted through the line.

WATER MEASURES—See Acre-foot, Acre-inch, Cubic Foot per Second, Hour-inch, Miner's Inch, Second Foot; Tables, page 274.

WATER POWER—Power created by a quantity of water passing from a higher to a lower level and susceptible to commercial and industrial utilization.

WATER POWER PLANT—A plant or mill which uses water power to operate its equipment. See also Hydroelectric Plant, Power Plant.

WATERPROOFING
1. To render impervious to water or dampness.
2. Any of the materials used to waterproof as a pitch or other bituminous materials.

WATER RIGHTS—A right to a definite or conditional flow (quantity) of water, usually for use at stated times and in stated quantities for irrigation or for hydroelectric power development. It may be a right acquired by prescription, for example, arising from the open, notorious, and undisputed use of water for the statutory term of years; or, a right acquired by appropriation, for example, a grant by an agency of government possessed of the right to distribute the unappropriated surplus waters of the state; or, a riparian right under the common law doctrine of riparian ownership of waters which wash the land. See also Riparian Rights.

WATERSHED—The drainage area contributing to the water found in the bordered stream. Used synonymously for drainage basin, as that of the Mississippi River.

WATER TABLE

1. The upper limit of that part of the soil (or underlying material) wholly saturated with water. The depth below the surface at which free water is found.
2. A projection at the bottom line of a building superstructure outside the vertical plane of the foundation, to provide a means of run-off for rain water. See illustration, page 306.

WATT—The power created by a current of one ampere flowing at one volt pressure.

WATT-HOUR—The commonly used measure of electrical energy; it is the product of the power in watts and the number of hours the power is maintained.

WEALTH—All things subject to ownership; the material objects themselves or evidences thereof, such as securities. In common usage, wealth includes money and/or anything which has a monetary value. Technically, money is not regarded as wealth, being a medium of exchange whereby wealth (objects) can be acquired.

WEATHERING—The physical and chemical disintegration and decomposition of rocks, minerals, and other organic materials or surfaces.

WEATHERSTRIP—A thin strip of metal, felt, wood, etc., used to cover the joint between a door or window sash and the jamb, casing, or sill; to keep out air, dust, rain, etc.

WEEP HOLES—A series of small holes in a retaining wall or similar structure which permits the drainage of water through the wall and hence reduces the pressure against the wall.

WEIGHTED AVERAGE—An average in which each component is adjusted by a factor which reflects its relative importance in the whole. It is obtained by multiplying each component by its assigned weight (frequency, degree of importance or reliability), adding each product and then dividing the sum of the products by the sum of the weights. See illustration, page 315. See also Band of Investment.

WEIGHTED RATE—A rate which has been adjusted to reflect its relative influence on a total result; a component of a weighted average rate; see also Band of Investment and Weighted Average.

WEIGHTED-USE FACTOR—The factor obtained by multiplying the use factor of each vegetative species on the range by its respective percentage of the composition and summing these products.

WEIR—A device installed in an irrigation ditch or a stream for use in the measurement of the quantity of water passing that point.

WELL—A hole drilled into the earth, generally by boring, to obtain water, petroleum, natural gas, etc.

WESTERN FRAMING—Framing in which the studding of each story rests on a sill, as opposed to balloon framing.

WHARF—A structure alongside which vessels can be held (docked) for loading and unloading; usually, constructed parallel with the shoreline. If built with the long dimensions extending into the water from the shore, it constitutes a pier.

WHEEL LEVELER—A small elevator used to raise the floor of a truck or trailer level with a loading dock by lifting the rear wheels.

WHOLE PROPERTY—See Larger Parcel.

WILD LAND—Land left in a state of nature, uninhabited, unoccupied, and uncultured, and not in use by the owner, his agent or lessee, for any artifical purpose.

WILL–CUT CRUISE—The estimated amount of lumber that can be sawed from the timber in a given area. It is obtained by deducting from the stand cruise an allowance for breakage or other waste.

WINDBREAK—Any physical feature sheltering a house from the wind, especially a tall hedge of trees or shrubs planted for that purpose.

WINDFALL—See Blowdown.

WIND LOAD—The amount of pressure exerted by wind on an exposed surface of a wall or roof, usually expressed in pounds per square foot of surface area.

WINDOW—A glassed opening in a wall or ceiling which provides natural light and ventilation. Types of window include awning, casement, circlehead or fan, clerestory, double-hung, fixed, and traverse or sliding, with their variations. See illustrations, page 301.

WINDOW SILL—The lower or base framing of a window opening.

WINDOW STOP—See illustration, page 310.

WINDOW WELL—See Light Well.

WING—A building section or addition projecting out from the main structure.

WINTER FAT—See Types of Range Vegetation, page 349.

WIRE GLASS—Window glass in which fine wire mesh is embedded to prevent shattering or breaking when exposed to extreme heat.

WITHE—See Wythe.

WITNESS CORNER—A survey corner (a monument) used to identify a point on the land surface which corresponds to a point in the legal description of a site.

WOOD FRAME CONSTRUCTION — Walls and partitions formed by wood framing of studs, or posts and girts, supporting wood roof and floor decks; may be enclosed by wood, metal, stucco, or composition siding or shingles; also may be veneered with brick or stone facing.

WOODLAND — Any land with trees. Generally, the term refers to wooded land of farms as distinct from cropland. Also, used to describe wooded land where the trees are either usable for timber or capable of growing to the point of timber.

WORKING ASSETS — Descriptive of assets intermediate in character between capital and current assets. Specifically, assets which are consumed in the activities carried on without themselves forming an integral part of the product, as supplies used in an operation.

WORKING CAPITAL — The readily convertible capital required in a business to permit the regular carrying forward of operations free from financial embarrassment. In accounting, the excess of current assets over current liabilities as of any date.

WORKING DRAWING — A drawing (usually in the form of a blueprint) for a whole structure or a portion thereof, drawn to scale and in such detail as to dimensions and instructions as is necessary to guide workmen on a construction job.

WORKINGHOUSE — A penthouse structure above the storage section of a grain elevator to house the mechanical equipment necessary to the operation of a grain elevator. Also known as a headhouse.

WRAPAROUND MORTGAGE — A mortgage subordinate to but inclusive of any existing mortgage(s) on a property. In general, a third party lender refinances the property by assuming the existing mortgage (and its debt service) and "wraps around" a new (junior) mortgage. The wraparound lender extends to the borrower an amount equal to the difference between the balance outstanding on the existing mortgage(s) and the face amount on the new mortgage.

WRIT OF CERTIORARI — See Certiorari.

WRIT OF EXECUTION — A legal order which directs a proper agent of a court (frequently a sheriff) to carry out an order of that court.

WROUGHT IRON — A comparatively pure form of iron, containing practically no carbon, and which is easily forged, welded, etc. Used to describe steel which has been molded and worked into ornamental shapes and patterns and used for railings, gates, furniture, etc.

WYE — A railroad juncture track, one track joining the main track from one direction, and the other joining the main track from another direction.

WYTHE—A masonry partition wall between flues in the same chimney stack.

YARD LUMBER—Lumber of all sizes and patterns which is intended for general building purposes. The grading of yard lumber is based on the intended use of the particular grade, and is applied to each piece with reference to its size and length when graded without consideration to further manufacture.

YEARLING—An animal approximately one year of age. A short yearling is from nine to twelve months of age, and a long yearling is from twelve to eighteen months.

YEAR-LONG GRAZING—Continuous grazing for a twelve-month period or a calendar year.

YIELD
1. Money paid or earned as a return on capital; analogous to interest but commonly used in connection with return on equity investments; as distinguished from interest paid on mortgage loans; "yield" may denote profits in total dollars or it may be used as a contraction of the term "equity yield rate," denoting the annual rate of return on equity capital.
2. The return per acre in bushels, pounds, or tons of agricultural crops.

YIELD TO MATURITY—The total yield on an investment, particularly a bond held to maturity, including the gains or losses from resale as well as regular earnings; the sum of all current yield and deferred yield; sometimes a contraction for the rate of yield to maturity; analogous to the equity yield rate and internal rate of return.

ZONAL SOIL—Any one of the great groups of soils having well-developed soil characteristics which reflect the influence of the active factors of soil genesis, such as climate and living organisms, chiefly vegetation.

ZONING—The public regulation of the character and intensity of the use of real estate through employment of police power. This is accomplished by the establishment of districts or areas in each of which uniform restrictions relating to improvements, structure heights, areas, bulk, density of population, and other limitations are imposed upon the use and development of private property.

ZONING MAP—A map depicting the various sections of the community and the division of the sections into zones of permitted land uses under the zoning ordinance.

ZONING ORDINANCE—A statute enacted by a legislative body for the exercise of police powers by the sovereign to regulate and control the use of real estate for the health, morals, safety, and general welfare.

ZONING VARIANCE—A change or variance in the use of property at a particular location which does not conform to the regulated use set forth in the zoning ordinance for the area surrounding that location. It is not an exception or change of the legally applicable zoning.

z-VALUE—The standard normal deviate. The value z represents the number of standard deviation units the random variable (observation) in a data set is above or below the mean. Tables for the area under a normal curve are constructed in terms of z values and for a given z; the table will provide the basis for determining the probability of an outcome between two values or the probability of an outcome being greater than or less than a specific value.

Appendixes

Abbreviations

AACI	Accredited Appraiser Canadian Institute
AASHO	American Association of State Highway Officials
AEC	Atomic Energy Commission
AFA	Association of Federal Appraisers
AGC	Associated General Contractors of America
AIA	American Institute of Architects
AIC	Appraisal Institute of Canada
AICPA	American Institute of Certified Public Accountants
AIHC	American Institute of Housing Consultants
AIP	American Institute of Planners
AIREA	American Institute of Real Estate Appraisers
ALDA	American Land Development Association
ALTA	American Land Title Association
ARA	Agricultural Research Administration
AREUEA	American Real Estate and Urban Economics Association
ARWA	American Right of Way Association
ASA	American Society of Appraisers
ASCP	American Society of Consulting Planners
ASFMRA	American Society of Farm Managers and Rural Appraisers
ASPO	American Society of Planning Officials
ASREC	American Society of Real Estate Counselors
BAB	Build America Better Program
BAC	Bureau of Agricultural Economics
BLM	Bureau of Land Management
BLS	Bureau of Labor Statistics
BOCA	Building Officials and Code Administrators International, Inc.
BOMA	Building Owners and Managers Association, International
BOR	Bureau of Outdoor Recreation
BRAB	Building Research Advisory Board
CAA	Civil Aeronautics Administration
CAB	Civil Aeronautics Board
CAE	Certified Assessment Evaluator, International Association of Assessing Officers
CAI	Community Associations Institute
CCC	Commodity Credit Corporation
CEA	Council of Economic Advisors; Commodity Exchange Authority
CED	Committee for Economic Development
CEQ	Council on Environmental Quality
CSC	Civil Service Commission

CSHA	Council of State Housing Agencies
DOT	Department of Transportation
ECM	European Common Market
EOC	Executive Officers Council
EPU	European Payments Union
ESA	Economic Stabilization Agency
FAA	Federal Aviation Agency
FCA	Farm Credit Administration
FCC	Federal Communications Commission
FCDA	Federal Civil Defense Administration
FDA	Food and Drug Administration
FDIC	Federal Deposit Insurance Corporation
FFLS	Federal Farm Loan System
FHA	Federal Housing Administration
FmHA	Farmers Home Administration
FHLBB	Federal Home Loan Bank Board
FHLMC	Federal Home Loan Mortgage Corporation
FIG	International Federation of Surveyors
FNMA	Federal National Mortgage Association
FPC	Federal Power Commission
FPHA	Federal Public Housing Authority
FRB	Federal Reserve Board
FSA	Federal Security Agency
FTC	Federal Trade Commission
GAO	General Accounting Office
GNMA	Government National Mortgage Association
GPO	Government Printing Office
GSA	General Services Administration
HEW	Department of Health, Education and Welfare
HUD	Department of Housing and Urban Development
IAAO	International Association of Assessing Officers
ICA	International Cooperation Administration
ICBO	International Conference of Building Officials
ICSC	International Council of Shopping Centers
IREF	International Real Estate Federation
IREM	Institute of Real Estate Management
IRS	Internal Revenue Service
MAI	Member Appraisal Institute
MBA	Mortgage Bankers Association of America
MEBIC	Minority Enterprise Business Investment Company
MSA	Mutual Security Agency
NAA	National Apartment Association
NABM	National Association of Building Manufacturers
NAHB	National Association of Home Builders of the United States
NAR	National Association of Realtors
NARC	National Association of Regional Councils
NAREB	National Association of Real Estate Brokers

NAREIT	National Association of Real Estate Investment Trusts
NASA	National Aeronautics and Space Administration
NAM	National Association of Manufacturers
NBS	National Bureau of Standards
NCDH	National Committee Against Discrimination in Housing
NCHP	National Corporation for Housing Partnerships
NFPA	National Forest Products Association
NHC	National Housing Corporation
NHOF	National Homeowners Foundation
NIFLB	National Institute of Farm and Land Brokers
NIREB	National Institute of Real Estate Brokers
NLRB	National Labor Relations Board
NSC	National Security Council
NSREA	National Society of Real Estate Appraisers
NTO	National Tenants Organization
OCZM	Office of Coastal Zone Management
PBS	Public Building Service
PCC	Production Credit Corporation
PHA	Public Health Administration
PHS	Public Health Service
PMA	Production and Marketing Administration
RDB	Research and Development Board
REA	Rural Electrification Administration
RESSI	Real Estate Securities and Syndication Institute
RFC	Reconstruction Finance Corporation
RM	Residential Member, Appraisal Institute
SBCC	Southern Building Congress International, Inc.
SBIC	Small Business Investment Company
SCS	Soil Conservation Service
SEC	Securities and Exchange Commission
SIR	Society of Industrial Realtors
SRA	Senior Residential Appraiser, Society of Real Estate Appraisers
SREA	Senior Real Estate Analyst, Society of Real Estate Appraisers
SRPA	Senior Real Property Appraiser, Society of Real Estate Appraisers
SREA	Society of Real Estate Appraisers
SSA	Social Security Administration
TVA	Tennessee Valley Authority
ULI	Urban Land Institute
UN	United Nations
UNESCO	United Nations Educational, Scientific and Cultural Organization
UNRRA	United Nations Relief and Rehabilitation Administration
URA	Urban Renewal Administration
USDA	United States Department of Agriculture
USGS	U.S. Geological Survey
USRA	United States Railway Association
USTC	United States Tariff Commission
VA	Veterans Administration

Areas of Plane Surfaces

Form	Name	Area
	Triangle	$\dfrac{\text{Altitude} \times \text{Base}}{2}$
	Trapezium irregular quadrilateral	Divide into two triangles and compute as above
	Parallel-ogram	Either parallel side $\times$ altitude
	Trapezoid	½ sum of parallel sides $\times$ altitude
	Regular Polygon	½ sum of all sides $\times$ inside radius
	Circle	$\pi = 3.1416$ πr^2 or $.7854\ d^2$ or $.0796\ cir.^2$
	Sector of Circle	$\dfrac{A^\circ}{360^\circ} \times \pi r^2$ or length of arc $\times$ ½ radius
	Segment of Circle	$\dfrac{r^2}{2}\left(\dfrac{\pi A^\circ}{180} - \sin A^\circ\right)$ or subtract triangle from sector
	Ellipse	Major axis $\times$ minor axis $\times$ .7854
	Parabola	Base $\times$ ⅔ altitude

Useful Rules

To Find Circumference

Multiply diameter by	3.1416
Or divide diameter by	0.3183

To Find Diameter

Multiply circumference by	0.3183
Or divide circumference by	3.1416

To Find Radius

Multiply circumference by	0.15915
Or divide circumference by	6.28318

To Find Side of an Inscribed Square

Multiply diameter by	0.7071
Or multiply circumference by	0.2251
Or divide circumference by	4.4428

To Find Side of an Equal Square

Multiply diameter by	0.8862
Or divide diameter by	1.1284
Or multiply circumference by	0.2821
Or divide circumference by	3.545

Square

A side multiplied by 1.4142 equals diameter of its circumscribing circle.
A side multiplied by 4.443 equals circumference of its circumscribing circle.
A side multiplied by 1.128 equals diameter of an equal circle.
A side multiplied by 3.547 equals circumference of an equal circle.

To Find the Area of a Circle

Multiply circumference by one-quarter of the diameter.	
Or multiply the square of diameter by	0.7854
Or multiply the square of circumference by	0.07958
Or multiply the square of ½ diameter by	3.1416

To Find the Surface of a Sphere or Globe

Multiply the diameter by the circumference.	
Or multiply the square of diameter by	3.1416
Or multiply four times the square of radius by	3.1416

To Find the Cubic Inches (Volume) in a Sphere or Globe

Multiply the cube of the diameter by .5236.

Signs and Symbols

÷	geometrical proportion	——W——	water line
≡	identical with	——G——	gas line
±	plus or minus	—·——·—	center line
∠	angle	—x——x—	fence line
∟	right angle	L^s	lengths
⊏ or >	greater than	L^l	lineal foot
⊐ or <	less than	▨ ⊞	per square foot
⊥	perpendicular	φ	diameter
⌣	difference	℞	plate
∫	integration	℄	center line
⊏○⊐	equivalent	P—	direction of pressure
∷	proportion	$\frac{A}{A}$ or $\frac{A}{A}$	{ indicates cross section of a drawing
⁃∶	difference, excess	▨▨▨▨	{ indicates exposed surface of a section cut
∴	therefore	#	{ pounds after a number number before a number
∵	because	☐	stadia station
∞	infinity	△	triangulation station
∞	varies as	⊙	transit traverse station
√	radical	⊕	indicates elevation point
°	degree	⊢3½⊣	{ dimension line. Number indicates distance between lines.
′	minute or foot	⟹	{ indicates that a section of a drawing, identical to the sections on either side of the symbol, has been omitted to reduce size.
″	second or inch	20° 5°	{ indicates dimensions of rise and span of a roof pitch.

Measures

The English System

Linear Measure

12 inches	= 1 foot
3 feet	= 1 yard
5.5 yards	= 1 rod
40 rods	= 1 furlong
8 furlongs	= 1 mile

Cubic Measure

1,728 cubic inches	= 1 cubic foot
27 cubic feet	= 1 cubic yard
128 cubic feet	= 1 cord
24.75 cubic feet	= 1 perch

Measure of Angles and Arcs

60 seconds	= 1 minute
60 minutes	= 1 degree
90 degrees	= 1 quadrant
360 degrees	= 1 full circle

Square Measure

144 square inches	= 1 square foot
9 square feet	= 1 square yard
43,560 square feet	= 1 acre
640 acres	= 1 square mile

Board Measure

1 board foot	= 144 cubic inches
1 board foot	= 1' × 1' × 1'
1 ton round timber	= 40 cubic feet
1 ton hewn timber	= 40 cubic feet

Nautical Measure

1.852 kilometers	= 1 nautical mile
1.150779 statute mile	= 1 nautical mile
6,076.11549 feet	= 1 nautical mile
1 nautical mile per hour	= 1 knot
6 feet	= 1 fathom
120 fathoms	= 1 cable length

Surveyor's or Land Measure

1 link = 7.92 inches
1 rod (or pole) = 25 links = 16½ feet
1 chain = 100 links = 4 rods = 66 feet
1 furlong = 40 rods = 10 chains = $\frac{1}{8}$ mile
1 mile = 320 rods = 80 chains = 5,280 feet
1 acre = 160 square rods = 43,560 square feet
1 square mile = 640 acres

Engineer's Chain

12 inches	= 1 link
100 links or 100 feet	= 1 chain
52.8 chains	= 1 mile

Dry Measure

(Grain, Fruit, etc.)

2 pints (pt.)	=	1 quart (qt.)	=	67.20 cu. in.	=	1.1012 liter (l.)
8 quarts	=	1 peck (pk.)	=	537.61 cu. in.	=	8.8096 l.
4 pecks	=	1 bushel (bu.)	=	2150.42 cu. in.	=	35.2383 l.
Imperial dry quart	=	1.0320 U.S. dry quarts				

Legal avoirdupois weight as fixed by U.S. government of 1 bushel (bu.) of:

```
      wheat = 60 lb.
     barley = 48 lb. (varies from 32 to 50 lb. in various states)
       oats = 32 lb.
        rye = 56 lb.
       corn = varies from 52 to 56 lb. in various states
Indian corn = 56 lb.
   potatoes = 60 lb. (North Carolina and West Virginia, 56 lb.)
```

Liquid Measure

4 gills (gi.)	=	1 pint (pt.)	=	28.875 cu. in.	=	0.4732 liter (l.)
2 pints	=	1 quart (qt.)	=	57.75 cu. in.	=	0.9463 l.
4 quarts	=	1 gallon (gal.)	=	231 cu. in.	=	3.7853 l.
31½ gallons	∷	1 barrel				

The Metric System

Measures of Length

10 millimeters (mm.)	= 1 centimeter	cm.
10 centimeters	= 1 decimeter	dm.
10 decimeters	= 1 meter	m.
10 meters	= 1 dekameter	Dm.
10 dekameters	= 1 hektometer	Hm.
10 hektometers	= 1 kilometer	Km.

1 meter	=	39.37 inches, 3.28083 feet, 1.0936 yards	1 kilometer = 0.62137 mile
1 centimeter	=	0.3937 inch	1 foot = 0.3048 meter
1 millimeter	=	0.03937 inch, or approximately 1/25 in.	1 inch = 2.54 centimeters, 25.4 millimeters
			1 yard = 0.9144 meters
			1 rod = 5.029 meters
			1 mile = 1.6093 kilometers

The Metric System (*continued*)

Measures of Surface

Myriameter	10,000 meters	6.2137 miles
Kilometer	1,000 meters	0.62137 miles
Hectometer	100 meters	328 feet 1 inch
Dekameter	10 meters	393.7 inches
Meter	1 meter	39.37 inches
Decimeter	0.1 meter	3.937 inches
Centimeter	0.01 meter	0.3937 inch
Millimeter	0.001 meter	0.0394 inch

1 square meter = { 10.764 square feet / 1.196 square yards / 1 centiare

1 square centimeter = 0.155 square inch

1 square millimeter = 0.00155 square inch

1 square yard = 0.836 square meter

1 square foot = 0.0929 square meter

1 square inch = { 6.452 square centimeters / 645.2 square millimeters

1 square rod = 25.29 square meters

1 acre = 0.4046 hectares

1 square mile = 259 hectares

Cuerda	3,930.40 square meters	0.97123 acres
Hectare	10,000 square meters	2.471 acres
Are	100 square meters	119.6 square yards
Centiare	1 square meter	1,550 square inches

Measures of Volume and Capacity

1 cubic meter = { 35.314 cubic feet / 1.308 cubic yards / 264.2 gallons (231 cubic inches) }

1 cubic decimeter = { 61.023 cubic inches / 0.0353 cubic feet }

1 cubic centimeter = 0.061 cubic inch

1 liter = { 1 cubic decimeter / 61.023 cubic inches / 0.0353 cubic foot / 1.0567 quarts (U.S.) / 0.2642 gallon (U.S.) / 2.202 lbs. of water at 62°F. }

1 cubic yard = 0.7645 cubic meter

1 cubic foot = { 0.02832 cubic meter / 28.317 cubic decimeters / 28.317 liters }

1 cubic inch = 16.393 cubic centimeters

Cord	3.625	steres
Liquid quart, U.S.	0.9463	liter
Dry quart, U.S.	1.101	liters
Quart, imperial	1.136	liters
Gallon, U.S.	3.785	liters
Gallon, imperial	4.546	liters
Peck, U.S.	8.810	liters
Peck, imperial	9.092	liters
Bushel, U.S.	35.24	liters
Bushel, imperial	36.37	liters

The Metric System (*continued*)

Measures of Weight

1 gram	=	15.432 grains	1 grain	=	0.0648 gram	
1 kilogram	=	2.2046 pounds	1 ounce			
		0.9842 ton of	avoirdupois	=	28.35	grams
		2240 lbs.	1 ounce Troy	=	31.103	grams
		19.68 hundred-	1 pound,			
1 metric ton =		weights	avoirdupois	=	0.4536 kilogram	
		(cwt.)	1 pound, Troy	=	0.3732 kilogram	
		2204.6 lbs.	1 ton, long	=	1.0160 metric tons	
			1 ton, short	=	0.9072 metric ton	

Miscellaneous

1 kilogram per meter	=	0.6720	pounds per foot
1 gram per square millimeter	=	1.422	pounds per square inch
1 kilogram per square meter	=	0.2084	pounds per square foot
1 kilogram per cubic meter	=	0.0624	pounds per cubic foot
1 degree centigrade	=	1.8	degrees Fahrenheit
1 pound per foot	=	1.488	kilograms per meter
1 pound per square foot	=	4.882	kilograms per square meter
1 pound per cubic foot	=	16.02	kilograms per cubic meter
1 degree Fahrenheit	=	0.5556	degrees centigrade
1 calorie (French Thermal Unit)	=	3.968	Btu (British Thermal Unit)
1 horse power	=	33,000	foot pounds per minute
		746	watts
1 watt (unit of electrical power)	=	0.00134	horse power
		44.22	foot pounds per minute
1 kilowatt	=	1,000	watts
		44,220	foot pounds per minute
		1.34	horse power

Conversion Factors for Measurement of Irrigation Water

1 second-foot = 1 cubic foot per second = 450 gallons per minute = about 1 acre-inch per hour.

1 cubic foot of water = 7.48 gallons.

A body of water under a head of 4 inches delivers through a hole 1 inch square 1/50 of a second-foot.

Legal miner's inch (California statutes, 1901) = 1 1/2 cubic feet per minute, measured under a 6-inch pressure, and is equivalent to a flow of 11 1/4 gallons per minute, or 1/40 cubic foot per second.

In practice, a miner's inch = 9 gallons per minute = 1/50 cubic foot per second.

1 acre-inch = 27,152 gallons, and will be supplied by a flow of 1 miner's inch in 50.4 hours.

Conversion Factors (*continued*)

Formula for Measuring Irrigation Water

1. Water measurement unit—cubic feet per second or second-feet.

$$\frac{\text{Number second-feet} \times \text{hours run}}{\text{Number acres}} = \begin{array}{l}\text{Acre-inches or inches}\\\text{depth on whole area.}\end{array}$$

2. Water measurement unit (Southern California)—miner's inch, 1/50 second-foot or 9 gallons per minute.

$$\frac{\text{Number miner's inches} \times \text{hours run}}{50 \times \text{number acres}} = \text{Acre-inches.}$$

3. Water measurement unit—statutory inches (1/40 second-foot or 11 1/4 gallons per minute).

$$\frac{\text{Number miner's inches} \times \text{hours run}}{40 \times \text{number acres}} = \text{Acre-inches.}$$

4. Pump—Gallons per minute.

$$\frac{\text{Gallons per minute} \times \text{hours run}}{450 \times \text{number acres}} = \text{Acre-inches.}$$

Water Measure

1 cubic foot = 7.4805 gallons
1 cubic foot = 62.42 pounds
1 gallon = 8.355 pounds

1 cubic foot per second = 50 miner's inches in Idaho, Kansas, Nebraska, New Mexico, and Southern California.

1 cubic foot per second = 40 miner's inches in Arizona, Montana, Oregon, and Northern California.

Selected Conversions *to* Metric Measures

Symbol	When you know	Multiply by	To find	Symbol
LENGTH				
in.	inches	2.540	centimeters	cm
ft.	feet	30.480	centimeters	cm
yd.	yards	0.9144	meters	m
mi.	miles	1.6093	kilometers	kn
AREA				
in.^{2}	square inches	6.542	sq. centimeters	cm^2
ft.^{2}	square feet	0.0929	sq. meters	m^2
yd.^{2}	square yards	0.836	sq. meters	m^2
mi.^{2}	square miles	2.590	sq. kilometers	km^2
	acres	0.4046	hectares	ha

Symbol	When you know	Multiply by	To find	Symbol
	MASS (weight)			
oz.	ounces	28.35	grams	g
lb.	pounds	0.4536	kilograms	kg
	short tons (2000 lbs.)	0.9072	tonnes (1000 kg)	t
	CAPACITY (liquid measure)			
fl. oz.	fluid ounces	29.573	milliliters	ml
pt.	pints	0.4732	liters	l
qt.	quarts	0.9463	liters	l
gal.	gallons	3.7853	liters	l
	CAPACITY (dry measure)			
pt.	pints	0.5506	liters	l
qt.	quarts	1.1012	liters	l
gal.	gallons	4.545	liters	l
pk.	pecks	0.009	cubic meters	m^3
bu.	bushels	0.036	cubic meters	m^3
	VOLUME			
$in.^3$	cubic inches	16.393	cubic centimeters	cm^3
$ft.^3$	cubic feet	0.028	cubic meters	m^3
$yd.^3$	cubic yards	0.765	cubic meters	m^3
	TEMPERATURE (exact)			
°F	Fahrenheit	5/9 (after subtracting 32)	Celsius	°C

Selected Conversions *from* Metric Measures

Symbol	When you know	Multiply by	To find	Symbol
		LENGTH		
mm	millimeters	0.0394	inches	in.
cm	centimeters	0.3937	inches	in.
m	meters	3.937	feet	ft.
m	meters	1.0936	yards	yd.
km	kilometers	0.62137	miles	mi.
		AREA		
cm^2	sq. centimeters	0.155	sq. inches	$in.^2$
m^2	sq. meters	1.196	sq. yards	$yd.^2$
km^2	sq. kilometers	0.386	sq. miles	$mi.^2$
ha	hectares (10,000 m^2)	2.471	acres	
		MASS (weight)		
g	grams	0.035	ounces	oz.
kg	kilograms	2.2046	pounds	lb.
t	tonnes (1000 kg)	1.1023	short tons (2000 lbs.)	
		CAPACITY (liquid measure)		
ml	milliliters	0.0338	fluid ounces	fl. oz.
l	liters	2.1134	pints	pt.
l	liters	1.0567	quarts	qt.
l	liters	0.2642	gallons	gal.
		CAPACITY (dry measure)		
l	liters	1.8162	pints	pt.
l	liters	0.9081	quarts	qt.
l	liters	0.2270	gallons	gal.
m^3	cubic meters	111.1111	pecks	pk.
m^3	cubic meters	27.7778	bushels	bu.
		VOLUME		
cm^3	cubic centimeters	0.00006	cubic inches	$in.^3$
m^3	cubic meters	35.7143	cubic feet	$ft.^3$
m^3	cubic meters	1.3072	cubic yards	$yd.^3$
		TEMPERATURE (exact)		
°C	Celsius	9/5 (then add 32)	Fahrenheit	°F

Energy Conversion Factors

The common unit of energy measure is the British thermal unit (Btu), which is the unit used to calculate and compare energy costs and savings. To convert between the common energy units, use the factors in this table.

To Convert	Into	Multiply By
Barrels, oil	gallons	42.0
Cubic feet, natural gas	therms	0.01
Cubic feet, natural gas	Btus	1,020
Gallons, No. 2 oil	Btus	138,000*
Gallons, No. 4 oil	Btus	145,000*
Gallons, No. 5 oil	Btus	148,000*
Gallons, No. 6 oil	Btus	150,000*
Gallons, kerosene	Btus	135,000*
Gallons, gasoline	Btus	125,000*
Gallons, diesel oil	Btus	138,700*
Horsepower-hours	Btus	2,544
Horsepower-hours	kWhs	0.7457
Horsepower	Btu/min	42.4176
Horsepower (boiler)	Btu/hr	33,479
Kilowatt-hours	Btus	3,413
mCF natural gas	Btus	1,000,000
Short ton, eastern steam coal	Btus	23,100,000*
Short tons, western coal	Btus	21,000,000*
Short tons, anthracite coal	Btus	25,400,000*
Short tons, bituminous steam coal	Btus	21,600,000*
Short tons, lignite, brown coal	Btus	14,000,000*
Steam, saturated (lbs.)	Btus	970
Therms, natural gas	cubic feet	100
Therms, natural gas	Btus	100,000
Tons, refrigeration	Btus/hr	12,000

*These are average values. Since exact Btu content varies with type and source, contact supplier when extreme accuracy is essential.

Conversion of Chains to Rods and Feet

Chains	Rods	Feet	Chains	Rods	Feet	Chains	Rods	Feet
1	4	66	15	60	990	28	112	1848
2	8	132	16	64	1056	29	116	1914
3	12	198	17	68	1122	30	120	1980
4	16	264	18	72	1188	31	124	2046
5	20	330	19	76	1254	32	128	2112
6	24	396	20	80	1320	33	132	2178
7	28	462	21	84	1386	34	136	2244
8	32	528	22	88	1452	35	140	2310
9	36	594	23	92	1518	36	144	2376
10	40	660	24	96	1584	37	148	2442
11	44	726	25	100	1650	38	152	2508
12	48	792	26	104	1716	39	156	2574
13	52	858	27	108	1782	40	160	2640
14	56	924						

Approximate Capacity of Round Silos

Estimated Weight In Tons of Corn Silage°
One Month or More After Filling

Depth in Feet	Inside Diameter in Feet					
	10	12	14	16	18	20
8	11	16	21	28	35	43
10	14	20	27	35	44	55
12	17	24	33	43	54	67
14	20	29	39	51	64	80
16	23	33	45	59	75	92
18	26	38	51	67	85	105
20	29	42	58	75	95	118
22	33	47	64	84	106	130
24	36	52	70	92	116	144
26	39	56	77	100	127	157
28	43	61	83	109	138	170
30	46	66	90	118	149	184
32	49	71	97	126	160	196
34	53	76	103	135	170	209
36	56	81	110	144	181	221
38	60	86	117	152	192	234
40	63	90	123	161	203	246
42			130	169	214	258
44			136	178	225	271
46			144	186	236	282
48			151	195	247	295

Source: *Farm and Ranch Brokers Mannual*, The National Institute of Farm Brokers. Chicago, 1959.

°Approximately 67% moisture. Grass silage usually contains more moisture and is from 10% to 15% heavier than corn silage, but contains about the same weight of dry matter per unit of space.

NOTE: To estimate the amount of silage remaining in a silo after part has been fed out, find the actual depth left and estimate the original total depth of silage after settling. Then subtract the tonnage fed out from the original to find the tonnage remaining.

Number of Shrubs or Plants for an Acre

Distance Apart	No. of Plants	Distance Apart	No. of Plants	Distance Apart	No. of Plants
3 × 3″	696,690	4 × 4′	2,722	13 × 13′	257
4 × 4″	392,040	4½ × 4½′	2,151	14 × 14′	222
6 × 6″	174,240	5 × 1′	8,712	15 × 15′	193
9 × 9″	77,440	5 × 2′	4,356	16 × 16′	170
1 × 1′	43,560	5 × 3′	2,904	16½ × 16½′	160
1½ × 1½′	19,360	5 × 4′	2,178	17 × 17′	150
2 × 1′	21,780	5 × 5′	1,742	18 × 18′	134
2 × 2′	10,890	5½ × 5½′	1,417	19 × 19′	120
2½ × 2½′	6,960	6 × 6′	1,210	20 × 20′	108
3 × 1′	14,620	6½ × 6½′	1,031	25 × 25′	69
3 × 2′	7,260	7 × 7′	881	30 × 30′	48
3 × 3′	4,840	8 × 8′	680	33 × 33′	40
3½ × 3½′	3,555	9 × 9′	537	40 × 40′	27
4 × 1′	10,890	10 × 10′	435	50 × 50′	17
4 × 2′	5,445	11 × 11′	360	60 × 60′	12
4 × 3′	3,630	12 × 12′	302	66 × 66′	10

Agricultural Products

Weights, Measures, and Conversion Factors

The following table on weights, measures, and conversion factors covers the most important agricultural products, or the products for which such information is most frequently asked of the U.S. Department of Agriculture. It does not cover all farm products nor all containers for any one product.

The information has been assembled from various sources within the Department and from State schedules of legal weights. For most products, particularly fruits and vegetables, there is a considerable variation in weight per unit of volume due to differences in variety or size of commodity, condition and tightness of pack, degree to which the container is heaped, etc. Effort has been made to select the most representative and fairest average for each product. For those commodities which develop considerable shrinkage, the point of origin weight or weight at harvest has been used.

The approximate or average weights as given in this table do not necessarily have official standing as a basis for packing or as grounds for settling disputes. Not all of them are recognized as legal weight. The table was prepared chiefly for use of workers in the U.S. Department of Agriculture who have need of conversion factors in statistical computations.

Agricultural Statistics

Weights and Measures

Commodity	Unit[1]	Approximate net weight	Commodity	Unit[1]	Approximate net weight
		Pounds			*Pounds*
Alfalfa seed	Bushel	60	Blackberries	24-quart crate	36
Apples	do	48	Bluegrass seed	Bushel	14-30
	Northwest box[2]	44	Broccoli	Wirebound crate	20-25
	Fiberboard box, cell pack	37-44	Broomcorn (6 bales per ton)	Bale	333
Apricots	Lug (Brentwood)[3]	24	Broomcorn seed	Bushel	44-50
Western	4-basket crate[4]	26	Brussels sprouts	Drums	25
Artichokes			Buckwheat	Bushel	48
Globe	1/2 box	20	Butter	Box	64
Jerusalem	Bushel	50	Cabbage	Open mesh bag	50
Asparagus	Crate	30		Wirebound crate[7]	50
Avocados	Lug[5]	12-15		Western crate[8]	80
Bananas	Fiber folding box[6]	40	Cantaloups	Jumbo crate[9]	83
Barley	Bushel	48	Carrots:		
Beans:			Without tops	Bushel	50
Lima, dry	do	56		Open mesh bag	50
Others, dry	do	60	Castor beans	Bushel	41
	Sack	100	Castor oil	Gallon	[10] 8
Lima, unshelled	Bushel	28-32	Cauliflower	W.G.A. crate	50-60
Snap	do	28-32		Fiberboard box, wrapper leaves removed film-wrapped, 2 layers	
Beets:			Celery	Crate[11]	23-35
Without tops	do	50	Cherries	Lug (Campbell)[12]	60
Bunched	Wirebound crate	45		Lug	16
Berries, frozen pack:			Clover seed	Bushel	20
Without sugar	50-gallon barrel	380			60
3 + 1	do	425			
2 + 1	do	450			

Weights and Measures

Commodity	Unit[1]	Approximate net weight (Pounds)
Corn:		
Ear, husked	Bushel	[13]70
Shelled	do	56
Meal	do	50
Oil	Gallon	[10]7.6
Sirup	do	11.72
Sweet	Mesh or paper bag	45–50
	Wirebound crate	40–60
Cotton	Bale, gross	[14]500
	Bale, net	[14]480
Cottonseed	Bushel	[15]32
Cottonseed oil	Gallon	[10]7.7
Cowpeas	Bushel	60
Cranberries	Barrel	100
	1/4–barrel box[16]	25
Cream, 40-percent butterfat	Gallon	8.38
Cucumbers	Bushel	48
Dewberries	24–quart crate	36
Eggplant	Bushel	33
Eggs, average size	Case, 30 dozen	47.0
Escarole	Bushel	25
Figs, fresh	Box, single layer[17]	6
Flaxseed	Bushel	56
Flour, various	Bag	100
Grapefruit:		
Florida and Texas	1/2–box mesh bag	40
Florida	1-3/5–bushel box	85
Texas	1-2/5–bushel box	80
California Desert Valleys and Arizona	Box[18]	[19]64
	Carton[20]	32
California, other than Desert Valleys	Box[18]	67
	Carton[20]	33-1/2
Grapes:		
Eastern	4–quart climax basket	6
	12–quart basket	18–20
Western	Lug[21]	28
	4–basket crate[22]	20
Hempseed	Bushel	44
Hickory nuts	do	50
Honey	Gallon	11.84
Honeydew melons	Jumbo crate[23]	44
Hops	Bale, gross	200
Horseradish roots	Bushel	35
Hungarian millet seed	Barrel	100
Kale	Bushel	48 and 50
Kapok seed	do	18
Lard	do	35–40
Lemons:	Tierce	375
California and Arizona	Box[24]	[19]76
	Carton[20]	38
Lentils	Bushel	60
Lettuce	Fiberboard box, carton	38–55
Lettuce, hothouse	24–quart basket	10
Limes (Florida)	Box	80
Linseed oil	Gallon	[10]7.7
Malt	Bushel	34
Maple sirup	Gallon	11.03

Weights and Measures (continued)

Commodity	Unit[1]	Approximate net weight (Pounds)
Meadow fescue seed	Bushel	24
Milk	Gallon	8.6
Millet	Bushel	48–50
Molasses, edible	Gallon	11.72
Molasses, inedible	do	11.74
Mustard seed	Bushel	58–60
Oats	do	32
Olives	Lug[21]	25–30
Olive oil	Gallon	[10] 7.6
Onions, dry	Sack	50
Onions, green bunched	Crate	60–65
Onion sets	Bushel	28–32
Oranges:		
Florida and Texas	1/2–box mesh bag	45
	Box[25]	90
California and Arizona	Box[18]	[19] 75
	Carton[20]	37-1/2
Orchardgrass seed	Bushel	14
Palm oil	Gallon	[10] 7.7
Parsnips	Bushel	50
	do	48
Peaches	Lug box[21]	20
	California fruit box	[26] 18
Peanut oil	Gallon	[10] 7.7
Peanuts, unshelled:		
Virginia type	Bushel	17
Runners, southeastern	do	21
Spanish:		
southeastern	do	25
southwestern	do	25
Pears:		
California	do	48
Other	do	50
Western	Box[27]	46
Peas:		
Green, unshelled	Bushel	28–30
Dry	do	60
Peppers, green	do	25–30
Perilla seed	Fiberboard carton	30–34
Pineapples	Bushel	37–40
	Crate[26]	70
Plums and prunes:		
California	4–basket crate[29]	28–34
Other	1/2–bushel basket	28
Popcorn:		
On ear	Bushel	[13] 70
Shelled	do	56
Poppy seed	do	46
Potatoes	Bushel	60
	Barrel	165
	Bag	100
Quinces	Bushel	48
Rapeseed	do	50 and 60
Raspberries	24–quart crate	36

Weights and Measures (continued)

Commodity	Unit[1]	Approximate net weight
		Pounds
Redtop seed	Bushel	50 and 60
Refiners' sirup	Gallon	11.45
Rice:		
Rough	Bushel	45
	Bag	100
	Barrel	162
Milled	Pocket or bag	100
Rosin	Drum, net	520
Rutabagas	Bushel	56
Rye	do	56
Sesame seed	do	46
Shallots	Crate (4–7 doz. bunches)	20–35
Sorgo:		
Seed	Bushel	50
Sirup	Gallon	11.55
Sorghum grain[30]	Bushel	56
Soybeans	do	60
Soybean oil	Gallon	[10]7.7
Spelt	Bushel	40
Spinach	do	18–20
Strawberries	24–quart crate	36
	12–pint crate	9–11
Sundangrass seed	Bushel	40
Sugarcane sirup (Sulfured or unsulfured)	Gallon	11.45
Sunflower seed	Bushel	[31]55
Sweetpotatoes	do	50
Tangerines, Florida	Crate / 4/5–bushel box	47 1/2

Commodity	Unit[1]	Approximate net weight
		Pounds
Timothy seed	Bushel	45
Tobacco:		
Maryland	Hogshead	775
Flue-cured	do	950
Burley	do	975
Dark air-cured	do	1,150
Virginia fire-cured	do	1,350
Kuntucky and Tennessee fire-cured	do	
Cigar-leaf	Case / Bale	1,500 / 250–365 / 150–175
Tomatoes	Crate / Lug box[21] / 2–layer flat	60 / 32 / 21
Tomatoes, hothouse	12–quart basket	20
Tung oil	Gallon	[10]7.8
Turnips:		
Without tops	Mesh sack	50
Bunched	Crate[8]	70–80
Turpentine	Gallon	7.23
Velvetbeans (hulled)	Bushel	60
Vetch	do	60
Walnuts	do	50
Water, 60°F.	Gallon	8.33
Watermelons	Melons of average or medium size	25
Wheat	Bushel	60
Various commodities	Short ton / Long ton	2,000 / 2,240

Conversion Factors

Commodity	Unit	Approximate equivalent
Apples	1 pound dried	7 pounds fresh; beginning 1943, 8 pounds fresh
Do	1 pound chops	5 pounds fresh
Do	1 case canned[32]	1.4 bushels fresh
Applesauce	do[32]	1.2 bushels fresh
Apricots	1 pound dried	6 pounds fresh
Barley	1 metric ton[33]	45.9296 bushels
Barley flour	100 pounds	4.59 bushels barley
Beans, lima	1 pound shelled	2 pounds unshelled
Beans, snap or wax	1 case canned[34]	0.008 ton fresh
Buckwheat flour	100 pounds	3.47 bushels buckwheat
Calves	1 pound live weight	0.557 pound dressed weight (1954–63 average)
Cattle	do	0.561 pound dressed weight (1954–63 average)
Cane sirup	1 gallon	5 pounds sugar
Cherries, tart	1 case canned[32]	0.023 ton fresh
Chickens	1 pound live weight	0.72 pound ready-to-cook weight
Corn	1 metric ton[33]	39.368 bushels
Corn, shelled	1 bushel (56 lbs.)	2 bushels (70 pounds) of husked ear corn
Corn, sweet	1 case canned[34]	0.030 ton fresh
Cornmeal:		
Degermed	100 pounds	3.16 bushels corn, beginning 1946
Nondegermed	do	2 bushels corn, beginning 1946
Cotton	1 pound ginned	3.26 pounds seed cotton, including trash[35]
Cottonseed meal	1 pound	2.10 pounds cottonseed
Cottonseed oil	do	5.88 pounds cottonseed
Dairy products:		
Butter	do	21.1 pounds milk
Cheese	do	10 pounds milk
Condensed milk, whole	do	2.3 pounds milk
Dry cream	do	19 pounds milk
Dry milk, whole	do	7.6 pounds milk
Evaporated milk, whole	do	2.14 pounds milk
Malted milk	do	2.6 pounds milk

Commodity	Unit	Conversion
Nonfat dry milk	do	11 pounds liquid skim milk
Ice cream[36]	1 gallon	15 pounds milk
Ice cream[36] (eliminating fat from butter and concentrated milk)		12 pounds milk
Eggs	1 case	47 pounds
Eggs, shell	do	39.5 pounds frozen or liquid whole eggs
Do	do	10.3 pounds dried whole eggs
Figs	1 pound dried	3 pounds fresh in California; 4 pounds fresh elsewhere
Flaxseed	1 bushel	About 2 1/2 gallons oil
Grapefruit, Florida	1 case canned juice[34]	0.64 box fresh fruit
Hogs	1 pound live weight	0.579 pound dressed weight, excluding lard (1954–63 average)
Linseed meal	1 pound	1.51 pounds flaxseed
Linseed oil	do	2.77 pounds flaxseed
Malt	1 bushel (34 lb.)	1 bushel barley (48 lb.)
Maple sirup	1 gallon	8 pounds maple sugar
Nuts:		
Almonds, imported	1 pound shelled	3 1/3 pounds unshelled
Almonds, California	do	2.22 pounds unshelled through 1949; 2 pounds thereafter
Brazil	do	2 pounds unshelled
Cashews	do	4.55 pounds unshelled
Chestnuts	do	1.19 pounds unshelled
Filberts	do	2.22 pounds unshelled through 1949; 2.5 pounds thereafter
Pecans:		
Seeding	do	2.78 pounds unshelled
Improved	do	2.50 pounds unshelled
Pignolias	do	1.3 pounds unshelled
Pistachios	do	2 pounds unshelled
Walnuts:		
Black	do	5.88 pounds unshelled
Persian (English)	do	2.67 pounds unshelled
Oats	1 metric ton[33]	68.8944 bushels
Oatmeal	100 pounds	7.6 bushels oats, beginning 1943

(continued overleaf)

Conversion Factors (continued)

Commodity	Unit	Approximate equivalent
Oranges, Florida	1 case canned juice [34]	0.53 box fresh
Peaches, California, freestone	1 pound dried	5-1/8 pounds fresh through 1918; 6 pounds fresh for 1919–28; and 6-1/2 pounds fresh from 1929 to date
Peaches, California, clingstone	do	7-1/2 pounds fresh
Peaches, clingstone	1 case, canned [32]	1 bushel fresh
Do	do	0.0230 ton fresh
Peanuts	1 pound shelled	1-1/2 pounds unshelled
Pears	1 pound dried	6-1/2 pounds fresh
Pears, Bartlett	1 case canned [32]	1.1 bushels fresh
Do	do	0.026 ton fresh
Peas, green	1 pound shelled	2-1/2 pounds unshelled
Do	1 case canned [34]	0.009 ton fresh (shelled)
Prunes	1 pound dried	2.7 pounds fresh in California; 3 to 4 pounds fresh elsewhere
Raisins	1 pound	4.3 pounds fresh grapes
Rice, milled (excluding brewers)	100 pounds	152 pounds rough or unhulled rice
Rye	1 metric ton [33]	39.368 bushels
Rye flour	100 pounds	2.23 bushels rye, beginning 1947
Sheep and lambs	1 pound live weight	0.482 pound dressed weight (1954–63 average)
Soybeans	1 metric ton [33]	36.7437 bushels
Soybean meal	1 pound	1.27 pounds soybeans
Soybean oil	do	5.49 pounds soybeans
Sugar	1 ton raw	0.9346 ton refined
Tobacco	1 pound farm-sales weight	Various weights of stemmed and unstemmed, according to aging and the type of tobacco. (See circular 435, U.S. Dept. of Agr.)
Tomatoes	1 case canned [34]	0.018 ton fresh
Turkeys	1 pound live weight	0.80 pound ready-to-cook weight
Wheat	1 metric ton [33]	36.7437 bushels
Wheat flour	100 pounds	2.30 bushels wheat [37]
Wool, domestic apparel shorn	1 pound greasy	0.48 pound scoured
Wool, domestic apparel pulled	do	0.73 pound scoured

1. Standard bushel used in the United States contains 2,150.42 cubic inches; and the standard fruit and vegetable barrel, 7,056 cubic inches; the gallon, 231 cubic inches; the cranberry barrel, 5,826 cubic inches of a heaped bushel, which would exceed somewhat the 2,150.42 cubic inches of a bushel basket level full. This also applies to such products as sweetpotatoes, peaches, green beans, green peas, spinach, etc.

2. Approximate inside dimensions, 10-1/2 by 11-1/2 by 18 inches.

3. Approximate inside dimensions, 4-5/8 by 12-1/2 by 16-1/8 inches.

4. Approximate inside dimensions, 4-1/2 by 16 by 16-1/8 inches.

5. Approximate dimensions, 4-1/2 by 13 -1/2 by 16-1/8 inches.

6. Approximate inside dimensions, 13 by 12 by 32.

7. Inside dimensions vary. Common sizes are 13 by 13 by 22-1/8 inches; and 13 by 15-1/8 by 23 inches.

8. Approximate inside dimensions, 13 by 18 by 21-5/8 inches.

9. Approximate inside dimensions, 13 by 13 by 22-1/8 inches.

10. This is the weight commonly used in trade practices, the actual weight varying according to temperature conditions.

11. Approximate inside dimensions, 9-3/4 by 16 by 20 inches.

12. Approximate inside dimensions, 4-1/8 by 11-1/2 by 14 inches.

13. The standard weight of 70 pounds is usually recognized as being about 2 measured bushels of corn, husked, on the ear, because it requires 70 pounds to yield 1 bushel, or 56 pounds, of shelled corn.

14. For statistical purposes the bale of cotton is 500 pounds or 480 pounds net weight. Prior to Aug. 1, 1946, the net weight was estimated at 478 pounds. Actual bale weights vary considerably, and the customary average weights of bales of foreign cotton differ from that of the American square bale.

15. This is the average weight of cottonseed, although the legal weight in some states varies from this figure of 32 pounds.

16. Approximate inside dimensions, 9-1/4 by 10-1/2 by 15 inches.

17. Approximate inside dimensions, 1-3/4 by 11 by 16-1/8 inches.

18. Approximate inside dimensions, 11-1/2 by 11-1/2 by 24 inches.

19. In California and Arizona from 1942 through 1953, the net weights as used by this Department were 77 pounds for oranges, 79 pounds for lemons, and 65 pounds for Desert Valleys grapefruit. Grapefruit in California areas, other than the Desert Valleys, averaged 68 pounds. The new weights effective in 1954 reflect the shift from the "box" to the ½-box carton as the container used.

20. Approximate inside dimensions, 10-1/4 by 10-11/16 by 16-3/8 inches for oranges or lemons, and 9-3/4 by 10-11/16 16-3/8 inches for grapefruit.

21. Approximate inside dimensions, 5-3/4 by 13-1/2 by 16-1/8 inches.

22. Approximate inside dimensions, 4-3/4 by 16 by 16-1/8 inches.

23. Approximate inside dimensions, 7-3/4 by 16 by 21-7/8 inches.

(Notes continued overleaf)

Notes *(continued)*

24. Approximate inside dimensions, 9-7/8 by 13 by 25 inches.
25. Approximate inside dimensions, 12 by 12 by 24 inches.
26. Approximate inside dimensions vary. Common size is 4-1/2 by 11-1/2 by 16-1/8 inches.
27. Approximate inside dimensions, 8-1/2 by 11-1/2 by 18 inches.
28. Approximate inside dimensions, 12 by 10-1/2 by 33 inches.
29. Inside dimensions vary. Ranges from 4 by 16 by 16-1/8 inches to 6 by 16 by 16-1/8 inches.
30. Includes both sorghum grain (kafir, milo, hegari, etc.) and sweet sorghum varieties.
31. This average of 55 pounds indicates the usual weight of sweetpotatoes when harvested. Much weight is lost in curing or drying and the net weight when sold in terminal markets may be below 55 pounds.
32. Case of 24 No. 2-1/2 cans.
33. 1 metric ton is equivalent to 2,204.6 pounds.
34. Case of 24 No. 303 cans.
35. Varies widely by method of harvesting.
36. The milk equivalent of ice cream per gallon is 15 pounds. Reports from plants indicate about 81 percent of the butterfat in ice cream is from milk and cream, the remainder being from butter and concentrated milk. Thus the milk equivalent of the milk and cream in a gallon of ice cream is about 12 pounds.
37. This is equivalent to 4.51 bushels of wheat per barrel (196 pounds) of flour and has been used in conversions, beginning July 1, 1957. Because of changes in milling processes, the following factors per barrel of flour have been used for earlier periods: 1790–1879, 5 bushels; 1880–1908, 4.75 bushels; 1909–17, 4.7 bushels; 1918 and 1919, 4.5 bushels; 1920, 4.6 bushels; 1921–44, 4.7 bushels; July 1944–Feb. 1946, 4.57 bushels; March 1946–Oct. 1946, average was about 4.31 bushels; and Nov. 1946–June 1957, 4.57 bushels.

Measure of Hay in Stacks*

Round Stacks

The volume in cubic feet of round stacks is best figured by:

Volume = [(0.4 × O) minus (.012 × C)] × C × C

In this formula, O equals the *over*, or distance in feet from the ground on one side up and over the peak down to the ground on the other side; it is advisable to take two measurements of O from different spots and then average them. C equals the *circumference*, or distance in feet around the stack at the ground.

Example: If O measures 40 ft. and C measures 60 ft., the volume in cu. ft. is figured this way:

Volume = [(.04 × 40) minus (.012 × 60)] × 60 × 60
Volume = [1.6 minus .72] × 60 × 60
Volume = .88 × 60 × 60
Volume = 3,168 cu. ft.

Oblong or Rectangular Stacks

The volume of an oblong or rectangular stack equals its length times the area of its cross section. The *length*, of course, can be easily measured, but an accurate formula is needed to figure the area of the cross section from the two other measurements obtainable, namely the *over* and the *width*. The *over*, O, is the distance from the ground on one side up and over the peak down to the ground on the other side. The *width*, W, is the width of the stack at the ground. The *length*, L, is the average length of the stack at the ground. The formulas for three types of stacks are:

For low, round-topped stacks.
Volume = [(.52 × O) minus (.44 × W)] × W × L
For high, round-topped stacks.
Volume = [(.52 × O) minus (.46 × W)] × W × L
For square, flat-topped stacks.
Volume = [(.56 × O) minus (.55 × W)] × W × L

Example: Determine cu. ft. in a square, flat-topped stack if L measures 50 ft., W measures 35 ft., and O measures 70 ft.

Volume = [(.56 × 70) minus (.55 × 35)] × 35 × 50
Volume = [39.20 minus 19.25] × 35 × 50
Volume = 19.95 × 35 × 50
Volume = 34,912.5 cu. ft.

---

*Source: *Farm and Ranch Brokers Manual.* The National Institute of Farm Brokers, Chicago, 1959.

Conversion of Hay in Barns and Stacks from Cubic Feet to Tons

(Cubic Feet Per Ton of Hay)

	Unsettled	Settled
	cu. ft.	cu. ft.
Timothy	640	625
Wild Hay	600	450
Alfalfa	485	470
Clover	512	500
Chopped Hay	225	210
Baled Hay (closely stacked)	150–200	150–200
Straw—Baled	200	200
Straw—Loose	1000	600–1000

Source: Doane Farm Book

Animal Units Per Month

	Age	Average lbs. TDN° required per day	Animal Units per month
Dairy Cattle			
Cows, 200 lbs. BF† per year	Mature	13.2	1.00
250 lbs. BF per year	Mature	14.5	1.10
300 lbs. BF per year	Mature	15.8	1.20
350 lbs. BF per year	Mature	16.5	1.25
400 lbs. BF per year	Mature	17.5	1.33
Bulls	Mature	13.2	1.00
Yearlings	1—2 yrs.	8.7	.66
Calves	3 mos.—1 yr.	5.3	.40
Sheep			
Ewes, nursing 2—4 months during year plus feed for lambs to 4 months of age	Mature	2.64	.20
Bucks	Mature	2.64	.20
Lambs, 40—100 lbs.	4—10 mos.	2.0	.15
Swine			
Sows (nursing), 2 litters per year	Mature	6.6	.50
Boars	Mature	5.6	.50
Pigs, 40—100 lbs.	2—4 mos.	3.3	.25
100—200 lbs.	4—6 mos.	5.3	.40
Beef Cattle			
Cows, nursing for 3 months during year	Mature	13.2	1.00
Bulls	Mature	13.2	1.00
Yearlings	1—2 yrs.	9.9	.75
Calves	3 mos.—1 yr.	6.6	.50
Steers, 2 years and over	2—4 yrs.	13.2	1.00

°TDN indicates total digestible nutrients   †BF indicates butterfat

U.S. Public Survey Diagram

Four Townships

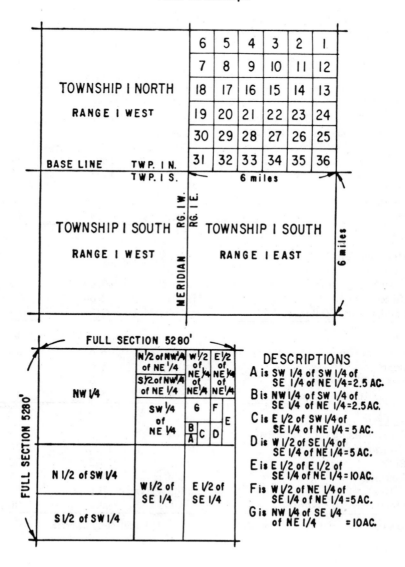

6	5	4	3	2	1
7	8	9	10	11	12
18	17	16	15	14	13
19	20	21	22	23	24
30	29	28	27	26	25
31	32	33	34	35	36

TOWNSHIP I NORTH

RANGE I WEST

BASE LINE   TWP. I N.
TWP. I S.   6 miles

RG. I W.
RG. I E.

TOWNSHIP I SOUTH

RANGE I WEST

MERIDIAN

TOWNSHIP I SOUTH

RANGE I EAST

6 miles

FULL SECTION 5280'

FULL SECTION 5280'

NW 1/4

N 1/2 of SW 1/4

S 1/2 of SW 1/4

N 1/2 of NW 1/4 of NE 1/4
S 1/2 of NW 1/4 of NE 1/4

W 1/2 of NE 1/4 of NE 1/4
E 1/2 of NE 1/4 of NE 1/4

SW 1/4 of NE 1/4

6   F
B C D E
A

W 1/2 of SE 1/4

E 1/2 of SE 1/4

DESCRIPTIONS

A is SW 1/4 of SW 1/4 of SE 1/4 of NE 1/4 = 2.5 AC.

B is NW 1/4 of SW 1/4 of SE 1/4 of NE 1/4 = 2.5 AC.

C is E 1/2 of SW 1/4 of SE 1/4 of NE 1/4 = 5 AC.

D is W 1/2 of SE 1/4 of SE 1/4 of NE 1/4 = 5 AC.

E is E 1/2 of E 1/2 of SE 1/4 of NE 1/4 = 10 AC.

F is W 1/2 of NE 1/4 of SE 1/4 of NE 1/4 = 5 AC.

G is NW 1/4 of SE 1/4 of NE 1/4 = 10 AC.

Standard Area Measures

American Standard Method of Floor Measurement
developed by the American Standards Association

Area measurement in office buildings is based in all cases upon the typical floor plans and barring structural changes which affect materially the typical floor, such measurements stand for the life of the building, regardless of readjustments incident to tenant layouts.

In the case of buildings designed for divided or multiple tenancy, this typical floor plan must permit of subdivision to accommodate usual tenant requirements with corridors that reach every reasonable office subdivision. The definition of "Net Rentable Area" applies to this typical floor, designed for tenant subdivision.

In the case of buildings designed for whole floor tenancy, where corridors are omitted, the definition of "Full Floor Rentable Area" applies.

NET RENTABLE AREA, OFFICE SPACE—The net rentable area of a multiple tenancy floor shall be the sum of all rentable areas on that floor. The rentable area of an office on a multiple tenancy floor shall be computed by measuring to the inside finish of permanent outer building walls, to the office side of corridors and/or other permanent partitions, and to the center of partitions that separate the premises from adjoining rentable areas. No deductions shall be made for columns and projections necessary to the building.

FULL FLOOR RENTABLE AREA, OFFICE SPACE—The rentable area of a single tenancy floor shall be computed by measuring to the inside finish of permanent building walls. Rentable area of a single tenancy floor shall include all area within outside walls, less stairs, elevator shafts, flues, stacks, pipe shafts and vertical ducts with their enclosing walls. Toilets, air conditioning rooms, fan rooms, janitors' closets, and electrical closets within and exclusively serving only that floor, shall be included in rentable area. No deductions shall be made for columns and projections necessary to the building.

STORE AREA—To determine the number of square feet in a rentable store area, measure from the building line in the case of street frontages and from the inner surface of other outer building walls and from the inner surface of corridor and other permanent partitions and to the center of partitions that separate the premises from adjoining rentable areas. No deduction should be made for vestibules inside the building line or for columns or projections necessary to the building. No addition should be made for bay windows extending outside the building line.

BASEMENT AREAS—If the rentable area extends beyond the building line under the sidewalk, measure from the curtain wall or finished surface of the retaining wall and from the inner surface of corridor and other permanent partitions and to the center of partitions that separate the premises from adjoining rentable areas.

If the rentable area is entirely inside the building line, measure from the inner surface of building walls and from the inner surface of corridor and other permanent partitions and to the center of partitions that separate the premises from adjoining rentable areas. No deduction should be made for columns, projections or footing stones necessary to the building.

Cubage Computation

See sketch on opposite page

	Cubic Feet
Basement — 28′ × 26′ × 7′	5,096
Main Portion of Building — 28′ × 26′ × 19′	13,832
Attic — 28′ × 26′ × 4.5′	3,276
°Open Porch — $\dfrac{8′ \times 26′ \times 12′}{3}$	832
Bay Window — 2.5′ × 7′ × 8′	140
Dormer — $\dfrac{4′ \times 8′ \times 5′}{2}$	80
	Total 23,256

°If enclosed, divisor should be 2. If enclosed, finished, and heated, consider as part of the house and use actual cube.

Cubic Contents Computation

Illustrative Drawing—Computation on Opposite Page

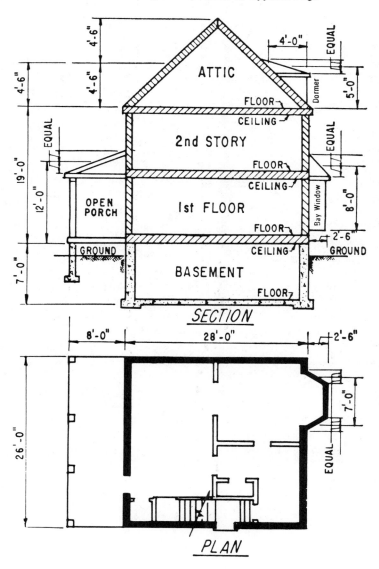

SECTION

PLAN

House Cross Section

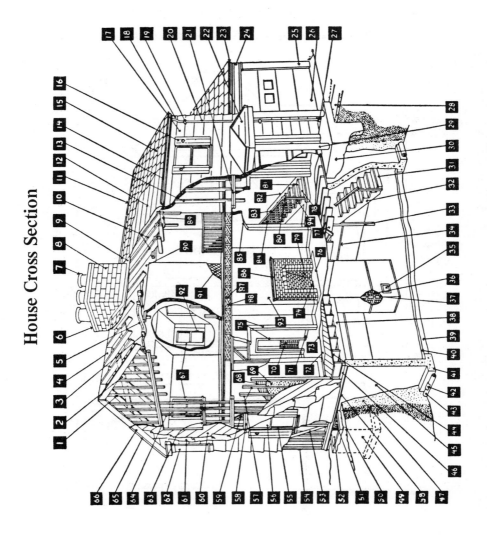

Description of Number Parts in House
(Cross Section)

1—Gable stud
2—Collar beam
3—Ceiling joist
4—Ridge board
5—Insulation
6—Chimney cap
7—Chimney pots
8—Chimney
9—Chimney flashing
10—Rafters
11—Ridge
12—Roof boards
13—Stud
14—Eave trough or gutter
15—Roofing
16—Blind or shutter
17—Bevel siding
18—Downspout or leader gooseneck
19—Downspout or leader strap
20—Downspout leader or conductor
21—Double plate
22—Entrance canopy
23—Garage cornice
24—Frieze
25—Door jamb
26—Garage door
27—Downspout or leader shoe
28—Sidewalk
29—Entrance post
30—Entrance platform
31—Basement stair riser
32—Stair stringer
33—Girder post
34—Chair rail
35—Cleanout door
36—Furring strips
37—Corner stud
38—Girder
39—Cinder or gravel fill
40—Concrete basement floor
41—Footing for foundation wall
42—Paper strip
43—Foundation drain tile
44—Diagonal subflooring
45—Foundation wall
46—Sill

47—Backfill
48—Termite shield
49—Areaway wall
50—Grade line
51—Basement sash
52—Areaway
53—Corner brace
54—Corner studs
55—Window frame
56—Window light
57—Wall studs
58—Header
59—Window cripple
60—Wall sheathing
61—Building paper
62—Pilaster

63—Rough header
64—Window stud
65—Cornice moulding
66—Frieze or barge board
67—Window casing
68—Lath
69—Insulation
70—Wainscoting
71—Baseboard
72—Building paper
73—Finish floor
74—Ash dump
75—Door trim
76—Fireplace hearth
77—Floor joists
78—Stair riser

79—Fire brick
80—Newel cap
81—Stair tread
82—Finish stringer
83—Stair rail
84—Balusters
85—Plaster arch
86—Mantel
87—Floor joists
88—Bridging
89—Lookout
90—Attic space
91—Metal lath
92—Window sash
93—Chimney breast
94—Newel

DIAGRAM SHOWING METHOD OF FIGURING LOADS FOR HOUSE FRAMING

Live load on roof = 30 lbs per sq ft of horizontal surface
Dead load of roof of wood shingle construction = 10 lbs per sq. ft.

Live load on Attic Floor, not used for living purposes = 20 lbs per sq ft.
Dead load of Attic Floor, not floored = 10 lbs per sq. ft.
Dead load of Attic Floor when floored = 20 lbs per sq ft.

Dead load of partitions = 20 lbs per sq ft of floor area

Live load on Second floor = 40 lbs per sq ft.
Dead load of Second floor = 20 lbs per sq ft.

Dead load of partitions = 20 lbs per sq. ft. of floor area

Live load on First Floor = 40 lbs per sq. ft.
Dead load of First Floor, ceiling not plastered = 10 lbs. per sq ft.
Dead load of First Floor, ceiling plastered = 20 lbs per sq ft.

Ceiling & Walls Plastered
Double flooring
Ceiling & Walls Plastered
Double Flooring
Girder
X = 12'-0"
24'-0"

Roof Types

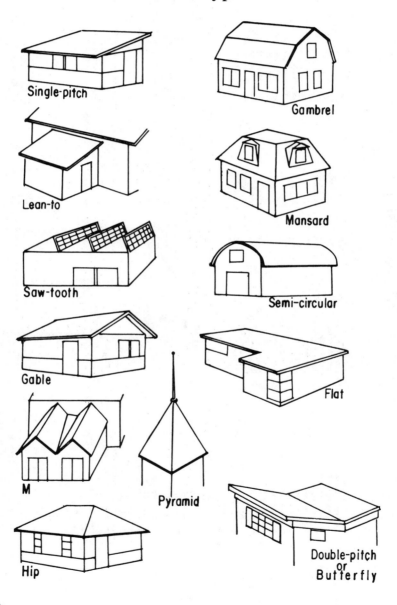

Single-pitch

Gambrel

Lean-to

Mansard

Saw-tooth

Semi-circular

Gable

Flat

M

Pyramid

Hip

Double-pitch
or
Butterfly

Window Types

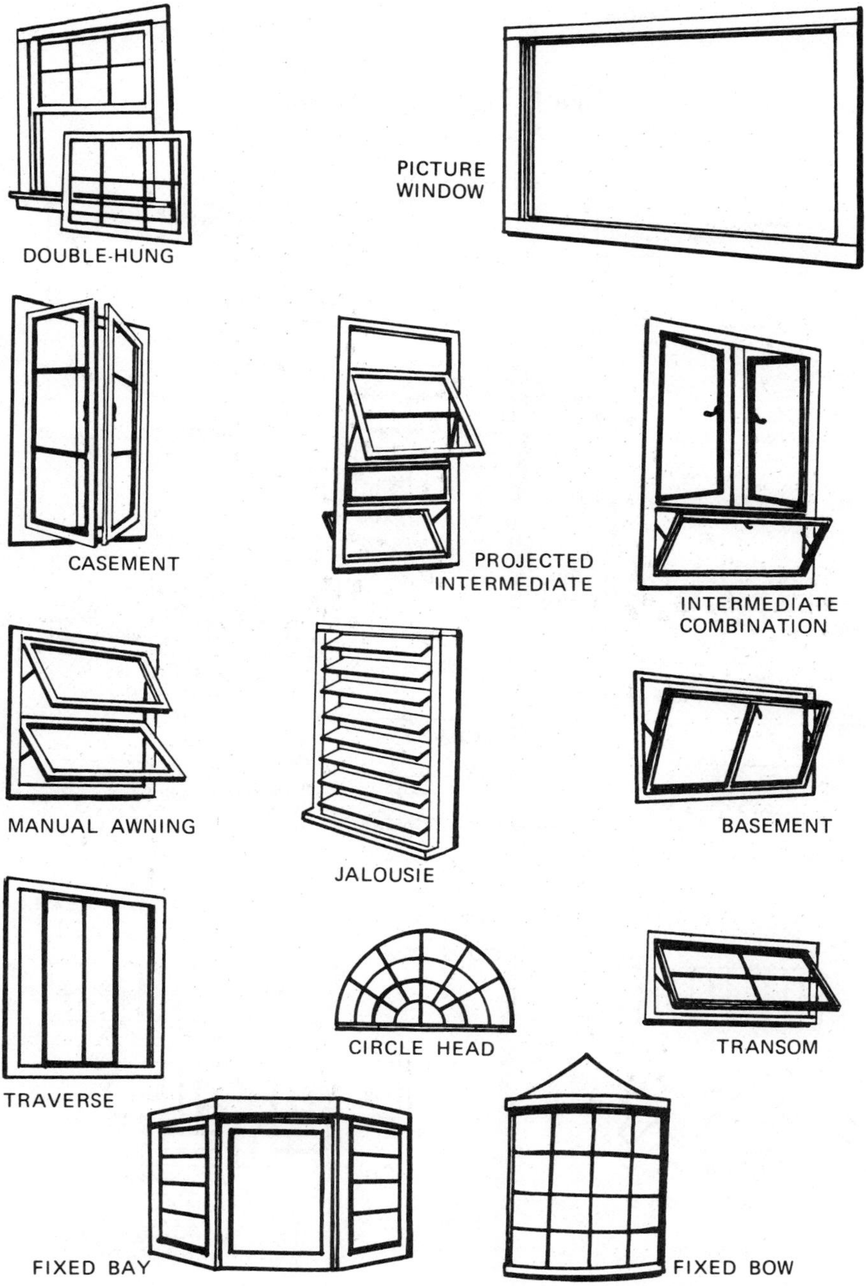

DOUBLE-HUNG

PICTURE WINDOW

CASEMENT

PROJECTED INTERMEDIATE

INTERMEDIATE COMBINATION

MANUAL AWNING

JALOUSIE

BASEMENT

TRAVERSE

CIRCLE HEAD

TRANSOM

FIXED BAY

FIXED BOW

Brick Masonry Bonds

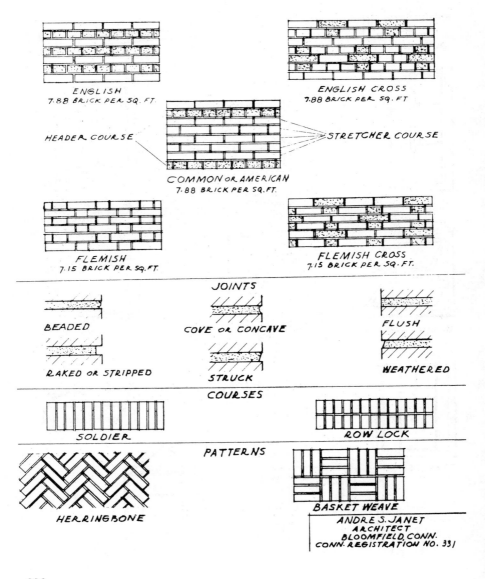

ENGLISH
7.88 BRICK PER SQ. FT.

ENGLISH CROSS
7.88 BRICK PER SQ. FT.

HEADER COURSE

STRETCHER COURSE

COMMON OR AMERICAN
7.88 BRICK PER SQ. FT.

FLEMISH
7.15 BRICK PER SQ. FT.

FLEMISH CROSS
7.15 BRICK PER SQ. FT.

JOINTS

BEADED

COVE OR CONCAVE

FLUSH

RAKED OR STRIPPED

STRUCK

WEATHERED

COURSES

SOLDIER

ROW LOCK

PATTERNS

HERRINGBONE

BASKET WEAVE

ANDRE S. JANET
ARCHITECT
BLOOMFIELD, CONN.
CONN. REGISTRATION NO. 331

Masonry Arches

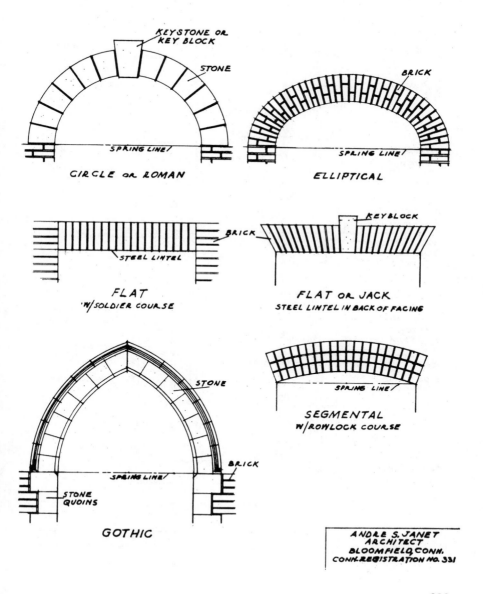

KEYSTONE OR KEY BLOCK

STONE

SPRING LINE

CIRCLE OR ROMAN

BRICK

SPRING LINE

ELLIPTICAL

BRICK

STEEL LINTEL

FLAT
W/SOLDIER COURSE

KEY BLOCK

FLAT OR JACK
STEEL LINTEL IN BACK OF FACING

STONE

SPRING LINE

SEGMENTAL
W/ROWLOCK COURSE

STONE

BRICK

SPRING LINE

STONE QUOINS

GOTHIC

ANDRE S. JANET
ARCHITECT
BLOOMFIELD, CONN.
CONN. REGISTRATION NO. 331

303

Door Framing

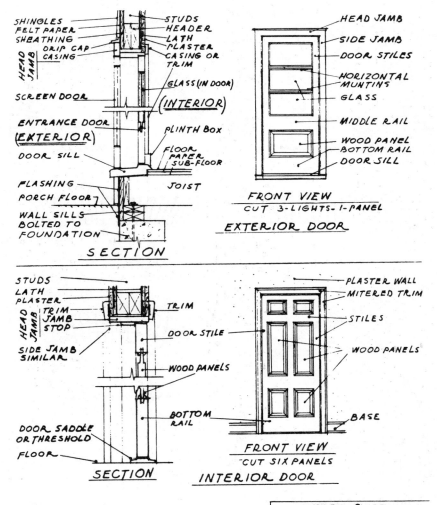

SECTION (upper left, exterior)

SHINGLES
FELT PAPER
SHEATHING
DRIP CAP
CASING
HEAD JAMB

STUDS
HEADER
LATH
PLASTER
CASING OR TRIM

GLASS (IN DOOR)

(INTERIOR)

SCREEN DOOR

ENTRANCE DOOR
(EXTERIOR)

DOOR SILL

PLINTH BOX

FLOOR
PAPER
SUB-FLOOR

FLASHING
PORCH FLOOR

JOIST

WALL SILLS
BOLTED TO
FOUNDATION

SECTION

FRONT VIEW

HEAD JAMB
SIDE JAMB
DOOR STILES
HORIZONTAL MUNTINS
GLASS
MIDDLE RAIL
WOOD PANEL
BOTTOM RAIL
DOOR SILL

FRONT VIEW
CUT 3-LIGHTS-1-PANEL

EXTERIOR DOOR

SECTION (lower left, interior)

STUDS
LATH
PLASTER
TRIM
JAMB
STOP
HEAD JAMB
SIDE JAMB SIMILAR

TRIM

DOOR STILE

WOOD PANELS

BOTTOM RAIL

DOOR SADDLE OR THRESHOLD

FLOOR

SECTION

FRONT VIEW (interior)

PLASTER WALL
MITERED TRIM
STILES
WOOD PANELS
BASE

FRONT VIEW
CUT SIX PANELS

INTERIOR DOOR

ANDRE S. JANET
ARCHITECT
BLOOMFIELD CONN.
CONN. REGISTRATION NO. 331

Roof and Wall Framing

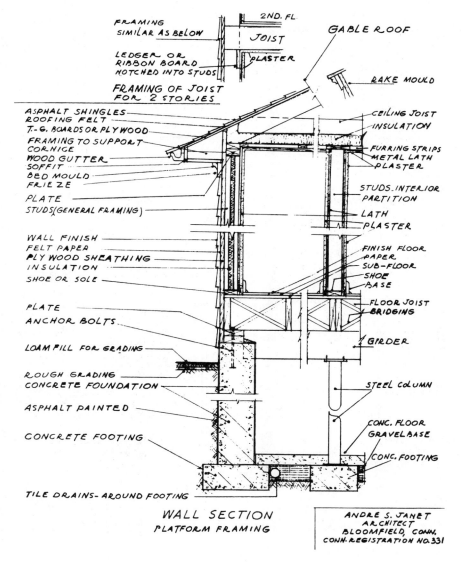

FRAMING SIMILAR AS BELOW

LEDGER OR RIBBON BOARD NOTCHED INTO STUDS

2ND. FL.

JOIST

PLASTER

FRAMING OF JOIST FOR 2 STORIES

GABLE ROOF

RAKE MOULD

ASPHALT SHINGLES
ROOFING FELT
T.-G. BOARDS OR PLYWOOD
FRAMING TO SUPPORT CORNICE
WOOD GUTTER
SOFFIT
BED MOULD
FRIEZE
PLATE
STUDS (GENERAL FRAMING)

CEILING JOIST
INSULATION

FURRING STRIPS
METAL LATH
PLASTER

STUDS. INTERIOR PARTITION
LATH
PLASTER

WALL FINISH
FELT PAPER
PLYWOOD SHEATHING
INSULATION
SHOE OR SOLE

FINISH FLOOR
PAPER
SUB-FLOOR
SHOE
BASE

PLATE
ANCHOR BOLTS

FLOOR JOIST
BRIDGING

LOAM FILL FOR GRADING

ROUGH GRADING
CONCRETE FOUNDATION

GIRDER

ASPHALT PAINTED

STEEL COLUMN

CONCRETE FOOTING

CONC. FLOOR
GRAVEL BASE

CONC. FOOTING

TILE DRAINS - AROUND FOOTING

WALL SECTION
PLATFORM FRAMING

ANDRE S. JANET
ARCHITECT
BLOOMFIELD, CONN.
CONN. REGISTRATION NO. 331

305

Roof Framing

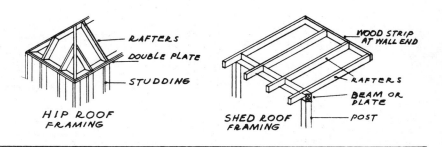

HIP ROOF FRAMING

WOOD STRIP AT WALL END — RAFTERS — BEAM OR PLATE — POST

SHED ROOF FRAMING

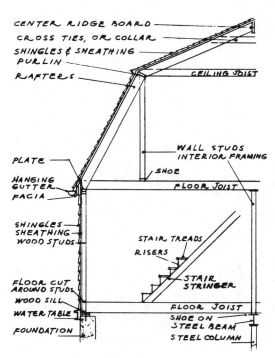

CENTER RIDGE BOARD

CROSS TIES, OR COLLAR

SHINGLES & SHEATHING

PURLIN

RAFTERS

CEILING JOIST

PLATE

HANGING GUTTER

FACIA

WALL STUDS INTERIOR FRAMING

SHOE

FLOOR JOIST

SHINGLES SHEATHING WOOD STUDS

STAIR TREADS

RISERS

STAIR STRINGER

FLOOR CUT AROUND STUDS

WOOD SILL

WATER TABLE

FOUNDATION

FLOOR JOIST

SHOE ON STEEL BEAM

STEEL COLUMN

WALL SECTION
BRACED FRAMING
GAMBREL ROOF

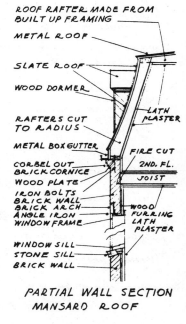

ROOF RAFTER MADE FROM BUILT UP FRAMING

METAL ROOF

SLATE ROOF

WOOD DORMER

RAFTERS CUT TO RADIUS

METAL BOX GUTTER

CORBEL OUT BRICK CORNICE

WOOD PLATE

IRON BOLTS
BRICK WALL
BRICK ARCH
ANGLE IRON
WINDOW FRAME

WINDOW SILL
STONE SILL
BRICK WALL

LATH PLASTER

FIRE CUT 2ND. FL.

JOIST

WOOD FURRING LATH PLASTER

PARTIAL WALL SECTION
MANSARD ROOF

ANDRE S. JANET
ARCHITECT
BLOOMFIELD, CONN
CONN. REGISTRATION No. 331

306

Interior Trim

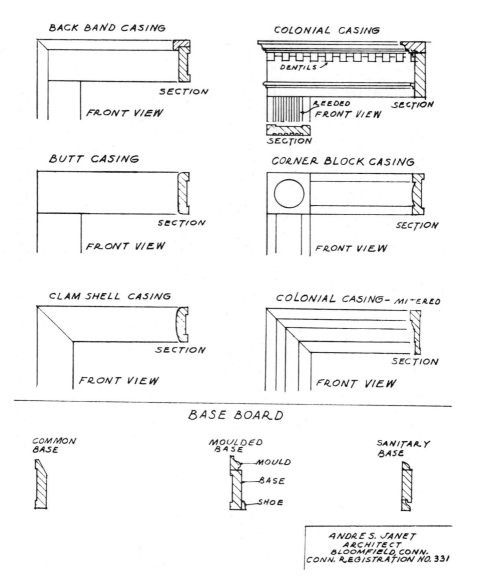

BACK BAND CASING

SECTION

FRONT VIEW

COLONIAL CASING

DENTILS

REEDED

FRONT VIEW

SECTION

SECTION

BUTT CASING

SECTION

FRONT VIEW

CORNER BLOCK CASING

SECTION

FRONT VIEW

CLAM SHELL CASING

SECTION

FRONT VIEW

COLONIAL CASING- MITERED

SECTION

FRONT VIEW

BASE BOARD

COMMON
BASE

MOULDED
BASE

MOULD

BASE

SHOE

SANITARY
BASE

ANDRE S. JANET
ARCHITECT
BLOOMFIELD, CONN.
CONN. REGISTRATION NO. 331

307

Window Framing—Casement

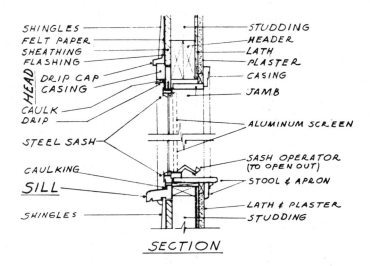

SHINGLES	STUDDING
FELT PAPER	HEADER
SHEATHING	LATH
FLASHING	PLASTER
HEAD DRIP CAP	CASING
CASING	JAMB
CAULK	
DRIP	
	ALUMINUM SCREEN
STEEL SASH	
	SASH OPERATOR (TO OPEN OUT)
CAULKING	
SILL	STOOL & APRON
	LATH & PLASTER
SHINGLES	STUDDING

SECTION

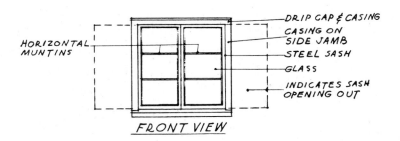

	DRIP CAP & CASING
HORIZONTAL MUNTINS	CASING ON SIDE JAMB
	STEEL SASH
	GLASS
	INDICATES SASH OPENING OUT

FRONT VIEW

ANDRE S. JANET
ARCHITECT
BLOOMFIELD, CONN.
CONN. REGISTRATION NO. 331

Window Framing—Double Hung—Metal

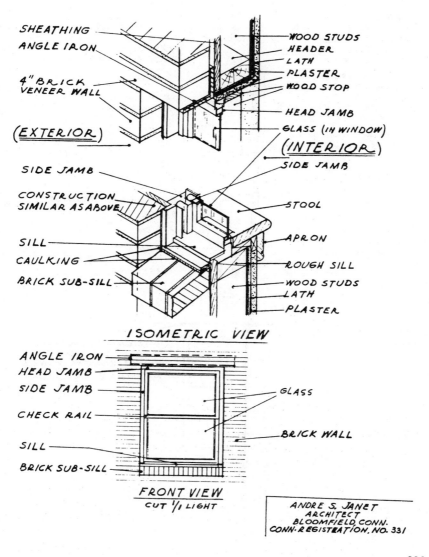

SHEATHING

ANGLE IRON

4" BRICK VENEER WALL

(EXTERIOR)

SIDE JAMB

CONSTRUCTION SIMILAR AS ABOVE

SILL

CAULKING

BRICK SUB-SILL

WOOD STUDS

HEADER

LATH

PLASTER

WOOD STOP

HEAD JAMB

GLASS (IN WINDOW)

(INTERIOR)

SIDE JAMB

STOOL

APRON

ROUGH SILL

WOOD STUDS

LATH

PLASTER

ISOMETRIC VIEW

ANGLE IRON

HEAD JAMB

SIDE JAMB

CHECK RAIL

SILL

BRICK SUB-SILL

GLASS

BRICK WALL

FRONT VIEW
CUT 1/1 LIGHT

ANDRE S. JANET
ARCHITECT
BLOOMFIELD CONN.
CONN. REGISTRATION. NO. 331

Window Framing – Double Hung – Wood

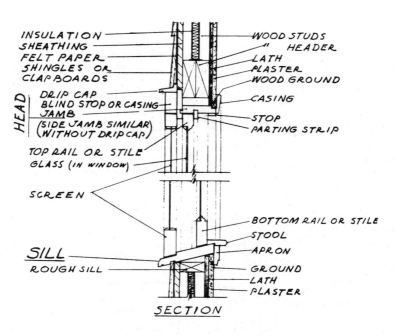

INSULATION
SHEATHING
FELT PAPER
SHINGLES OR
CLAPBOARDS

WOOD STUDS
" HEADER
LATH
PLASTER
WOOD GROUND

HEAD

DRIP CAP
BLIND STOP OR CASING
JAMB
(SIDE JAMB SIMILAR)
(WITHOUT DRIP CAP)

CASING

STOP
PARTING STRIP

TOP RAIL OR STILE
GLASS (IN WINDOW)

SCREEN

BOTTOM RAIL OR STILE
STOOL

SILL

APRON

ROUGH SILL

GROUND
LATH
PLASTER

SECTION

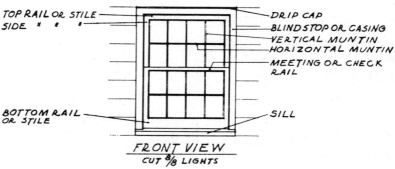

TOP RAIL OR STILE
SIDE " " "

DRIP CAP
BLIND STOP OR CASING
VERTICAL MUNTIN
HORIZONTAL MUNTIN
MEETING OR CHECK
RAIL

BOTTOM RAIL
OR STILE

SILL

FRONT VIEW
CUT 8/8 LIGHTS

ANDRE S. JANET
ARCHITECT
BLOOMFIELD, CONN.
CONN. REGISTRATION NO. 331

Electric Symbols

OUTLETS

⊖   DUPLEX CONVENIENCE — FLOOR
⊣⊖ DUPLEX CONVENIENCE — WALL
⊣⊖ W.P. WATER PROOF
Ⓒ   CLOCK OUTLET
Ⓕ   FAN OUTLET
⊣⊖ RANGE OUTLET
◐   SPECIAL PURPOSE
⊣⊖Ⓡ RADIO & CONVENIENCE
⊡   PUSH BUTTON
⊏⁄   BUZZER
⊏ₒ   BELL
◇   ANNUNCIATOR
⊡   DOOR OPENER
Ⓜ   MAID SIGNAL

FIXTURES

○   CEILING HUNG
○ₚ𝒸 CEILING HUNG — PULL CHAIN
Ⓟ   CLOSET, WITH SWITCH ON DOOR JAMB
▣   RECESSED OR CEILING MOUNTED
⟠   INDIRECT - CEILING MOUNTED
⊸○   WALL BRACKET
⊸Ⓝ   NITE LIGHT
⊸Ⓟ   PILOT LIGHT
▭   ULTRA-VIOLET GERMICIDAL LAMP
▭   FLUORESCENT
≡   SINGLE ROW SLIMLINE
≣   THREE ROW SLIMLINE
⊥   FLUORESCENT, WITH STEMS

   CORNICE LIGHTING

   COVE LIGHTING

ANDRE S. JANET
ARCHITECT
BLOOMFIELD, CONN.
CONN. REGISTRATION NO. 331

Electric Symbols (*Continued*)

SWITCHES

S   SINGLE POLE

S_2 DOUBLE POLE

S_3 THREE WAY

S_4 FOUR WAY

WIRING

——————— BRANCH CIRCUIT— CONCEALED IN CEILING

— · — ·   "   "   —   "   IN FLOOR

- ·· ---   "   " — EXPOSED

—///—   "   " — 3 WIRE

—//—//—   "   " — 4 WIRE

——▶   HOME RUN TO PANELBOARD

WIRING PLATES

WATERPROOF DUPLEX
CONVENIENCE OUTLET

AUTOMATIC
DOOR SWITCH

GROUNDING TYPE
4-WIRE

RANGE OUTLET

GROUNDING TYPE
3-WIRE

CLOCK HANGER

ANDRE S. JANET
ARCHITECT
BLOOMFIELD, CONN.
CONN. REGISTRATION NO. 331

Plumbing Symbols

PLAN VIEWS
BATH TUBS

4'-0" x 4'-1" x 16" RECESSED

5'-3" x 3'-8" x 12" SHOWER OR FOOT

4'-0" x 4'-1" x 16" CORNER

4'-6" TO 6'-0" x 16" RECESSED

ROLL RIM.

LAVATORIES

FLAT TOP FOR COUNTER

LOW BACK PEDESTAL OR LEGS

SHELF BACK WALL HUNG

ANGLE WALL HUNG

SHOWERS

BAKED ENAMEL CABINET PLASTIC CURTAIN

BUILT-IN WALL GLASS DOOR

URINALS

FLOOR TYPE

WALL HUNG

TROUGH TYPE

PEDESTAL TYPE

WATER CLOSETS

LOW TANK WALL HUNG

FLUSH VALVE FLOOR OR WALL HUNG

BIDET

KITCHEN EQUIPMENT

FLAT RIM SINK

SINK & TRAY COMBINATION

LAUNDRY TRAYS SINGLE — DOUBLE

CABINET UNIT- WITH DISHWASHER.

MISCELLANEOUS

AUTOMATIC WASHER

AUTOMATIC DRYER

COUNTER UNIT WATER HEATER

WATER HEATER

ANDRE S. JANET
ARCHITECT
BLOOMFIELD, CONN.
CONN. REGISTRATION NO. 331

Measures of Central Tendency and Dispersion

CENTRAL TENDENCY

The purpose of a measure of central tendency is to represent a group of individual values in a simple and concise manner such that there is a general understanding of the size of the individual values in the group. In other words, the measure of central tendency summarizes, represents and/or describes the "typical" value of a distribution of any size. Further, this measure may serve as a base for inferences that might be made about the population that the statistic represents.

Of the various measures of central tendency the most common are the mean, the median and the mode. Each is discussed below with emphasis on its calculation both from ungrouped and grouped data. For purposes of illustration, the following sample of 11 Gross Rent Multipliers will be used throughout in the calculation of both measures of central tendency and dispersion. All 11 GRM's are presumed to have been calculated from sales prices and annual gross rents of 11 separate but comparable properties.

Sample of 11 Gross Rent Multipliers
(in order obtained)

5.9
6.3
6.1
6.1
6.7
5.6
6.3
5.8
7.0
6.3
5.9

Calculation of Mean $(\bar{X})$ — Ungrouped Data

Formula: $\bar{X} = \dfrac{\Sigma X}{n}$

Where: Σ = summation sign

X = individual (observed) values of Gross Rent Multipliers

n = number of observations

Thus: $\Sigma X = 68.0$

              $n = 11$

Therefore: $\overline{X} = \dfrac{68.0}{11} = 6.18$

Calculation of Mean ($\overline{X}$) — Weighted Mean

Formula: $\overline{X} = \dfrac{\Sigma f X}{n}$

Where: f = weight (frequency)

           n = sum of weights (frequencies)

The ungrouped data is now arranged in a frequency distribution as follows:

X	f	fX
5.6	1	5.6
5.8	1	5.8
5.9	2	11.8
6.1	2	12.2
6.3	3	18.9
6.7	1	6.7
7.0	1	7.0
	$n = 11$	$\Sigma f X = 68.0$

Therefore: $\overline{X} = \dfrac{68.0}{11} = 6.18$

Calculation of Mean ($\overline{X}$) — Grouped Data

Formula: $\overline{X} = \dfrac{\Sigma f X_i}{n}$

Where: f = frequency (number of observations within interval)

           X_i = midpoint of class interval

The ungrouped data from above is now arranged in classes according to a pre-computed formula:

$$\frac{R}{1 + 3.322 \log n}$$

Where: R = Range = 1.4

           n = 11

           $\log n = \log 11 = 1.0414$

and where: Number of Intervals $= 1 + 3.322 \log n = 1 + (3.322 \cdot 1.0414) = 4.46$ (rounded to 5)

Size of Interval $= \dfrac{R}{1 + 3.322} \log n = \dfrac{1.4}{4.46} =$ .314 (rounded to .3)

Therefore:

GRM Interval	Number (f)	Interval Midpoint (X_i)	fX_i
5.6−5.89	2	5.75	11.5
5.9−6.19	4	6.05	24.2
6.2−6.49	3	6.35	19.05
6.5−6.79	1	6.65	6.65
6.8−7.09	1	6.95	6.95
	$n = 11$		$\Sigma fX_i = 68.35$

$$\bar{X} = \frac{68.35}{11} = 6.21$$

Calculation of Median (Md) — Ungrouped Data

Formula: $Md = \dfrac{n + 1}{2}$

Where: n = number of observations

Therefore: $Md = \dfrac{11 + 1}{2} = \dfrac{12}{2} = 6$

The median is that number which lies in the middle of a series of data (once the data has been arrayed from low to high or vice versa). Note: If there are an even number of observations, interpolation is required. For example, had there been 12 observations in our data set then the median would be located between the sixth and seventh items in the array, i.e., $\dfrac{n + 1}{2} = \dfrac{12 + 1}{2} = 6.5$.

For our ungrouped data from above, however, the median is the sixth item in the array. Thus, arranging the data from low to high:

$$
\begin{array}{l}
5.6 \\
5.8 \\
5.9 \\
5.9 \\
6.1 \\
6.1 \quad \leftarrow \text{median} \\
6.3 \\
6.3 \\
6.3 \\
6.7 \\
7.0
\end{array}
$$

The median is identified as 6.1.

Calculation of Median (Md) – Grouped Data

Formula: $Md = L + \dfrac{1(n/2-F)}{f}$

Where:
L = the lower limit of the median class
i = the median class interval, i.e., the width of the median class
n = the total number of observations
F = the cumulative frequency for all classes *below* the median class
f = the frequency for the median class

Thus, from the grouped data above:

L = 5.9
i = 0.3
n = 11
F = 2
f = 4

Therefore:

$$Md = 5.9 + \dfrac{.3(11/2-2)}{4} = 5.9 + \dfrac{.3(3.5)}{4} =$$

$$5.9 + 0.26 = 6.16$$

Calculation of Mode (Mo): Ungrouped Data

The mode represents the most frequent observation. Therefore, from the ungrouped data above, the mode is 6.3

Calculation of Mode (Mo): Grouped Data

Formula: $Mo = L + \left(\left[\dfrac{\Delta_1}{\Delta_1 + \Delta_2} \right] \cdot i \right)$

Where:
L = lower limit of modal class
Δ_1 = the absolute difference (i.e., ignore signs) between the frequency of the modal class and the frequency of the *premodal* class
Δ_2 = the absolute difference (i.e., ignore signs) between the frequency of the modal class and the frequency of the *post modal* class
i = the modal class interval, i.e., the width of the modal class

Thus, from the grouped data above:

L = 5.9
Δ_1 = 2
Δ_2 = 1
i = 0.3

Therefore:

$$Mo = 5.9 + (\tfrac{2}{3} \cdot 0.3) = 5.9 + .2 = 6.1$$

Summary Comparisons of Measures of
Central Tendency

Sample of 11 Gross Rent Multipliers

	Ungrouped Data	Grouped Data
Mean	6.18	6.21
Median	6.10	6.16
Mode	6.30	6.10

DISPERSION

As noted above, measures of central tendency (averages) summarize the typical value of a distribution of any size such that different distributions may be distinguished from each other by the different values of these descriptive (typical) measures. Even greater precision in the description of the typical value of a distribution (set of data) can be obtained by showing how the data vary about the measure of central tendency. This is accomplished by a measure of dispersion (scatter) and provides (1) a determination of the reliability of the measure of central tendency and (2) serves as a basis for control of the variability itself.

While other measures of dispersion exist, the more common measures used in analysis (and to be covered here) are the range, average deviation and standard deviation. Each is discussed below, utilizing the same data presented above in the calculations of the measures of central tendency.

Calculation of the Range (R)

Formula: $R = H-L$

Where: $H =$ the highest value of the variables in a set of data (array).

$L =$ the lowest value of the variables in a set of data (array).

Thus: $H = 7.0$
$L = 5.6$

Therefore: $R = 7.0-5.6 = 1.4$

The range, then, represents the total spread between the highest and lowest variables in a distribution. It represents the simplest of all measures of dispersion.

Calculation of Average Deviation ($A.D.$) – Ungrouped Data

Formula: $A.D. = \dfrac{\Sigma |X-\bar{X}|}{n}$

Where: X = individual observations in data set
                $\overline{X}$ = mean value of data
                n = number of observations
                $||$ = absolute difference (ignore signs)

Therefore:

X	$\overline{X}$	$|X-\overline{X}|$
5.6	6.18	0.58
5.8	6.18	0.38
5.9	6.18	0.28
5.9	6.18	0.28
6.1	6.18	0.08
6.1	6.18	0.08
6.3	6.18	0.12
6.3	6.18	0.12
6.3	6.18	0.12
6.7	6.18	0.52
7.0	6.18	0.82
		$\Sigma|X-\overline{X}| = 3.38$

and,

$$A.D. = \frac{3.38}{11} = 0.31$$

Calculation of Average Deviation ($A.D.$) — Frequency Distribution

Formula: $A.D. = \dfrac{\Sigma f|X-\overline{X}|}{n}$

Where: f = the frequency with which each item appears in the distribution

Therefore:

X	$\overline{X}$	$|X-\overline{X}|$	f	$f|X-\overline{X}|$
5.6	6.18	0.58	1	0.58
5.8	6.18	0.38	1	0.38
5.9	6.18	0.28	2	0.56
6.1	6.18	0.08	2	0.16
6.3	6.18	0.12	3	0.36
6.7	6.18	0.52	1	0.52
7.0	6.18	0.82	1	0.82
				$\Sigma f|X-\overline{X}| = 3.38$

and,

$$A.D. = \frac{3.38}{11} = 0.31$$

Calculation of Average Deviation ($A.D.$) – Grouped Data

Formula: $A.D. = \dfrac{\Sigma f |X_i - \overline{X}|}{n}$

Where: X_i = midpoint of class interval

Therefore:

X_i	$\overline{X}$	$|X_i - \overline{X}|$	f	$f|X_i - \overline{X}|$
5.75	6.21	0.46	2	0.92
6.05	6.21	0.16	4	0.64
6.35	6.21	0.14	3	0.42
6.65	6.21	0.44	1	0.44
6.95	6.21	0.74	1	0.74

$$\Sigma f |X_i - \overline{X}| = 3.16$$

and,

$$A.D. = \frac{3.16}{11} = 0.29$$

Note: In a sample, approximately 57.5% of the observations are in the interval $\overline{X} \pm A.D.$

Calculation of Standard Deviation (s) – Ungrouped Data

Formula: $s = \sqrt{\dfrac{\Sigma (X - \overline{X})^2}{n-1}}$

In the calculation of the standard deviation, the differences between the mean and other observations in the data are squared so as to eliminate the problem of negative deviations.

Therefore:

X	$\overline{X}$	$X - \overline{X}$	$(X - \overline{X})^2$
5.6	6.18	−0.58	0.34
5.8	6.18	−0.38	0.14
5.9	6.18	−0.28	0.08
5.9	6.18	−0.28	0.08
6.1	6.18	−0.08	0.01
6.1	6.18	−0.08	0.01
6.3	6.18	0.12	0.01
6.3	6.18	0.12	0.01
6.3	6.18	0.12	0.01
6.7	6.18	0.52	0.27
7.0	6.18	0.82	0.67

$$\Sigma (X - \overline{X})^2 = 1.63$$

and,

$$s = \sqrt{\frac{1.63}{10}} = \sqrt{.163} = .40$$

Calculation of Standard Deviation (s) — Frequency Distribution

Formula: $s = \sqrt{\dfrac{\Sigma f(X - \overline{X})}{n-1}}$

Where: f = the frequency with which each item appears in the distribution

Therefore:

X	$\overline{X}$	$X - \overline{X}$	$(X - \overline{X})^2$	f	$f(X - \overline{X})^2$
5.6	6.18	−0.58	0.34	1	0.34
5.8	6.18	−0.38	0.14	1	0.14
5.9	6.18	−0.28	0.08	2	0.16
6.1	6.18	−0.08	0.01	2	0.02
6.3	6.18	0.12	0.01	3	0.03
6.7	6.18	0.52	0.27	1	0.27
7.0	6.18	0.82	0.67	1	0.67

$$\Sigma f(X - \overline{X}) = 1.63$$

and,

$$s = \sqrt{\frac{1.63}{10}} = \sqrt{.163} = .40$$

Calculation of Standard Deviation (s) — Grouped Data

Formula: $s = \sqrt{\dfrac{\Sigma f(X_i - \overline{X})^2}{n-1}}$

Where: X_i = midpoint of class interval

Therefore:

X_i	$\overline{X}$	$X_i - \overline{X}$	$(X_i - \overline{X})^2$	f	$f(X_i - \overline{X})^2$
5.75	6.21	−0.46	0.21	2	0.42
6.05	6.21	−0.16	0.03	4	0.12
6.35	6.21	0.14	0.02	3	0.06
6.65	6.21	0.44	0.19	1	0.19
6.95	6.21	0.74	0.55	1	0.55

$$\Sigma f(X_i - \overline{X}) = 1.34$$

and,

$$s = \sqrt{\frac{1.34}{10}} = \sqrt{.134} = .37$$

Note: In a sample,   68% confidence interval = $\overline{X} \pm s$
95% confidence interval = $\overline{X} \pm 1.96s$
(2s often used)
99% confidence interval = $\overline{X} \pm 2.575s$
(3s often used)

Summary Comparisons of Measures of Dispersion

Sample of 11 Gross Rent Multipliers

	Ungrouped Data	*Grouped Data*
Range	1.4	—
Average Deviation	0.31	0.29
Standard Deviation	0.40	0.37

Simple Linear Regression*

Regression analysis is one of the most widely used statistical tools, partially because it provides a structure and basis for analyzing and understanding the relationships among variables. Regression analysis may be performed under controlled circumstances (as in many scientific applications) or uncontrolled circumstances (as are more common in real estate). In each situation, it can be a powerful vehicle in explaining market operations, environmental conditions, and associations of sets of data; in forecasting future expectancies; in testing the reliability of variables to be used in analysis; and in analyzing of forecasts.

It is particularly important to note that in traditional appraisal analysis, the data used represent a sample that is rarely random and are generally biased by the appraiser's collection method and specific selection process. Further, even though an abundance of sales data may be available, the process tends to encourage reduction in the amount of data actually processed for manageability and for ease in explaining the variance observed among all data compared. Because of these processes, there are few, if any, methods available to traditional processes which allow formal testing of the data base or of conclusions drawn from a study of that data base for reliability or representativeness. Regression analysis offers one alternative to many of these difficulties.

*Courtesy of E. Roger Everett, SREA, MAI, and SREA Course 301.

The Data Set

Sale Number	Y (dependent variable) Price	X (independent variable) Square Feet	Price/S.F.
1	$36,500	1,550	$23.55
2	38,000	1,700	22.35
3	39,000	1,700	22.94
4	40,000	1,850	21.62
5	41,500	1,800	23.06
6	42,000	1,900	22.11
7	42,000	1,950	21.54
8	44,000	2,150	20.47
9	44,500	2,000	22.25
10	46,000	2,200	20.91

Average (Mean) Sales Price ($\overline{Y}$) = $41,350

Standard Deviation of Sales Price (s) = $3,010

Coefficient of Variation for Sales Prices $\left(\dfrac{s}{\overline{Y}}\right)$ = 0.0728

Average (Mean) Area ($\overline{X}$) = 1,880 sq. ft.

Standard Deviation of Areas (s) = 204.4 sq. ft.

Coefficient of Variation for Areas $\left(\dfrac{s}{\overline{X}}\right)$ = 0.1087

Average (Mean) Price per sq. ft. ($\overline{A}$) = $22.08

Standard Deviation of Price per sq. ft. (s) = $0.97

Coefficient of Variation for Price per sq. ft. $\left(\dfrac{s}{\overline{A}}\right)$ = 0.0438

Data Plotted

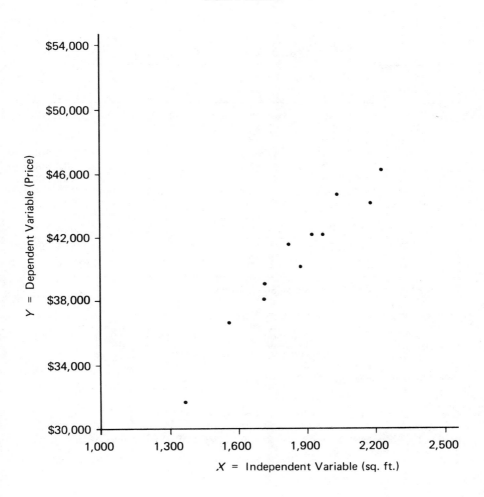

Value: Central Tendency and Dispersion

Sale Number	Price	$(X-\overline{X})$ (price−mean)	$\mid(X-\overline{X})\mid$	$(X-\overline{X})^2$
1	$ 36,500	$−4,850	$ 4,850	$23,522,500
2	38,000	−3,350	3,350	11,222,500
3	39,000	−2,350	2,350	5,522,500
4	40,000	−1,350	1,350	1,822,500
5	41,500	150	150	22,500
6	42,000	650	650	422,500
7	42,000	650	650	422,500
8	44,000	2,650	2,650	7,022,500
9	44,500	3,150	3,150	9,922,500
10	46,000	4,650	4,650	21,622,500
	$413,500	−0−	$23,800	$81,525,000
	ΣX	$\Sigma(X-\overline{X})$	$\Sigma\mid X-\overline{X}\mid$	$\Sigma(X-\overline{X})^2$

Average Price: $413,500 \div 10 = \$41,350\,(\overline{X})$

Average Deviation: $23,800 \div 10 = \$2,380\left(\dfrac{\Sigma\mid X-\overline{X}\mid}{n}\right)$

Standard Deviation: $\sqrt{\dfrac{81,525,000}{10-1}} = \$3010\left[\sqrt{\dfrac{\Sigma(X-\overline{X})^2}{n-1}}\right]$

Coefficient of Dispersion: $\$2380 \div \$41,350 = 0.0576\left(\dfrac{A.D.}{\overline{X}}\right)$

Coefficient of Variation: $\$3010 \div \$41,350 = 0.0728\left(\dfrac{s}{\overline{X}}\right)$

Note: To be consistent with regression analysis, all these values of sales price could be designated as y.

Linear Regression Calculations

Number	Col. 1 Y	Col. 2 $Y-\bar{Y}$	Col. 3 $(Y-\bar{Y})^2$	Col. 4 X	Col. 5 $X-\bar{X}$	Col. 6 $(X-\bar{X})^2$	Col. 7 $(Y-\bar{Y})(X-\bar{X})$
1	$365(00)	-48.5	2,352.25	15.5(0)	-3.3	10.89	160.05
2	380	-33.5	1,122.15	17.0	-1.8	3.24	60.30
3	390	-23.5	552.25	17.0	-1.8	3.24	42.30
4	400	-13.5	182.25	18.5	-.3	.09	4.05
5	415	1.5	2.25	18.0	-.8	.64	-1.20
6	420	6.5	42.25	19.0	.2	.04	1.30
7	420	6.5	42.25	19.5	.7	.49	4.55
8	440	26.5	702.25	21.5	2.7	7.29	71.55
9	445	31.5	992.25	20.0	1.2	1.44	37.80
10	460	46.5	2,162.25	22.0	3.2	10.24	148.80
	$4,135	-0-	8,152.50	188.0	-0-	37.60	529.50
			$\Sigma(Y-\bar{Y})^2$	ΣX		$\Sigma(X-\bar{X})^2$	

$\bar{Y} = \$413,500 \div 10 = \$41,350$

$\bar{X} = 18,800 \div 10 = 1,880$

$b = \dfrac{(Y-\bar{Y})\ (X-\bar{X})}{(X-\bar{X})^2} = \dfrac{529.50}{37.60} = \$14.08$

$\left(b = \dfrac{\Sigma XY - \bar{X}\,\Sigma Y}{\Sigma X^2 - \bar{X}\,\Sigma X} = \dfrac{5,295,000}{376,000} = 14.0824 \right)$

$b_0 = \bar{Y} - [b(\bar{X})] = 41,350 - [14.0824(1,880)] = \$14,875$

$Y_c = b_0 + b(X) = \$14,875 + \$14.08X$

$\Sigma X^2 = \$35,720,000$

$\Sigma Y^2 = \$17,179,750,000$

$\Sigma XY = \$782,675,000$

$s_Y = \sqrt{\dfrac{8,152.50}{10}} = \$2,855.26$

$s_X = \sqrt{\dfrac{37.60}{10}} = \$193.91$

$$Y_c = \$14{,}875 + \$14.08\ (1{,}300\ S.F.) = \$33{,}179$$
$$Y_c = \$14{,}875 + \$14.08\ (1{,}900\ S.F.) = \$41{,}627$$
$$Y_c = \$14{,}875 + \$14.08\ (2{,}500\ S.F.) = \$50{,}075$$

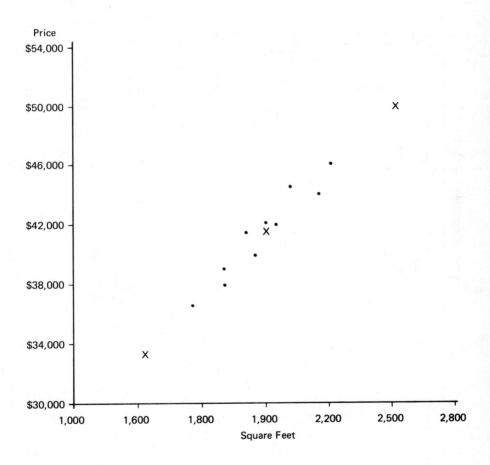

Using Regression Equation to Estimate Prices

Sale Number	b_0	±	$b(X)$	Y_c
1	14,875	+	14.08(1,550)	$36,702
2	14,875	+	14.08(1,700)	38,815
3	14,875	+	14.08(1,700)	38,815
4	14,875	+	14.08(1,850)	40,928
5	14,875	+	14.08(1,800)	40,223
6	14,875	+	14.08(1,900)	41,632
7	14,875	+	14.08(1,950)	42,336
8	14,875	+	14.08(2,150)	45,152
9	14,875	+	14.08(2,000)	43,040
10	14,875	+	14.08(2,200)	45,856

Note: *b* value actually calculated is used for arithmetic extensions (14.0824).

Comparison of Actual and Projected Prices

Sale Number	Actual Price	Y_c	Absolute Difference
1	$ 36,500	$ 36,702	$ 202
2	38,000	38,815	815
3	39,000	38,815	185
4	40,000	40,928	928
5	41,500	40,223	1,277
6	42,000	41,632	368
7	42,000	42,336	336
8	44,000	45,152	1,152
9	44,500	43,040	1,460
10	46,000	45,856	144
		$413,499	$ 6,867

Average Y_c = $413,499 ÷ 10 = $41,350

Average Deviation = $6,867 ÷ 10 = $686.70

Coefficient of Dispersion: $686.70 ÷ $41,350 = 0.017

Correlation Coefficient: $R = 1 - \dfrac{b s_X}{s_Y} = \dfrac{2730.25}{2855.26} = 0.9562$

Coefficient of Determination: $R^2 = \dfrac{b \Sigma (Y - \bar{Y})\ (X - \bar{X})}{\Sigma (Y - \bar{Y})^2}$

$$R^2 = \frac{14.08\,(529.50)}{8152.5} = .91$$

$$R^2 = [0.9562]^2 = 0.9144$$

Standard Error of the Estimate

$$Syx = \sqrt{\frac{\Sigma y^2 - \bar{y}\,\Sigma y - b\,(\Sigma xy - \bar{x}\,\Sigma y)}{n - m}}$$

$$Syx = \sqrt{\frac{1{,}717{,}975 - 148.75\,(4{,}135) - 14.082447\,(78{,}267.5)}{8}}$$

$$Syx = 9.326233 \times 100 = \$932.62$$

Necessary Calculations

x	y	xy
1,550	$36,500	56,575,000
1,700	38,000	64,600,000
1,700	39,000	66,300,000
1,850	40,000	74,000,000
1,800	41,500	74,700,000
1,900	42,000	79,800,000
1,950	42,000	81,900,000
2,150	44,000	94,600,000
2,000	44,500	89,000,000
2,200	46,000	101,200,000

$$\Sigma xy = 782{,}675{,}000$$

OR

$$Syx = \sqrt{\frac{\Sigma (y - y_c)^2}{n - m}}$$

$$Syx = \sqrt{\frac{6{,}958{,}927}{8}}$$

$$Syx = \$932.67$$

This is the standard deviation of the column of residuals.

Graphic Analysis

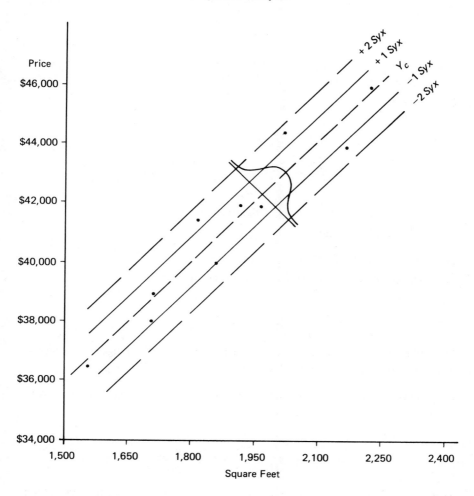

Standard Error of the Regression Coefficient

$$s_b = \frac{Syx}{\sqrt{\Sigma(x-\bar{x})^2}}$$

$$s_b = \frac{932.62}{\sqrt{376,000}} = 1.5209$$

Test of b:

$$\frac{b}{s_b} = t \text{ statistic}$$

$$\frac{14.08}{1.5209} = 9.2576$$

Compare to t table 5% level of significance 8 $D.F.$ = 2.306

b is highly significant

Confidence interval for the regression line:

The standard error of Yc (S_{y_c}), is defined as:

$$S_{y_c} = S_{yx}\sqrt{\frac{1}{n} + \frac{(X-\bar{X})^2}{\Sigma(X-\bar{X})^2}}$$

It should be noted that S_{y_c} is not uniform throughout the range of the regression line, but varies for each level of X.

Confidence interval for the individual forecast:

The standard error of the forecast (S_{y-y_c}) is defined as:

$$S_{y-y_c} = S_{yx}\sqrt{1 + \frac{1}{n} + \frac{(X-\bar{X})^2}{(X-X)^2}}$$

Note the formula for S_{y-y_c} is identical to the formula for S_{y_c} with "one" added to the term under the radical.

Basic Formulas: Compound Interest (Compound Discount) Tables

Amount of One (Future Worth of One *or* Amount of One at Compound Interest *or* Compound Amount of One)

Formula: $S^n = (1 + i)^n$

Where:

S^n = Balance of $1 deposit at the end of "n" periods; the future amount to which $1 will accumulate if invested at time period zero at "i" interest rate for "n" periods.

i = Rate at which interest is paid on the current balance at the end of each compounding period.

n = Total number of periods over which compounding takes place.

Example:

Invest $100 today for a period of 5 years earning 9 percent compound annually.

Thus:

i = 9% or .09

n = 5 years

$$(1 + i)^n = (1.09)^5 = 1.538642$$

Therefore:

$$S^n = (1 + i)^n = 1.538642$$
$$\text{and } \$100 \cdot S^n = \underline{\$153.86}$$

Amount of One per Period (Future Worth of an Annuity of One *or* Accumulation of One per Period *or* Compound Amount of One Per Period)

Formula: $S_{\overline{n}|} = \dfrac{S^n - 1}{i}$

Where:

$S_{\overline{n}|}$ = Total dollar balance of a series of equal investments; the future amount to which "n" equal periodic payments will accumulate as each earns "i" interest rate, with payments at the *end* of each period.

333

Example:
Invest $100 one year from today and each year thereafter for a total of 5 years at an 8 percent interest rate.

Thus:

$$i \quad = \quad 8\% \text{ or } .08$$
$$n \quad = \quad 5 \text{ years}$$
$$\frac{S^n - 1}{i} = \frac{(1.08)^5 - 1}{.08} = 5.866601$$

Therefore:

$$\$100 \cdot S_{\overline{n|}} = \frac{S^n - 1}{i} \cdot \$100 = 5.866601 \cdot \$100 = \underline{\$586.66}$$

Sinking Fund Factor (Amortization Rate)

Formula: $1/S_{\overline{n|}} = \dfrac{i}{S^n - 1}$

Where:

$$1/S_{\overline{n|}} = \text{Sinking fund factor}$$

Example:
An amount of $10,000 must be available at the end of 5 years. Determine the uniform annual investment necessary that will accumulate to this amount if funds invested earn 5 percent.

Thus:

$$i \quad = \quad 5\% \text{ or } .05$$
$$n \quad = \quad 5 \text{ years}$$
$$\frac{1}{S_{\overline{n|}}} = \frac{.05}{(1.05)^5 - 1} = .180975$$

Therefore:

$$\$10,000 \cdot 1/S_{\overline{n|}} = \$10,000 \cdot .180975 = \underline{\$1,809.75}$$

Present Worth of One (Present Value Reversion of One *or* Reversion Factor)

Formula: $V^n = \dfrac{1}{S^n}$

Where:

$$V^n = \text{Reversion factor}$$

Example:

An amount of $5,000 is to be received 5 years hence. Determine the amount to be paid today for the right to receive that single lump-sum payment if the discount rate is 10 percent.

Thus:

$$i \; = \; 10\% \text{ or } .10$$
$$n \; = \; 5 \text{ years}$$
$$V^n \; = \; \frac{1}{S^n} \; = \; \frac{1}{(1+i)n} \; = \; \frac{1}{(1.10)^5} \; = \; .620921$$

Therefore:

$$\$5,000 \; \cdot \; V^n \; = \; \$5,000 \; \cdot \; .620921 \; = \; \underline{\$3,104.61}$$

Present Worth of One per Period (Present Value of an Ordinary Annuity of One per Period *or* Level Annuity Factor *or* Inwood Factor)

Formula: $a_{\overline{n}|} \; = \; \dfrac{1 - V^n}{i}$

Where:

$a_{\overline{n}|}$ = Annuity factor, or present value of $1 per year payable in arrears for n years

Example:

An amount of $1,000 is to be received annually for 5 years. Determine the amount to be paid today for the right to receive this series of uniform payments if the discount rate is 8.5 percent.

Thus:

$$i \; = \; 8.5\% \text{ or } .085$$
$$n \; = \; 5 \text{ years}$$
$$a_{\overline{n}|} \; = \; \frac{1 - \dfrac{1}{(1+i)n}}{i} \; = \; \frac{1 - \dfrac{1}{(1.085)^5}}{.085} \; = \; 3.940642$$

Therefore:

$$\$1,000 \; \cdot \; a_{\overline{n}|} \; = \; 3.940642 \; \cdot \; \$1,000 \; = \; \underline{\$3,940.64}$$

Partial Payment (Installment to Amortize One *or* Annuity Capitalization Rate)

Formula: $\dfrac{1}{a_{\overline{n}|}} \; = \; \dfrac{i}{1 - V^n}$

Where:

$1/a_{\overline{n}|}$ = Partial Payment

Example:

An amount of $10,000 is invested today. Determine the annual payments to fully amortize the investment over 5 years if the interest (discount) rate is 9.5 percent.

Thus:

$$i = 9.5\% \text{ or } .095$$
$$n = 5 \text{ years}$$

$$1/a_{\overline{n}|} = \frac{1 - \dfrac{1}{(1+i)^n}}{i} = \frac{1 - \dfrac{1}{(1.095)^5}}{.095} = .260436$$

Therefore:

$$\$10,000 \cdot 1/a_{\overline{n}|} = \$10,000 \cdot .260436 = \underline{\$2,604.36}$$

Depreciation Methods

Section 167 of the Internal Revenue Code makes provision for the depreciation of real estate over its useful (economic) life. Specifically, the depreciation charges allowed as a deduction from real estate income afford the owner the opportunity to recoup his investment in a capital asset held for production of income. Such charges account for the wearing out or exhaustion of the capital asset and involve improvements only, i.e., land is not depreciable. The right to depreciate real estate remains intact even though it is recognized that much (if not most) real estate appreciates in value over time. Further, a capital asset such as real estate can be depreciated more than once by successive owners. Finally, the depreciation charge against income is a *non-cash* expense, i.e., money does not flow from the operation as it does in the case of other expenses. As such, depreciation represents the major tax-shelter feature of real estate ownership.

There are various methods of calculating depreciation charges (discussed below) but their respective availability for use has been specified under the provisions of the Tax Reform Act of 1969. In general, however, classification of methods may be placed in two categories—straight-line and accelerated. It is within the latter category that the major variation lies with respect to method. It is also to be noted that under the accelerated methods of depreciation, the periodic dollar amount allocated for depreciation purposes actually declines over time since it is computed on the basis of the *undepreciated balance* of the property which is also declining over time or as in the case of sum of the years'-digits, a declining fraction as determined by formula is applied to the initial depreciable cost. Each form of depreciation method is discussed below with an illustration of its respective calculation. (In each case, for exposition purposes, an asset with a cost of $100,000 and a useful life of 10 years is assumed ignoring salvage value in the case of the straight-line and sum of the years'-digits calculations and, in all cases, ignoring IRS guidelines as to the *minimum* period over which depreciation may be calculated.)

Straight-Line

Annual depreciation charges are determined on the basis of depreciable costs less salvage value divided by useful (economic) life. Using the example noted above and ignoring salvage value, the computation of annual depreciation charges would be simply: $100,000 ÷ 10 or $10,000 annually. A schedule of annual depreciation and the cumulative total appears on the next page.

Straight-Line

Year	Annual Depreciation	Cumulative Depreciation
1	$10,000	$10,000
2	10,000	20,000
3	10,000	30,000
4	10,000	40,000
5	10,000	50,000
6	10,000	60,000
7	10,000	70,000
8	10,000	80,000
9	10,000	90,000
10	10,000	100,000

Sum of the Years'-Digits

Annual depreciation charges are computed on the basis of a fraction which changes over time (declines) applied to the initial depreciable cost of an asset. The numerator of the fraction represents the remaining useful (economic) life of the asset and changes each year, while the denominator represents the sum of all the years'-digits and remains constant. The generalized formula for this fraction is:

$$\frac{N}{N(N+1)/2}$$

Thus, the fraction representing the proportion of depreciation in the first year is $10/55$; and for the second year $9/55$, and so on. A schedule of annual depreciation, the cumulative total and the annual fraction utilized in the computation appears below:

Sum of the Years'-Digits

Year	Annual Depreciation	Cumulative Depreciation	Fraction
1	$ 18,181.82	$ 18,181.82	10/55
2	16,363.66	34,545.48	9/55
3	14,545.45	49,090.93	8/55
4	12,727.27	61,818.20	7/55
5	10,909.09	72,727.29	6/55
6	9,090.91	81,818.20	5/55
7	7,272.73	89,090.93	4/55
8	5,454.54	94,545.47	3/55
9	3,636.36	98,181.83	2/55
10	1,818.17	100,000.00	1/55

Declining Balance

Annual depreciation charges are determined on the basis of some fixed multiple (125%, 150% or 200%) of the straight-line depreciation rate as applied to the *undepreciated balance* of the property. In our example, from above, the straight-line depreciation rate is 10 percent [computed by either taking the reciprocal of the useful (economic) life of the property or relating the annual dollar depreciation charges ($10,000) to the original depreciable cost ($100,000)].

For the 125% declining balance method, the appropriate annual rate to apply would be one and one-quarter times the straight-line rate or 12.5%; for the 150% declining balance method, it would be one and one-half times the straight-line rate or 15%; and for the 200% declining balance method, it would be twice the straight-line rate or 20%. A schedule of annual depreciation and the cumulative total for each of these declining balance methods appears below:

Declining Balance

| | 125% | | 150% | | 200% | |
| | Annual | Cumulative | Annual | Cumulative | Annual | Cumulative |
Year	Depreciation	Depreciation	Depreciation	Depreciation	Depreciation	Depreciation
1	$12,500.00	$12,500.00	$15,000.00	$15,000.00	$20,000.00	$20,000.00
2	10,937.50	23,437.50	12,750.00	27,750.00	16,000.00	36,000.00
3	9,570.31	33,007.81	10,837.50	38,587.50	12,800.00	48,800.00
4	8,374.02	41,381.83	9,211.87	47,799.37	10,240.00	59,040.00
5	7,327.27	48,709.10	7,830.09	55,629.46	8,192.00	67,232.00
6	6,411.36	55,120.46	6,655.58	62,285.04	6,553.60	73,785.60
7	5,609.94	60,730.40	5,657.24	67,942.28	5,242.88	79,028.48
8	4,908.70	65,639.10	4,808.66	72,750.94	4,194.30	83,222.78
9	4,295.11	69,934.21	4,087.36	76,838.30	3,355.44	86,578.22
10	3,758.22	73,692.43	3,474.25	80,312.55	2,684.35	89,262.57

Allowable Methods of Depreciation (By Property Type)

It is perhaps obvious from the above calculations that the more rapid the write-off of the cost of the property via depreciation, the more money should be available to the owner-investor. As noted previously, although depreciation is charged against income, it is a non-cash expense. It, therefore, reduces taxable income and thus provides the opportunity to retain cash which may be reinvested.

Depreciation as a tax shield was severely restricted by the Tax Reform Act of 1969. The owner-investor still may elect to use that method which provides the maximum shelter for his specific property as long as it falls within the limitations now imposed by that Act. A synopsis of the restrictions which have been placed on the use of the different methods is given on the next page.

SYNOPSIS OF DEPRECIATION METHODS
ALLOWABLE

Type of Property	Restrictions	Method (s) Allowable
	New	
Residential Rental	80% of gross rents must be non-transient residential	200% declining balance, *or* sum of the years'-digits, *or* straight-line
	Used	
Residential Rental	20 years or more remaining economic life	125% declining balance, *or* straight-line
	New	
Non-residential Rental	Commercial and Industrial	150% declining balance, *or* straight-line
Other	Not Listed Above	Straight-line
Low-income Rental Housing	Rehabilitation expenditures not to exceed $20,000 per unit excluding cost of building acquisition	Straight-line with 5 year (60 month) useful life
Historical Structures	Rehabilitation expenditures (no limit) excluding cost of building acquisition	Straight-line with 5 year (60 month) useful life

Depreciation Recapture

The depreciation recapture rules under the Tax Reform Act of 1969 were enlarged, thus representing even further restrictions on the tax shield aspects of depreciation. Recapture occurs when the property is sold, and the total depreciation actually charged against the property under one of the accelerated methods exceeds that which would have been charged had straight-line depreciation been used. This "excess" amount is subject to ordinary tax rates, rather than capital gain rates.

Recapture rules in effect prior to January 1, 1970 allowed the owner-investor to avoid the recapture provisions if he held the property for ten years or used straight-line depreciation. The new ruling provides for a holding period of 16 years, eight months for residential rental property and rehabilitation costs. The wording of the ruling on depreciation recapture for residential rental property (other than FHA 221 (d) (3) and 236 rental properties constructed before 1975) and for rehabilitation expenditures was changed in essence from "100% minus 1% for each full month after 20 months" (total 120 months or 10 years) to "100% minus 1% for each full month after 100 months" (total 200 months or

16 years, eight months). For other real property, excess depreciation is fully recaptured.

Component Depreciation

For both new and used property, the opportunity exists to produce a depreciation deduction substantially greater than that available under the traditional methods discussed above. In effect, a building is divided into its component parts (e.g., structural, plumbing system, central heating and air conditioning, electrical work and the like) such that they may be depreciated separately over their useful (economic) life. For new property, such a breakdown must be made while the building is under construction and may include an allocation of indirect costs, as for example, architectural and legal fees, to the various component parts. For used property, an appraisal dividing the building into its component parts is required. Due to the fact that those components, other than the structural component, normally have a lower useful (economic) life and that accelerated methods may be applied to each, the tax shelter opportunities are enhanced. It is suggested that competent tax counsel be retained should this method be utilized.

Symbols, Valuation Models, Rates, and Relationships

Symbols

a_n — Present worth of $1 per period for n periods at specified rate. See Basic Formulas.

app — Appreciation as fraction of original price or value. Note: app relates to total price or value in formulas involving R and r; app relates to original equity or downpayment in formulas involving the equity dividend rate R_e and the equity yield rate Y.

C — The mortgage coefficient.

d — Annual dividend (same as NOI).

d_e — Annual equity dividend.

dep — Depreciation as fraction of original price or value. Note: dep relates to total property price or value in formulas involving R and r; dep relates to original equity or downpayment in formulas involving the equity dividend rate R_e and the equity yield rate Y.

e — Denotes equity when used as a subscript in the symbol d_e shown above.

e — Denotes the natural constant 2.718282 . . . when used in continuous growth formulas.

EGI — Effective gross income.

ETR — Effective tax rate.

f — The "annual constant" for debt service (12 × monthly installment per dollar of loan, 4 × quarterly installment, etc.). Also, R_m.

f_p — The "annual constant" which would be required to amortize the entire loan within a projection period p.

i — Effective interest rate.

I — Nominal annual interest rate (divide by number of conversion periods per year to obtain periodic effective interest rate i). Also, used to denote Income (in this use I is the same as NOI or d).

J — Income adjustment factor used in Ellwood formulas and obtainable from Ellwood Tables.

M — Loan to value ratio.

n — Number of compounding periods in compound interest formulas; in mortgage-equity formulas the symbol n represents the projection period in years.

NOI — Net operating income (same as d). Sometimes referred to as NIBR — Net Income Before Recapture.

NIBT — Net income before taxes (equivalent of NOI plus annual property taxes).

P — Fraction of loan paid off in projection period.

p — Projection period or contemplated period of ownership (used as a subscript — see f_p and S_p).

PGI — Potential gross income.

R — In appraisal formulas R typically represents the overall rate. *Caution: R* is a popular symbol in other disciplines and may represent other quantities such as the annual payment or *R*ent on an annuity contract. Also, R_0.

R_e — Annual equity dividend rate.

r — Denotes basic rate in mortgage-equity formulas. Denotes continuous growth rate in continuous growth formulas. *Caution: r* is a popular symbol in other disciplines and may represent other quantities such as the annual payment or annual *r*ent of an annuity whose present worth is one dollar.

S — One dollar plus the interest per dollar per period; the base. See Basic Formulas.

S^n — The future worth of $1 which growth with compound interest at a specified rate for n periods. See Basic Formulas.

$S_{\overline{n}|}$ — The future worth of $1 per period growing with interest at a specified rate for n periods. See Basic Formulas.

S_p — The amount to which $1 will grow with interest at the effective rate during the projection period p.

V — Value.

V^n — The present worth of $1 due n periods hence discounted at a specified rate. See Basic Formulas.

Y — Equity yield rate.

Valuation Models

Universal Valuation Formula:

$$V = I/R \text{ or } V = d/R \text{ (Ellwood)}$$

Where: V = Value
$I = d$ = NOI
R = Overall Rate or Composite Rate (Ellwood)

Thus: $I = V \cdot R$
$R = I/V$
and,
$R = 1/\text{Factor or Factor} = 1/R$

Therefore: $V = I \cdot F$ $\quad I = \dfrac{V}{F}$ $\quad F = \dfrac{V}{I}$

Ellwood Formula:

General Formula:

$$R = Y - MC \pm \frac{\text{dep.}}{\text{app.}} \, 1/S_{\overline{n}|}$$

Where:

R	=	Composite Rate (Overall Rate) = R_0
Y	=	Equity Yield Rate
M	=	Loan to Value Ratio
C	=	Mortgage Coefficient°
dep.	=	Expected decline in value over holding period (in percentage terms)
app.	=	Expected increase in value over holding period (in percentage terms)
$1/S_{\overline{n}|}$	=	The Sinking Fund Factor at the Equity Yield Rate for the projection period

$$°C = Y + P \, 1/S_{\overline{n}|} - f$$

Where:

P	=	Portion of mortgage paid off°°
f	=	Mortgage Constant = R_m

$$°°P = \left(\frac{f}{I} - 1\right)(S_p - 1) \text{ or } P = \frac{f - I}{f_p - I}$$

Where:

I	=	Nominal annual interest rate on the mortgage
S_p	=	Future worth of one at end of the income projection period compounded for the periodic intervals of mortgage payments at the effective mortgage interest rate.

Expanded Formula:

$$R_0 = Y - M\left\{Y + \left[1/S_{\overline{n}|}\left(\frac{f}{I} - 1\right)\left(S_p - 1\right)\right] - f\right\} \pm \frac{\text{dep.}}{\text{app.}} \, 1/S_{\overline{n}|}$$

Other Manipulations:

$$r = Y - MC$$

Where:

r = Basic Rate

$\dfrac{R - r}{1/S_{\overline{n}|}}$ = Appreciation when negative *or* depreciation when positive expressed as a fraction of original value.

Mortgage Equity Formula:

Percentage Debt $\times$ f = weight

Percentage Equity $\times$ Y = weight

Weighted Average

Less: Allowance for Equity Build-up°

Basic Rate (r)

Less: Adjustment for Appreciation°°

or

Plus: Adjustment for Depreciation°°

Overall Rate (R_0)°°°

°Equity Build-up = Loan to Value Ratio × Portion of Mortgage Paid off × Sinking Fund Factor at the Equity Yield Rate for the Holding Period.

°°Allowance for Capital Loss (or Gain) = Forecast Fraction of Depreciation (or Appreciation) × Sinking Fund Factor at the Equity Yield Rate for the Holding Period.

°°°Equivalent to the Composite Rate in the Ellwood Formulation.

Rates and Other Relationships

Discount Rate: DR

Percentage of Mortgage Loan to Value _times_ Mortgage Interest Rate _plus_ Percentage of Equity to Value _times_ the Equity Yield Rate _equals_ the Discount Rate

_or_

$\dfrac{\text{Mortgage Loan}}{\text{Value}}$ $\times$ 1 = required % on total property investment to cover interest on mortgage

$+ \dfrac{\text{Equity}}{\text{Value}}$ $\times$ Y = required % on total property investment to cover return on equity

= Discount Rate (also called composite interest rate).

Capital Recovery Rate: CRR (For Assets with Limited Economic Life)

(1) Straight-line Premise: The reciprocal of the Remaining Economic Life of the Asset

_or_

$$CRR = \frac{1}{REL \text{ (in years)}}$$

(2) Level Annuity Premise: The sinking fund factor at the Discount Rate as determined by the Remaining Economic Life of the Asset

(3) Safe Rate Premise: The sinking fund factor at the Safe Rate as determined by the Remaining Economic Life of the Asset

Capitalization Rate: CR. Also R_B

The sum of the Discount Rate and the Capital Recovery Rate (under either the Straight-line, Level Annuity, or Safe Rate Premise)

or

Discount Rate (DR)

+ Capital Recovery Rate (CRR)

= Capitalization Rate

Overall Rate: OAR (See also Mortgage Equity and Ellwood Formulations). Also, R_0

(1) $\dfrac{\text{Net Operating Income}}{\text{Sales Price}}$ = OAR

(2) Weighted Average Overall Rate (Physical Components);

Note: Assumes Stable Land Value and Limited Building Life.

(a) Discount Rate *times* the percentage of investment in site *plus* the Capitalization Rate *times* the percentage of investment in improvements	=	weight
	=	weight
	=	OAR
(b) Discount Rate *times* 1 (100% of investment) *plus* the Capital Recovery Rate *times* the percentage of investment in improvements	=	weight
	=	weight°
	=	OAR

°Represents *Effective CRR*

(3) Simple Mortgage Equity Overall Rate (Financial Components):

Mortgage constant (see below) *times* Loan to Value Ratio	=	weight
Equity Dividend Rate *times* Equity to Value Ratio	=	weight
	=	Simple Mortgage Equity OAR

Equity Dividend Rate: R_e

$$\dfrac{\text{Cash Throw Off}}{\text{Equity Investment}} = R_e$$

or

$$\dfrac{\text{Net Operating Income} - \text{Debt Service}}{\text{Dollar Investment in Equity}} = R_e$$

Equity Yield Rate: Y

The return on equity risk capital—the Internal Rate of Return

The return produced by both income and reversion to the equity position expressed as an annual rate. It is that rate which discounts all flows (income and reversion) such that they equal the original equity investment, i.e., that rate which discounts all flows such that $NPV = 0$.

The yield rate (IRR) is *never* known until the complete investment experience is a matter of history. It cannot be calculated *precisely* until after the property has been bought, operated over a span of time, and then resold. Therefore, it is incorrect to say that buyers demand this or that yield. The only plausible and supportable opinion is that "good prospects" for a yield of "X" percent or better would probably attract a buyer.

The yield on equity investment will be significantly influenced by the *source of recapture*, and this in turn will be determined by the relative magnitudes of *periodic income* and *proceeds for resale* or *"reversion."*

Equity Yield Formulas (for approximating Y with trial rates):

$$Y \pm \frac{\text{dep.}}{\text{app.}} \times 1/S_{\overline{n}|} = R_e$$

$$R_e \pm \frac{\text{app.}}{\text{dep.}} \times 1/S_{\overline{n}|} = Y$$

Mortgage Constant: f or R_m

The relationship (ratio) between (of) annual debt service and the *original* principal amount of the mortgage

or

$$\frac{\text{Debt Service}}{\text{Original Principal Amount}} = f = R_m$$

In the case of the transfer of property where the existing mortgage is to be assumed by the buyer, the remaining balance on the mortgage is to be substituted in the above formula to determine f.

Gross Income Multiplier: *GIM* or *GRM*

The relationship between sales price and *either* potential gross income or effective gross income—these relationships are not to be intermingled, i.e., there must be consistency in the multipliers used for analysis.

$$\frac{\text{Sales Price}}{\text{Potential Gross Income}} = GIM$$

or

$$\frac{\text{Sales Price}}{\text{Effective Gross Income}} = GIM$$

Mortgage Balances: *Refinancing and Reversions*

Viewing the mortgage as annuity, the calculation of remaining balance (as a percentage of the original balance) at any point in time becomes a simple matter of dividing the annuity factor for the remaining term of the mortgage by the annuity factor for the full term of the mortgage. This calculation is particularly useful (for that matter, necessary) in the determination of net cash reversion to the equity interest.

$$\frac{\begin{array}{c}\text{Annuity Factor}\\\text{(Remaining Term of Mortgage)}\end{array}}{\begin{array}{c}\text{Annuity Factor}\\\text{(Full Term of Mortgage)}\end{array}} = \begin{array}{c}\text{Mortgage Balance}\\\text{as}\\\text{Fraction of}\\\text{Initial Principal}\end{array}$$

The *complement* (1–mortgage balance as fraction of initial principal) of the above calculation is the fraction of the mortgage paid-off *or* the cumulative/ total equity build-up as a percentage of initial mortgage principal. This calculation is useful in the determination of the amount to be refinanced at some future point in time.

Ad Valorem Tax Problem:

When the purpose of an appraisal is to estimate value as a basis for taxation or to test the fairness of existing taxes, it may be necessary to employ a technique which capitalizes income before deducting taxes, on the premise that value must be established before ad valorem taxes can be computed.

To capitalize net income before property taxes, use the following equation:

$$\frac{\text{NIBT}}{R + \text{ETR}} = \text{Value}$$

where NIBT is net income before taxes, R is the overall rate which would be appropriate for capitalizing the net income remaining after deducting property taxes (NOI), and ETR is the effective tax rate. See for definition of overall rate, net operating income and effective tax rate.

Note: The above equation presumes these relationships:

$$
\begin{array}{rcl}
\text{NOI} + \text{Taxes} & = & \text{NIBT}\\
\text{Value} \times \text{ETR} & = & \text{Taxes}\\
\text{NOI}/R & = & \text{Value}
\end{array}
$$

Properties of Exponents:

$$\frac{1}{a^n} = a^{-n}$$

$$a^m \cdot a^n = a^{m+n}; \quad \frac{a^m}{a^n} = a^{m-n}; \quad (a^m)^n = a^{mn}$$

$$(ab)^n = a^n b^n \quad \text{and} \quad \left(\frac{a}{b}\right)^n = \frac{a^n}{b^n}$$

Continuous Growth:

$1 growing with interest at rate r compounded continuously for n periods will grow to $\$e^{rn}$ where e is the natural constant, 2.718282. . . .

Types of Range Vegetation

ANNUALS—A type of range vegetation in which annual forbs or annual grasses constitute the dominant vegetation. Abandoned lands often fall in this class.

BARREN—This type includes all areas on which there is naturally no vegetation, such as intermittent lake beds, saline flats, active sand dunes, shale, rock slides, and lava flows. Areas that have been denuded should not be confused with areas naturally barren, nor should areas containing annuals for but part of the year be classified under this type.

BROAD—LEAVED TREES—A type of range vegetation including all deciduous trees such as aspen, cottonwood, birch, and alder.

BROWSE—SHRUB—This type includes foothill or mountain ranges where browse, except sagebrush, is predominant. Characteristically it occupies the transition zone of the lower foothill or mountain slopes.

CONIFER—Any of an order of trees or shrubs, as evergreens and pines, which bear cones. As range vegetation, type includes all range lands dominated by coniferous timber with supporting grasses, forbs, or browse.

CREOSOTE BUSH—This type includes areas where creosote (Covillea) constitutes the predominant vegetation.

DESERT SHRUB—This is a general type that includes areas where desert shrubs, aside from those separated into individual types dominate. It includes several genera such as blackbush (Coleogyne), coffee berry (Simmondsia), cat's claw (Acacia and Mimosa), gray molly (Kochia), hopsage (Grayia), horse brush (Tetradymia), and little rabbit brush (Crysothamnus stenophyllus); but pure types of each are so limited as not to justify a separate type.

GRASSLAND—This type includes all grasslands other than meadow. Perennial grasses predominate although forbs and browse may be present.

GREASEWOOD—This type includes areas where greasewood (Sarcobatus) is the predominant vegetation.

HALF SHRUB—Semiwoody perennials of low stature such as Aplopappus, Gutierrezia, Artemisia frigida, and Eriogonum wrightii. They commonly consist of woody caudex from which herbaceous stems are produced that die back annually.

MEADOW—As a type of range vegetation it includes areas where sedges, rushes, and mesic grasses predominate and which usually remain wet or moist throughout the summer.

MESQUITE—This type includes areas where various species of mesquite (Prosopis) predominate.

PERENNIAL FORB—This type includes areas where perennial forbs predominate. There is little true forb type, for a forb cover is usually temporary in character and soon is replaced by a permanent type if the disturbing factor is removed.

PINON—JUNIPER—This type includes pinon, juniper, and digger pine.

SAGEBRUSH—This type includes all lands where species of sagebrush predominate.

SALTBRUSH—This type includes areas where various salt desert shrubs such as Atriplex predominate.

WASTE—This type includes all vegetated areas that have insufficient value to be used economically owing to inaccessibility, denseness of timber, or sparseness of forage growth. Large areas of sparse forage, unless within easy reach of a better type, are classified as waste (for grazing) because of the impracticability of running stock over large areas to get a small amount of feed.

WINTER FAT—This type includes areas where winter fat (Eurotia) constitutes the predominant vegetation.

Types of Soil

ACID SOIL—A soil which has an acid reaction; more particularly it is a soil which has a preponderance of hydrogen ions over hydroxyl ions in the soil solution. A pH of 7 represents the neutral point in soil solution and any value below is acid. See also, pH.

ADOBE—A term describing a soil which cracks deeply upon drying and breaks into irregular but roughly cubical blocks. Adobe soils are usually heavy textured and have a content high in colloidal clay.

AELOIAN SOIL—Soil developed from material transported and deposited by the wind.

ALKALINE SOIL—The opposite of acid soil. Any soil which is alkaline in reaction. It has a pH above 7.

ALLUVIAL SOIL—An azonal soil forming from materials (alluvion) transported by flowing water. Such soil is unstable.

AZONAL SOIL—A soil without horizons, one insufficiently developed, thus lacking a definite soil profile.

BOG SOIL—An intrazonal group of marshy or swampy soils underlain with peat, common to humid or subhumid climates.

CALCAREOUS SOIL—One containing carbonate of calcium (limestone).

CATENA—A group of soils within one zonal region developed from similar parent material but different in solum characteristics owing to differences in relief and/or drainage.

CHERNOZEM—A zonal group of soils having a deep, dark colored to nearly black surface horizon, rich in organic matter, which grades into lighter colored soils and finally into a layer of lime accumulation; developed under tall and mixed grasses in a temperate to cool subhumid climate.

CLAY—Small mineral soil grain, less than 0.005 mm. in diameter; plastic when moist but hard when baked or fired.

CLAY LOAM—A textural term describing a soil which contains a moderate amount of fine material mixed with coarser soil grains. When the moist soil is pinched between the thumb and finger, it will form a thin "ribbon" which will break readily, barely sustaining its own weight. The moist soil is plastic and will form a cast that will bear much handling. When kneaded in the hand it does not crumble readily but tends to work in a heavy, compact mass.

CLAYPAN—A dense and heavy soil horizon underlying the upper part of the soil which because of the characteristics of clay interferes with water movement or root development.

COARSE TEXTURED SOIL—A soil which contains a preponderence of soil grains larger than 0.25 mm. Sandy loams, gravelly sandy loams, and loamy sands are classed as coarse textured soils.

COLLUVIAL SOIL—Soil material found at the base of a steep hill or slope which has been transported by gravity or water.

DESERT SOIL—A zonal group of soils having a light colored surface soil usually underlain by calcareous material and frequently by a hardpan. They develop under an extremely scant shrub vegetation in areas having warm to cool arid climates.

DROUTHY SOIL—A loose textured soil with poor water holding capacity due to such conditions as sand or gravel subsoil.

FINE SANDY LOAM—A soil with a fine sandy loam texture containing much sand but which has enough silt and clay to make it coherent. The sands contain 50% or more of fine sand, or less than 25% fine gravel, coarse, and medium sand. Thus the fine sandy loam type contains a larger percentage of fine sand than does the sandy loam type.

FINE TEXTURED SOIL—A soil which contains a high percentage of fine particles 0.005 mm. in diameter or less. Such soils are also referred to as clays.

GLACIAL SOIL—Parent material of soil that has been moved and redeposited by glacial activity.

GUMBO SOIL—A silty, fine textured soil which becomes very sticky when wet and has a greasy appearance.

HARDPAN—A layer of silt, clay, or any soil material cemented together. A hardened soil horizon which will not dissolve to any appreciable extent in water. The soil may have any texture and be compacted or cemented by iron oxide, organic material, silica, calcium carbonate, or other substances.

HEAVY SOIL—A term sometimes used to describe a clay soil. See, Clay; Fine Textured Soil.

IMMATURE SOIL—A young or imperfectly developed soil; one lacking individual horizons.

IMPERVIOUS SOIL—Not allowing the passage of water, air, or plant roots.

LACUSTRINE SOIL—Soils formed from materials deposited by the waters of lakes and ponds, usually fine textured and heavy.

LIGHT TEXTURED SOIL—A term sometimes used to denote a sandy or coarse textured soil.

LOAM—A soil having a mixture of different grades of sand, silt, and clay in such proportions that the characteristics of no one predominate. It is mellow with a gritty feel, and when moist is slightly plastic. Squeezed when dry, it will form a cast that will require careful handling. The cast formed by squeezing when moist can be handled freely without breaking. See also, Clay Loam, Fine Sandy Loam, Sandy Loam, Silt Clay Loam, Silt Loam.

LOESS – Wind blown material. It differs from till and water sediment in that it is uniformly silty.

MARINE SOIL – A soil formed from materials deposited by the oceans and seas and later exposed by upward movement; for example, the coastal plain soils of Maryland and Virginia.

MEDIUM TEXTURED SOIL – Sometimes used to designate loams, fine sandy loams, and clay loams.

MELLOW – A soil is termed mellow when it can be easily worked due to its friable and loamy characteristics.

MUCK – Fairly well decomposed organic soil material, relatively high in mineral content, dark in color, and accumulated under conditions of imperfect drainage.

NEUTRAL SOIL – A soil that is not significantly acid or alkaline which is a desirable condition. It has a pH between 6.6 and 7.3.

ORGANIC SOIL – A general term used in reference to any soil, the solid part of which is predominantly organic matter.

PEAT SOIL – Unconsolidated soil material consisting largely of undecomposed or slightly decomposed organic matter accumulated under conditions of excessive moisture.

PEDALFERS SOIL – A soil in which there has been a shifting of alumina and iron oxide downward in the soil profile but with no horizon or carbonate accumulation.

PEDOCAL SOIL – A soil with a horizon of accumulated carbonates in the soil profile.

PHASE SOIL – That part of a soil unit or soil type having minor variations in characteristics used in soil classification from the characteristics normal for the type, although they may be of great importance. The variations are chiefly in such external characteristics as relief, stoniness, or accelerated erosion.

PODZOL – A zonal group of soils having an organic mat and a thin organic-mineral layer above a gray leached layer which rests upon an alluvial dark brown horizon, developed under the coniferous or mixed forest, or under vegetation in a temperate to cold moist climate.

PRAIRIE SOILS – The zonal group of soils having a dark brown or grayish brown surface horizon, grading through brown soil to the lighter colored parent material at two to five feet, developed under tall grasses, in a temperate relatively humid climate. The term has a restricted meaning in soil science and is not applied to all dark colored soils of the treeless plains but only to those in which carbonates have not been concentrated in any part of the profile by soil-forming processes.

PRIMARY SOIL—A soil formed in place from the weathering of the underlying rock and minerals.

RECENT SOIL—A secondary soil of such recent deposition that the weathering or aging processes have made little or no change in the profile.

RESIDUAL SOIL—Soil formed in place by the weathering of mineral material or, in other words, by the disintegration and decomposition of rock in place.

SALINE SOIL—A soil containing enough common alkali salts to injuriously affect plant growth.

SANDY LOAM—A soil containing much sand and enough silt and clay to make it somewhat coherent; the sand grains can be felt. It will form a weak cast when dry and squeezed in the hand.

SECONDARY SOILS—A soil that has been transported by water or wind and redeposited; alluvial soil.

SILT CLAY LOAM—A soil made up of moderate amounts of fine grades of sand and moderate amounts of clay but more than 50% silt and clay, and contains more clay than silt loam. It is cloddy when dry; when wet it has the tendency to "ribbon" upon being squeezed between finger and thumb.

SILT LOAM—A soil made up of moderate amounts of the fine grades of sand, small amounts of clay, and one-half or more silt. It appears cloddy when dry but has a smooth feel when wet and will not "ribbon."

TRANSPORTED SOIL—Secondary soils; soils that have been moved and redeposited by water or wind.

UPLAND SOIL—Soils developed through the disintegration and decomposition of rocks in place and the weathering of the resulting debris; primary soils; usually occupying hilly to mountainous terrain.

Sources of Information

Bibliographies and Reference Guides

Advisory Commission on Intergovernmental Relations (ACIR). *Library Periodical Index.* Bimonthly.

Ahn, Michad. *Industrial Bibliography.* Washington, D.C.: The Urban Land Institute, 1974.

Akerson, Charles B. *Study Guide—AIREA Course I—B: Capitalization Theory and Techniques.* Cambridge, Massachusetts: Ballinger Publishing Company, 1980.

American Institute of Real Estate Appraisers. *The Appraisal Journal Bibliography: 1932—1969.* Chicago, 1970.

_____. *Golf Courses: A Guide to Analysis and Valuation.* Chicago, 1980.

_____. *Real Estate Appraisal Bibliography.* 1st and 2nd eds. Chicago, 1964 and 1973.

American Society of Appraisers. *Appraisal and Valuation Manual.* nine volumes. Washington, D.C.: American Society of Appraisers, 1956—1972.

Arnold, Alvin L., and Jack Kusnet. *The Arnold Encyclopedia of Real Estate.* Boston, Massachusetts: Warren, Gorham & Lamont, 1978.

Boyce, Byrl N., ed. *Real Estate Appraisal Terminology* (AIREA—SREA). Rev. ed. Cambridge, Massachusetts: Ballinger Publishing Company, 1980.

Daniells, Lorna M. *Business Information Sources.* Berkeley: University of California Press, 1976.

Denne, Robert C. *Bibliographic Series: Computer-Assisted Appraisal and Assessment Systems.* Chicago: International Association of Assessing Officers, 1977.

Dombal, Robert W. *Residential Condominiums: A Guide to Analysis And Appraisal* (AIREA). Cambridge, Massachusetts: Ballinger Publishing Company, 1973.

Dumouchel, J. Robert, ed. *Dictionary of Development Terminology.* New York: McGraw-Hill Book Company, 1975.

Friedman, Edith J., ed. *Encyclopedia of Real Estate Appraising.* 3rd ed. Englewood Cliffs, New Jersey: Prentice-Hall, Inc., 1978.

Garrett, Robert L. et al. *The Valuation of Shopping Centers* (AIREA). Cambridge, Massachusetts: Ballinger Publishing Company, 1976.

Gimmy, Arthur E. *Tennis Clubs and Racquet Sport Projects: A Guide to Appraisal, Market Analysis, Development and Financing* (AIREA). Cambridge, Massachusetts: Ballinger Publishing Company, 1979.

Graaskamp, James A. *A Guide to Feasibility Analysis.* Chicago: Society of Real Estate Appraisers, 1980.

Hanford, Lloyd D. *Feasibility Study Guidelines.* Chicago: Institute of Real Estate Management, 1972.

Harrison, Henry S. *Houses – The Illustrated Guide to Construction Design and Systems.* Rev. ed. Chicago: Realtors National Marketing Institute, 1976.

Himstreet, William C. *Writing Appraisal Reports.* Rev. ed. Chicago: American Institute of Real Estate Appraisers, 1974.

International Association of Assessing Officers. *Demonstration Appraisal Report Series.* Chicago: International Association of Assessing Officers, 1969–1979.

Johnsich, John R., ed. *Real Estate Books and Periodicals in Print.* Sacramento, California: Real Estate Publishing Company, 1977 (supplement, 1978–1979).

Kerl, Klaus J. *Selected Annotated Bibliography of Office Building Feasibility Studies.* Chicago: American Society of Real Estate Counselors, 1975.

Kinnard, William N., Jr., and Byrl N. Boyce. *An Introduction to Appraising Real Property.* Rev. ed. Chicago: Society of Real Estate Appraisers, 1978.

Kinnard, William N., Jr., and E. Roger Everett. *A Guide to Appraising Apartments.* Rev. ed. Chicago: Society of Real Estate Appraisers, 1979.

Kinnard, William N., Jr., et al. *Special Applications of Appraisal Analysis.* Rev. ed. Chicago: Society of Real Estate Appraisers, 1980.

MacBride, Dexter D., ed. *The Bibliography of Appraisal Literature.* Washington, D.C.: The American Society of Appraisers, 1974.

National Association of Home Builders. *Homes and Homebuilding: 1979.* Washington, D.C.: National Association of Home Builders, 1978.

National Association of Realtors. *Bibliography Series.* Chicago: Herbert U. Nelson Memorial Library, National Association of Realtors, revised periodically.

Realtors National Marketing Institute. *Guide to Commercial Property Leasing.* Chicago: Realtors National Marketing Institute, 1974.

Rushmore, Stephen. *Selected Bibliography on Hotels, Motels and Restaurants.* New York: Helmsley–Spear Hospitality Services, Inc., 1979.

_____. *The Valuation of Hotels and Motels* (AIREA). Cambridge, Massachusetts: Ballinger Publishing Company, 1978.

Shenkel, William M. *A Guide to Appraising Industrial Property.* Chicago: Society of Real Estate Appraisers, 1967.

Society of Industrial Realtors and National Association of Industrial and Office Parks. *Guide to Industrial Site Selection.* Washington, D.C.: Society of Industrial Realtors, 1979.

Society of Real Estate Appraisers. *Appraisal Information Sources.* Vol. I and II. Chicago: Society of Real Estate Appraisers, 1971 and 1979.

_____. *A Compendium: A Guide to Appraising Specific Property Types.* Chicago: Society of Real Estate Appraisers, 1973.

_____. *A Guide to Appraising for Federal Agencies.* Chicago: Society of Real Estate Appraisers, 1979.

_____. *A Guide to Narrative Demonstration Appraisal Reporting.* Chicago: Society of Real Estate Appraisers.

Stebbins, Grady, Jr. *A Guide to Appraising Residences.* Chicago: Society of Real Estate Appraisers, 1976.

Tandy, Janet K., and Mickey T. C. Wu. *Computer Applications in Real Estate: A Selected Bibliography with Annotations.* Rev. ed. Lexington: Center for Real Estate and Land Use Analysis, University of Kentucky, 1978.

Trowbridge, Carl R. *Office Guide to Real Estate Appraisal Reporting.* Englewood Cliffs, New Jersey: Prentice-Hall, Inc., 1974.

U.S. Department of Housing and Urban Development. *Housing and Urban Development References.* Bimonthly.

Books and Monographs

American Institute of Real Estate Appraisers. *The Appraisal of Real Estate.* 7th ed. Chicago: American Institute of Real Estate Appraisers, 1978.

_____. *Readings in the Income Approach to Real Property Valuation.* Vol 1. Cambridge, Massachusetts: Ballinger Publishing Company, 1977.

_____. *Readings in Real Estate Investment Analysis.* Vol. 1. Cambridge, Massachusetts: Ballinger Publishing Company, 1977.

_____. *Readings in Real Property Valuation Principles.* Vol 1. Cambridge, Massachusetts: Ballinger Publishing Company, 1977.

Atteberry, William, et al. *Real Estate Law.* 2nd ed. Columbus, Ohio: Grid Publishing Company, 1978.

Babcock, Frederick M. *The Valuation of Real Estate.* New York: McGraw-Hill Book Company, 1932.

Beckett, John A. *Management Dynamics: The New Synthesis.* New York: McGraw-Hill Book Company, 1971.

Bloom, George F., and Henry S. Harrison. *Appraising the Single Family Residence.* Chicago: American Institute of Real Estate Appraisers, 1978.

Boyce, Byrl N., and Stephen D. Messner. *Management of an Appraisal Firm.* Chicago: Society of Real Estate Appraisers, 1972.

Britton, James A., Jr., and Lewis O. Kerwood, eds. *Financing Income-Producing Real Estate.* New York: McGraw-Hill Book Company, 1977.

Burchell, Robert W., and David Listokin. *Fiscal Impact Handbook.* New Brunswick, New Jersey: Center for Urban Policy Research, 1978.

Church, Albert M., and Robert H. Gustafson. *Statistics and Computers in the Appraisal Process.* Chicago: International Association of Assessing Officers, 1976.

Clark, Louis E., Jr., and F. H. Treadway, Jr. *Impact of Electric Power Transmission Line Easements on Real Estate Values* (AIREA). Cambridge, Massachusetts: Ballinger Publishing Company, 1977.

Conway Publications, Inc. *Industrial Park Growth.* Atlanta, 1979.

_____. *Pitfalls in Development.* Atlanta: Conway Publications, Inc., 1978.

Cook, Charles C., ed. *Proceedings of Colloquium on Computer Assisted Mass Appraisal Potential for Commercial and Industrial Real Property.* Cambridge, Massachusetts: Lincoln Institute of Land Policy, 1978.

Costonis, John J. *Space Adrift.* Urbana: University of Illinois Press, 1974.

Dasso, Jerome. *Computerized Assessment Administration.* Chicago: International Assocation of Assessing Officers, 1973.

Desmond, Glenn M., and Richard E. Kelley. *Business Valuation Handbook.* Llano, California: Valuation Press, 1977.

Dilmore, Gene. *The New Approach to Real Estate Appraising.* Englewood Cliffs, New Jersey: Prentice-Hall, Inc., 1971.

Elzey, Freeman F. *A First Reader in Statistics.* Belmont, California: Wadsworth Publishing Company, 1974.

French, William B., and Harold F. Lusk. *Law of the Real Estate Business.* Homewood, Illinois: Richard D. Irwin, Inc., 1979.

Gipe, George W. *Mass Appraisal of Apartments with Comparable Sales.* Cambridge, Massachusetts: Lincoln Institute of Land Policy (Monograph no. 77–8), 1977.

Greer, Gaylon E. *Real Estate Investor and the Federal Income Tax.* Rev. ed. New York: Wiley Interscience, 1978.

Grier, Eunice, and George Grier. *Equality and Beyond: Housing Segregation and the Goals of the Great Society.* Berkeley: University of California Press, 1966.

Higgins, J. Warren. *Impact of Federal Taxation on Real Estate Decisions.* 3rd ed. Storrs: Center for Real Estate and Urban Economic Studies, University of Connecticut (Real Estate Report No. 31), 1980.

Hoagland, Henry E., et al. *Real Estate Finance.* 6th ed. Homewood, Illinois: Richard D. Irwin, Inc., 1977.

Hoover, Edgar M. *An Introduction to Regional Economics.* New York: Alfred A. Knopf, 1971.

Institute of Real Estate Management. *Lease Escalators and Other Pass–Through Clauses.* Chicago: Institute of Real Estate Management, 1979.

International Association of Assessing Officers. *Assessing and the Appraisal Process.* 5th ed. Chicago, 1974.

_____. *Property Assessment Valuation.* Chicago, 1977.

_____. *Use–Value Farmland Assessments: Theory, Practice, and Impact.* Chicago, 1974.

Jensen, David L. *The Role of Cluster Analysis in Computer Assisted Mass Appraisals.* Cambridge, Massachusetts: Lincoln Institute of Land Policy, 1977.

Kahn, Sanders A., and Frederick E. Case. *Real Estate Appraisal.* 2nd ed. New York: Ronald Press, 1977.

Kain, John F., and John M. Quigley. *Housing Markets and Racial Discrimination.* New York: Columbia University Press, 1975.

Kinnard, William N., Jr. *An Appraisal Report Primer for Residential Lenders and Underwriters.* Storrs: Center for Real Estate and Urban Economic Studies, University of Connecticut (General Series No. 10), 1978.

_____. *Income Property Valuation.* Lexington, Massachusetts: Lexington Books, 1971.

Kinnard, William N., Jr., et al. *Industrial Real Estate.* 3rd ed. Washington, D.C.: Society of Industrial Realtors, 1979.

_____. *Valuation and Analysis of Interests in Participation Financed Properties.* Chicago: Society of Real Estate Appraisers, 1972.

Kratovil, Robert. *Real Estate Law.* 7th ed. Englewood Cliffs, New Jersey: Prentice–Hall, Inc., 1979.

Lewman, Harry. *Managing an Appraisal Office* (AIREA). Cambridge, Massachusetts: Ballinger Publishing Company, 1971.

Lukens, Reaves C., Jr. *The Appraiser and Real Estate* (AIREA). Cambridge, Massachusetts: Ballinger Publishing Company, 1972.

Lusht, Kenneth M. *The Behavior of Appraisers in Valuing Income Property: A Status Report.* University Park: Pennsylvania University Press, 1979.

McClave, James T., and P. George Benson. *Statistics for Business and Economics.* Rev. ed. San Francisco: Dellen Publishing Company, 1979.

McMichael, Stanley L. *McMichael's Appraising Manual.* 4th ed. Englewood Cliffs, New Jersey: Prentice–Hall, Inc., 1951.

McMichael, Stanley L., and Paul T. O'Keefe. *Leases: Percentage, Short and Long Term.* 6th ed. Englewood Cliffs, New Jersey: Prentice–Hall, Inc., 1974.

Maisel, Sherman J., and Stephen E. Roulac. *Real Estate Investment and Finance.* New York: McGraw–Hill Book Company, 1976.

Messina, John P. *Real Estate Appraisers and the Problems of Malpractice.* Chicago: Society of Real Estate Appraisers, 1977.

Messner, Stephen D., et al. *Analyzing Real Estate Opportunities: Market and Feasibility Studies.* Chicago: Realtors National Marketing Institute, 1977.

———. *Marketing Investment Real Estate: Finance, Taxation, Techniques.* Chicago: Realtors National Marketing Institute, 1975.

Morton, T. Gregory. *Regression Analysis Appraisal Models: Selected Topics and Issues.* Storrs: Center for Real Estate and Urban Economic Studies, University of Connecticut (Real Estate Report No. 19), 1976.

Murray, William G. *Farm Appraisal and Valuation.* 5th ed. Ames: The Iowa State University Press, 1969.

National Association of Home Builders. *Cost Effective Site Planning: Single Family Development.* Washington, D.C., 1976.

North, Lincoln W. *Real Estate Investment Analysis and Valuation.* 2nd ed. Winnipeg, Canada: Saults & Pollard Ltd., 1976.

O'Mara, W. Paul, et al. *Residential Development Handbook.* Washington, D.C.: Urban Land Institute, 1978.

Rockham, J.B., and T.F. Smith, eds. *Automated Mass Appraisal of Real Property.* Chicago: International Association of Assessing Officers, 1974.

Rams, Edwin M. *Analysis and Valuation of Retail Locations.* Reston, Virginia: Reston Publishing Company, 1976.

———. *Rams' Real Estate Appraisal Handbook.* Englewood Cliffs, New Jersey: Prentice–Hall, Inc., 1975.

Ratcliff, Richard U. *Valuation for Real Estate Decisions.* Santa Cruz, California: Democrat Press, 1972.

Ring, Alfred A. *The Valuation of Real Estate.* 2nd ed. Englewood Cliffs, New Jersey: Prentice–Hall, Inc., 1970.

Rose, Jerome G., ed. *Transfer of Development Rights.* New Brunswick, New Jersey: Center for Urban Policy Research, 1975.

Roulac, Stephen E. *Modern Real Estate Investment.* San Francisco: Property Press, 1976.

_____. *Tax Shelter Sale–Leaseback Financing.* Cambridge, Massachusetts: Ballinger Publishing Company, 1976.

Saliba, David J. *Real Estate Valuation in Court.* Chicago: International Association of Assessing Officers, 1972.

Schmutz, George L. *The Appraisal Process.* 3rd ed. rev. Manhattan Beach, California: The author, 1959.

Seldon, Maury, ed. *The Real Estate Handbook.* Homewood, Illinois: Dow Jones–Irwin, 1980.

Seldin, Maury, and Richard H. Swesnik. *Real Estate Investment Strategy.* 2nd ed. New York: Wiley–Interscience, 1979.

Shenkel, William M. *Modern Real Estate Appraisal.* New York: McGraw–Hill Book Company, 1978.

Sherwood, Gerald E. *New Life for Old Dwellings: Appraisal and Rehabilitation.* Washington, D.C.: U.S. Government Printing Office, 1975.

Smith, Halbert C. *Real Estate Appraisal.* Columbus, Ohio: Grid, Inc., 1976.

Smith, Halbert C. et al. *Real Estate and Urban Development.* Rev. ed. Homewood, Illinois: Richard D. Irwin, Inc., 1977.

Spurr, William S., and Charles P. Bonini. *Statistical Analysis for Business Decisions.* Rev. ed. Homewood, Illinois: Richard D. Irwin, Inc., 1973.

Stafford, Howard A. *Principles of Industrial Facility Location.* Atlanta: Conway Publications, Inc., 1979.

Suter, Robert C. *The Appraisal of Farm Real Estate.* Danville, Illinois: The Interstate Printers & Publishers, Inc., 1974.

Sutte, Donald T., Jr. *Appraisal of Roadside Advertising Signs.* Chicago: Aldine, 1965 (reprinted in paperback by Athenum, 1972).

Urban Land Institute. *Industrial Development Handbook.* Washington, D.C., 1978.

_____. *Shopping Center Development Handbook.* Washington, D.C., 1977.

Von Furstenburg, George M., ed. *Patterns of Racial Discrimination: Housing.* Lexington, Massachusetts: Lexington Books, 1974.

Weimer, Arthur M. et al. *Real Estate.* 7th ed. New York: Wiley Book Company, 1977.

Wendt, Paul F. *Real Estate Appraisal Review and Outlook.* Athens: The University of Georgia Press, 1974.

Wendt, Paul F., and Alan R. Cerf. *Real Estate Investment Analysis and Taxation.* 2nd ed. New York: McGraw–Hill Book Company, 1979.

Building Cost Services and Data

Architectural Design Cost and Data. Pasadena, California. Monthly.

Boeckh Building Cost Guides (Residential, Commercial, Light Industrial, Institutional, Agricultural, and Mobile Home). Milwaukee: Boeckh Publications (Division of American Appraisal Associates, Inc.), Annual.

Boeckh Building Cost Index Numbers. Milwaukee: Boeckh Publications. Looseleaf; bimonthly.

Boeckh Building Valuation Manual. Milwaukee: Boeckh Publications. Looseleaf; bimonthly.

Boeckh General Estimate Manual. Milwaukee: Boeckh Publications. Looseleaf; semiannual.

Building Cost File (regional editions). New York: Construction Publishing Company, Inc. Annual.

Building Construction Cost Data. Duxbury, Massachusetts: Robert Snow Means Company. Annual.

Dodge Building Cost Calculator & Valuation Guide. New York: McGraw—Hill Information Systems Company. Looseleaf; quarterly.

Marshall Valuation Service. Los Angeles: Marshall and Swift Publication Company. Looseleaf; monthly.

Real Estate Evaluation Guide. Milwaukee: Boeckh Publications. Monthly.

Residential Cost Handbook. Los Angeles: Marshall and Swift Publication Company. Looseleaf; quarterly.

Capitalization, Amortization, Compound Interest and Related Tables

Akerson, Charles B. *The Internal Rate of Return in Real Estate Investments* (AIREA). Cambridge, Massachusetts: Ballinger Publishing Company, 1976.

_____. *An Introduction to Mortgage Equity Capitalization* (AIREA). 2nd ed. Cambridge, Massachusetts: Ballinger Publishing Company, 1973.

Bogen, Jules J., ed. *Financial Handbook.* 4th ed. New York: Ronald Press, 1968.

Ellwood, L.W. *Ellwood Tables for Real Estate Appraising and Financing* (AIREA). 4th ed. Cambridge, Massachusetts: Ballinger Publishing Company, 1977.

Financial Publishing Company. *Capitalization Rate Tables.* AIREA edition. Boston, 1974.

_____. *Financial Compound Interest and Annuity Tables.* 4th ed. Boston, 1966.

Hughes, James W. *Methods of Housing Analysis.* New Brunswick, New Jersey: Center for Urban Policy Research, 1977.

Johnson, Irvin E. *The Instant Mortgage—Equity Technique.* Lexington, Massachusetts: Lexington Books, 1972.

_____. *Mini—Math for Appraisers.* Chicago: International Association of Assessing Officers, 1972.

Kent, Frederick C., and Maude E. Kent. *Compound Interest and Annuity Tables.* New York: McGraw—Hill, Inc., 1963.

Stiebritz, H.R. *Mathematics for Real Estate Appraisers.* Winnipeg, Canada: Appraisal Institute of Canada, 1975.

Condemnation

American Institute of Real Estate Appraisers. *Condemnation Appraisal Practice.* 2 vols. Chicago, 1974, 1973.

American Association of State Highway Officials. *Acquisition for Right of Way.* Washington, D.C., 1962.

American Right of Way Association. *Proceedings of the Annual National Seminar.* Los Angeles. Annual.

Institute of Planning, Zoning, and Eminent Domain. *Proceedings.* Albany, New York: Matthew Bender and Company. Annual.

Just Compensation. Sherman Oaks, California: Just Compensation, Inc. Monthly.

MacBride, Dexter D. *Power and Process: A Commentary on Eminent Domain and Condemnation.* Washington, D.C.: American Society of Appraisers, 1969.

National Cooperative Highway Research Program. *Reports.* Washington, D.C. Irregular series.

Orgel, Lewis. *Valuation Under the Law of Eminent Domain.* 2nd ed. 2 vols. Charlottesville, Virginia: The Michie Company, 1953.

Rams, Edwin M. *Valuation for Eminent Domain.* Englewood Cliffs, New Jersey: Prentice–Hall, Inc., 1973.

Right of Way. Los Angeles: American Right of Way Association. Bimonthly.

Rohan, Patrick J., and Melvin A. Reskin. *Condemnation Procedures and Techniques; Forms.* Albany, New York: Matthew Bender and Company. Looseleaf service.

Sackman, Julius L., and Patrick J. Rohan. *Nichols' Law of Eminent Domain.* 3rd ed. rev. Albany, New York: Matthew Bender and Company. Looseleaf service.

Schmutz, George L. *Condemnation Appraisal Handbook.* Revised and enlarged by Edwin M. Rams. Englewood Cliffs, New Jersey: Prentice–Hall, Inc., 1963.

Operating Expense Standards and Business Operating Ratios

Building Owners and Managers Association International. *Downtown and Suburban Office Building Experience Exchange Report.* Washington, D.C. Annual.

Dun & Bradstreet, Inc. *Key Business Ratios in 125 Lines.* New York. Annual.

Harris, Kerr, Forster & Company. *Clubs in Town and Country.* New York. Annual.

_____. *Trends in Hotel–Motel Business.* New York. Annual.

Horwath & Horwath International and Laventhal & Horwath. *Worldwide Lodging Industry.* Philadelphia: Laventhal & Horwath. Annual.

Institute of Real Estate Management. *Income/Expense Analysis: Apartments.* Chicago. Annual.

_____. *Income/Expense Analysis: Condominiums, Cooperatives and Planned Unit Development.* Chicago. Annual.

_____. *Income/Expense Analysis: Suburban Office Buildings.* Chicago. Annual.

Laventhal & Horwath. *Restaurant Operations.* Philadelphia. Annual.

_____. *U.S. Lodging Industry.* Philadelphia. Annual.

National Retail Merchants Association, Controllers' Congress. *Department Store and Specialty Store Merchandising and Operating Results.* New York. Annual.

____. *Financial and Operating Results of Department and Specialty Stores.* New York. Annual.

Robert Morris Associates. *Sources of Composite Financial Data — A Bibliography.* 4th ed. Philadelphia, 1976.

Stauss, George, and Harry Lewman. *Ratios and Methodology in Apartment House Valuation* (AIREA). Cambridge, Massachusetts: Ballinger Publishing Company, 1975.

Troy, Leo. *Almanac of Business and Industrial Financial Ratios.* Englewood Cliffs, New Jersey: Prentice–Hall, Inc., 1976.

Urban Land Institute. *Dollars and Cents of Shopping Centers.* Washington, D.C., 1978.

Periodicals

AIM. Appraisal Institute of Canada, Winnipeg, Canada. Quarterly.

American Industrial Properties Report. Indprop Publishing Company, Inc., Red Bank, New Jersey. Bimonthly.

Apartment Management Report. Apartment Owners and Managers Association of America, Watertown, Iowa. Monthly.

Apartment Owner–Builder. Apartment News Publication, Inc., Long Beach, California. Monthly.

Appraisal Briefs. Society of Real Estate Appraisers, Chicago, Illinois. Semimonthly.

Appraisal Digest. New York State Society of Real Estate Appraisers, Albany, New York. Quarterly.

Appraisal Institute Digest. Appraisal Institute of Canada, Winnipeg, Canada. Semiannual.

Appraisal Journal. American Institute of Real Estate Appraisers, Chicago, Illinois. Quarterly.

Appraisal Review. National Association of Independent Fee Appraisers, St. Louis, Missouri. Quarterly.

Appraisal Review Journal. National Association of Review Appraisers, St. Paul, Minnesota. Three times a year.

The Appraiser. American Institute of Real Estate Appraisers, Chicago, Illinois. Monthly, except in July and August.

Area Development. Halcyon Business Publishing, Inc., New York, New York. Monthly.

AREUEA Journal. American Real Estate and Urban Economics Association, Dallas, Texas. Quarterly.

Assessment and Valuation Legal Reporter. International Association of Assessing Officers, Chicago, Illinois. Monthly; looseleaf.

Assessors Digest (formerly *International Assessor*). International Association of Assessing Officers, Chicago, Illinois. Bimonthly.

Assessors Journal. International Association of Assessing Officers, Chicago, Illinois. Quarterly.

Assessors Review. Institute of Municipal Assessors of Ontario, Ontario, Canada. Quarterly.

Builder. National Association of Home Builders, Washington, D.C. Monthly.

Building Owner and Manager. Building Owners and Managers Association International, Washington, D.C. Monthly.

Buildings. Stamats Publishing Company, Cedar Rapids, Iowa. Monthly.

Chain Store Age Executive. Lebhar–Friedman Publications, Inc., New York, New York. Monthly.

Chartered Surveyor. Royal Institute of Chartered Surveyors, Linden, England. Monthly.

Cornell Hotel and Restaurant Administrations Quarterly. Cornell University, Ithaca, New York. Quarterly.

Downtown Idea Exchange. Alexander Reports Corporation, New York, New York. Biweekly.

DRDC News. Downtown Research and Development Center, New York, New York. Quarterly.

Economic Geography. Clark University, Worchester, Massachusetts. Quarterly.

Environmental Affairs. Environmental Law Center, Boston College School of Law, Newton Centre, Massachusetts. Quarterly.

Environmental Comment. Urban Land Institute, Washington, D.C. Monthly.

Farm and Land Realtor. Farm and Land Institute, Chicago, Illinois. Monthly.

Housing (formerly *House & Home*). McGraw–Hill, Inc., New York, New York. Monthly.

Housing Market Report. National Press Building, Washington, D.C. Biweekly.

HUD Newsletter. U.S. Department of Housing and Urban Development, Washington, D.C. Weekly.

Income Property Finance Report. IPFR Publishing Corporation, New York, New York. Eighteen issues a year.

Industrial Development. Conway Research, Inc., Atlanta, Georgia. Bimonthly.

Journal of the American Institute of Architects. American Institute of Architects, Washington, D.C. Monthly.

Journal of the American Institute of Planners. American Institute of Planners, Washington, D.C. Quarterly.

Journal of the American Society of Farm Managers and Rural Appraisers. American Society of Farm Managers and Rural Appraisers, Denver, Colorado. Semiannual.

Journal of Housing. National Association of Housing and Redevelopment Officials, Washington, D.C. Monthly.

Journal of Property Management. Institute of Real Estate Management, Chicago, Illinois. Monthly.

Journal of Real Estate Taxation. Warren, Gorham & Lamont, Inc., Boston, Massachusetts. Quarterly.

Land Economics. University of Wisconsin Press, Madison, Wisconsin. Quarterly.

Land Use Law and Zoning Digest. American Society of Planning Officials, Chicago, Illinois. Monthly.

Lawyers Title News. Lawyers Title Insurance Corporation, Richmond, Virginia. Bimonthly.

Legal Bulletin. U.S. League of Savings Associations, Chicago, Illinois. Bimonthly.

Mortgage Banker. Mortgage Bankers Association of America, Washington, D.C. Monthly.

Mortgage and Real Estate Executives Report. Warren, Gorham & Lamont, Inc., Boston, Massachusetts. Biweekly.

Multi—Housing News. Gralla Publications, New York, New York. Monthly.

NARA Previews. National Association of Review Appraisers, St. Paul, Minnesota. Bimonthly.

National Market Letter. Real Estate Research Corporation, Chicago, Illinois. Monthly.

National Property Law Digests. Washington, D.C. Monthly.

National Real Estate Investor. Communication Channels, Inc., New York, New York. Monthly.

National Savings & Loan League Journal. National Savings & Loan League, Washington, D.C. Monthly.

National Tax Journal. National Tax Association, Washington, D.C. Monthly.

New Zealand Valuer. New Zealand Institute of Valuers, Wellington, New Zealand. Quarterly.

Professional Builder. Cahners Publishing Company, Inc., Denver, Colorado. Monthly.

Property Tax Report. Institute of Property Taxation, Washington, D.C. Monthly.

The Real Estate Appraiser and Analyst. Society of Real Estate Appraisers, Chicago, Illinois. Bimonthly.

Real Estate & Construction. Touche Ross & Company, New York, New York. Bimonthly.

Real Estate Investment Ideas. Institute for Business Planning, Englewood Cliffs, New Jersey. Twice a month.

Real Estate Investors Report. Warren, Gorham & Lamont, Inc., Boston, Massachusetts. Monthly.

Real Estate Issues. American Society of Real Estate Counselors, Chicago, Illinois. Semiannual.

Real Estate Law Journal. Warren, Gorham & Lamont, Inc., Boston, Massachusetts. Quarterly.

Real Estate Law Report. Warren, Gorham & Lamont, Inc., Boston, Massachusetts. Monthly.

Real Estate Report. Real Estate Research Corporation, Chicago, Illinois. Quarterly.

Real Estate Review. Warren, Gorham & Lamont, Inc., Boston, Massachusetts. Quarterly.

Real Estate Tax Ideas. Warren, Gorham & Lamont, Inc., Boston, Massachusetts. Monthly.

Real Estate Today. Realtors National Marketing Institute, Chicago, Illinois. Monthly.

Real Property, Probate and Trust Journal. American Bar Association, Chicago, Illinois. Quarterly.

RESSI Review. Real Estate Securities and Syndication Institute, Chicago, Illinois. Monthly.

Right of Way. American Right of Way Association, Los Angeles, California. Bimonthly.

Savings Bank Journal. National Association of Mutual Savings Banks, New York, New York. Monthly.

Savings and Loan News. U.S. League of Savings Associations, Chicago, Illinois. Monthly.

Shopping Center World. Atlanta, Georgia. Monthly.

Site Selection Handbook. Conway Research, Inc., Atlanta, Georgia. Annual.

Title News. America Land Title Association, Washington, D.C. Monthly.

Traffic Quarterly. Eno Foundation, Inc., Westport, Connecticut. Quarterly.

Urban Land. Urban Land Institute, Washington, D.C. Monthly.

Valuation. American Society of Appraisers, Washington, D.C. Three issues a year.

Valuer. Australian Institute of Valuers, New South Wales, Australia. Quarterly.

Valuer. Incorporated Society of Valuers and Auctioneers, London, England. Eleven issues a year.

Washington Report. National Association of Regional Councils, Washington, D.C. Monthly.

Zoning and Planning Law Report. Clark Boardman Company, Ltd., New York, New York. Monthly.

Real Estate Market Data

Annual Housing Survey. Washington, D.C.: U.S. Department of Commerce, Bureau of the Census. Annual.

Bureau of the Census Catalog. Washington, D.C.: U.S. Department of Commerce. Quarterly; monthly supplements.

Business Conditions Digest. Washington, D.C.: U.S. Department of Labor, Bureau of Economic Analysis. Monthly.

1977 Census of Construction Industries. Washington, D.C.: U.S. Department of Commerce, Bureau of the Census, 1978.

1977 Census of Manufactures (Geographic Area and Industry Series). Washington, D.C.: U.S. Department of Commerce, Bureau of the Census, 1978.

1977 Census of Retail Trade (Geographic Area Series). Washington, D.C.: U.S. Department of Commerce, Bureau of the Census, 1978.

1977 Census of Wholesale Trade (Geographic Area Series). Washington, D.C.: U.S. Department of Commerce, Bureau of the Census, 1978.

City and County Data Book. Washington, D.C.: U.S. Department of Commerce, Bureau of the Census, 1977.

County Business Patterns. Washington, D.C.: U.S. Department of Commerce, Bureau of the Census, 1977.

Current Construction Reports (Series C–20, C–21, C–22, C–25, C–27, C–30, C–40, C–41, and C–50). Washington, D.C.: U.S. Department of Commerce, Bureau of the Census. Monthly and Quarterly.

Current Housing Reports (Series H–111 and H–130). Washington, D.C.: U.S. Department of Commerce, Bureau of the Census. Quarterly and annual summary.

Current Population Reports (Series P–20, P–23, P–25, P–26, P–28, and P–60). Washington, D.C.: U.S. Department of Commerce, Bureau of the Census. Monthly and quarterly.

Current Retail Trade. Washington, D.C.: U.S. Department of Commerce, Bureau of the Census. Monthly.

Current Wholesale Trade. Washington, D.C.: U.S. Department of Commerce, Bureau of the Census. Monthly.

Economic Indicators. Washington, D.C.: U.S. Government Printing Office. Monthly.

Economic News Notes. Washington, D.C.: National Association of Home Builders. Monthly and quarterly.

Employment and Earnings. Washington, D.C.: U.S. Department of Labor. Monthly.

Existing Home Sales. Washington, D.C.: National Association of Realtors, Economics and Research Division. Monthly.

Federal Home Loan Bank Board Journal. Washington, D.C.: Federal Home Loan Bank Board. Monthly.

Federal Home Loan Bank Board News. Washington, D.C.: Federal Home Loan Bank Board. Biweekly.

Federal Reserve Bulletin. Washington, D.C.: Board of Governors of the Federal Reserve System. Monthly.

Housing and Urban Development Trends. Washington, D.C.: U.S. Department of Housing and Urban Development. Quarterly.

Monthly Catalog of U.S. Government Publications. Washington, D.C.: U.S. Government Printing Office. Monthly.

Statistical Abstract of the United States. Washington, D.C.: U.S. Department of Commerce, Bureau of the Census. Annual.

Survey of Buying Power. New York: Sales & Marketing Management. Annual.

Survey of Current Business. Washington, D.C.: U.S. Department of Labor, Bureau of Economic Analysis. Monthly.